Banking and Monetary Policy from the Perspective of Austrian Economics

Annette Godart-van der Kroon • Patrik Vonlanthen
Editors

Banking and Monetary Policy from the Perspective of Austrian Economics

Springer

Editors
Annette Godart-van der Kroon
Ludwig von Mises Institute Europe
Brussels, Belgium

Patrik Vonlanthen
Swiss Mises Institute
Zürich, Switzerland

ISBN 978-3-030-09332-7 ISBN 978-3-319-75817-6 (eBook)
https://doi.org/10.1007/978-3-319-75817-6

Printed on acid-free paper

This Springer imprint is published by the registered company Springer International Publishing AG part of Springer Nature.
The registered company address is: Gewerbestrasse 11, 6330 Cham, Switzerland

Preface

After having organised several conferences related to this topic and motivated by the upcoming changes for the ECB and the changing mentality on financial policies, the Ludwig von Mises Institute Europe and the Swiss Mises Institute have decided to publish the book "Banking and Monetary Policy from the Perspective of Austrian Economics".

For a while there has indeed been a feeling of discontent about the policy of the European Central Bank (ECB). That is not only applicable to experts and academics, but also to other people. To show the arguments against the inflationary ECB policy, several prominent academics have given their thoughts on this topic, but there are also introductory articles explaining the several aspects of the theories of the Austrian School.

The editors would like to express their gratitude to first of all the authors of this book, Jure Otorepec for finishing the heavy task of proofreading the texts and Louisa Kelly for her translation.

Brussels, Belgium
Zürich, Switzerland

Annette Godart-van der Kroon
Patrik Vonlanthen

Information About the Institutes

Ludwig von Mises Institute Europe

The institute is a non-partisan think tank fostering an open and free society and primarily aims at:

- Exchanging and reintroducing the basic values and principles of Liberalism, especially the ideas of the Austrian School.
- Acting as an interface between the academic, the political and the business world.
- Connecting liberal-minded individuals and organizations at national and international levels.

The Ludwig von Mises Institute-Europe has successfully organized a variety of conferences, symposia, discussions, targeted dinner debates and lunch debates.

Members include former Prime Ministers, MEPs, former European Commissioners, key politicians, senior academics, business leaders and prominent journalists.

The Swiss Mises Institute

Patrik Vonlanthen is founder and president of the Swiss Mises Institute.

The institute he leads pursues liberty at its core. This implies that liberty is an approach to life rather than the elaboration of mere thoughts or ideas.

Contents

List of Contributors

William Barnett II Department of Economics, Joseph A. Butt, S. J. College of Business Administration, Loyola University New Orleans, New Orleans, LA, USA

Walter Block Harold E. Wirth Endowed Chair in Economics, Department of Economics, Joseph A. Butt, S. J. College of Business Administration, Loyola University New Orleans, New Orleans, LA, USA

Brendan Brown Mises Institute, Auburn, AL, USA

Hudson Institute, Washington, DC, USA

MUFG, Tokyo, Japan

Nicolas Cachanosky Department of Economics, Metropolitan State University of Denver, Denver, CO, USA

Annette Godart-van der Kroon Ludwig von Mises Institute Europe, Brussels, Belgium

J. G. Hülsmann Université d'Angers, Angers, France

Andreas Hoffmann Institute for Economic Policy, Leipzig University, Leipzig, Germany

Jesús Huerta de Soto King Juan Carlos University, Madrid, Spain

Alistair Milne Loughborough University, Loughborough, UK

Chikako Nakayama Faculty of Graduate School of Global Studies, Tokyo University of Foreign Studies, Tokyo, Japan

Makoto Nishibe School of Economics, Senshu University, Tokyo, Japan

Max Rangeley Cobden Center, London, UK

Gunther Schnabl Universität Leipzig, Leipzig, Germany

Arkadiusz Sieroń Institute of Economic Sciences, University of Wroclaw, Wrocław, Poland

Patrik Vonlanthen Swiss Mises Institute, Zurich, Switzerland

Erich Weede University of Bonn, Bonn, Germany

Introduction

Annette Godart-van der Kroon and Patrik Vonlanthen

For a while there has been a feeling of discontent about the policy of the European Central Bank (ECB) that is not only applicable to experts and academics but also to other people. To show the arguments against the inflationary ECB policy, several academics have given their thoughts on this topic, but there are also introductory articles explaining the several aspects of the theories of the Austrian School. Before going deeper into the content, the following points should be indicated.

Firstly, in this book other arguments than the usual Keynesian arguments are used to explain the causes of the latest crisis and how to solve it and to propose new techniques. Secondly, this publication is important, because there is not only a feeling of discontent about the low interest rate policy of the European Central Bank (ECB) but there is a deep divide between countries who have a rather healthy financial system and other countries who want a policy of redistribution. Thirdly, the timing is also important, because when Mario Draghi will end his term by the end of October 2019, the question who is going to be his successor will become urgent. Not only it is important which country is going to provide the new president of ECB, but also what kind of banking policy will prevail.

While Draghi's term as president runs until the end of October 2019, speculation is already building on who might inherit his position. However, the process of determining a successor hasn't yet begun. The chancellor and her finance minister are set "to push for Bundesbank President Jens Weidmann to become the fourth guardian of the single currency, arguing it's finally Germany's turn after the Netherlands, France and Italy," Spiegel reported, without revealing where it got the information.

A. Godart-van der Kroon (✉)
Ludwig von Mises Institute Europe, Brussels, Belgium
e-mail: annette.godart@vonmisesinstitute-europe.org

P. Vonlanthen
Swiss Mises Institute, Zurich, Switzerland
e-mail: patrik@mises.ch; patrik.vonlanthen@isispirit.ch

A. Godart-van der Kroon, P. Vonlanthen (eds.), *Banking and Monetary Policy from the Perspective of Austrian Economics*,
https://doi.org/10.1007/978-3-319-75817-6_1

Weidmann is willing to accept the post if it were to be offered to him, according to the prerelease of an article published on Friday, May 19, 2017. This was contested by the German government and the Bundesbank as too premature. In France, led by political newcomer Emmanuel Macron, Bank of France Governor Francois Villeroy de Galhau is tipped to be a contender for the job. Melvyn Krauss, a senior fellow at the Hoover Institution at Stanford University, argued in an article in Germany's "Die Zeit" newspaper that "Macron's victory paves the way for the Frenchman to claim the ECB prize."

Skepticism of the ECB's policies runs high in a country where monetary orthodoxy is enshrined in the national DNA. ECB appointments are not democratic. The parliament has no power to block ECB appointments, and the president of the ECB cannot be held accountable for his decisions. The ECB presents this unaccountability as an advantage, as they claim to be "politically independent." But as Rothbard (1994[1]) was keen to point out, government agencies have to be accountable to the people and their elected representatives and therefore should be "dependent on politics." Otherwise, the people lose their ability to influence ECB appointments, and those appointments are made entirely according to the whim of the ruling elite. Draghi has managed to make his position a most important one, although he has not been elected. His decisions, like the lowering of the interest rate, influence European politics in a far-reaching way. Since a few years, Mario Draghi can be called the *fifth* power in Europe. In short it should be possible to hold the ECB president accountable for his decisions.

Lastly, the book features articles from some of the most prominent authors in their respective disciplines, who gave the book fascinating contributions from their unique perspectives. They are experts concerning banking and financial policy and were able to present their visions for new and better banking and monetary policies.

The articles in this book are not only excellent in their technical aspects, they also go deeper and give a broader view, which makes these articles indispensable for whoever is interested in the topics covered.

1 Part I

In the first part, "Mises's and Hayek's Ideas on Banking and Monetary Policy from a Historical, Economic Point of View," Guido Hülsmann gives a very good overview of the several theories on money since the classical revolution and Adam Smith to the bullion controversy, Ricardo and the Currency School and the Banking School, while ending with the theories of von Mises.

In his article, *Mises Geldtheorie*, professor Guido Hülsmann explains that the "initial publication of Ludwig von Mises' *Theorie des Geldes und der Umlaufsmittel*

[1]The Case Against the Fed, 1994, page 5. Publisher: The Ludwig von Mises Institute, Auburn, Alabama.

in 1912 represents an important turning point in political economy. At the time, Mises developed a new theory of money and banking that he fit into the subjectivist value theory developed by Carl Menger."

Mises criticized the Currency School and the Banking School. Both schools had their flaws, but by recognizing them, he developed a famous crisis theory, arguing that the artificial expansion of the money supply has a tendency to lead to intertemporal imbalances within the production structure. Several aspects are discussed: the nature and value of money, the theory of fiduciary media, and the money and banking policy. One of the most important discoveries von Mises made was that inflationary development is more harmful than its deflationary counterpart. This is due to the fact that price inflation leads to capital consumption and, ultimately, to a relatively impoverished society. In particular, it reduces the incentives for savings; therefore, less capital is available for investment. It also distorts business accounting, because of the reporting of phantom profits. Excessive profits would be paid out and consumed, thus leading to a progressively shrinking capital base for the entire economy.

Barnett and Block, in their contribution, *Money: Capital Good, Consumer Good or (Media of) Exchange Good* ?, argue that exchange is a form of production, and consequently, there are only two types of goods, consumers' goods and capital goods, and that money is, then, a capital (producers') good. Use money *as* money to facilitate trade. That is to say, it must be understood in terms of the meaning attributed to it by a relevant human mind. Note that this means that the monetary good, e.g., gold coins, may be (1) a consumers' good, (2) a money capital good, or (3) a non-money capital good. Any asset, including durable consumers' goods or even non-durable consumers' goods, is a store of value and thus a capital good. If one is holding the coins as a media of exchange, then they are capital goods, specifically money; if one is holding the coins for investment purposes, then they are investment goods—an inventory of "junk" gold coins of an inventory or numismatically valuable gold coins.

Knies K. (1885)[2] *Geld und Kredit* cited in Mises (1980) proposed a threefold division into means of production, objects of consumption, and media of exchange.

Mises, here, makes the most important finding: the essential aspect of a good is not its physical properties but, rather, its "significance for satisfying human wants." Strictly speaking those goods should be called goods of the first order. "Our civilization is inseparably linked with our methods of calculation. It would perish if we were to abandon this most precious tool of acting" according to Mises. However, "Economic calculation cannot comprehend things which are not sold and bought against money" (Mises 1996). Therefore, we may conclude that Mises understood that, contrary to the statement supra, even though money is not necessary for production in an underdeveloped society, it certainly is in a modern capitalist economy.

---

[2]Knies K. *Geld und Kredit* cited in Mises (1980).

The problem is that Mises does not recognize that an exchange in the ownership rights to an article alters its utility to the individuals concerned. And, since money is that which par excellence provides exchange services, it is de facto a capital good. But the foundation of commerce consists not of the legal system alone; money is every bit as much a foundation of commerce as are any of these other institutions correctly mentioned by Mises in this regard. Therefore, by that criterion, money is a capital good.

The problem here is Mises' failure to see that a change in the quantity of money does affect the welfare of members of a community. Friedman maintains that:

> It is a commonplace of monetary theory that nothing is so unimportant as the quantity of money expressed in terms of nominal money units—dollars, or pounds, or pesos. The situation is very different with respect to the real quantity of money—the quantity of goods and services that the nominal quantity of money can purchase, or the number of weeks' income to which the nominal quantity of money is equal.

This real quantity of money has important effects on the efficiency of operation of the economic mechanism, on how wealthy people regard themselves as being, and, indeed, on how wealthy they actually are. Barnett and Block (2004) argue that the optimum quantity of a commodity money is whatever amount is provided in a free market. They also maintain that the optimum quantity of a fiat money is the extant amount; i.e., that amount of fiat money should be frozen. In that case, a general decline in market determined prices would cause an increase in real money, the increase of which would be optimal in that institutional setting. Therefore, money, the good that facilitates exchanges, is, indubitably, a capital good. Furthermore, as shown supra by Mises himself, money is essential to production in a modern capitalist society; without it there neither would nor could be any such society.

Production goods derive their value from that of their products. Not so money, for no increase in the welfare of the members of a society can result from the availability of an additional quantity of money. The laws which govern the value of money are different from those which govern the value of production goods and from those which govern the value of consumption goods. In sum, because money is "the" good used in exchange and exchange transforms goods from higher to lower order and production is action which transforms goods from higher to lower order, money, too, is a producers' good, i.e., a capital good.

> Yet money is demonstrably *not* a future good. In fact, when the money is spent—in the future—it loses all its utility for the present owner. It has utility only while and insofar as it is *not* spent, and its character as a present good stems from the omnipresent human condition of *uncertainty*.

Nishibe argues in his article, *The Trend of economic thinking of market and money: what is Hayek's position on the issues?,* that the process of Hayek's transformation of his conception of the market, or any economist's transformation in many cases, occurred in the following order: (1) vision, (2) theory, and (3) methodology.

Hayek used the terms *Weltanschauung* and 'world view' in order to critically describe the characteristics of socialism in a fairly negative light.

In fact, according to Nishibe, Hayek was deeply disappointed by the fact that socialism had won over liberalism after WWII.

It is probably true that economic analysis has never been the product of detached intellectual curiosity about the *why* of social phenomena but of an intense urge to reconstruct a world which gives in to profound dissatisfaction. To study the teleological property of economics, Hayek regards the facts of the social sciences:

> In short, in the social sciences the things are what people think they are. Money is money, a word is a word, a cosmetic is a cosmetic, if and because somebody thinks they are.

Hayek was concerned about these topics, because he was strongly concerned with the difficulty of realizing liberalism compared to socialism. The result is that in economics you can never establish a truth once and for all but will always have to convince every generation anew—and that you may find much more difficult when things appear to yourself no longer as simple as they once did.

Hayek also said that "I seriously believe that any such striving for popularity— at least till you have very definitely settled your own convictions, is fatal to the economist and that above anything he must have the courage to be unpopular."

Hayek's socioeconomics since 1960 was not only the result of his philosophical and methodological turns but also from a change of his vision of the market that is a complex of some basic theoretical concepts. The key concept for Hayek in breaking with the general equilibrium theory and reaching a new market image was his vision of competition as a rival and discovery process since 1946, not the subjective and dispersive knowledge since 1937. Hayek's image of the market as "a rival and dispersive discovery procedure for knowledge" should be a vision for establishing a new theory of the market as a self-organizing complex system or a "spontaneous order." That is the basic idea of Hayek. Nishibe refers to the importance Hayek attributed to the role of intellectuals and their influence on public opinion. Socialists dared to be utopian; that is why Hayek proposed a liberal utopia.

> The reason why Hayek was so pessimistic to be an economist is concerned with the nature of knowledge created and obtained in economics. Such pessimism and fear as Hayek attributes to economics arises from the general character of economics, i.e. its inclusion of self-evaluation of scientific statements and proposition of social affairs in economics and its validity and applicability depending on public perception or popularity of the theory. It is evident that Hayek's sorrow and fear of being an economist is much deeper. We should be fully aware of the unique nature of economics and social sciences in general.

But apart from this contemporary mood, "the ideas of economists and political philosophers, both when they are right and when they are wrong, are more powerful than is commonly understood," but success can be only achieved "in the long run." Hayek's idea here is that the economist has a strong influence on the public through his vision and theory, but it takes a long time to take effect, so that the old dominant theories tend to form the public's world view or public opinions, and as a result, the present theory is often neglected or unaccepted by the public.

According to Hayek, world view is the old, previous, dominant, popular, amateurish, simplified, and distorted pseudo-theory formed and diffused by the intellectuals and firmly held by the public. Accordingly, the formation of vision of the economist is more or less influenced by reality as well as the world view or public opinion.

2 Part II

In the second part, "The Measures Taken by the ECB Considered in the Light of the Ideas of Mises and Hayek," Brendan Brown starts in his *What Is Wrong with the 2% Inflation Target*? with the following sentence:

> The fable of the Emperor's new clothes describes aptly the situation of central bankers today. They claim that their box of non-conventional tools enables them to strongly influence long-term interest rates. And more fundamentally they boast of having the ability to steer the overall inflation rate so as to achieve with remarkable precision a given target (2% p.a.) for this variable over say 2 year intervals. Their patchy successes in both endeavours have won them some acclaim. And yet on closer examination they have little power if any on either score – except as derives from public gullibility. There are unfortunately many who would not dare to challenge the existence of such power for fear of revealing their own lack of understanding.

Inflation targeting and the tools used in its pursuance are in fact harmful to economic prosperity and more narrowly financial stability. It is the principal purpose of his paper to demonstrate that conclusion. How can we be so sure that the vaunted powers of the central bank to fix the inflation rate and strongly influence long-term interest rates are at best make-believe and at worst destructive? As regards the power to stabilize the inflation rate at 2% PA (Per Annum) over 2-year periods, how could this be possible?

In the Austrian school economic tradition, there is an aversion to defining inflation in terms of movements of the "price level" and a preference for a monetary interpretation not itself based on pseudoscience. The advocates of sound money point out that though there is no guarantee of stable prices on average over the long run, the amount of inflation and more generally monetary turmoil (what J.S. Mill described as the money monkey wrench getting into all the other machinery of the economy) should be less than in any alternative monetary regime, including that where the official aim is stable prices or stable inflation (Salerno 2012) .

A dislodged monetary pivot means price inertia and institutionalism. Some potential catalysts are one-offs and could include in present circumstances (2017) policies of economic nationalism in the United States which might boost upward pressure on wages (e.g., tax changes which favor production in the United States rather than abroad). Historically, high inflation or hyperinflations have usually emanated from government inability or unwillingness to tap savings via capital markets at a going market rate consistent with a sound money regime.

But the question arises: How did we get to the 2% inflation standard? Janet Yellen, then a Fed Governor, gave a paper in favor of calling a halt, fundamentally arguing that a little inflation was pro-growth given a whole list of inflexibilities in the wage-price mechanisms (including the hoary Keynesian topic of money illusion) and also making reference to biases in inflation calculation (even though in fact if this were estimated the same way as in the 1950s or earlier, it would have been near 4% pa at this time).

There was no formal decision taken by the FOMC (Federal Open Market Committee) on Yellen's advocacy, and some objections were raised by fellow members (e.g., Shouldn't Congress be consulted?), and one member, Larry Lindsey, focused on the issues of tax frictions and disincentives under a regime of permanently low inflation. Greenspan summarized the sense of the meeting as to proceed with considerable care and trial and error in pursuing the objective of price stability once inflation came down to low levels. This was in July 1996.

In broad brush, we could describe the almost finished first two decades of the twenty-first century as hosting a global 2% inflation standard. In the aftermath of the 2008–2010 recession and panic, the Fed led the way in a campaign to boost the inflation rate up to its 2% inflation target—and to do so designed and opened a box of non-conventional tools not previously used. The argument here has been that 2% inflation is a deeply flawed standard. It conflicts with the natural rhythm of prices in a capitalist economy, and the conflict shows up as bouts of eventually painful asset price inflation (booms and bust). It strengthens forces of inertia which can cripple the invisible hand and hinder the path to prosperity. But how can we do this in the context of our present fiat monies?

Gold bullion has unique properties as a candidate for high-powered money for which there is no equivalent under a fiat money system. It enjoys a large natural and stable demand, and there are no close ersatz substitutes. Here are a few suggestions by Brendan Brown: Reserves at the central bank, like gold, must not pay interest. Obstacles to a vibrant use of cash in the economy should be demolished (e.g., antitrust action against credit card companies which use their power to force retailers to accept their cards without charging fees, issuance of high denomination notes to satisfy demand for these as medium of exchange). Bank demand for reserves (which would be held voluntarily not as a legal reserve requirement) would be boosted by the curtailing and ideally abolition of too big to fail, lender of last resort, and deposit insurance (as above).

In sum, the journey away from the 2% inflation standard to sound money can be driven only by a strong political momentum in its favor. There lies the challenge. It is plausible that the political momentum would be greatest after an episode of deep monetary failure. But where this failure has had as most visible consequence asset market boom and bust rather than high goods and services inflation, it is notoriously difficult for advocates of sound money to put together a winning coalition. There are so many potential scapegoats against which popular rage can be directed by parties with an alternative agenda (to sound money)—and it is not at all obvious through all the fog that unsound money was enemy no. 1.

In their article, *Unintended Consequences of ECB Policies on Europe's Periphery*, Hoffman/Cachanosky wants to show that in particular the Mises-Hayek or Austrian business cycle theory (*ABCT*) has been rediscovered to explain what went wrong.

"Economists at the Bank of International Settlements were among the first to warn central bankers about global credit booms and worrisome financial imbalances in the 2000s, suggesting that—in line with Hayek's work—holding inflation at bay alone does not guarantee long-term macroeconomic stability" (Hoffmann/Cachanosky). In the spirit of this research, the authors revisit the unintended consequences of the European Central Bank's (ECB) low interest rate policies with a focus on the periphery countries of the European Union (EU) since the 2000s, from a modern

Austrian perspective. To this end, they draw heavily upon their own empirical and theoretical work in which they augmented the Mises-Hayek theory to consider risk, explain (recurring) international credit cycles as well as resource misallocations. They show, however, that ECB policies were not successful in stimulating bank lending and investment. The main beneficiaries of holding rates at low levels are governments, who use the financial leeway to delay painful reforms. The authors suggest that the ECB's policy has unintentionally slowed down the recovery in the crisis economies and worsened Europe's growth prospects since 2009.

According to the Austrian School, aggressive ECB policies may fail to restore confidence necessary to bolster a takeoff of investment and lending—at least in the short run as malinvestment is not undone during the recession. The fear of outstanding structural adjustments may result in a lower innovation and growth potential of the crisis economies and lead to a further decline in natural interest rates. In their conclusion the authors contend that "among these credit boom theories, the Austrian theory emphasizes how monetary policy mistakes may trigger unsustainable credit booms and increase the depth and duration of the subsequent crisis." In particular, they apply the Austrian, or Mises-Hayek, business cycle theory and the *law of unintended consequences*.

Absent established bailout institutions, the ECB had become the main player in dealing with the complex evolution of the crisis. Moreover, ECB policies coincide, for instance, with new regulatory initiatives that may be counterproductive as well as governments that are unwilling to reform. However, the authors have provided evidence that, in contrast to its objectives, the main beneficiaries of ECB policies seem to be governments. As governments find it easier to refinance, the ECB provides them with leeway to delay unpopular reforms. Rather than successfully combating the crisis, ECB policy, thereby, unintentionally increases crisis duration and (indirectly) prevents a sustainable takeoff of the European economy.

In the introduction of his contribution, *The Failure of ECB Monetary Policy from a Mises-Hayek Perspective*, Günther Schnabl remarks

> It is shown how since the turn of the millennium an overly expansionary monetary policy contributed to unsustainable overinvestment booms in the southern and western periphery of the European Monetary Union, and more recently in Germany. To explain idiosyncratic business cycles within the euro area before and since the outbreak of the European financial and debt crisis, the overinvestment theories are combined with the literature on optimum currency areas and on the role of fiscal policies in a monetary Union. Therefore, a timely exit from the ultra-expansionary monetary policy is recommended.

The causes and consequences of cyclical and structural imbalances within the European Monetary Union based on the monetary overinvestment theory by Mises and Hayek are analyzed. The overinvestment theory allows us to identify an overly loose monetary policy as a reason for unsustainable overinvestment and speculation booms. To understand the heterogeneous economic development within the monetary union, the overinvestment theory is combined with the theory on optimum currency areas.

Schnabl proceeds to discuss the Monetary Overinvestment Theories and Boom-and-Bust Cycles. He explains the reasons for the European financial and debt crisis and the implications of monetary policy crisis management. A lasting stagnation and zombification in the crisis countries was the result. It is a counter hypothesis to views, which see—based on Keynes—the European financial and debt crisis (euro crisis) as the outcome of a random shock, like De Grauwe contended in 2011. It also contradicts the views that the gradual decline of growth rates in the industrialized countries including the member states of the European Monetary Union is due to a savings glut originating in ageing societies and an exogenous gradual fall of the marginal efficiency of investment. Schnabl concluded that the monetary policy of the European Central Bank is from a Mises-Hayek perspective a failure in several regards. He gives the following reasons:

Firstly, the ECB's overly loose monetary policy stance is at the roots of the unsustainable investment, real estate, and consumption booms in the southern and western euro area countries (and beyond), which have triggered the still lingering European financial and debt crisis (euro crisis). Secondly, the time-varying emergence of crisis in the different parts of the European Monetary Union is due to a constructional flaw of a heterogeneous monetary union with decentralized fiscal policies. The Maastricht fiscal criteria have failed and are failing to indicate excessive spending during the speculative upswings as unsustainable tax revenues were/are produced. Thirdly, the attempts of the European Central Bank to cure the European financial and debt crisis with zero and negative interest rates as well as with extensive government bond purchases have paralyzed investment and growth in all parts of the European Monetary Union. The reason is that the ECB's monetary policy rescue measures in combination with relatively tight fiscal policies stimulate capital outflows, i.e., capital flight. Given the global low interest rate environment, foreign investment has a large likelihood to become malinvestment and therefore to become a quasi-transfer in favor of the debtor countries. Fourthly, because the low-cost liquidity provision of the European Central Bank paralyzes productivity gains and growth in the European Monetary Union, while at the same time having redistribution effects, redistribution conflicts within the euro area have emerged and are likely to further intensify. This is the case within every single euro area member state, because the monetary policy rescue measures redistribute via asset markets in favor of the older generations (at the cost of the younger generations). Furthermore, at a supranational level, the TARGET2 system redistributes from Germany, Luxemburg, Finland, and the Netherlands to a larger number of euro area countries, which are more or less strongly in crisis mode. The large number of the recipient countries of the TARGET2 quasi-transfer mechanism explains the political acceptability of the monetary policy rescue measures in the board of the ECB. The danger exists that because of this redistribution an exit of donor countries from the European Monetary Union is going to be more likely in the course of time.

Government bond purchases of the European Central Bank should be ended at once. The main refinancing rate should be lifted slowly but decisively to prompt a gradual adjustment of banks, enterprises, and governments to the reconstitution of the allocation and the signaling function of the interest rate. Only a tightening of monetary policy will lead to a revival of productivity gains and thereby a recovery of growth, which is the basis for real wage increases all over Europe. Only if market principles are restored, the fundament for integration, wealth, cohesion, and peace in Europe will be reconstituted. His conclusion was that the monetary policy failure will turn out to be a threat to the European integration process.

The article of Arkadiusz Sieroń, *Hayek and Mises on Non-Neutrality of Money. Implications for Monetary Policy,* contributes to the debate on the benefits and costs of expansionary monetary policy, including that conducted by the European Central Bank. The neutrality (or non-neutrality) of money is the key issue of monetary economics addressed by each school of economic thought.

Each School of Economics emphasizes different causes of the non-neutrality of money, such as price rigidity (new Keynesians) or incomplete information (new classical economists). However, there is a consensus that money is non-neutral in the short term.

The aim of this article is to examine the concept of neutral money in the light of the Austrian school's ideas. The author focuses on Hayek's and Mises's writings, as these two economists presented the most far-reaching criticism of the neutrality of money, showing that changes in the money supply are never neutral, even in the long term.

Sieron also mentions the role of Cantillon ([1755] 1959), who provided the first attempt to "trace the actual chain of cause and effect between the amount of money and prices," pointing out that the impact of a monetary injection depends on the nature of the injection. This phenomenon—that Blaug (1985) calls the Cantillon effect—makes money non-neutral, both in the short and long run.

In his conclusion Sieron examines the impact of neutral money. The Austrian economists formulate strong arguments against the concept of neutral money. They argue that the neutrality of money not only violates methodological individualism but also cannot be actually achieved in the real world, partially due to the Cantillon effect, which mainstream economists overlook. The non-neutrality of money should be taken into account. Indeed, as one can read on the ECB's official website "this purpose is considered to be the natural role of monetary policy, since "monetary policy can affect real activity only in the shorter term. But ultimately it can only influence the price level in the economy" (ECB).

There are three main implications of the above analysis for monetary policy, in particular for the ECB's actions. First, the Austrians' arguments for the non-neutrality of money enrich the literature about the limits of monetary policy and strengthen the case against the overly loose monetary policy conducted by the central banks, including the ECB. From the Austrian perspective, the increase in money supply does not lead to merely temporary changes but permanently affects the real side of the economy. Hence, the non-neutrality of money is a strong argument against the view that central banks should respond to real disturbances or changes in money demand, as monetary inflation does not neutralize monetary deflation and undo its social consequences, but as von Mises formulated, it "simply add[s] to it the social consequences of a new change." Second, the failure of central banks is to take into account that the Cantillon effect leads to an underestimation of the negative effects of monetary inflation, including quantitative easing. Third, the non-neutrality of money postulated by the Austrian economists is a strong argument against price stability as the aim of monetary policy. According to mainstream economics, money is neutral (introduced by Wicksell), and the increase in money supply does not affect the economy, as long as the price level remains stable (Hayek). However, if money is not neutral, monetary impulses always affect the economy. Hence, inflationary monetary policy may entail negative consequences for the economy—such as business cycles or asset price bubbles—even when the general price level remains stable. This is because what matters for the economy is not a mere increase in the money supply but also the channel of monetary inflation: the effects of monetary policies on the real economy differ depending on the channels of monetary injections. Such a disaggregated analysis of monetary policy and credit expansion in the spirit of Cantillon's seminal work (Cantillon [1755] 1959)—going beyond the large aggregates (such as the general price level) and the focus on narrowly defined price stability—would be a real boon to the development of monetary theory and monetary policy conducted by the ECB and other central banks.

Erich Weede starts in his article, *Managing Decline by Expanding Government: The Case of Germany*, with some considerations about human nature. In essence, he argues that markets can handle human fallibility much better than governments and that therefore limited government is a necessity. Thereafter there might be a short discussion about econometric evidence demonstrating a link between economic freedom or small government, on the one hand, and prosperity or growth, on the other hand. Finally, he discusses the German climate and energy policies, the rescuing of the Euro, and ultimately migration policies. Under Merkel, these policies always rely on expanding government. This is likely to overburden Germany and to lead to decline. Given the weight of the German economy in Europe, as well as the geographic location of the country, German problems are likely to affect, or even infect, all of Europe.

Human fallibility necessitates limited government and economic freedom.

Philosophy as well as all the social sciences, economics included, should start from the insight of human fallibility, as formulated by Popper. What economists call rationality is merely the *attempt* to maximize benefits and to minimize costs. In Weede's view, one could go a step further: rationality is the attempt to cope with human fallibility.

In different spheres of life, there are different mechanisms to overcome error or poor solutions to problems. Competition on price and quality in the market serves a similar function as do scientific debates or competition between parties in politics. It is the easiest to institutionalize.

That is "why democracies choose bad policies" (Caplan 2007).

Expanding public decision-making or government has the following effects. As outlined by Hayek, it makes the mobilization of individual knowledge much less likely. Moreover, collective decision-making is a powerful impediment to innovation, according to the economic historians Rosenberg and Birdzell. Economic freedom and a capitalist market economy are synonyms. Following Hayek, one may justify individual freedom by the insight in the limitation of human knowledge and by hopes for unpredictable progress.

The basic principle of a capitalist society is that everyone produces whatever he/she wants. Liberty and entrepreneurship imply the opportunity to mobilize the knowledge which is scattered across thousands or millions of heads. Since knowledge cannot be centralized, capitalist societies are superior to planned economies. Discussing the future of the Euro, Weede remarks that some time ago, Goldman Sachs estimated German liabilities for Eurozone debt to be 949 billion Euros, whereas the damage from the dissolution of the Eurozone for Germany might be 800 billion Euro (FAZ 2013: 23). We seem to have a choice between terror without end or an end with terror. Inside the German government as well as outside of Germany, the economic power of Germany is much overestimated.

Rescuing the Euro is likely to result in a catastrophic overburdening of future generations living in Germany and other donor economies. The two ways of transferring debt are from the voting generation to the next one. An inefficient climate policy of a comparatively small country with a decreasing demographic and economic weight in the world is more likely to contribute to overburdening the German economy than to save the climate, as well. Inspired by Hayek, we have to consider the limits of government. No one can seriously argue that government enjoys a comparative advantage over private organizations in the provision of charity.

One gets the impression that many politicians take the size of the burden they place on taxpayers, consumers, and future generations as an indicator of their own greatness and importance.

3 Part III

In the third part, "Proposed Monetary Reforms for the Future," Jesús Huerta de Soto attacks in his paper *Anti-deflationist Paranoia* the current anti-deflationist paranoia from the point of view of the Austrian School of Economics. After discussing three different types of deflation (that are deliberately provoked by the authorities, the inevitable credit deflation after a crisis, and the good deflation based on increasing productivity), Huerta de Soto answers one by one the standard arguments normally given against deflation, concluding that in many instances they are defended by specific political and pressure groups that only benefit from inflationary environments. Inflation is always very popular and precisely for that reason is so perverse and does so much damage. Deflation, on the contrary, is not popular, but it is very necessary to promote the necessary economic reforms and to discipline the behavior of all the agents operating in the economy and the political arena.

No one can have failed to hear the widespread outcry that for months has been sounding against deflation. In all the media we are met with a dismal, apocalyptic scene in which deflation is the worst of all worlds. The voices most often heard come from an amalgam of New Keynesians, or of neoclassical economists, or of monetarists... Though they believe their views are diametrically opposed from a theoretical standpoint, they nevertheless all agree that deflation is the worst of all worlds. Hence, there is a kind of phobia of deflation, a serious psychological illness which Huerta de Soto calls a "anti-deflationist paranoia."

According to Mises, deflation is a monetary change which consists of a decrease in the money supply (Mises). Or, to put it another way, an increase in the demand for money (to decrease supply is to increase demand).

Huerta de Soto explains the three types of deflation as follows:

First, deflation deliberately provoked by the state. The second is the inevitable result after a boom. All recurrent, cyclical economic problems spring from this error of institutional design, from this odious privilege granted to banks, by which they can act outside general legal principles and neglect to maintain a 100 percent reserve ratio on demand deposits. Consequently, the money supply behaves like an accordion. Just as easily as it expands, due to the generation of "virtual" money, it later contracts.

There is also a third type of deflation, which is "good" deflation.

An example of *the first* type of deflation is the most talked-about case: the monumental error committed by the Chancellor of the Exchequer of the United Kingdom in 1925, Mr. Winston Churchill. Churchill insisted on reintroducing the gold standard after World War I, but at the pound's gold parity prior to World War I. This was a very grave error, because World War I was financed, as always, by inflation. The market was flooded with sterling notes, which meant that the de facto parity of sterling banknotes with gold fell dramatically. Many theorists claim it was a great error, but the only error was that their opponents insisted on returning to the gold standard at the pre-World War I parity. Of course, it was key to return to the gold.

The *second* type of deflation is that which inevitably occurs in a system like ours, which has rested on a fractional reserve ever since Peel's Bank Charter Act of 1844.

> The bubble leads to systematic errors of investment and seriously distorts the real structure of the market, which is very dynamically efficient and reveals the investment errors sooner or later. At that moment, a financial crisis erupts, because it becomes clear that a large number of the loans banks granted during the stage of credit expansion were granted for unviable or unsustainable investment projects. Deflation is inevitable. This is the second type of deflation.

This is because economic agents discover that many of the investments they so eagerly made during the bubble stage were pointless. In short, much of the virtual money created during the bubble stage disappears, and the money supply inevitably contracts in the form of deflation.

We simply hit a raw nerve when we point out that the origin of the crisis does not lie in deflation (which everyone mistakenly identifies as the cause of the evils) but rather in the previous stage, that of the speculative bubble. For this reason, the entire banking system must be redesigned and a 100 percent reserve requirement established on demand deposits and their equivalents. As he has already pointed out, after every bubble, the deflationary process, which can be more intense or less, is inevitable.

We also have the famous Japanese example, which is the one always cited to scare us about deflation. We are told that because of its deflation, Japan has spent years without a recovery and with very insignificant growth. This is the crude, short-sighted, erroneous argument of many who lack training in economics. Moreover, if Japan has faced slight deflation (for in today's colloquial terms, the drop in prices has not been drastic) for over a decade, this deflation has not put the country in its decidedly weak economic state (incidentally, the economic weakness is relative, given that Japan has a huge amount of accumulated capital and any visitor to the country can see how prosperous it is, especially with respect to 20 years ago). All they have managed to achieve is to become one of the most indebted countries in the world and to maintain their rigidity indefinitely.

The *third* type of deflation is when the money supply remains relatively stable, and little by little, an increase in productivity occurs. It is then that the third "deflation" scenario begins to unfold. This is why it is referred to as "good" deflation and results from an increase in productivity with a relatively constant monetary supply.

Even in the academic sphere, we must admit, as Mises did, that a sound, suitable, and complete theory of deflation is sorely missing. To remedy this academic deficiency, Professors Huerta de Soto and Philipp Bagus have devoted their efforts in several writings.

One of the periods of the greatest prosperity in the United States began at the end of the Civil War in 1865 and lasted almost until the beginning of the twentieth century. It was a period of cumulative growth, year after year, of between 2 and 4 percent, with secular deflation, year after year, of around 1 percent. To wrap up, he would like to finish with the following question: "What are the psychological and sociological reasons for the hostility toward deflation? What is the origin of this serious psychological illness called "anti-deflationist paranoia"?

Inflation is a drug. It is an extremely dangerous drug, a great and deadly temptation for the whole social body.

Also delighted with inflation are trade unionists. Inflation covers their backs, since the devastating effects of union policies, which tend to make the labor market more rigid (artificial increases in wages, the minimum wage, etc.), are concealed in an inflationary environment. However, in an environment of zero inflation, or of deflation, these effects are fully exposed, and we immediately realize that such policies, mentioned previously, are harmful.

Entrepreneurs are confronted by countless daily problems in their companies. If they are offered a very cheap and easy short-term loan with flexible repayment options, they all end up falling for it, just like they did during the bubble stage.

That is why inflation is so popular. That is why it is so perverse and does so much damage. That is why it is a drug so lethal to society. And that is why deflation is so necessary.

Chikako Nakayama in *The reconsideration of Hayek's Idea on the De-nationalization of Money: Taking the Growing Tendency of Digital Currencies in Consideration* starts to recite the beginnings of Bitcoin.

At the end of the twentieth century in 1999, when there was no influential digital currency yet, Friedman expressed his view in an interview, "I think that the Internet is going to be one of the major forces for reducing the role of government. The one thing that's missing, but that will soon be developed, is a reliable e-cash, a method whereby on the Internet you can transfer funds from A to B, without A knowing B or B knowing A." Some interpret this statement to predict Bitcoin and praised Friedman's foresight. Here the author investigates some arguments on money, focusing on the relation of money to the market concept of the Austrian School of Economics, taking our contemporary development of digital money in view.

Growing tendencies of digital currencies include the birth of Bitcoin and its impact. As is well-known, the idea of Bitcoin was originally shown in 2008 in a paper by Satoshi Nakamoto whose personality, career, affiliation, or profile could not further be detected. His paper was rather brief consisting of nine pages, not published in any journal with peer reviews, but distributed to some mailing list as a kind of design paper.

In 2012, the European Central Bank published a rough but schematically classifying report on virtual currencies in general, placing Bitcoin in this context as one of the most prominent cases "to compete against real currencies as a medium of exchange." But according to Nakamoto, transaction costs tend to increase to avoid mediating disputes and fraud, even though it was still impossible to eliminate such irregularity completely. The problem of high transaction cost might be popular among many people who have a high cost of remittance, especially for payments beyond national boundaries.

Nakamoto hence proposed an electronic payment system based on the cryptographic proof, using a time stamp server for the whole chronological line of transactions to protect both sellers and buyers. He emphasized that it then enables any two willing parties to transact directly without any third party, which means cryptology is the replacement for people's trust in financial institutions. But the paper itself was brimmed with rich ideas for further development in many directions so that by 2016, the technology of cryptology of blockchain has become independently discussed for its own potential, not necessarily being connected with Bitcoin. Some indicated—after pointing out Bitcoin's complexity, which makes it possible to describe it as a protocol, a currency, a payment system, or a technology platform—that it is open-source software at its core.

Antonopoulos, described Bitcoin as a network of *trust* "that could also provide the basis for so much more than just currencies."

"The realization that 'this isn't money, it's a decentralized trust network…' (*Ibid.*)." Perhaps he was cautious enough to distinguish between currency and money, but it is evident here that his attention was laid more on the decentralized network of trust than on the possible birth of a new digital currency.

Besides, the existence of the authority and power of nation-states to set the currency plays an important role there, on which the whole international monetary system is constructed. In order to analyze this point, Hayek's treatise on this theme in 1976 has been the most important reference for those who have treated the theme of Bitcoin. Money had gradually come to be seen to have three functions: as a medium of exchange, unit of account, and store of value. These forms of money were followed by the creation and development of the World Wide Web in the mid-1990s, which engendered virtual communities and their own digital currencies, although other local, unregulated currencies had already existed before that. Finally, Bitcoin was discussed as the heir of these successions in this overview.

The problem was, even though Bitcoin was originally planned only as a medium of exchange, that is, to have only exchange value, it was possible that "the 'mining' activity . . .leads to money creation without the receipt of funds" (ECB 2012), and "users of the system actually exchange real currency for computing bits". But the Japanese government, being remarkably unfamiliar with this problem, issued an official statement in 2014 that they regarded Bitcoin neither as a currency nor as a financial commodity, but taxable as a commodity under Japanese law. Then at the end of April to May 2016, the Japanese government enacted a bill, with which Bitcoin became defined as an "asset-like value."

What Nakamoto originally strove for was to avoid double spending and the intervening destruction by greedy attackers. The legal and social aspects of Bitcoin bring us back to the issue of trust. It has been discussed as people's belief, collective belief, or confidence in money that makes the money valid and effective in a society. According to Williamson, the concept of trust has been an elusive one for economic theorists, especially those who laid importance on institutions and transaction cost. He warned that it was redundant or misleading to use the term "trust" easily or its absence where contractual safeguards or their absence was discussed. He then classified three kinds of trust as the outcome of many different questions and comments. Hence, she adds: "we ask whether this kind of semi-security of identity would eventually be contradictory to the principle of a free market system as Hayek had explored".

The historical background of Hayek's *Denationalisation of Money* in 1976 was the following. It was a time when the international system of fixed exchange rate was suddenly abandoned by the abolishment of the "gold standard": the Nixon shock in 1971, the decisive crisis of the reserve currency of US dollar, which shook the whole international economic system and was the catalyst for it to be reconsidered and reconstructed. It was natural for economists to explore monetary issues fundamentally. Setting the problem in a way to question. What Hayek believed was that "a fixed rate of redemption in terms of gold or other currencies ... prevented monetary authorities from giving in to the demands of the ever-present pressure for cheap money."

Hayek's motivation to write it was closely connected to his hopelessness of "finding a politically feasible solution ... to stop inflation." Hence, he gradually went on to reach a somehow surprising idea that governments should be deprived of its monopoly of the issue of money. This claim for denationalization of money could be seen as Hayek's declaration of political stance of liberalism against the state, with the conviction against totalitarianism. Hayek claimed that we could not easily change the system of money and credit arranged and controlled by governments. He listed up three fundamental reasons for this.

The third was the large volume of government expenditure. Further he gave some more detailed explanation of the first one there.

Money, which is current only because people have been forced to accept it, is wholly different from money that has come to be accepted because people trust the issuer to keep it stable. Here his usage of the concept trust is remarkable. From his statements, the national currencies in Europe were not recognized any more as the only or the most trusted ones by more and more people, opening the possibility to use dollars' accounts there. For Hayek, "money is not a tool of policy. . . but it should be part of the self-steering mechanism." He argued that "competition would certainly prove a more effective constraint, forcing the issuing institutions to keep the value of their currency constant," a deviation from Hayek's expectations. For example, Friedman gave the following argument: "we have ample empirical and historical evidence ... (that) private currencies which offer purchasing power security would not drive out governmental currencies." Hayek quoted this critical attitude of Friedman and commented that he was surprised that Friedman had so little faith in competition to make a better institution prevail.

But the discrepancy may come from other different ideas on the relation among the trusted financial institutions which consist of private banks, the central bank and the government, or in principle the state, instead of the government of the day, which authorizes the whole system.

> As this statement shows, Hayek's long-term vision of monetary order was not the cutthroat struggle for the only seat, but rather some peaceful plurality of good currencies with communities using them being flexible and partly overlapping speculative directions, which gave rise to the whole stories of offshore markets, tax havens etc. In this sense, Hayek's vision of the open market mechanism for competing currencies was not exactly hitting the mark.

Vital is the reasoning of Chikako Nakayama with respect to the meaning of trust in relation to market and transaction costs. Beyond the expectation of Hayek, as Nakamoto explicitly stated, banks have to take appropriate measures for avoiding fraud, disputes, conflicts, or any kind of troubles and for keeping the privacy of their customers. These measures are necessary in order to gain people's trust but inevitably increase the transaction costs, some part of which banks impose on the side of customers as a fee. Hence there came such attempts as Bitcoin to dispense with such transaction costs once and for all. In other words, the question Bitcoin has raised was whether the transactions within and beyond such institutional trust could in fact be replaced by the cryptographic proofs.

Besides, the necessity for banks to keep the privacy of customers is contradictory to the openness of all the information in the market of competing currencies Hayek believed in. To gain people's trust, banks make an effort to keep their information secret, which would damage the transparency of markets and possibly induce illegal transactions in some cases. It will not necessarily be a bank that keeps information secret, and the way to secure the privacy in BTC against the intervention by powers and institutions will match to this aspect.

Alistair Milne elaborates in his contribution *Cryptocurrencies from an Austrian Perspective* the potentially fundamental reform of the monetary arrangements through the usage of cryptocurrency technology by using a single mutually distributed ledger for financial transactions.

He starts in his work by outlining challenges posed while restoring free markets of money and credit according to insights of Austrian economics. As a solution, he acknowledges the need for a radical decentralization of payments without any need for a state-controlled monetary base or centralized settlement. This could be accomplished with this novel technology commonly labeled "blockchain." Therewith, many of the key Austrian monetary policy objectives for monetary arrangements could be fulfilled. Milne outlines the major elements as:

- All commercial and central bank money takes form in a distributed, electronic equivalent.
- Decentralization is achieved via a mutual distributed ledger.
- No subsequent settlement using central bank reserves.
- No distinction between the medium of exchange and money substitutes.
- Deposits not on the ledger but with the promise of immediate redemption on demand into ledger money are loans at risk of potential temporary suspension or permanent default.
- All payment instruments become mechanisms for instructing transfers of ledger money.
- The central bank's fiat issue is permanent and cannot be withdrawn, while commercial bank issue is only temporary.
- Two mechanisms ensure repayment and prevent an inflationist exploitation of money issue.
- Repayment onto the ledger is covered by a "triple lock."
- Bank money so securitized is "overcollateralized."
- Bank transaction deposits are no longer bank liabilities.

What role is played in this schema by information technology and cryptography? The distributed ledger technology developed for cryptocurrencies such as Bitcoin provides the essential decentralized immediate real-time accounting framework that makes this schema workable.

Milne puts in his proposal special emphasis on the transition phase for this new arrangement and proposes an imminent coordination role for the state which he understandably attributes as a rather "impure" version of Austrian thinking. Hence, there are limitations on anonymity since identities remain intact and payments can be traced.

Milne also reflects in his work on the changing nature of the medium of exchange while pointing out that Austrian monetary thinking makes a clear distinction between the medium of exchange and money substitutes. Further, money, as a social institution, is also not a creation of the state, but Milne acknowledges that still the state may have the power to influence monetary arrangements.

Milne then dispels the two "myths" about cryptocurrencies. "One is that the suggestion that an unpermissioned open-source cryptocurrency could serve as a monetary standard outside of state control. A second is that current unpermissioned cryptocurrencies could easily compete with established fiat currencies for widespread use in everyday domestic exchange."

Milne summarizes his arguments about these "myths":

> All this indicates that the future of cryptocurrencies in the medium to long term will belong to permissioned private sector alternatives—supporting much quicker and more resource efficient processing with more flexible and practical governance that adapts to changing economic and business circumstances.

This though is a quite different model; permissioning means also a need for control of identities and therefore integration into existing banking networks based on fiat currencies; so the outcome is not separate competing currencies but just separate competing means of payments. Such developments may effectively challenge the market power of banks in payment and transaction services, but they are not a fundamental change to monetary arrangements. The main exceptions where unpermissioned open-course cryptocurrency may continue to develop are those countries where governments seek to assert control over economic and social activity, through controls on foreign exchange and other regulatory limitations on financial transactions. There unpermissioned cryptocurrency are likely to continue to be attractive as unregulated and unregulatable alternatives to repressed domestic and international payments.

In a later part of the article, Milne describes operational details on how bank payments are accomplished without settlements by using a mutual distributed ledger and gives historical perspectives *in order to make the key point that settlement is not an inherent and indivisible aspect of payments*.

He finally describes what implications for banking and bank regulations would result and as such what the future role of the central banks could be. For this, the prospects of the adaption are of utmost importance to Milne and elaborated accordingly in the article.

Milne concludes that fundamental problems caused by state incursion into the provision of money and credit can be addressed with a technological solution. Cryptocurrency technologies allow to put all bank transaction deposits and fiat money in a single "mutual distributed ledger" and therefore allow an almost complete withdrawal of the role of the state in banking industry and the provision of money and credit allowing a market-based response to our current monetary and macroeconomic economic challenges.

Max Rangeley looks in his article *Blockchain: The New Intellectual Battleground in Economics* at three key areas related to the Austrian School of Economics where according to Rangeley blockchain will have a defining character. Blockchain not only supports the tenets of the Austrian School of Economics but even overhauls tenets of other schools of economics. In his contribution Rangeley looks firstly at the Austrian School conception of the nature of money. Secondly, he takes a look at Hayek's notion of the fatal conceit and, thirdly, looks at Austrian business cycle theory and how blockchain will both lead to new thinking in this area and serve as a natural complement to traditional Austrian thinking. So for Rangeley the battle is not about whether blockchain will or will not become used but rather what type of economy it will lead to.

In the first part, Rangeley starts with Menger's discourse on the nature of money, putting emphasis on how money arises out of the free market without the need for state intervention. He then looks at the connection of the Austrian conception of money and the blockchain technology.

Taking Hayek's book *The Fatal Conceit* as reference, Rangeley explains the difficulties for a rightful adaption of this new technology due to the nature of the state as described by Hayek therein.

He cites in his part also a remarkable speech from the Deputy Governor of the People's Bank of China Fan Yifei with "Digital currencies have shown considerable promise...[our research] suggests that the best way to take advantage of these innovations is for central banks to take the lead, both in supervising private digital currencies and in developing digital legal tender of their own."

Then Rangeley reflects on how blockchain impacts characteristic features in the Austrian Business Cycle-Theory of Boom-and-Bust and asks: How does this new technology fit to the theory? For him the changes in the ledger system are not a continuation of the familiar technological "disruption" similar to retailers selling online rather than through catalogues or movies being streamed over the Internet rather than television, but rather a philosophical shift in the very nature of what constitutes money and credit.

Counter to the traditional economics discourse, the Austrian tradition looks at time preferences which must be coordinated by interest rates just as prices coordinate preferences for goods in other parts of the economy rather than the procyclical tightening during a recession according to mainstream economics.

Rangeley continues to build his case for Bitcoin by pointing out that "if radical monetary policy such as negative interest rates is continued to being pursued by central banks then more widespread trading on blockchain(s) would make substitution out of the currency viable and easy, likely forcing a tighter monetary policy on the central bank."

He then looks at Friedman's critique of Hayek's *The Denationalisation of Money* "pointing out that there is no law preventing voluntary exchange between two parties using any medium they choose and yet the adoption of competing currencies has not been widespread." Rangeley identifies the cause in no realistic alternatives to the current monetary ledger structure prior to Bitcoin.

On a blockchain-based economy, what constitutes "money" would be continuously evolving, and therefore consumers and firms could easily move out of a central bank currency into a near-money asset on the blockchain such as gold—a commodity with which one would currently not be able to pay for goods at the local supermarket but which would likely have a high degree of moneyness on a blockchain economy. The European Central Bank supports this idea with their view that a substitution effect could be deleterious to monetary policy instruments:

> In this regard, a widespread substitution of central bank money by privately issued virtual currency could significantly reduce the size of central banks' balance sheets, and thus also their ability to influence the short-term interest rates. Central banks would need to look at their existing tools to deal with this risk (for instance, trying to impose minimum reserve requirements on virtual currency schemes).

From an Austrian School position, the matching of time preferences through normalized interest rates will lead to a capital structure which reflects the desires and constraints of consumers in complementary time periods. As Mises put it with respect to the gold standard, which also restricted credit creation:

> In a market economy the rate of interest has a tendency to correspond to the amount of this difference in the valuation of future goods and present goods. True, governments can reduce the rate of interest in the short run. They can issue additional paper money. They can open the way to credit expansion by the banks. They can thus create an artificial boom and the appearance of prosperity. But such a boom is bound to collapse sooner or later and to bring about a depression.

> The gold standard put a check on governmental plans for easy money. It was impossible to indulge in credit expansion and yet cling to the gold parity permanently fixed by law. Governments had to choose between the gold standard and their—in the long run disastrous—policy of credit expansion.

Credit markets on a blockchain free of influence by central banks would likely take a different form to even Austrian School-inspired "free banking." Hayek's *Conceit of Knowledge* prefigured the idea that we should not try and predict the exact nature of how genuinely free credit markets might develop on a blockchain substrate, but we can take it as an assumption that the underlying economic nature of interest rates will not change; people and institutions will lend to each other at a rate that reflects the demand and supply of savings as well as, of course, the creditworthiness of the borrower.

For Rangeley's proposition it matters that the interest rates are set by the free market rather than by central banks. As long as this is the case, then any credit markets taking place on blockchains will serve to mitigate the effects of artificial credit expansion by central banks and help to realign time preferences once a recession arrives. If the standard Austrian axioms are accepted—that resources must be reallocated following a recession so that the capital structure can return to an undistorted state, that further stimulus will delay this necessary adjustment, and that the best way to achieve the reordering is through the unhampered interactions between agents in a free market—then the ability to trade on blockchains using assets that are not manipulated by a central bank will accelerate the readjustment process and will mean that it can occur with greater transparency.

Rangeley concludes, "Blockchain technology constitutes one of the most innovative developments in ledger systems since the invention of modern accounting techniques during the Renaissance. It is already bringing about, and will continue to bring about, significant changes not only in how we use money but in how we conceptualise money itself..[. . .]..blockchain technology complements the Austrian framework and in fact realises some of the concepts which have hitherto not been given sufficient attention in economics such as competing currencies."

As blockchain technology develops and the related protocols become increasingly optimized and more widely used, there will be increasing attention to Austrian School ideas with respect to money. Some of the very ideas that are axiomatic to Keynesianism, at least with respect to monetary policy, become not just impractical but increasingly nonsensical as blockchains become more widely adapted in finance and other sectors. Monetary stimulus, one of the cornerstones of modern macroeconomics, will become increasingly untenable if trading on private blockchains occurs more frequently as it relies on central bank manipulation of the money supply. This is likely to happen not just because people wish to use another form of "money," but because trading in general on blockchains will be more efficient and hitherto unthought of money systems will be increasingly embedded into these new frameworks.

For the neoclassical synthesis, this implies a weaker economy as monetary authorities will increasingly lack the ability to stimulate the economy through interest rate manipulation and other instruments of monetary policy; for the Austrian School, it will mean the possibility of a revitalized economy as interest rates become increasingly set by the market and monetary "stimulus" becomes impossible, thus allowing free exchange and genuinely free markets.

Part I
Mises's and Hayek's Ideas on Banking and Monetary Policy from a Historical, Economic Point of View

Mises' Monetary Theory

J. G. Hülsmann

Mises developed a new theory of money and banking that he fit into the subjectivist value theory developed by Carl Menger. He also provided numerous suggestions and clarifications to specific theoretical questions. Thus he placed the general theory of subjective value on the foundation of the logic of choice; he developed a subjectivist classification system of money as well as a systematic theory of the causes and effects of monetary prices; he researched the international impact of the changing supply of and demand for money and became a pioneer in international monetary economics; he studied the principles of price formation in unorganized markets; and he criticized mechanistic approaches to the quantity theory of money and to value theory, index number theory, as well as the theories of the Currency School and the Banking School. Last but not the least, he developed a famous crisis theory, arguing that the artificial expansion of the money supply has a tendency to lead to intertemporal imbalances within the production structure.

The present chapter builds on and extends the studies of Pallas (2004) and Hülsmann (2007, 2012). We will present the historical context of Mises' monetary thought and then give an outline of his *The Theory of Money and Credit*.

The present chapter is a revised translation of "Mises' Geldtheorie" in T. Polleit (ed.), *Mises für Einsteiger* (Munich: Finanzbuch-Verlag, 2013), pp. 40–82.

J. G. Hülsmann (✉)
Université d'Angers, Angers, France
e-mail: Guido.Hulsmann@univ-angers.fr

A. Godart-van der Kroon, P. Vonlanthen (eds.), *Banking and Monetary Policy from the Perspective of Austrian Economics*,
https://doi.org/10.1007/978-3-319-75817-6_2

1 Historical Background

The importance of Mises' monetary theory can be stated in one phrase: it rebuilds classical monetary theory on a completely new and more solid foundation, thus awakening it out of the slumber into which it had sunken after 1844 and making it relevant again for political decision-making. We shall therefore start off by considering the peculiarities of classical monetary policy and the causes for its decline. For simplicity's sake, we will begin with Adam Smith.

1.1 The Classical Revolution

Smith is the founding father of classical economics. His fame derives from the fact that in *The Wealth of Nations*, he had convincingly argued that aggregate wealth is not dependent on the *level* of monetary expenditure. While he considered the use of money to be an indispensable precondition for a widespread division of labor, he saw the amount and extent of monetary expenditure as irrelevant. Aggregate wealth could only grow as a result of an increase in the division of labor and of a higher rate of savings for the purposes of capital formation. In his view, wealth does not increase through the availability of a larger supply of money or by more extensive monetary expenditure. Therefore, all measures and policy interventions aimed at increasing either of these variables were effectively pointless.

With this perspective, Adam Smith opposed what he called "mercantilism," a doctrine that had been dominant for centuries. According to mercantilism, the level of monetary expenditure was the central driving force behind economic development. Governmental authorities tried to increase monetary expenditure by using a variety of measures, such as providing as much support as possible to banks for the purposes of creating money. Above all, government spending was seen as one of the most important causes of national wealth. Supporters of this doctrine rejected any demands for a more frugal government and for greater limitations on state activities. In their eyes, such demands were the outgrowth of stubbornness, unworthy of Her Majesty's subjects.

Adam Smith and his followers, the classical economists, reduced mercantilism to ashes. This was not an overnight revolution. It was the result of a long-winding battle of ideas, stretching out over several decades. Eventually there was a political breakthrough for classical liberalism in the period between 1840 and 1870. In monetary policy, too, the classical approach came to be applied. Since the quantity of money was seen as irrelevant, the primary goal in monetary policy was to provide the market with *unadulterated* silver and gold coins. The role of the state should be limited to that of an overseer, or rather, a guarantor of the coinage. Essentially, the money stock should be regulated through a competitive mining industry with minimal influence by the state.

In the decades following 1840, the classical approach received opposition before being completely discarded. This decline was only made worse by theoretical shortcomings, and, in turn, practical failures.

Adam Smith's intellectual edifice suffered from two weaknesses related to price theory. First and fundamentally, he believed that the price of goods was determined primarily by the production costs and only indirectly by supply and demand. Using this incorrect assumption as his basis, Smith made a second and fatal error when analyzing the particular case of convertible paper money (promissory notes).

According to Smith (1994 [1776], Bk. II, chap. II, pp. 318f), the issuance of such paper money could not lead to a lasting increase in the total money stock and in the price level. Smith believed that convertibility should ensure that paper money has the same purchasing power as the corresponding specie or precious metal, and these values would be objectively fixed by the production costs. *Since the purchasing power does not change, the overall demand for money would also remain unchanged.* If, for some reason, the banks began to increase the total amount of money by putting more paper money into circulation, then there would not be any domestic demand for this new money. The superfluous money units would then be exported. The problem is that promissory notes do not enjoy the same trust abroad as they do domestically. Therefore, it would not be possible to export these notes. Instead, the corresponding amount would have to be exported in the form of precious metals. The issuance of additional promissory notes is thus accompanied by a reduced use of precious metals. One medium of exchange (specie) is displaced by the other medium of exchange (paper money). According to Smith, this would not have a lasting impact domestically on the overall money supply and demand. For this reason, he saw the introduction of convertible paper money as desirable. An expensive good (gold) could be replaced with a cheap good (paper), and the resources saved in this process would be diverted elsewhere to increase the overall wealth of the nation (ibid., pp. 320–322).

The influence and authority of Adam Smith was so great that it took two major debates before economists began to liberate themselves from his errors. However, as we shall see in the following section, his misconceptions were compounded by additional errors that arose in the wake of those debates. Ultimately, the reputation of classical monetary theory declined, and the old theory of mercantilism, the one Smith fought against, made a resurgence, first in economic policy before finding its way to academia.

1.2 The Bullion Controversy

The first of these debates—the so-called Bullion controversy—took place in the first decade of the nineteenth century in the British House of Commons (Cannan 1925; Hollander 1910–1911). During the Napoleonic Wars, the Bank of England suspended gold payments and increased the issuance of notes considerably as a way to finance the wars. The natural consequence was an increase in the price of goods and the emergence of a premium on gold. Bank representatives did not want to admit this relationship, though. They thought that it was not possible to put so many notes into circulation that it exceeded public demand. This dispute, which involved David Ricardo and Henry Thornton (see Thornton (1939 [1802]), ended with the publication of a report by an appointed parliamentary committee. The *Bullion Report of 1810* found the Bank's issuance of notes caused the prices of goods to rise. The Bank was able to put more notes into circulation than the public needed because it had suspended the redemption of issued notes. It was, therefore, recommended to restore the convertibility to gold back to the prewar level as soon as possible. This recommendation was implemented in 1821.

The question remained whether the issuance of *convertible* notes might also lead to an increase in the overall money supply and its potential resulting consequences. This was especially applicable to notes, which were backed either not at all or only partially by the corresponding gold stocks in the vaults of the issuers (fractional-reserve principle). Were these notes *added* to the circulation of money (increasing the quantity of money), or did they simply *displace* the gold that would have been used in their place (leaving the overall quantity of money unchanged)?

During the period between 1820 and 1870, these questions became the focus of intense debates on monetary and banking policy going on throughout the Western world. These debates included the opposing schools of thought of the Currency School and the Banking School (overview in Claassen 1970, pp. 7–21).

1.3 Ricardo and the Currency School

The ideas of Ricardo and Say were the origin of the Currency School. Their doctrines dealt much more thoroughly with monetary theory than those of their teacher Adam Smith. They included two especially important insights. First, they emphasized much more clearly that changes in the money supply do not lead to lasting advantages and disadvantages to the *overall economy* but do affect *specific sectors* within the economy. The increase in the money supply was associated with an income and wealth gain for certain economic actors, which was counterbalanced by the corresponding losses of other actors. In particular, Ricardo (1992 [1817], p. 247) rejected the notion that the Bank of England had provided aid to commerce in general by lending "money below the market rate of interest." Rather, in his eyes, the overall effect of such lending was that "a part of the traders of the country are unfairly, and for the country, unprofitably benefited, by being enabled to supply themselves with an instrument of trade at a lesser charge than those who must be influenced only by a market price."

In the public lectures given in the 1820s at the Collège de France, Jean-Baptiste Say explained that the issuance of uncovered promissory notes was the true cause of the first modern banking crisis in Europe, the British "Panic of 1825." According to Say, the additional notes had entailed an excessive easing of financial terms for firms: "The directors of many firms have been able [...] to extend the size of their firms in disproportion to their capital."[1] The extension of the money supply led to a discount of the notes as compared to specie, and thus the owners of the notes rushed to the banks for redemption. This forced the banks to scramble for cash. They no longer extended the credits as they had routinely done before, and this ruined the successful operation of all those business extensions that had been initiated thanks to cheap credit and which depended on ongoing credit to keep going. Thus the banking crisis turned into an economic crisis, forcing firms to panic sell the products they had on stock, spurring unemployment and entailing widespread bankruptcy (see Say 1852, p. 475).

Ricardo died in 1823 and Say 9 years later. At this point, the pernicious effects of the fractional-reserve principle were barely visible. In the subsequent decades, there were numerous banking crises, and the teachings of Ricardo and Say attracted more and more followers, who assembled themselves into the Currency School.[2] These economists drew practical conclusions from Ricardo's doctrine. They emphasized that variations "in the amount of currency [i.e. promissory notes, JGH] are seldom, if ever; the original and exciting cause of fluctuations in prices and in the state of trade" (Jones-Loyd 1857, p. 167). Anticipating hereby the twentieth-century analyses by Irving Fisher, Maurice Allais, and many other economists, they argued that, even though the issue of uncovered promissory notes usually was not the initial cause of such fluctuations, it did nevertheless "exert a considerable influence in restraining or augmenting the violence of commercial oscillations" (ibid.). They frequently suggested a strict level of proportionality between the money supply and the price level. Their political ambitions primarily focused on reducing the issuance of unsecured notes. In the words of Samuel Jones-Loyd (Lord Overstone), "not only must that paper be convertible into metallic money, but the whole of its oscillations must be made to correspond exactly, both in time and amount, with what would be the oscillations of a metallic currency, as indicated by the state of bullion" (ibid., p. 138). This principle is known as the "currency principle."

They did, however, believe that they would also be able to do without the same restrictions on unsecured demand deposits and bank overdrafts since their use was more as credit than money. These belonged to "the ordinary banking business of deposit and discount" (ibid., p. 122).

---

[1]The full passage reads as follows: "La crise commerciale qui a eu lieu en Angleterre est propre à faire sentir les inconvénients qui peuvent naître de cette faculté illimitée de multiplier l'argent de la circulation. Les banques ont abusé de cette facilité et se sont servies de leurs billets pour escompter une trop grande quantité d'effets de commerce. Les chefs de beaucoup d'entreprises ont pu, au moyen de ces escomptes, donner à leurs entreprises une extension disproportionnée avec leurs capitaux" Say (1852, pp. 474f).

[2]In Great Britain, members included among others Thomas Joplin, James McCulloch, Mountifort Longfield, Richard Torrens, and Samuel Jones-Loyd; in Germany, Wilhelm Tellkampf, Philipp Geyer, Carl Knies, Otto Hübner, and Otto Michaelis; and in France u.a. Henri Cernuschi and Léon Wolowski (see Smith 1990 [1936], p. 145).

1.4 The Banking School

The members of the Banking School[3] responded that the Currency School was greatly mistaken in postulating a fundamental difference between banknotes and demand deposits. The fallacy of this idea became obvious when considering that demand deposits, too, can be used (via checks) as a means of payment. The only difference here was the *form* of money: demand deposits were scriptural money or accounting money. But there was no *material* difference as compared to banknotes.

They also emphasized that there was no mechanical connection between the money supply and the price level, an assumption frequently held by economists of the Currency School. A 10% increase in the money supply would by no means entail a rise of the price level by exactly 10%. It was not even certain that they would rise at all. The reason was that the price of goods was not singularly influenced by the money supply, or the quantity of money, but also by the demand for money (by the hoarding of notes and demand deposits). If, for example, the supply and the demand of money rose simultaneously and at the same rate, then the overall price level would remain unchanged.

With these considerations in mind, the economists of the Banking School developed their central thesis. They argued that *uncovered* (but convertible) bank money—whether in the form of notes or of demand deposits—could play an indispensable role in the economy and, therefore, that it should play such a role. It was precisely *because* such money could be created for free and so to say out of nothing that the available amount of money could be constantly adapted to meet the demand for money. Quite in the spirit of Adam Smith, they pointed out that, in a competitive environment, the supply of money could never deviate permanently from the demand for money. Unwanted bank money—meaning money that no one would want to hold on to—would eventually be returned to the issuers who would redeem it for gold (law of reflux). On the other hand, any additional money demand would be reflected in additional loan requests, and the banks could then fulfill these requests through an increase in the money supply without affecting the price level. Hence, it was precisely the creation of uncovered bank money that would make the money supply "elastic" and closely match the money demand, while adhering to money rigidly backed by metals would have led to a rollercoaster of rising and falling prices for goods.

Additionally, the Banking School advocates argued there were two other consequences that were highly desirable from the classical perspective. The first was that expensive precious metals would be replaced by low-cost bank money. The second was that the creation of money would lead to an increase in the savings rate. Indeed, each unit of money that was kept in circulation (rather than flowing back to the

[3]In Great Britain, members included among others Thomas Tooke, John Fullarton, James Wilson, and H.D. Macleod; in Germany Adolph Wagner and Leopold Lasker; and in France Charles Coquelin, Jean-Gustave Courcelle-Seneuil, Michel Chevalier, and J.E. Horn (see Smith 1990 [1936], p. 145).

issuer) was after all held by someone, and this someone thereby demonstrated his desire to save rather than consume this part of his wealth.

1.5 Peel's Act and the Consequences

The dispute between the two schools of thought ended with the provisional victory of the Currency School, which put its stamp on the Bank Charter Act of 1844, otherwise known as Peel's Act after the prime minister at the time Robert Peel. The law sought to cap the circulation of banknotes while leaving deposit banking largely unregulated. To put a lid on banknote production, the Bank of England's banknote monopoly was strengthened, and the other banks were press-ganged into managing demand deposits rather than issuing their own notes. No special arrangements were made for the creation of deposits out of thin air, however. Here the commercial banks were able to go and act as they pleased.

What happened next is only too clear in retrospect. Deposit banking continued to experience exponential growth through the creation of uncovered accounting money, which was handed out to its beneficiaries in the form of credit (see Fig. 1). This in turn implied a weakening of the liquidity of the banks. The less prudent banks defaulted periodically, resulting in repeated crises of the entire banking system. The first of these large crises, in the years following 1844, occurred in 1848 and was initially attributed to the year's unique historical circumstances. In the following years, however, events repeated outside of a revolutionary atmosphere. There were banking crises in Great Britain and several other countries in 1857, 1866, 1873, 1882, 1893, and 1897.

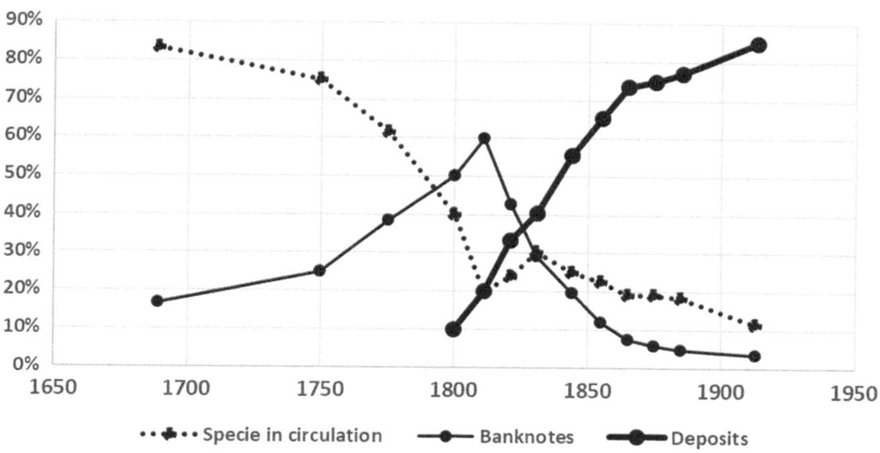

Fig. 1 M1 components in England and Wales, 1689–1913. Data source: R.E. Cameron et al. (1967, p. 42), quoted from Mathias (1983, p. 460, Table 39)

Peel's Act did not meet its high level of expectation. In spite of the capping of note circulation, there was still a cycle of bull and bear markets. Banking crises continued and actually became more volatile. The failure of the Currency School's theory in practice undermined its reputation, as well as that of Ricardo, and ultimately led to the decline of classical economics as a whole.

1.6 A New Orthodoxy

The lessons of the Banking School were now on the upswing, especially theories related to elastic currency and the expediency of stable prices. In the course of the nineteenth century, there was growing evidence that banking crises were embedded in price fluctuations (Juglar 1862; Fisher 1963 [1911]). This led to the idea that a crisis could be avoided by stabilizing the price level as much as possible. To achieve this end, an elastic bank money was essential, since gold production followed the demand for money only slowly and indirectly. Without bank money, the money supply would constantly lag behind its demand, especially in a dynamically growing economy, leading to a tendency for the price of goods to fall. This was precisely the tendency that prevailed throughout the nineteenth century on the British Isles (see Fig. 2). In the aftermath of the international banking crisis of 1873, this price-deflationary tendency became equally dominant on the continent.

During the last quarter of the nineteenth century, the ideas of the Banking School became dominant in Western monetary thought. Their outstanding representatives up to World War II include John Stuart Mill, Alfred Marshall, and D.H. Robertson.

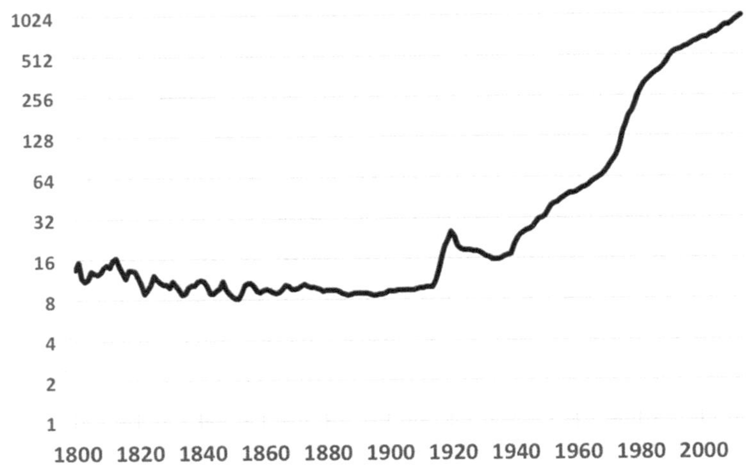

Fig. 2 Evolution of UK CPI, 1800–2013. Data source: ONS, dataset MM23, long-term indicator of prices of consumer goods and services; Jan 1974=100

Even up until today, this doctrine is the basis for the practice of central banks and is fairly unchallenged in most university curricula.

And also another idea with origins in the Banking School now became ever more popular. We have already pointed out that the economists of the Banking School interpreted the increased holding of money that resulted from the ex nihilo creation of money as increased saving. In the eyes of their opponents, this was one of the most serious errors of the Banking School. If this view were correct, then any increase in the amount of money would almost automatically entail an increase in the savings rate. After all, there was always someone who was holding each unit of money in circulation. Thus there could be "savers" who had not in fact saved any part of their income but simply received a bank loan created from nothing. That is the exact opposite of Adam Smith's doctrine. The overall wealth of society could then improve not only by a frugal lifestyle and restrained consumption but also by the more comfortable way of money creation.

In response to this objection, the economists of the Banking School, just as Adam Smith before them, brought up the real bills doctrine. The creation of money, they claimed, is not baseless or "from nothing." It is by no means an arbitrary action by commercial banks. On the contrary, the creation of credit is simply a reflection of simultaneous events in the real economy. Banks grant credit only if an appropriate collateral is provided. For example, if a hat manufacturer finishes 100 hats and sells them to retailers for the total price of 1000 thalers, then on the basis of this exchange, the bank can create a sum of 1000 thalers (e.g., in the form of scriptural money) and issue a loan. The newly created money "represents" the real value of the 100 new hats and is therefore ultimately a real economic variable. This, the champions of the Banking School claimed, would also be in line with classical economics. A real good, in the form of a subsistence fund, has been established first, and, as a result, its monetary equivalent could then be lent out.

1.7 Departure from Classical Economics

The aforementioned objection from the Currency School was also handled in a completely different way. The Scottish jurist and economist Henry Dunning Macleod agreed with the central element of that objection. He argued that the Currency School was right in claiming that money creation ultimately springs from the initiative of the banks. It was *not* a mere reflection of any previous or simultaneous events happening in the real economy. Bank loans do not "passively" follow any occurrences within the real economy. The banks were not simply middlemen who facilitated the flow of one person's savings to another person's project. Banks *created* loans that were *not* based in prior savings.

While Macleod and the Currency School agreed on this point, they radically differed when it came to assessing its economic significance. The economists of the Currency School believed that loans without savings were some sort of foul play. In a natural economy, loans depended on savings. True savings were made out of revenue earned, in the context of a given overall money stock. A portion of that money stock was saved in cash, and a portion of these cash savings would then be used for loans. Clearly, things were quite different when loans were made by creating money out of thin air. In this case there were not any true savings involved. For the Currency School, this was not an advantage but a major shortcoming. Such loans were not a stroke of genius to dispense with the necessity of savings before granting loans. They were a questionable banking practice that was likely to lead straight to payment defaults and crises.

Macleod completely disagreed with this assessment. In a monetary economy, he argued it was not the case that part of the money stock was saved and then part of these savings were passed on as credit. In fact, the causal link was the exact opposite. Granting credit was not just a possible *allocation* of available money. It was its actual *origin*. By its very nature, money was a form of credit. It was a right, a claim on other people (see Macleod 1856, 1889, p. 82).

With this line of argumentation, Macleod made a radical departure from classical economics. As we have seen, the Banking School held the somewhat original interpretation that money creation was a reflection of real economic savings. But just like the Currency School, it did not doubt the foundational dependency between savings and investments. There could be an increase in investment only through increased savings. Macleod reversed this cause-and-effect sequence. It was not demand deposits that led to credit but rather credit created from nothing that led to demand deposits.

Macleod presented these ideas in a very polemical form, and because of this, his writings were often met with rejection. Yet the practical failures of the Currency School created fertile ground for his theories. At the time, the principles of the Banking School were the leading doctrine, but this new orthodoxy had a rather obvious weak spot: the artificial interpretation of money creation as "saving." Just like the Currency School, Macleod underscored this weakness, and his approach offered a radical but intellectually appealing alternative to the discredited Currency School.

In the following decades, this approach was further developed, especially in England and the German-speaking world, and eventually led to a triumphant resurrection of mercantilism. Josef Alois Schumpeter, Albert Hahn, and John Maynard Keyes laid the most important milestones of this process.

Schumpeter (1911) argued that financing credit from nothing was intimately related to entrepreneurship as well as to the crises of the capitalist economies. Bank credit out of thin air paved the way to innovation, and innovation entailed adjustment crises of rival companies working with outdated technology. An economy that grew steadily and organically was, therefore, an unattainable ideal. Growth was primarily caused through innovative breakthroughs, but these could not be had without crises.

Hahn (1920) and Keynes (1936) pushed Macleod's approach to its logical conclusion. It was not savings that led to (credit-financed) investment but (credit-financed) investment that led to savings. Thus they had finally arrived at the exact antithesis of classical economics. If investments could easily be made without saving, then it would be superfluous to explore profound theories on the real economic importance of foregoing consumption. The classical concepts of a "wage fund" and of a "subsistence fund" (the sum total of all funds saved from consumption and available for investment) thus fell into oblivion. After the World War II, they were mentioned in textbooks only as a curious idea of the nineteenth century (see Braun 2012, 2014). Previously, cutting consumption was considered an indispensable prerequisite for the production of goods. Now it appeared to be superfluous, *at best*. More realistically, it appeared as a potential disruptive factor. After all, at least some part of income that was not spent on consumers' goods would not be spent at all, but hoarded, with corresponding losses for "aggregate demand" and thus for production.

From a Keynesian perspective, saving is an individualistic luxury with potentially adverse consequences for broader society. Just like their mercantilist predecessors, Keynesian economists tend to reject all bourgeois demands for a frugal lifestyle as self-serving and a danger to the public.

Hahn (1949) later recanted his fallacies. Keynes never did. He devoted much of his energy to hammering out a supposedly new economic philosophy, which, upon closer inspection, was a newer edition of the exact same fundamental concepts that had already been rejected by Adam Smith. According to Keynes, there was not enough money spent on the free market ("aggregate demand" was too low), and thus production remained below its potential capacity. The state could remedy this problem by providing entrepreneurs with suitable information (and also through propaganda and media manipulation if necessary) to boost optimism. It could also pursue redistribution policies to favor groups that typically spend more money than regular taxpayers. It could inflate the money supply by controlling the central bank. Finally, it could also spend more money itself, particularly, by putting macroeconomic investments under its supervision and control (socialization of investments).

1.8 Welcome to State Dirigisme

In 1936, Keynes published *The General Theory of Employment, Interest, and Money* triumphantly bringing Macleod's approach and the older related ideas of John Law (1705) into the world of academic economics. But the "Keynesian Revolution" had even more far-reaching dimensions. Keynesian-style "dirigisme through the printing press" was also connected to various radical intellectual movements of the nineteenth century that had not made it into the mainstream debates of their own times. The classical economists had not paid any attention to these advocates. They had dismissed them as money cranks.

More than 100 years before Keynes, pioneers in socialism had recognized that socialism could be realized relatively easily and without resistance if the state controlled the banking system. They saw the creation of a central bank as a decisive step in the fight for central economic planning to improve overall efficiency against the "anarchy" of the market.

The leaders in this school of thought were Barthélémy Prosper Enfantin (1796–1864) and Saint-Amand Bazar (1791–1832). Both were fierce adherents of the philosopher Henri de Saint-Simon (1760–1825), who advocated for a performance-orientated egalitarianism or meritocracy. With the help of the central bank, the Saint-Simonians wanted to make sure that all available resources were actually used; and that they were used by people who in their (the Saint-Simonians') opinion would use them most sensibly (see Enfantin et al. 1831).

In the revolutionary year of 1848, Karl Marx and Friedrich Engels published their *Communist Manifesto* (1848), in which they presented similar considerations and demands. At the same time, the socialist anarchist Pierre-Joseph Proudhon also strongly recommended the creation of a central bank at the time. Unlike the Saint-Simonians and Marx-Engels, however, he was by no means recommending state-controlled (and paternalistic) governance over all economic processes. On the contrary, he believed that a central bank would allow for an unlimited amount of money and could therefore resolve all financing issues. The bank should rather be an instrument of individual emancipation from the constraints of scarcity.[4]

Sixty years later, Rudolf Hilferding (1947 [1910]) argued that there was no need to bring about the centralization of money and banking through political interventions. It was an inevitable tendency inherent in mature capitalism.

Keynes (1936, Chap. 23) avoided mentioning these socialist forerunners to his readers. He only highlighted such predecessors who, from a technical rather than ideological standpoint, argued that savings, and especially money hoarding, represented a hindrance to economic development. This included Thomas Malthus, Silvio Gesell, and John A. Hobson. Keynes also spoke favorable of Clifford Hugh Douglas, although he considered his criticism of interest rates to be excessive.

2 A Masterpiece from Vienna

When Ludwig von Mises began developing his *Theory of Money and Fiduciary Media* in 1906, the classical approach to monetary theory had already been pushed into the background for quite some time. The dominance of the Banking School was challenged only by a few old men who were somehow "left over" from the previous era. Younger scholars typically adhered to the principles of the Banking School, and some of them had started walking in the footsteps of Macleod and Marx.

[4]The exchange between Proudhon and Frédéric Bastiat (1863) is worth reading because both positions are expressed in a particularly clear and eloquent manner.

2.1 The Austrian School of Economics

At the time, Mises was a regular participant of a seminar taught by Eugen von Böhm-Bawerk at the University of Vienna. Böhm-Bawerk had achieved international fame through his book *Capital and Interest* (Böhm-Bawerk 1921). He fully adhered to the classical thought on the wealth of nations. In the same way as his mentor Carl Menger, he worked on rectifying and strengthening the ideas of Adam Smith. Böhm-Bawerk spent even less time than Menger dealing with monetary theory. And up until the 1880s, there had been little reason, due to the prevalence of classical economics. Even the disputes between the Currency and Banking Schools appeared to simply be an argument *within* the classical approach. At the beginning of the twentieth century, however, the movement inspired by Macleod became progressively stronger, and this also brought the ideas found in the nineteenth-century socialist underground onto a broader stage for the first time.

Böhm-Bawerk's seminar provided a fertile ground for the confrontation of these great intellectual movements, for it counted in its ranks three young pioneers of the twentieth-century monetary theory: Rudolf Hilferding, Josef Schumpeter, and Ludwig von Mises. Hilferding and Schumpeter were fully committed to the new lines of thought. Their writings solidified and accelerated the general departure from classical economics. Ludwig von Mises had also started off by following the contemporary mainstream. In 1903, however, he discovered Carl Menger's *Principles of Economics* (Menger 1871) and thereafter lost his former convictions.

Mises now recognized the importance of Adam Smith and understood the great improvements that Smith's doctrine had received from the hands of his countrymen. He also saw ample room for similar improvements in the field of monetary theory and the urgency with which they were needed. Therefore, he chose this field to make his own contribution. He started working on a *Habilitation* thesis in monetary theory, which he eventually published in 1912 under the title *Theorie des Geldes und der Umlaufsmittel*.[5] A revised second edition was published in 1924, and this edition was then translated into English and first published in 1934 under the title *Theory of Money and Credit*.

Initially, Mises planned on giving a systematic exposition of his encompassing new approach to monetary economics. He wanted to begin with the fundamentals of value and price theory and then build on these foundations to present the theory of money. The approaching First World War partly destroyed his plan. Mises feared that there would not be enough time remaining to complete his work as planned. Therefore, he resolved to postpone work on the fundamentals and instead focus on questions related to monetary theory. It was not until many years later when he wrote *Nationalökonomie* (1940), which later became *Human Action* (1949), that Mises

[5]The habilitation diploma is best understood as a professional license for professors who seek employment in the universities of Central Europe. It is obtained on the basis of a comprehensive habilitation thesis dealing with an entire field of inquiry (typically written after a doctoral thesis, which deals with more narrowly defined problems).

finally executed the original plan when he presented his entire doctrine as one coherent whole (see Mises 2009 [1978], p. 95).

2.2 The Nature of Money

The first part of the habilitation thesis deals with some questions regarding value and price theory that Mises envisaged in his original plan. The title of this first section is "The Nature of Money," but it also focuses on some deeper problems in value theory. For example, Mises discusses the arguments of Irving Fisher, who claimed that there are quantitative laws of the utility of goods. Mises (1981, p. 218) dismissed this theory, and more generally he rejected the notion that quantitative constants exist in the economy.

Carl Menger had shown that the subjective value judgments of acting persons were at the very heart of price theory. Starting from this insight, Mises sought to build his theory of money prices. The first step was acknowledging that the formation of money prices depends on the nature of the specific type of money that was being exchanged. Therefore, it was necessary to first classify the various forms of money in a way that corresponded to the particularities of their valuation and price formation (Fig. 3).

Mises, much like J.B. Say (1841, Chap. XXX, 1852, Chap. XVII), made a clear distinction between "money in the narrower sense" and "money substitutes."

Money substitutes are "perfectly secure and immediately convertible claims to money" (p. 65), much like token coin, a promissory note issued by a bank, or a demand deposit held at a commercial bank. The value of these substitutes is derived entirely from the legal obligation the issuer has to exchange or redeem them at the

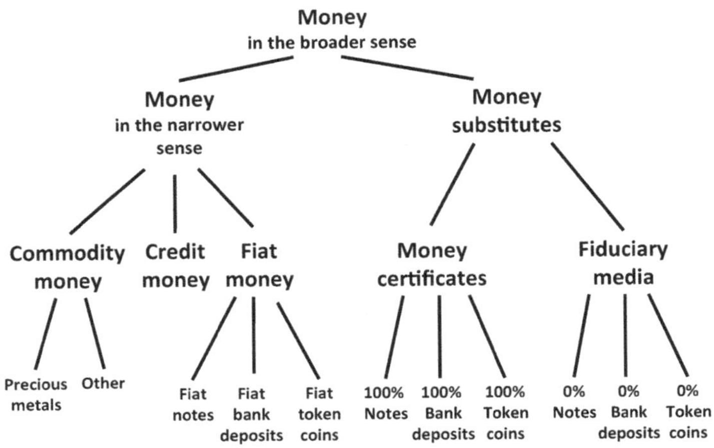

Fig. 3 Classification of monetary goods according to Mises. Source: Hülsmann (2012, p. 34)

owner's request and, of course, on the safe expectation that this obligation will be fulfilled. One might think that redemption would be particularly secure if the relevant substitute were 100% covered by a corresponding monetary sum held by the issuer (Mises refers to such a substitute as a "money certificate"). But according to Mises, even those substitutes that are not actually covered at all (he calls them *Umlaufsmittel* or "fiduciary media") can be redeemable and secure monetary claims. It all comes down to the personal or subjective perspective of the money users. Such uncovered monetary substitutes can therefore be exchanged, too, and their prices would result from the same mechanisms as the prices of the money certificates (although the quantitative exchange relationship would be different).

In contrast to monetary substitutes, the value of money in the narrower sense (which today is commonly referred to as "base money") does not spring from a legal obligation to redeem it into other goods. Mises distinguished three main categories of base money: commodity money, credit money, and fiat money.

It is not necessary to discuss these distinctions in detail. Let us rather underscore the punch line. Mises argued that *the forms of money—which alone are relevant from the point of view of value and price theory—have nothing to do with the physical properties of the goods that are used as money*. For example, precious metal coins are not in and of themselves already money in the narrow sense. They *can* be base money, if they are subject to independent valuation. They *can* also be money certificates or fiduciary media, if money users have the expectation that these coins can be redeemed into base money. The same thing holds true for any paper note. It can be base money (paper money), but it can also be a money certificate or a fiduciary medium. The physical properties do not indicate the economic character. The latter derives from business practices, contracts, and legislation—in short, from a man-made context in which the type of money is used.

As can be inferred from the original German-language title of his book—which literally translates into "*Theory of Money and Fiduciary Media*"—Mises considered fiduciary media to be a very particular and very important form of money.[6] Their importance stems from the fact that they allow an almost costless and thus almost unlimited extension of the money stock. This is quite different from the cases of commodity money and of money certificates. The production of precious metals and other forms of commodity money is costly, and thus, the amount of money in this form cannot be increased as quickly and arbitrarily as desired. Similarly, money certificates do not alter the total amount of money either since they are entirely backed by base money. On the other hand, the production of fiduciary means is limited only by accidental circumstances, such as a lack of coordination between issuers (the banks) or banking regulations.

[6]This was lost in the 1934 Batson translation, which rendered "fiduciary media" systematically as "credit" and thus blurred some of the major distinctions that Mises stressed in his book. Credit and fiduciary media are two very distinct phenomena, even though they are today (as in Mises' time) usually combined in the practice of banking. Mises stressed that there can be credit without fiduciary media and that fiduciary media do not need to be issued via credit. On the problems of the Batson translation, see Hülsmann (2012, pp. 32–34).

In the third part of his work, Mises examines the consequences these facts have for economic activity. This leads him to address the great questions that had already held center stage in the debate between the Currency and Banking Schools. It leads him to fully espouse the "currency principle" while correcting the numerous mistakes of the Currency School in relatively minor matters (Hülsmann 2000, 2007; Salerno 2012; McCaffrey 2012). And it leads him to make an original contribution to the doctrine of that school, namely, a crisis theory, which he develops out of Böhm-Bawerk's theory of capital.

Before venturing into the arguments of the third part, it is important to consider the core concepts of the second part. Here Mises leaves aside all questions related to fiduciary media. He considers a hypothetical economy that uses only money in the narrower sense and money certificates, but not fiduciary media. Which factors determine the subjective value of money, and which determine money prices, in such an economy?

2.3 The Value of Money

The classical economists thought that the price of money corresponded to its production costs. Carl Menger had argued that this theory does not hold up. The market prices of all economic goods ultimately did not result from costs but from the subjective valuation of acting persons. Menger himself had demonstrated his argument only for the special case of consumer goods. Then Böhm-Bawerk went on to show that Menger's theory also held true for capital goods. In regard to money, however, there was still no such proof.

There was a very old theory stating that money is merely some sort of an "assignment" of value of all other goods—just as a warehouse receipt assigns this or that good, held in storage, to the owner of the receipt. (Macleod's credit theory of money, too, was a variant of this conception.) From this perspective, the question of the value of money was quite easy to answer: the value of money was simply determined by the value of the real goods it represented and for which it could so to say be redeemed.

This theory, however, was unsatisfactory because money in and of itself is not an assignment for other goods. Some forms of money (money substitutes) are indeed assignments, and *their* value could thus be explained this way. But money in the narrower sense is not similar to a warehouse receipt but rather to an independent commodity, as Menger (1968 [1909]) had pointed out. What then is the explanation for the subjective value of such a monetary commodity? How can its market prices be explained?

At the time, several influential economists, such a Knut Wicksell and Karl Helfferich, maintained that these questions could not be answered at all with the help of Menger's theory of value. According to Menger, the market price of economic goods stemmed from their subjective use value. But this scheme of thought could not be applied to the special case of money, because its use value was dependent on its purchasing power (on its market prices). The upshot would be circular reasoning, money prices being explained as a consequence of the subjective use value of money, and the latter being explained as a consequence of money prices.

How to get out of this vicious circle? Friedrich von Wieser, a student of Menger, had tackled this problem very much along the lines of the nineteenth-century German economists (see Hülsmann 2007, pp. 225–240; Gabriel 2012). Wieser argued that *today's* subjective value of money is derived from *yesterday's* money prices. Yesterday's money prices spring from yesterday's subjective value of money, which in turn is based on other money prices prevailing in the day *before* yesterday, etc. In other words, the alleged logical circle was an optical illusion. It arose from the false assumption that the subjective value of money at any particular time *t* was determined by the money prices prevailing *at the same time*.

Mises refined Wieser's approach and later named it "regression theorem" (Mises 1998 [1949], p. 406). He emphasized that determining the subjective value of money from previous money prices by no means established an endless chain of causation, thus producing a *regressus ad infinitum*. The chain of causation ended on the day on which the commodity in question was used as money for the first time. *Up until that day*, the market prices of this commodity resulted exclusively from the subjective value of its non-monetary uses. *On that day*, monetary demand came into play as well, and the subjective value of its monetary use could then be derived from its already existing purchasing power.

After clarifying the basic principles of the value of money and money prices, Mises sought to examine the consequences of changes in the supply and demand of money. In particularly, he highlighted three fundamental ideas.

Firstly, Mises demonstrated that changes in the money supply had no mechanical effect on money prices. There was no fixed quantitative relationship, such as a percentage change of X in the money supply resulting in a percentage change of Y in the price level. More generally, the objective conditions under which human beings act had an impact on market prices only through individual choices. It is true that an increase in the amount of money tends to reduce the value of each individual unit of money, but how much the value diminishes depends on the people affected, and the valuations of each individual do not need remain constant over time.[7]

Secondly, Mises stressed that there is no *systematic* relationship between the money stock and aggregate production. Increasing the quantity of money does not benefit the production of goods, and reducing it does not hinder production. "An increase in the quantity of money can no more increase the welfare of the members of a community, than a diminution of it can decrease their welfare" (Mises 1981, p. 102).

This was, of course, the basic idea of classical economy theory as represented by the Currency School. Mises repeated this idea in numerous sections of his work (see Mises 1912, pp. 78, 83, 96, 156, 225, 227f, 230, 235, 262f, 402f). He was aware that,

---

[7]This phenomenon is now known as the "Cantillon effect," after the economist who first researched it in the eighteenth century. See Cantillon (2011 [1755], pp. 147ff).

in this respect, he was in direct contradiction with the Banking School and the majority of his contemporaries in economics. Changes in the money stock could lead only here and there, only *accidentally*, to positive and negative repercussions on aggregate production. This could result in particular from the fact that changes in the money stock entailed reallocations of wealth and income, which had an influence on capital formation (see Mises 1981, p. 239).

Finally, Mises emphasized that any change in the supply or demand of money influenced the distribution of income and wealth. *Overall* economic prosperity—what Smith called the wealth of nations—is not connected with monetary factors. But this does not hold true on the *microeconomic* level. Individual households and firms may very well gain or lose as a result of a change in the money supply or of the demand for money.

2.4 Theory of Fiduciary Media and Fiduciary Credit

After discussing the foundations of value and price theory in the second part of his book, Mises could finally address questions related to fiduciary media and fiduciary credit. Although fiduciary media could also be issued without granting credit at the same time (Mises called this the non-banking style or "nicht-bankmäßige" issue), the primary way to issue fiduciary media at the time and even up until today was in conjunction with a bank credit (banking style or "bankmäßige"). Therefore, the discussion around fiduciary media was closely related to the analysis of "fiduciary credit"—credit made available in the form of fiduciary media, created out of nothing.

Now the scientific literature on banking theory was, according to Mises, in a much less satisfactory condition than monetary theory (where one could at least rely on the works of Menger and Wieser). He felt the contemporary literature on banking was merely descriptive of the technical, organizational, and juridical aspects of the business. It had failed to tackle the economic problems (see Mises 1912, pp. IXf). What were these problems? In the third part of his book, Mises dealt with six major research questions:

1. What is the difference between true (commodity) credit and artificial (fiduciary) credit?
2. Are there any limits to the production of fiduciary media?
3. Is the production of fiduciary media "elastic" in the sense that it flexibly adjusts to changes in the demand for money?
4. Which impact do the banks' cash reserves have on the demand for fiduciary media?
5. Is the issuance of fiduciary media liable to entail macroeconomic imbalances?
6. Which is the appropriate course of action for monetary and banking policy?

Mises built his banking theory on the foundations established by the classical economists and by the Currency School. He concurred with their approach in regard to the essential points and disagreed only on relatively minor issues (even if these had had far-reaching consequences in practice). He assessed the scientific value of the Banking School in the exact opposite way. The latter was correct on the minor issues but wrong on the main points. The Banking School had correctly pointed out that there was no significant difference between bank deposits and banknotes from an economic perspective. It had also rightly rejected the rigid quantity theory, which claimed there was a mechanical link between the quantity of money and the price level. However, the Banking School idea of an "elastic" supply of fiduciary media was completely fallacious. In his words:

> The fatal error of Fullarton and his disciples was to have overlooked the fact that even convertible banknotes remain permanently in circulation and can then bring about a glut of fiduciary media the consequences of which resemble those of an increase in the quantity of money in circulation. Even if it is true, as Fullarton insists, that banknotes issued as loans automatically flow back to the bank after the term of the loan has passed, still this does not tell us anything about the question whether the bank is able to maintain them in circulation by repeated prolongation of the loan. The assertion that lies at the heart of the position taken up by the Banking School, namely, that it is impossible to set and permanently maintain in circulation more notes than will meet the public demand, is untenable; for the demand for credit is not a fixed quantity; it expands as the rate of interest falls, and contracts as the rate of interest rises. But since the rate of interest that is charged for loans made in fiduciary media created expressly for that purpose can be reduced by the banks in the first instance down to the limit set by the marginal utility of the capital used in the banking business, that is, practically to zero, the whole edifice built up by Tooke's school collapses. (Mises 1981, pp. 383f)

In other words, the Banking School—much like Adam Smith in this regard—believed in the erroneous idea that the demanded amount of fiduciary media (of fiduciary credit) is independent from the price of such credits or rather that the credit price is independent from the supply of fiduciary credits. By pointing out this fundamental error, Mises refuted the theory of elastic bank credit in all its forms. In particular, he thereby also refuted the "real bills" doctrine. We have already seen that this theory was premised on the notion that the market prices of the commodities serving as collateral for the "real bills" (and therefore for money and credit creation) are independent from money creation. Mises saw through the fallacy of this premise. When fiduciary media are created from nothing and used for payment, commodity prices are inevitably higher than they otherwise would have been. Mises (1981, p. 346) draws the following conclusion:

> The circulation of fiduciary media is in fact not elastic in the sense that it automatically accommodates the demand for money to the stock of money without influencing the objective exchange value of money, as is erroneously asserted. It is only elastic in the sense that it allows of any sort of extension of the circulation, even completely unlimited extension, just as it allows of any sort of restriction. The quantity of fiduciary media in circulation has no natural limits. If for any reason it is desired that it should be limited, then it must be limited by some sort of deliberate human intervention—that is by banking policy.

Thus Mises comes to essentially the same practical conclusions as the Currency School, albeit with a more refined and in-depth explanation. He also added a new element to their framework. Building on Böhm-Bawerk's capital theory, Mises developed a new theory of economic crises—known today as the Austrian business cycle theory—which had particular relevance during the subsequent decades and even for our present day.

Much like J. B. Say, the representatives of the Currency School had already pointed out that the issuance of fiduciary media could lead to liquidity crises. They had not found it necessary to also examine what would happen if the banks suddenly had an unlimited amount of liquidity. They assumed that *only a few banks* would push forward with the issuance of fiduciary media so that they would sooner or later fall prey to a liquidity shortage, as they would be obliged to make ever higher payments to other banks (external drain). Now, could this not be avoided if *all banks simultaneously* increased their issuances (e.g., by creating a banking cartel)? Or if gold were simply replaced with some immaterial base money, therefore allowing the central bank to provide unlimited liquidity?

Such questions had been raised already by Joseph Proudhon and a few other writers of the nineteenth century. But mainstream economists, who at the time were thoroughly committed to classical economics, considered them absurd. Hardly anybody bothered to deal with such cranky nonsense. Now, as a result of the historical events discussed above, at the beginning of the twentieth century, these crazy ideas had spread quite widely and had become the subject of a much broader discussion. It was time for the matter to be investigated. Mises (1981, p. 390) wrote: "The problem that is before us is usually referred to by the catch-phrase 'gratuitous nature of credit.'" It is the "chief problem in the theory of banking." In the first edition, he had added: "and one of the most difficult problems of economics" (Mises 1912, p. 417).

Many economists at the time did not share the view that this was the central issue of banking theory. The theorists of the Banking School even held that this supposed problem simply did not exist. For them, it was impossible to increase the money supply to the point of surpassing the needs for trade. Therefore, the interest rate could not fall to zero. Credit could never be gratuitous.

Swedish economist Knut Wicksell held a different opinion. A few years before Mises, he realized that this was a serious and fundamental problem (see Wicksell 1898). Wicksell presented two considerations to prove the existence of natural limits to the creation of credit. On the one hand, commercial banks would sooner or later be concerned about the redeemability of their notes and demand deposits. Even if they could count on the support of the other banks (cartel), they would therefore abstain from creating any more fiduciary media. On the other hand, increases in the money supply would tend to increase the price level and thus the price of gold. But then people would sooner or later start to redeem their fiduciary media in gold, and the banks would have to forgo more issuances or reduce previous issuances.

Mises found Wicksell's argumentation unsatisfactory. The second argument would only apply to commodity money systems, but not to fiat money systems. Even the first proof was not sound because it violates Wicksell's own assumption that all money would have already been completely replaced by fiduciary media. In such a scenario, where the banks enjoy the full trust of their customers, there just would not be any redemptions of fiduciary media into base money.

If Wicksell's arguments were not correct, then why should the ever-increasing issuance of fiduciary media ever lead to a crisis? Mises developed his own theory by referring to Wicksell's distinction between the "natural interest rate" and the "money interest rate." Without issuing fiduciary media, the money interest rate would have a tendency to approach the natural interest rate, and the economy would find itself with an intertemporal balance between the production of consumers' goods and capital goods. This would change through the issuance of fiduciary media via fiduciary credits. The money interest rate would be pushed below the natural interest rate, thus disrupting the intertemporal equilibrium. The production of capital goods would then be artificially stimulated, yet without the real resources—the "subsistence fund"—that are necessary to achieve an overall extension of production. In other words, artificially low interest rates would lead to either too many or too lengthy production projects that could ultimately not be completed with the available real resources. Sooner or later, some of the already initiated projects would have to be stopped due to lack of funds. In Mises' words,

the situation is as follows:

> despite the fact that there has been no increase of intermediate products and there is no possibility of lengthening the average period of production, a rate of interest is established in the loan market which corresponds to a longer period of production; and so, although it is inadmissible and impracticable from an overall point of view, a lengthening of the period of production becomes at first profitable. But there cannot be the slightest doubt as to where this will lead. A time must necessarily come when the means of subsistence available for consumption are all used up although the capital goods employed in production have not yet been transformed into consumption goods. This time must come all the more quickly inasmuch as the fall in the rate of interest weakens the motive for saving and so slows up the rate of accumulation of capital. The means of subsistence will prove insufficient to maintain the laborers during the whole period of the process of production that has been entered upon. (Mises 1912, pp. 430f)[8]

Mises' theory differs from the liquidity crisis theory of the Currency School in that he stresses that the crisis is one of the *real* economy (even though it has a monetary origin, as in the liquidity crisis theory). This is precisely why it cannot be avoided by unfaltering and resolute issuances of fiduciary media or of immaterial base money. Such issuances may temporarily postpone a crisis, but only at the price of ever-increasing imbalances in the real economy.

2.5 Monetary and Banking Policy

In conclusion, we now turn to Mises' views on monetary policy. A comparison of the first and second editions of his *Theory of Money and Credit* demonstrates a radicalization of his political thinking between the years 1912 and 1924.

[8]Notice that we quote the first edition (our translation). On the changes that this passage underwent in subsequent editions of the book, see Hülsmann (2012, p. 21, footnote 41).

In the first edition published in 1912, Mises's thinking—much like that of his predecessors—revolved around the supposed ideal of money having a stable purchasing power. Just like the classical economists, however, he rejected a purely immaterial fiat money system. Just like Ricardo, he praised the gold standard because it largely restricted the possibilities for the state to abuse the system. He also stressed that it was practically impossible to measure changes in the monetary values with sufficient precision and that powerful lobbyists and interest groups would exploit these inevitable gray zones. But most of all, as we have seen, he made the case that any artificial increase of the money stock by central or commercial banks would initiate a new business cycle. This also held true when the objective was to stabilize the price level. Loaning out additional money would entail an artificial reduction of the interest rate, and thus new "roundabout" production projects would be *launched*. But it would not be possible to *complete* all of these projects with the available resources.

In the following years, then, Mises personally witnessed wartime inflation, the hyperinflations in Austria (1922) and in Germany (1923), and the socialist experiments financed by printing banknotes in Austria and other European countries. In the light of these experiences, he thoroughly reconsidered the traditional arguments of monetary policy.

In the first edition of his book, he had emphasized the fact—well-known at the time—that any artificial expansion in the money supply must cause a redistribution of income and wealth. The initial users of this new money could spend it while the price level was still relatively low, whereas later users—especially the last ones—would have to pay higher prices for a time, even though their own income would not yet have risen.

In the second edition of 1924, then, Mises made three decisive additions.

First, he stressed that *monetary stabilization policies, too, modified the distribution of incomes and wealth*. In other words, it was spurious to believe that monetary stabilization could be a tool to prevent distributional conflicts. In a best-case scenario, it could prevent an unfair redistribution between creditors and debtors, but by doing this, it would itself create a redistribution between the early and the later users of the new money units.

Second, Mises stressed that the redistribution between creditors and debtors could be prevented even without any monetary policy whatsoever—and was actually prevented in practice. Changes in the price level do not per se lead to an unequal distribution of wealth. This concerns especially the cases in which such changes are predictable (relatively uniform inflation and relatively uniform deflation) so that the contractual partners can take these factors into account.

Third, an absolutely stable price level was quite irrelevant from a practical point of view. Entrepreneurs bought and sold at concrete and individual unit prices, not at some abstract price level. They were not concerned with the general *level* of prices but with price *differences*. These differences—the price structure—were liable to permanent change under the impact of the market process, and they change even when the officially measured price level remains stable. It was therefore wrong to assert that money becomes better when its purchasing power became more stable.

Money with a perfectly stable purchasing power is not perfect money (see also Mises 1928).

With these considerations, Mises revolutionized the economic analysis of inflation and monetary policy. His central insight was that using state intervention to perfectly stabilize the purchasing power of money was pointless. It was therefore just as pointless to impose any kind of artificial money on the market in order to reach that goal.

Mises' thinking also developed in an entirely different direction. While he argued in the first edition of his book that price inflation was as equally undesirable as price deflation, he now came to the conclusion that an inflationary development was much more harmful than its deflationary counterpart (see Mises 1981, pp. 251–268). This is due to the fact that price inflation leads to capital consumption and, ultimately, to a relatively impoverished society. In particular, it reduces the incentives for savings; therefore less capital is available for investment. It also distorts business accounting, because of the reporting of phantom profits. Excessive profits would be paid out and consumed, thus leading to a progressively shrinking capital base for the entire economy.

In this light, monetary theory and policy need a complete revamp. The focus on micromanaging the value of money is misdirected. The central question is how to prevent significant mistakes leading to price inflation and political abuse of monetary policy. In 1924, Mises (1981, p. 435) answered that competition was the most effective means to avoid these problems (see Hülsmann 2008). It was the best way to limit abuses of the monetary system by private actors and, more importantly, by the state.

References

Bastiat, F. (1863). Gratuité du crédit. *Œuvres complètes*. Paris: Guillaumin (Bd. V, S. 94-335. New English translation forthcoming in J. de Guenin and D. Hart (eds), *The Collected Works of Frédéric Bastiat*, vol. 4 (Indianapolis: Liberty Fund)).

Braun, E. (2012). The subsistence fund in Ludwig von Mises's explanation of the business cycle. In J. G. Hülsmann (Ed.), *Theory of money and fiduciary media* (pp. 193–208). Auburn, AL: Mises Institute.

Braun, E. (2014). *Finance behind the veil of money*. West Palm Beach: Liberty.me.

Cameron, R. E., et al. (1967). *Banking in the early stages of industrialisation*. New York: Oxford University Press.

Cannan, E. (1925). *The paper pound of 1797–1821*. London: King & Son.

Cantillon, R. (2011 [1755]). *An essay on economic theory*. Auburn, AL: Mises Institute.

Claassen, E.-M. (1970). *Analyse des liquidités et théorie du portefeuille*. Paris: Presses Universités de France.

Enfantin, B.-P., Carnot, H., Fournel, H., & Duveyrier, C. (1831). *Doctrine de Saint-Simon: Exposition. Première année. 1828–1829* (3rd ed.). Paris: Bureau de l'Organisateur.

Fisher, I. (1963 [1911]). *The purchasing power of money: Its determination and relation to credit, interest, and crises*. New York: Augustus M. Kelley.

Gabriel, A. (2012). Why was the reception of the first edition of Mises's theory of money and credit so lukewarm? In J. G. Hülsmann (Ed.), *Theory of money and fiduciary media* (pp. 37–61). Auburn, AL: Mises Institute.

Hahn, A. (1920). *Volkswirtschaftliche Theorie des Bankkredits*. Tübingen: Mohr.
Hahn, A. (1949). *The economics of illusion*. New York: New York Institute of Finance.
Hilferding, R. (1947 [1910]). *Das Finanzkapital*. Berlin: Dietz.
Hollander, J. H. (1910–1911). The development of the theory of money from Adame Smith to David Ricardo. *Quarterly Journal of Economics, 25*, 429–470.
Hülsmann, J. G. (2000). Théorie et théoriciens de la banque libre – Commentaire de Le Maux. *Journal des Economistes et des Etudes Humaines, 10*(1), 157–167.
Hülsmann, J. G. (2007). *Mises – The last knight of liberalism*. Auburn, AL: Mises Institute.
Hülsmann, J. G. (2008). Mises on monetary reform: The private alternative. *Quarterly Journal of Austrian Economics, 11*(3), 208–218.
Hülsmann, J. G. (2012). The early evolution of Mises' monetary thought. In idem (Hg.), *Theory of money and fiduciary media* (pp. 1–36). Auburn, AL: Mises Institute.
Jones-Loyd, S. (Lord Overstone). (1972 [1857]). *Tracts and other publications on metallic and paper currency*. Clifton, NJ: Kelley.
Juglar, C. (1862). *Des crises commerciales et de leur retour périodique en France, en Angleterre et aux Etats-Unis*. Paris: Guillaumin.
Keynes, J. M. (1936). *General theory of employment, interest, and money*. London: Macmillan.
Law, J. (1705). *Considérations sur le numéraire et le commerce*. The Hague.
Macleod, H. D. (1856). *The theory and practice of banking*. London: Longman, Brown Green, and Longmans.
Macleod, H. D. (1889). *The theory of credit*. London: Longmans, Green & Co..
Marx, K., & Engels, F. (1848). *Manifest der kommunistischen Partei*. London: Bildungs-Gesellschaft für Arbeiter.
Mathias, P. (1983). *The first industrial nation* (2nd ed.). London: Routledge.
McCaffrey, M. (2012). The influence of the currency-banking dispute on early Viennese monetary theory. In J. G. Hülsmann (Ed.), *Theory of money and fiduciary media* (pp. 127–165). Auburn, AL: Mises Institute.
Menger, C. (1871). *Grundsätze der Volkswirthschaftslehre*. Wien: Manz.
Menger, C. (1968 [1909]). "Geld" *Handwörterbuch der Staatswissenschaften* (3. Aufl., Vol. IV, pp. 1–124). Tübingen: Mohr (reprinted in *Gesammelte Werke*).
Pallas, C. (2004). *Ludwig von Mises als Pionier der modernen Geld- und Konjunkturlehre*. Marburg: Metropolis.
Ricardo, D. (1992 [1821]). *The principles of political economy and taxation* (3rd ed.). London: J.M. Dent.
Salerno, J. T. (2012). Ludwig von Mises as currency school free banker. In J. G. Hülsmann (Ed.), *Theory of money and fiduciary media* (pp. 95–125). Auburn, AL: Mises Institute.
Say, J.-B. (1841). *Traité d'économie politique* (6th ed.). Paris: Guillaumin.
Say, J.-B. (1852). *Cours complet d'économie politique pratique* (3rd ed.). Paris: Guillaumin.
Schumpeter, J. A. (1911). *Theorie der wirtschaftlichen Entwicklung*. Leipzig: Duncker & Humblot.
Smith, V. C. (1990 [1936]). *The rationale of central banking*. Indianapolis: Liberty Fund.
Smith, A. (1994 [1776]). *The wealth of nations*. New York: Modern Library.
Thornton, H. (1939 [1802]). *An inquiry into the nature and effects of the paper credit of Great Britain*. London: London School of Economics.
von Böhm-Bawerk, E. (1921). *Kapital und Kapitalzins* (4. Aufl.). Jena: Fischer.
von Mises, L. (1912). *Theorie des Geldes und der Umlaufsmittel* (1st ed.). Leipzig: Duncker & Humblot.
von Mises, L. (2005 [1924]). *Theorie des Geldes und der Umlaufsmittel* (Reprint of the 2nd ed.). Berlin: Duncker & Humblot.
von Mises, L. (1928). *Geldwertstabilisierung und Konjunkturpolitik*. Jena: Fischer.
von Mises, L. (1940). *Nationalökonomie*. Genf: Editions Union.
von Mises, L. (1998 [1949]). *Human action*. Auburn, AL: Mises Institute.
von Mises, L. (2009 [1978]). *Memoirs*. Auburn, AL: Mises Institute.
von Mises, L. (1981). *Theory of money and credit*. Indianapolis: Liberty Fund.
Wicksell, K. (1898). *Geldzins und Güterpreise*. Jena: Fischer.

Money: Capital Good, Consumers' Good, or (Media of) Exchange Good?

William Barnett II and Walter Block

1 Introduction

Several Austrians, Mises foremost among them, maintain that money is neither a capital good nor a consumers' good.

It is usual to divide economic goods into the two classes of those that satisfy human needs directly and those which only satisfy them indirectly: that is consumption goods or goods of the first order and production goods or goods of higher orders. The attempt to include money in either of these groups meets with insuperable difficulties. It is unnecessary to demonstrate that money is not a consumption good. It seems equally incorrect to call it a production good.

Of course, if we regard the twofold division of economic goods as exhaustive, we shall have to rest content with putting money in one group or the other. This has been the position of most economists; and since it has seemed altogether impossible to call money a consumption good, there has been no alternative but to call it a production good.

This apparently arbitrary procedure has usually been given only a very cursory vindication. Roscher, for example, thought it sufficient to mention that money is "the chief instrument of every transfer" . . . (Mises 1980, pp. 95–96, footnote omitted).

In this paper, we argue that exchange is a form of production, and, consequently, there are only two types of goods, consumers' goods and capital goods; and that

W. Barnett II (✉)
Department of Economics, Joseph A. Butt, S. J. College of Business Administration, Loyola University New Orleans, New Orleans, LA, USA
e-mail: wbarnett@loyno.edu

W. Block
Harold E. Wirth Endowed Chair in Economics, Department of Economics, Joseph A. Butt, S. J. College of Business Administration, Loyola University New Orleans, New Orleans, LA, USA
e-mail: wblock@loyno.edu

A. Godart-van der Kroon, P. Vonlanthen (eds.), *Banking and Monetary Policy from the Perspective of Austrian Economics*,
https://doi.org/10.1007/978-3-319-75817-6_3

money is, then, a producers' good. The method we shall use is to quote at length from and then analyze cited material. In Sect. 2 we address this topic from the perspective of "The Theory of Money and Credit" (Mises 1980 [1912]).[1] We take issue with Rothbard (1970) on this matter in Sects. 3 and 4 and focus on it using Hoppe et al. (1998) as a case in point. Each of these quotes is followed by our analysis and commentary. A brief summary and conclusions in Sect. 5 end the paper. Throughout Sect. 2 all page-number-only cites are to Mises (1980); the same applies to Rothbard (1970) in Sect. 3 and Hoppe et al. (1998) in Sect. 4.

This is not to deny that a good that serves as money may not also be a consumers' good. A monetary good most certainly can be used for purposes of consumption. We do not at all dispute this. You can paper your wall with paper money. You can take a swim in gold and/or greenbacks (as did Scrooge McDuck of comic book fame). You can burn paper money or melt down gold and study the chemical effects of such a process. You can even light your cigar with a $20 bill. But in none of these cases are you using gold or paper bills *as* money, e.g., to facilitate trade. When you do that, money is necessarily a capital good.[2]

It must be noted that "to facilitate trade" must be understood in terms of the meaning attributed to it by a relevant human mind. Consider a good, say gold coins, that is a monetary good, i.e., it serves as money, in a particular society during the time period under consideration. It may either be held by A, or A may exchange the coins with B for some non-monetary item, X. In the former case, the good is money if A holds it with the intent of exchanging it at some, perhaps as yet undetermined, point in the future, for some other, also perhaps as yet undetermined, product. That is, the coins are money in such a case, not just during the process of monetary exchange, but also during any period in which they are being held for that purpose, and as such they are capital goods. However, if A holds the coins for numismatic purposes, they are not money; rather they constitute a coin collection. And, if the coin collection is held for personal aesthetic pleasure, it constitutes a consumers' good; however, if it is held as an investment,[3] e.g., a "store of value," then it is no different than any other asset held as an investment; i.e., it is a capital good. Note that this means that the monetary good, e.g., gold coins, may be (1) a consumers' good; (2) money—a capital good; or (3) a non-money capital good. Any asset, including durable consumers' goods or even non-durable consumers' goods,[4] is a store of value and thus a capital good. If one is holding the coins as media of exchange, then they are capital goods, specifically money; if one is holding the coins for investment

[1]Mises (1990 [1932], p. 55) maintains the same position.

[2]We thank our colleague, Stuart Wood, for this important point that he made in his commentary on our paper given at the Austrian Scholars' Conference of 2003, held at the Mises Institute in Auburn AL. Moreover, the material in the next five (5) paragraphs of the text deals with issues that arose in subsequent conversations with him, for which, also, we thank him.

[3]The same analysis applies, mutatis mutandis, if A is holding the coins for any other non-monetary purpose(s).

[4]For example, Rothbard's (1993 [1962], p. 7) ham sandwich in the making.

purposes, then they are investment goods—an inventory of "junk" gold coins of an inventory or numismatically valuable gold coins.

In the latter case, if A, holding the coins as money, exchanges them to B for X, they are money to A. However, they may not be money to B if he intends to acquire them for numismatic purposes. In that case, B understands the exchange as a barter transaction—the trade of X for a coin collection—and the coins are not money to B.[5] Similarly, if A is holding the coins for numismatic purposes and understands the exchange as a barter transaction—exchanging his coin collection for X—the coins, even during the exchange process, are not money to A.[6]

In sum, even when used in an exchange process, the gold coins may be money to both parties, neither party, or to only one and that one, either, party. A good acquires its character as money depending upon the meaning attributed to it by the relevant party or parties. The question is, "What meaning is attributed to the good?" Then, in any particular historical instance in which the answer is "money," the good is necessarily a capital good.

Moreover as with other goods, the character of an item used as money can be transformed. For example, gold coins intended as money can be converted to a coin collection, in which case they are transformed from a capital good to a consumers' good; or they can be smelted and changed to an industrial use, in which case they are altered from one type of capital good to another, say electrical contacts in some piece of industrial equipment. This is in principle no different than taking scrap steel that had been part of a steel building used for industrial purposes, i.e., being used as a capital good and recycling into steel: (1) embodied in an automobile used for pleasure, i.e., converting it into a consumers' good or (2) embodied in a truck used for commercial purposes, i.e., converting it into a different type of capital good.

Implicit in the foregoing is that, as with other goods, the one used as money may show up, simultaneously, anywhere in the structure of production (Hayek 1931; Rothbard 1993 [1962]), whether as a consumers' good or as a higher order good, and its location in the structure may shift from higher to lower and vice versa. However, as money it must of necessity, we contend, show up only as a higher order good. And, of course, one and the same commodity (e.g., gold) can appear simultaneously at different places in the capital structure, i.e., the structure of production excluding the lowest, i.e., consumers' goods and order (Lachmann 1956; Garrison 2001). Further, it can move around in the structure from lower order to higher, and vice versa.

[5]The same analysis applies, mutatis mutandis, if B is acquiring the coins for any other non-monetary purpose(s).

[6]The same analysis applies, mutatis mutandis, if A was holding the coins for any other non-monetary purpose(s).

2 Mises

In opposition to Roscher, Knies made room for money in the classification of goods by replacing the twofold division into production goods and consumption goods by a threefold division into means of production, objects of consumption, and media of exchange. His arguments on this point, which are unfortunately scanty, have hardly attracted any serious attention and have been often misunderstood. Thus, Helfferich attempts to confute Knies's proposition that a sale-and-purchase transaction is not in itself an act of production but an act of (interpersonal) transfer, by asserting that the same sort of objection might be made to the inclusion of means of transport among instruments of production on the grounds that transport is not an act of production but an act of (interlocal) transfer and that the nature of goods is no more altered by transport than by a change of ownership (Mises 1980, p. 96, footnote omitted).

Mises maintains that Knies (1885) was right. His argument (Mises 1980, pp. 95–102), in essence, is that the ambiguity of the German word, *Verkehr*, led to confusion between transfers through space and interpersonal transfers and, consequently, to the confounding of money, the means of interpersonal transfers, with the transportation goods, the means of transfers through space. The common nomenclature of the two meanings, as also their incidental confusion, may well be attributable to the fact that exchange transactions often, but by no means always, go hand in hand with acts of transport, through space and vice versa. But obvious1y this is no reason why science should impute an intrinsic similarity to these essentially different processes (Mises 1980, p. 97, footnote omitted).

This is correct; however, it is a non sequitur to maintain, as Mises does, that because on those grounds, science should not link them; they should not be linked at all. Indeed, there may be, and are, other valid grounds for such a link.

In fact, the role played by man in production always consists solely in combining his personal forces with the forces of nature in such a way that the cooperation leads to some particular desired arrangement of material. No human act of production amounts to more than altering the position of things in space and leaving the rest to nature (Mises 1980, p. 97, footnote omitted).

This is highly problematic. Unless "desired arrangement of material" and "altering the position of things in space" are to take on entirely trivial meanings, these statements rule out the provision of many services (e.g., the services of doctors and lawyers in conveying advice orally) as acts of production.

It is often overlooked that, among other natural qualities, the position of a thing in space has important bearings on its capacity for satisfying human wants. Things that are of perfectly identical technological composition must yet be regarded as specimens of different kinds of goods if they are not in the same place and in the same state of readiness for consumption or further production.... The only water that can quench the thirst of the traveler in the desert is the water that is on the spot, ready for consumption (Mises 1980, pp. 97–98).

Mises, here, makes a most important finding: the essential aspect of a good is not its physical properties but, rather, its "significance for satisfying human wants."

Although he makes the point that, for acting man, drinking water in the desert and drinking water in a well-watered mountain district are "totally different," he does not also acknowledge that for A and B in the desert, drinking water in the desert owned by A is "totally different" from that owned by B. If A owns the water and B does not, then if B cannot meet A's price, unless B is prepared to coerce A, B must go thirsty, though A has surfeit. But, of course, coercion is outside the realm of the market—the realm of voluntary human interactions (Rothbard 1970).

Strictly speaking, only those goods should be called goods of the first order which are already where they can immediately be consumed. All other economic goods, even if they are ready for consumption in the technological sense, must be regarded as goods of higher orders which can be transmuted into goods of the first order only by combination with the complementary good, "means of transport." Regarded in this light, means of transport are obviously production goods (Mises 1980, p. 98).

Again Mises makes clear that, "for the purposes of economics," "it is better to regard" two goods physically identical save for their locations "as goods of different kinds." However, in the very next sentence, he uses the phrase "where [goods] can immediately be consumed" to determine whether said items are consumers' goods. "Can," in this context, means "physically able to." However, if there is a candy bar on the desk between you and me, it can be consumed by either of us. However, assuming it is owned by one of us, it may not be consumed by the other, without permission. For the owner it is a consumers' good; for the other party, it is something of a higher order that first requires neither physical transformation nor spatial relocation but, rather, a transfer of ownership rights, i.e., exchange, for it to become a consumers' good of his. But, the transformation of a good from higher to lower order is, precisely, what is meant by production.

We have seen that transfer through space is one sort of production; and means of transport, therefore, so far as they are not consumption goods such as pleasure yachts and the like, must be included among production goods. Is this true of money as well? Are the economic services that money renders comparable with those rendered by means of transport? Not in the least. Production is quite possible without money. There is no need for money either in the isolated household or in the socialized community. Nowhere can we discover a good of the first order of which we could say that the use of money was a necessary condition of its production (Mises 1980, pp. 98–99).

That money is not a capital good because it is not necessary to production is a non sequitur. That production of cooked fish was, and is, possible without the existence of steel mills does not mean they are not capital goods. Moreover, it is incorrect to say that there are no consumers' goods for the production of which "the use money is a necessary condition." It would be impossible to produce many (most?) of the goods provided by a modern capitalist economy without the use of money. Or as Mises well understood in a different context: "Our civilization is inseparably linked with our methods of calculation. It would perish if we were to abandon this most precious tool of acting" (Mises 1996, p. 230). However, "Economic calculation cannot comprehend things which are not sold and bought against money" (Mises 1996, p. 214). Therefore, we may conclude that Mises understood that, contrary to the statement supra, even though money is not necessary for production in an underdeveloped society, it certainly is in a modern capitalist economy.

Böhm-Bawerk's argument leaves out of consideration the difference between transport, which consists in an alteration of the utility of things, and exchange, which constitutes a separate economic category altogether. It is illegitimate to compare the part played by money in production with that played by ships and railways (Mises 1980, p. 100).

To say that transport alters the utility of goods and, implicitly, that exchange does not is incorrect. The problem is that Mises does not recognize that an exchange in the ownership rights to an article alters its utility to the individuals concerned. And, since money is that which par excellence provides exchange services, it is de facto a capital good.

Every sort of economic organization needs not only a mechanism for production but also a mechanism for distributing what is produced. It will scarcely be questioned that the distribution of goods among individual consumers constitutes a part of production, and that in consequence we should include among the means of production not only the physical instruments of commerce such as stock exchanges, ... account books, ... but also everything that serves to maintain the legal system which is the foundation of commerce, as, for example, ... law courts ... (Mises 1980, p. 101).

The implication is that because the legal system is "the" foundation of commerce, everything that serves to maintain it is a capital good. But, the foundation of commerce consists not of the legal system alone; money is every bit as much a foundation of commerce as are any of these other institutions correctly mentioned by Mises in this regard. Therefore, by that criterion, money is a capital good.

What prevents us nevertheless from reckoning money among these "distribution goods" and so among production goods (and incidentally the same objection applies to its inclusion among consumption goods) is the following consideration. The loss of a consumption good or production good results in a loss of human satisfaction; it makes mankind poorer. The gain of such a good results in an improvement of the human economic position; it makes mankind richer. The same cannot be said of the loss or gain of money.... An increase in the quantity of money can no more increase the welfare of the members of a community, than a diminution of it can decrease their welfare. Regarded from this point of view, those goods that are employed as money are indeed what Adam Smith called them, "dead stock, which... produces nothing" (Mises 1980, pp. 101–102, footnote omitted).

The problem here is Mises' failure to see that a change in the quantity of money does affect the welfare of members of a community. Friedman (1969, p. 1) maintains that:

> It is a commonplace of monetary theory that nothing is so unimportant as the quantity of money expressed in terms of nominal money units—dollars, or pounds, or pesos. The situation is very different with respect to the real quantity of money—the quantity of goods and services that the nominal quantity of money can purchase, or the number of weeks' income to which the nominal quantity of money is equal. This real quantity of money has important effects on the efficiency of operation of the economic mechanism, on how wealthy people regard themselves as being and, indeed, on how wealthy they actually are.

And, Hutt (1956, p. 198) states:

> Now Mises himself, and several other economists, maintain explicitly that the amount of money which individuals and firms decide to hold is determined by the marginal utility of its services. Yet for some reason they have not made the next small step needed to recognize this prospective yield (of 'utilities') which invites the holding of money, as the normal return to investment.

The prospective yield from investment in money assets consists, I suggest, (a) of a prospective *pecuniary yield*, in which case the money assets are producers' goods; (b) of a prospective *nonpecuniary yield* in personal convenience, in which case the money assets are consumers' goods; or (c) of a prospective "real," i.e., *nonpecuniary* speculative yield, in which case the money assets are producers' goods, whether held privately or in the course of business.

Thus, for Hutt, people hold money because it provides a yield, i.e., a benefit, to them. Moreover, Hutt (1956, p. 208) states that: "The mere fact, however, that a particular economic good is capable of being diluted is no proof that it is not useful or productive." Then, in a footnote, (Hutt 1956, p. 208, n71) he distinguishes between "the 'number of money units' and, 'the amount of money in real terms'," clearly implying that an increase in the "number of money units" (i.e., "nominal money") does not confer an additional yield or benefit to society, whereas an increase in "money in real terms" (i.e., "real money") does.

Barnett and Block (2004) argue that the optimum quantity of a commodity money is whatever amount is provided in a free market. They also maintain that the optimum quantity of a fiat money is the extant amount, i.e., that the amount of fiat money should be frozen. In that case, a general decline in market-determined prices[7] would cause an increase in real money, which increase would be optimal in that institutional setting.[8]

However, as an economist qua economist, all that can be said is that in a commodity-money economy, some individuals voluntarily add to the stock of money, e.g., by causing newly mined gold to be minted into coins. It is true that this reduces the value of the existing stock of money below what it otherwise would be, but that can no more be said to violate the rights of someone whose money holdings are so decreased in value than can the production of additional units of any other good that reduces the value of preexisting units of that good. That is, actions that are within the rights of the individuals cannot be said to improperly harm others because they cause a decline in value of the others' possessions, regardless of whether the goods in question are money or something else. In point of fact, additions to the stock of a commodity money or of the real, though not nominal, stock of fiat money provide net benefits; else they would not be made. To argue otherwise is to argue that money constitutes, in effect, a case of "market failure." That is, the implicit claim here is that the free market will misallocate resources to the production of money, which resources could be put to better use elsewhere (Mises 1996, pp. 421–422). Should that be the case, governmental intervention into the monetary system cannot be ruled out

[7]Such a decline would be normal in a growing economy with a fixed stock of fiat money.

[8]See, also, Canaan (1921).

on logical grounds. Rather, it becomes a historical/empirical issue: do the benefits of governmental intervention outweigh the costs thereof?

Money, in fact, is indispensable in our economic order. But as an economic good, it is not a physical component of the social distributive apparatus in the way that account books, prisons, or firearms are. No part of the total result of production is dependent on the collaboration of money even though the use of money may be one of the fundamental principles on which the economic order is based (Mises 1980, p. 102).

The problem here is the failure to see that the social distributive apparatus is not solely concerned with the physical distribution of goods but also with the distribution of the rights to them. Moreover, that money is not a physical component of the social distributive apparatus (which of course it is in a commodity-money society[9]) is irrelevant; if something plays a role in transforming a good from a higher to a lower order, it is, de facto, a capital good. But that is exactly what happens in every exchange, and, therefore, money, the good that facilitates exchanges, is, indubitably, a capital good. Furthermore, as shown supra by Mises himself, money is essential to production in a modern capitalist society; without it there neither would nor could be any such society.

Production goods derive their value from that of their products, not so money; for no increase in the welfare of the members of a society can result from the availability of an additional quantity of money. The laws which govern the value of money are different from those which govern the value of production goods and from those which govern the value of consumption goods (Mises 1980, p. 102).

The argument that additions to the stock of money do not increase the welfare of the members of society has been dealt with, supra. It is not correct to say that the laws that govern the value of money are different from those that govern the value of other goods. The value of any good is determined by the contribution it is expected to make (directly, in the case of consumers' goods or indirectly, in the case of capital goods) to the satisfaction of human wants.

In sum, because money is "the" good used in exchange, and exchange transforms goods from higher to lower order, and production is action which transforms goods from higher to lower order, money, too, is a producers' good, i.e., a capital good. That the transformations in which money is involved are not physical in nature but, rather, are of an intangible nature—"merely" concerning ownership rights—is irrelevant. Money is just as important, indeed, probably far more important, for the production process than any other single capital good such as steel or cement. It would be far easier to conceive of a modern civilization without either of the latter two, than the former.

There is yet another series of ways in which goods can be transformed from higher to lower orders in the structure of production without moving them

[9]We are certainly aware of the fact that our present social arrangements do not at all feature a commodity money or, indeed, many of the other attributes of a laissez-faire economy. This point notwithstanding, we are attempting to address present realities, not only theoretical considerations. It cannot be denied that fiat money and central banks, for example, play very important roles in modern societies.

geographically or changing them physically. This method, too, is thus analogous to the role played by money, in transferring items from the ownership and control of one person to another. We refer here to the functions of advertising, marketing, brokering, insuring, and in all other ways bringing material closer to the realm of the final consumer without chemically or physically transforming it. On the somewhat superficial distinction made between selling and production costs, Kirzner had this to say:

> Every aspect of the product (including such extras as friendly service, free parking, and the like) has been produced (and the associated outlays undertaken) strictly in the belief that it would enhance the salability of the whole product. No single penny of the outlay—even those usually considered as strictly production, rather than selling, costs—can be perceived as anything but costs incurred in order to 'sell.' (Kirzner 1973, p. 144)

The point is that there is a direct analogy between activities such as advertising, marketing, brokering, etc., as intermediating agencies on the one hand, which bring goods and services out of the wilderness of the higher order area and into or closer to the more salutary arena of consumption, and on the other hand, money, which does precisely the same thing. The purpose of product markets and capital goods is, after all, the bringing of them into fruition as items of use to consumers; they have no intrinsic value in and of themselves apart from this necessary "mission" of theirs. If the former deserve to be considered part and parcel of higher order or capital goods and services, and they do, then so does the latter.

3 Rothbard

Here is a statement from Murray Rothbard on matters pertaining to our subject:

> We are now on the threshold of a great economic law, a truth that can hardly be overemphasized, considering the harm its neglect has caused throughout history. An increase in the supply of a producers' good increases, *ceteris paribus*, the supply of a consumers' good. An increase in the supply of a consumers' good (when there has been no decrease in the supply of another good) is demonstrably a clear *social benefit*; for someone's "real income" has increased and no one's has decreased [footnote omitted].

Money, on the contrary, is solely useful for exchange purposes. Money, per se, cannot be consumed and cannot be used directly as a producers' good in the productive process. Money per se is therefore unproductive; it is dead stock and produces nothing. Land or capital is always in the form of some specific good, some specific productive instrument. Money always remains in someone's cash balance (Rothbard 1970, p. 670).

An analogy arises between money and what is called a "catalyst" in the field of chemistry. Rothbard quite correctly maintains that money, per se, is not used up[10] as

---

[10]Gold, of course, is subject to wear and tear as it is used, certainly in the case of jewelry and teeth fillings, but also as it passes from hand to hand in its monetary use.

it is utilized in its task of facilitating trade. But the same can be said for the role of catalysts in chemical reactions. They assist in these processes without, themselves, being used up. Yet, it would be the rare chemist who would go so far as to say that, therefore, a catalyst "per se is therefore unproductive."

It is much the same with money. Even on Rothbard's own grounds that money is not used up when it plays its exchange facilitating role, it hardly follows that money is therefore "dead stock and produces nothing." Very much to the contrary, the monetary commodity is a highly useful one. If, in fact, money is dead stock and produces nothing, i.e., adds no value, why would people give up valuable goods and resources to acquire it? And yet we know that they do.

Then there is the point that "money always remains in someone's cash balance." To be sure, it does. But no less could be said in behalf of any other economic good. While it is of course true that items such as steel, shoes, and sugar do not enter anyone's cash balance, let alone remain there, these goods are also always under the ownership and control of someone, no matter how quickly they may travel from hand to hand in terms of turnover of property from one person to another. Thus, if (part of) the reason that Rothbard considers money "unproductive" is that it is always owned, then all other economic goods must also be "unproductive" because they also are owned.[11] But the latter position is unacceptable, as all other goods most certainly are "productive;" therefore, it cannot be maintained that money is unproductive because it is always in someone's cash balance.[12]

4 Hoppe et al.

Although Hoppe et al. (1998, pp. 19–50)[13] do not directly address the issue with which we are concerned, it does arise indirectly in their discussion of money as a present good and not a future good.[14] According to Rothbard (1993 [1962], pp. 60–61):

> Goods being directly and presently consumed are *present goods*. A *future good* is the present expectation of enjoying a consumers' good at some point in the future. A future good may be

[11]That is, if we accept the analogy between money always being in someone's cash balance and economic goods always being owned by someone.

[12]This is neither the time nor the place to critically examine Rothbard's view that "An increase in the supply of money confers no social benefit whatever." See on this Barnett and Block (2004).

[13]The careful reader will note that Block is a co-author both of the present paper and the one now undergoing criticism in this section of it. The correct implication of this strange phenomenon is that Block has changed his mind as concerns the proper status of money as a present or future good. However, nothing said in the present paper can properly be interpreted as criticism of the main contention of Hoppe et al. (1998), to wit that fractional reserve banking is incompatible with the operations of a free enterprise system.

[14]The purpose of Hoppe, Hülsmann, and Block is to refute the normative and positive positions of Selgin and White (1996). The conclusions of that paper stand independently of the arguments herein.

a claim on future consumers' goods or it may be a capital good, which will be transformed into a consumers' good in the future. Since a capital good is a way station (and nature-given factors are original stations) on the route to consumers' goods, capital goods and nature-given factors are both future goods.

If Rothbard is correct, as we think him to be, then money cannot be a present good, as only "[g]oods being directly and presently consumed are *present goods*" (Rothbard 1970, pp. 59–60). Moreover, it is no more "a claim on future consumers' goods" than it is a claim on present or future capital goods. The logical conclusion, based on Rothbard, is that it is a capital good. That is, it is a good, and there are only consumers' goods and capital goods. Of course, there are claims thereto, from which these must be distinguished, but these are not the goods themselves.

However, Hoppe et al. (1998, p. 43) state:

Yet money is demonstrably *not* a future good. In fact, when the money is spent—in the future—it loses all its utility for the present owner. It has utility only while and insofar as it is *not* spent, and its character as a present good stems from the omnipresent human condition of *uncertainty* [footnote omitted].

Compare the paragraph above with the following one, in which the present authors have substantively substituted the word "inventory" for the word "money" and also non-substantively substituted "exchanged" for "spent," with the following:

Yet inventory is demonstrably *not* a future good. In fact, when the inventory is exchanged—in the future—it loses all its utility for the present owner. It has utility only while and insofar as it is *not* exchanged, and its character as a present good stems from the omnipresent human condition of *uncertainty*.

This latter sentence is obviously incorrect. Inventories of any kind are not present goods; rather, it is the characteristic of being "directly and presently consumed" that makes a good a present good, and money qua money is never consumed. This applies, even, to goods that would otherwise and ordinarily be considered "consumer" goods. Suppose a person has an inventory of apples, for example. Now, apples, typically, are considered consumer, not producer, goods. But with an inventory of them, this can no longer be the case. Only those apples that are consumed in any given time period can be considered consumer, not intermediate, goods. The ones that are to be consumed later are at present intermediate goods.[15] We conclude that money is not a present good. Therefore, it must be a future good, and because it is a future good, it must be a capital good.[16]

---

[15]On this point, see the text to which is appended footnote 27, infra, and Rothbard (1993 [1962], pp. 6–8).

[16]Money is not the only good that is a claim to other goods. Properly understood any good is a claim against other goods; it is just that money is the most efficient good for the purpose of being a claim; in a commodity money world, money is also a commodity and in a paper money world, paper money is also paper. However, there are some claims that are not goods in themselves but solely and merely claims to underlying goods, e.g., stocks and bonds. If gold coins were no longer money because people shifted to platinum coins, the gold coins would still have value as a commodity that could be traded with (i.e., used as a claim against) other goods. However, if paper money were no longer money because people shifted to commodity coins, the paper money would be virtually worthless, save for any collectors' value or scrap value it might have. The same can be said for the

To be sure, the main function of money for most people[17] is to bridge the gap between present and future, which is necessitated[18] by the uncertainty of the latter. If the future were known with certainty, there would be no need for money. But precisely the same state of affairs obtains with regard to inventory. There would also be no benefit in holding inventory either, were it not for this omnipresent uncertainty. Indeed, inventories of goods play much the same role in dealing with future uncertainty as do monetary holdings. Yet no one would be tempted to claim that stocks of goods whose purpose is to mediate between input and output are not higher order, or intermediate goods; no one would be tempted to categorize them as present or consumer goods.

Compare also, the following two (2) paragraphs.

The error in classifying *money* as a future good can be revealed in a twofold manner. On the one hand, negatively, it can be shown that this assumption still leads to contradiction. In support of their thesis, Selgin and White claim that "holding *money* for later *spending*, rather than *spending it on* consumption *now*, does defer consumption to the future," implying that the holding of *money* involves the exchange of a future good (satisfaction) for a present one. In the next sentence, they admit that *money* held is *spent neither* on consumer goods *nor* on producer goods. Yet they fail to notice that this implies also, as a further consequence, that holding *money* for later *spending*, rather than *spending it on* production *now*, does defer *production* (and hence *future* consumption) to the future. If the holding of *money* defers consumption and production, however, then it becomes impossible to maintain that the holder of *money* has thereby invested in a *future* good, because *there* are *no future goods—whether* consumer or producer goods—which result from the act of holding *money* and to which its holder could thus be entitled. Yet as claims to no future goods whatsoever, *money* would be worthless. By implication, if *money* is not worthless (and no one would hold *money* if it had no value), then its value must be that of a *present* good (Hoppe et al. 1998, pp. 43–44).

Again, a similar word substitution is employed in the next paragraph as between "money" and "inventory."

The error in classifying *inventory* as a future good can be revealed in a twofold manner. On the one hand, negatively, it can be shown that this assumption still leads to contradiction. In support of their thesis, Selgin and White claim that "holding

stock and bonds of a corporation, the assets of which were totally destroyed. Thus a bond is not a good but a claim to a good; only goods have value, and the bond's value is derivative from the good it is a claim against—destroy the good and you destroy the claim. The same could be said of gold coins—destroy the good (the gold coins) and you destroy the claim the gold coins constitute against other goods. One can destroy the bond (the claim) without destroying the goods underlying it; but if you destroy the good, you destroy the value of the bond, though it may continue to exist physically. However, from an economic point of view, mere physical existence takes on a secondary role.

[17]Exceptions include misers such as Scrooge McDuck, who reveled in daily "swims" through his money bin. Fora positive spin on this economic actor, see Block (1991, pp. 105–109).

[18]"Necessitated" might be too strong a word, since it cannot be denied that people did exist under barter.

inventory for later *exchanging*, rather than *exchanging it for* consumption *now*, does defer consumption to the future," implying that the holding of *inventory* involves the exchange of a future good (satisfaction) for a present one. In the next sentence, they admit that *inventory* held is *exchanged neither for* consumer goods *nor for* producer goods. Yet they fail to notice that this implies also, as a further consequence, that holding *inventory* for later *exchanging*, rather than *using it in* production *now*, does defer *production* (and hence *future* consumption) to the future. If the holding of *inventory* defers consumption and production, however, then it becomes impossible to maintain that the holder of *inventory* has thereby invested in a *future* good, because *there* are *no future goods—whether* consumer or producer goods—which result from the act of holding *inventory* and to which its holder could thus be entitled. Yet as claims to no future goods whatsoever, *inventory* would be worthless. By implication, if *inventory* is not worthless (and no one would hold *inventory* if it had no value), then its value must be that of a *present* good.

These word substitutions, again, are our attempt to illustrate the point that just because, undeniably, money is the par excellence means of dealing with doubt about future events, it by no means logically follows that it is a present good. Very much to the contrary, stocks of goods on the shelves of the retailer are also employed to this end, and no one would think to characterize them as present or consumers goods because of this fact.

An earlier example from Hoppe of a similar analysis is:

> Matters become somewhat more complex under conditions of uncertainty, with money actually in use, but the praxeological independence of money and interest remains fully intact. Under these conditions, man invariably has three instead of two alternatives as to how to allocate his current income. He must not only decide how much to allocate to the purchase of present goods and how much to future goods (i.e., how much to consume and how much to invest), but also how much to keep in cash. There are no other alternatives. (Hoppe 1993, p. 119)

Compare, also, the following two (2) paragraphs based upon a quote from Mises that appears in Hoppe et al. (1998, p. 44):

> In a system without change in which there is no uncertainty whatever about the future, nobody needs to hold *cash*. Every individual knows precisely what amount of money he will need at any future date. He is therefore in a position to lend all the funds he receives in such a way that the loans fall due on the date he will need them (Mises 1996, p. 249).
>
> In a system without change in which there is no uncertainty whatever about the future, nobody needs to hold *inventory*. Every individual knows precisely what amount of inventory he will need at any future date. He is therefore in a position to lend all the inventory he receives in such a way that the loans fall due on the date he will need them.

Hoppe et al. (1998, p. 44) also state [emphasis added]:

> The source of the utility of a consumer good is its direct and present serviceability, and the source of the utility of a producer good is its indirect future serviceability. Money, by contrast, is neither consumed nor employed in production. It is neither directly serviceable (as consumer goods are) nor indirectly useful as a way station to future consumer goods (as producer goods are). Rather, the utility of money must be that of an *indirectly* yet presently serviceable good.

However, as we have seen supra, money is a capital good. It is used in production to transform goods from higher orders to lower orders; that is its function. That is, the entire function of money qua money is to be a more efficient means of transforming higher order goods to lower orders than barter exchange. Of course, the transformation is not physical, but rather is part and parcel of ownership. And, it most certainly is "indirectly useful as a way station to future consumer goods;" again, think of the alternative, barter. The problem seems to be thinking that transforming goods requires some physical change in the good or its location. But that is not correct.

Thus, we have shown that money is not some third type of good, distinct from consumers' goods or capital goods, but, rather, it is a type of capital good; moreover, it is not a present good, but, rather, a future good.

Consider the following analysis by Rothbard (1993 [1962], pp. 6–8) of the lowly "ham sandwich" as further evidence in support of our claim regarding money as a future not a present good. In this economist's view, the final good in this regard is not the creation of the sandwich by Jones' wife who "expend(s) energy in unwrapping the bread, slicing the ham, placing the ham, between bread slices and carrying it to Jones." No, this is only "the labor of the housewife." This, coupled with "bread in the kitchen, ham in the kitchen and a knife to slice the ham" plus time and land upon which to stand, constitute "first order producers' goods, since, in this case, these co-operate in the production of the consumers' good."

Where then does money figure into this idyllic picture of domestic bliss? Is it a consumers' good? Not a bit of it; rather, Rothbard informs us, "the consumers' good" in this little story is "the ham sandwich at the point of being eaten." Money is certainly not as close to this final consumption as is foodstuff at the very point of being consumed. How does it stack up in comparison with the "first order producers' goods" necessary to construct this culinary delight, that is, "bread in the kitchen, ham in the kitchen and a knife to slice the ham?" That is, which comes first in time, in the ordinary case of putting together this concoction? Surely, the use of money is prior to anything properly included in this category, since "bread in the kitchen, ham in the kitchen, etc." come after the purchase of them in the market.

Rothbard continues his meticulous and careful analysis by identifying "second order producers' goods" as "bread-in-retail-shop and housewife's labor in carrying it (plus the ever-present land-as-standing-room and time." Again we ask, where does money fit into this scenario, in terms of the temporal order? Clearly, if we were but to include it, as Rothbard does not, at least not this early in his magnum opus, we would have to count "bread-in-retail-shop," along with ham, lettuce, and mustard in the store, as even higher order goods. This would leave money as an intermediate order production or capital good, in that it is through the intermediation of money, in between the higher and lower orders, that material in the latter is transformed into material in the former. That is, money is a necessary concomitant of the production process in the absence of barter, and its contribution takes place somewhere in between the higher order good (bread and ham in the store, owned by the retailer) and the lower order good (bread and ham on the street, under the possession of the housewife) on its way into the kitchen.

If Rothbard is so meticulous as to consider even bread and ham in the kitchen not as a final consumption good, but rather as a first order production good, how much stronger is the case that money, which appears in this story before that stage, should be considered not only a capital good but one of a higher order than this?

In the analysis of the present authors (see listing below), bread and ham[19] in the store is the sixth order capital good; money, which transmits these intermediate goods into the housewife's possession is the fifth; material in the grocery bag en route home is the fourth; the raw materials in the kitchen the third; the put-together sandwich in the kitchen the second; and when it arrives on the plate in front of Jones, this constitutes the lowest, or first order intermediate or capital good.

Capital or intermediate goods 6 – bread and ham in the store

Capital or intermediate goods 5 – money and bread and ham in the process of exchange

Capital or intermediate goods 4 – bread and ham in the housewife's possession, on the street, being carried to the home

Capital or intermediate goods 3 – bread and ham in the kitchen

Capital or intermediate goods 2 – ham placed on the bread in the form of a sandwich, but still located in the kitchen

Capital or intermediate goods 1 – ham sandwich placed in front of Jones, in his very hands

Consumer goods – the ham sandwich, at the very point of being eaten by Jones

Although at first blush money might seem out of place in this list because the other items all refer to steps in the transformation of raw materials into a ham sandwich; however, to make this objection is to consider the production process from the perspective of an "engineer," not that of an economist. To the economist it is not the physical transformation that is important, but rather the value transformation, i.e., the value added. So as any of the other steps add value by advancing the work-in-process closer to its end—a consumer good being consumed—so also does the change of ownership effectuated by use of the money as a capital good in the exchange process, as per our argument in Sect. 2, supra.

5 Conclusion

Admittedly, if there are categories of action and goods other than those of consumption and production, the most likely would be exchange; then there would be a certain coherence in selecting money, out of all other possibilities, to be placed in the third grouping. However, there is simply no warrant for any such exception to the general rule that when man acts, he does so for the purpose of either consuming now and in the present or rendering the future more to his liking than that situation which would have obtained had he not acted, that is, of increasing his store of capital or

[19]"Plus etcetera" is always to be implicitly understood in all these cases.

intermediate goods. There is, unfortunately for the theories of those economists we have criticized above, no third option. Money might appear to be an exception, but as we have shown, it, too, must be successfully subsumed under the rubric of one of these categories, to wit producers' goods.

Acknowledgment We thank two anonymous referees of this review for their helpful suggestions; the usual caveats apply: any remaining errors or infelicities are our own responsibility.

References

Barnett, W., II, & Block, W. (2004). On the optimum quantity of money. *Quarterly Journal of Austrian Economics, 7*(1), 39–52.

Block, W. (1991). *Defending the undefendable*. New York: Fox and Wilkes.

Canaan, E. (1921). Application of the theoretical apparatus of supply and demand to units of currency. *Economic Journal, 31*, 453–461.

Friedman, M. (1969). The optimum quantity of money. In *The optimum quantity of money, and other essays* (pp. 1–50). Chicago, IL: Aldine Publishing.

Garrison, R. W. (2001). *Time and money: The macroeconomics of capital structure*. London: Routledge.

Hayek, F. A. (1931). *Prices and production*. London: Routledge.

Helfferich, K. (1923 [1924]). *Das Geld* [Money] (6th ed.). London: Leipzig (Cited in Mises (1980:96)).

Hoppe, H.-H. (1993). *The economics and ethics of private property: Studies in political economy and philosophy*. Boston: Kluwer.

Hoppe, H.-H., Hülsmann, J. G., & Block, W. (1998). Against fiduciary media. *Quarterly Journal of Austrian Economics, 1*(1), 43–44.

Hutt, W. (1956). The yield from money held. In M. Sennholz (Ed.), *On freedom and free enterprise* (pp. 196–216). Princeton, NJ: Van Nostrand.

Kirzner, I. M. (1973). *Competition and entrepreneurship*. Chicago, IL: University of Chicago Press.

Knies, K. (1885). *Geld und Kredit*. Bd. I. Berlin: Weidmann (Cited in Mises (1980:96)).

Lachmann, L. M. (1956). *Capital and its structure*. London: London School of Economics and Political Science.

Roscher, W. (1906). *System der Volkswirtschaf.* Ed. Pöhlmann (24th ed.). Stuttgart (Cited in Mises (1980:96)).

Rothbard, M. N. (1970). *Power and market: Government and the economy*. Menlo Park, CA: Institute for Humane Studies.

Rothbard, M. N. (1993 [1962]). *Man, economy and state*. Auburn, AL: Ludwig von Mises Institute.

Selgin, G. A., & White, L. H. (1996). In defense of fiduciary media—or, we are *Not* Devo (lutionists), we are Misesians! *RAE, 9*(2), 83–107.

Smith, A. (1930 [1776]). *The wealth of nations*. In Cannan's (Ed.). London: Methuen (Cited in Mises (1980:102)).

von Mises, L. (1980 [1912]). *The theory of money and credit*. Indianapolis: Liberty Classics.

von Mises, L. (1990 [1932]). The position of money among economic goods. In R. M. Ebeling (Ed.), *Money, method, and the market process*. Norwell, MA: Kluwer Academic Publishers.

von Mises, L. (1996). *Human action* (4th ed.). San Francisco: Fox & Wilkes.

The Trend of Economic Thinking on Markets and Money: What Is Hayek's Position on These Issues?

Makoto Nishibe

1 Introduction: Vision and World View

In my article "Hayek's Transformation of Market-Images in the 1930–1940s" (Nishibe 2010), I argued that Hayek transformed his vision of the market during the 1930s and the 1940s and that a crucial breakthrough in adopting the concept of rivalrous competition lied in his 1946 paper "The Meaning of Competition" rather than in his 1937 famous essay on dispersive knowledge. I also emphasized the important role of vision for an economist to form his theory and suggested that the process of Hayek's transformation, or any economist's transformation in many cases, occurred in the following order: (1) vision, (2) theory, and (3) methodology.

In this article, I shed light on the issue of world view or public opinion: a different aspect of economics from vision held by an economist. I examine in what way and why Hayek was interested in the issue of world view and which positions he took regarding vision and world view in the theory of the market and money. While an economist's vision has an indespensable role in creating any new theory and thought, "world view" (Weltanschauung) or "prevailing opinion" of the public has an important role in diffusing economic theories and thoughts and thereby transforming the present reality.[1] Finally, after briefly reviewing the issues and contrasting them with the arguments of other researchers, I will present, along the lines of Hayek, my interpretation of a comprehensive picture of economics that is comprised of vision, world view, theory, methodology, and reality.

---

[1]We clearly distinguish Schumpeter's "vision" that economists hold to define the economic realm from Hayek's "world view" as the prevailing public opinion on the economic reality. However, Maki fused the latter into the former without making such a distinction between them (Maki 2001, pp. 4–5).

M. Nishibe (✉)
School of Economics, Senshu University, Tokyo, Japan
e-mail: nishibe@isc.senshu-u.ac.jp

A. Godart-van der Kroon, P. Vonlanthen (eds.), *Banking and Monetary Policy from the Perspective of Austrian Economics*,
https://doi.org/10.1007/978-3-319-75817-6_4

2 Vision and Public Opinion in Hayek's "The Trend of Economic Thinking"

In his eminent book *The Road to Serfdom*, Hayek used the terms *Weltanschauung* and "world view" in order to critically describe the characteristics of socialism in a fairly negative light as follows.

> And, indeed, socialists everywhere were the first to recognize that the task they had set themselves required the general acceptance of a common *Weltanschauung*, of a definite set of values. It was in these efforts to produce a mass movement supported by such a single world view that the socialists first created most of the instruments of indoctrination of which Nazis and Fascists have made such effective use (Hayek 1944b, p. 85).

It was in totalitarian situations where "the general acceptance of a common *Weltanschauung*, of a definite set of values," was first created and utilized as the instrument of indoctrination by socialists. Then, Nazis and Fascists polished it up to work more efficiently. It is clear from the passage that the change of a generally accepted world view in a society will result in the change of values, attitudes, and actions of the people and in the change of actual performance and the state of affairs in a society. There are few cases where Hayek had used in other publications the term "world view," which is a calque of the German philosophical term "Weltanschauung."[2] On the contrary, Hayek had often used the term "public opinion" instead of it (Hayek 1933a, 1944a, 1954, 1960). After I have checked up several cases, I have come to see that "public opinion" is used almost as a synonym for "world view" but in a better sense.

Since Hayek dealt with the problem of "public opinion" at the very beginning of his academic career, I am convinced that he had been aware of the importance of the issue long before then. Hayek mentioned it in "The Trend of Economic Thinking" when he made his inaugural lecture at LSE in 1933.

> The aspect which I wish chiefly to emphasize is (...) the role played by purely scientific progress—the growth of our insight into the interdependence of economic phenomena—in bringing about these changes in his attitude to practical problems. (...) But, in fact, the cause of the great historical changes which I am discussing seems to me to be of a more subtle kind. It consists neither of a change in the underlying ethical valuations nor of a refutation of the validity of certain analytical propositions but rather in a change of view regarding the relevance of that knowledge for practical problems. It was not a change of ideals nor a change of reasoning but a change of view with regard to the applicability of such reasoning which was responsible for the characteristic features of the popular economics of today. (...)

[2]The term "Weltanschauung" was initially used by Immanuel Kant in *Critique of Judgment* (1790) and ever since has been widely used by many German philosophers and writers as Dilthey, Husserl, Jaspers, Mannheims, Freud, Heidegger, and Gadamer. It is also well known that Adolf Hitler frequently used the term in his book, Mein Kampf. So such a connection to the term might have prevented Hayek from frequent use of the term "world view."

> It is probably true that economic analysis has never been the product of detached intellectual curiosity about the *why* of social phenomena, but of an intense urge to reconstruct a world which gives to profound dissatisfaction. This is as true of the phylogenesis of economics as of the ontogenesis of probably every economist. As Professor Pigou has aptly remarked: "It is not wonder, but the social enthusiasm which revolts from the sordidness of mean streets and the joylessness of withered lives, that is the beginning of economic science" (Hayek 1933a [1991], p. 18).

Here it should be noted that "a change of view regarding the relevance of that knowledge for practical problems," viz. " a change of view with regard to the applicability of such reasoning which was responsible for the characteristic features of the popular economics of today" is not "a change in the underlying ethical valuations of the validity of certain analytical propositions" nor "a refutation of the validity of certain analytical propositions," viz. "not a change of ideals nor a change of reasoning." Here Hayek indicated the very peculiar characteristics of social sciences, especially of economics. He had noticed and warned that the object of economics is, unlike in natural sciences, social phenomena which are affected by subjective cognitions, actual actions, and changeable passions of humans and that economists must be aware that economics is largely affected by popular reputation or public evaluation on the analytical propositions of a positive science as well as ethical propositions of a normative science. In other words, Hayek refers to the "teleological" property of economics as a tool containing in itself self-referential propositions or meta-evaluations in terms of applicability and relevancy to practical problems. In order to fully understand what the teleological property of economics means, now let us reconfirm how Hayek regards the facts of the social sciences.

> Take such things as tools, food, medicine, weapons, words, sentences, communications, and acts of production—or any one particular instance of any of these. (...) They abstract from *all* the physical properties of the things themselves. They are all instances of what are sometimes called "teleological concepts," that is, they can be defined only by indicating relations between three terms: a purpose, somebody who holds that purpose, and an object which that person thinks to be a suitable means for that purpose. (...) In short, in the social sciences, the things are what people think they are. Money is money, a word is a word, and a cosmetic is a cosmetic, if and because somebody thinks they are (Hayek 1943a [1948], pp. 59–60).
>
> No superior knowledge the observer may possess about the object, but which is not possessed by the acting person, can help us in understanding the motives of their actions (ibid. 60).

If we replace "the object," "the observer," and "somebody (the acting person)" with "economics," "the economist," and "the public," respectively, then it follows that "economics is economics if and because the public thinks it is", notwithstanding what the economist thinks it is. This is the factual definition of economics as a social science for Hayek. It should at least include the teleological property of economics for the public.

The reason why Hayek could recognize this fact is not because he wanted to raise his reputation as a prominent economist but because he was strongly concerned with the difficulty of realizing liberalism compared to socialism. Furthermore, because of his acute perception of the peculiarity of economics, which depends on the influence of "public opinion" or "popularity", it would be quite difficult to achieve a nice balance between intellectual sincerity, the truth, and concessions to popular prejudice.

> In our field no knowledge can be regarded as established once and for all and that, in fact, knowledge once gained and spread is often, not disproved, but simply lost and forgotten. (...) The result is that in economics you can never establish a truth once and for all but have always to convince every generation anew—and that you may find much more difficult when things appear to yourself no longer so simple as they once did (Hayek 1944a [1991], p. 38).
>
> The reason why I think that too deliberate striving for immediate usefulness is so likely to corrupt the intellectual integrity of the economist is that immediate usefulness depends almost entirely on influence, and influence is gained most easily by concessions to popular prejudice and adherence to existing political groups. I seriously believe that any such striving for popularity—at least till you have very definitely settled your own convictions—is fatal to the economist and that above anything he must have the courage to be unpopular (ibid. 44).

Hayek thus himself declared paradoxically that he cannot strive for "immediate usefulness" and "popularity" and that "he must have the courage to be unpopular" to maintain the intellectual integrity of an economist.

Caldwell (1988b) referred to the article "The Trend of Economic Thinking" and indicated that Hayek despairs over the direction of current "public opinion," which preferred increasing state intervention in the economy and that such popular concepts of planning had its origins in the German historical school. Hayek touches upon a number of themes that were to engage him for the remainder of his career, but it is not a blueprint, but a manifesto or rather a starting point.

I surely admit that Hayek's article in 1933 contains many potential "visions" that would have flourished to create important propositions and new theories later on, but here I am concerned with the article because of his attention to the idea that "public opinion" related to the peculiarity of economics in the time of the expansion of socialism. In the next section, I will take a look at the transformation of Hayek's vision of the market. Thereafter, I will examine the role of public opinion in the case of modern microeconomics and its rapid propagation of the conventional vision, which formed even after Hayek's insightful vision of the market, and consider the relation between vision and world view and their impact on public opinion.

3 Hayek's Transformation of His Vision of the Market

It is common knowledge that Hayek changed his theoretical and methodological positions a few times during his lifetime, but there is still disagreement on the number of times and contents of his transformations and their implications for Hayek's whole thoughts and theories (Caldwell 1988a, 2004; Fleetwood 1995; Foss 1995; Hutchison 1981; Lawson 1994).

I have joined the arguments and presented my account on the issue (Nishibe 2010). I contend that Hayek's turn of his market images is the key factor of his two-time transformations in 1946 (Hayek 1946) and 1960 (Hayek 1960). Hayek's battle with the market socialists in the socialist economic calculation debate was crucial because it enabled him to transform his vision of the mechanistic market based on equilibrium into one of market process with rivalry and discovery in the late 1940s and further into one of a spontaneous order based on social rules of conduct in 1960 and thereafter. Hayek's socioeconomics since 1960 was not only the result of his philosophical and methodological turns but also from a change of his vision of the market that is a complex of some basic theoretical concepts.

To put it more precisely as to how it developed, Hayek started as an orthodox neoclassical economist to tackle monetary business cycle theory in view of Austrian capital and interest theory in the 1920s and participated in the controversy on the feasibility of centrally planned economies in the 1930s (Hayek 1935) that was initiated by Mises in 1920 (Mises 1920). By debating such market socialists as Taylor and Lange, he recognized in the 1940s that the vision of a mechanical centralized market with an auctioneer of general equilibrium that underlies the whole theory of conventional economics and forms the foundation of market socialism is a fundamental defect that misleads the whole argument. Hayek could criticize the general equilibrium theory for the first time when he began dealing not just with allocation and exchange of scattered knowledge in a society as he did in his famous papers in 1937 (Hayek 1937a) and 1945 (Hayek 1945) but also with the discovery and creation of new knowledge through the process of competition among multiple agents in the market as he did in 1946 (Hayek 1946). Hayek thus eventually reached a new vision of the dispersive network of economic transactions.

It is notable that the transformation involves not only methodology or theory but also vision. Here vision can work as a catalyst to grasp reality and help create a new theory and methodology in science. The key concept for Hayek in breaking with general equilibrium theory and reaching a new market image was his vision of competition as a rivalrous and discovery process since 1946, not subjective and dispersive knowledge since 1937. This break was mainly caused by his struggle with Lange's trial and error method. This method can be regarded as the practical application of Walrasian general equilibrium model with *tâtonnement* and "parametric function of prices" that are supposed to work almost in the same manner and with the same theoretical conditions to make general equilibrium an orthodox pure theory of economics, which can then be used as an ingenious strategy to endorse market socialism and make it feasible in the debate.

It is conceivable that Hayek's transformation has taken place in the order of (1) vision, (2) theory, and (3) methodology. To put it in general terms, the ontogenesis of a theory would be as follows. Vision gradually turns into theory. Once theory is established, methodology is abstracted from theory as metatheory, and it fundamentally determines or constrains the basic structure of theory. It is often observed that a shift in methodology is not the cause, but the result of change of theoretical endeavors as substantive scientific activities to grapple with reality. Methodology does not transform itself nor automatically creates a new theory.

Vision in substantive economics is no less important than methodology, particularly in order to discover a new finding, create a new framework, and improve scientific knowledge of reality. Vision offers a metaphor, an analogy, or an image to activate *abduction* different from deduction or induction, which consists in a cognitive movement from surface phenomena (event/action) in an empirical domain to some deeper mechanisms, structures, rules, tendencies, power, or relations. So it is recognized that vision is necessary for scientific hypothetical reasoning that enables the creation of new theories or conceptions. Once vision transforms, it requires a change of methodology in order to present an integrative and consistent basis of a new theory so that it can formally systemize itself. The vision of a theory is the frame of reference for key concepts in economics, even though it cannot be expressed in an explicit manner in the first place; vision is not less important than methodology in order for economics to explore the unknown reality of our socioeconomic world.

Hayek's case of transformation exemplifies the propositions on the relation of vision, theory, and methodology. He had experienced his philosophical turns through all three; however, the transformation in methodology had not taken place by itself. Such particular fundamental concepts such as equilibrium, competition, and knowledge have gradually changed the prevailing vision of the market that was to be replaced by a new one at some threshold. The vision of the market is a complex system constituted by those concepts that support a total structure of a theory, so its change is potentially able to overturn the economic theory as a whole. Methodological shifts followed these changes in order to build the foundations.

Hayek's image of the market as "a rivalrous and dispersive discovery procedure for knowledge" should be seen as a vision for establishing a new theory of the market as a self-organizing complex system or a "spontaneous order," which is Hayek III's basic idea after he transformed his thinking twice in *The Meaning of Competition* (1946) and *The Constitution of Liberty* (1960), even though Hayek himself had not accomplished to develop a new theory of the market. Hayek's vision can still help us create a more articulate and realistic theory of the market.

Now I would like to explain the main reason why I must pay special attention to the rivalry of multiple independent ends and the discovery of dispersive and unknown knowledge in Hayek's image of the market depicted in a series of articles after 1946 (Hayek 1946, 1947, 1968). This is because modern extensive versions of neoclassical economics that encompass the development of informational economics and even parts of the Austrian school tend to take Hayek's "Economics and Knowledge" (Hayek 1937a) as an epoch-making breakthrough toward a new view of the market as "a telecommunications system" and especially toward informational economics. It is plausibly told that Hurwicz (1960, 1971), by inheriting Hayek's vision of the market, pioneered the notions of incentive compatibility and informational efficiency and developed the theory of mechanism design.

But I doubt if the development of informational economics is not largely based on the idea of a concentrated market with an auctioneer or the parametric function of prices and if it was built in Hayek's vision of the dispersive market. This is why I consider that interpreting Hayek as the founder of informational economics is due to a lack of understanding of the essence of his position on the issue of the market, and it is utterly misleading. We had better think that this is a battle among many schools of economics not for scientific truth and validity but for justification for the throne and for public popularity. The notion of "vision" is not sufficient to understand the dynamic process of this kind of phylogenesis of economics. We will come back to this point once again when we come up against "world view" in the next section.

4 World View of the Market and Its Error

On Hayek's transformations of vision of the market, we have thus focused on the crucial role of "vision" of an economist as a creator of new theories because we were interested in the process of innovation in economics. Here, in order to consider how new theories of economics can diffuse among people and influence public opinion and economic policies, we would like to shed light on the other side of the thing, i.e., the important role of "world view" (Weltanschauung) of the intellectuals as propagators of new theories.

Hayek paid attention to the peculiar role of the intellectuals. A strong belief prevailed that the influence of the intellectuals on politics is negligible, but they in fact exercised a great power of influence by shaping "public opinion" when they performed the role as intermediary in the spreading of ideas. In this respect, Hayek, assuming that socialism won the victory over liberalism in the year of 1949 after WWII, endeavored to understand the reason why so many intellectuals are inclined toward socialism and write out a prescription (Hayek 1949 [1997]).

His conclusion is that "the main lesson which the true liberal must learn from the success of the socialists is that it was their courage to be Utopian which gained them the support of the intellectuals and therefore an influence on public opinion which is daily making possible what only recently seemed utterly remote" (ibid. 237). He encourages to create "a new liberal program which appeals to the imagination, (. . .) a liberal Utopia, a program which seems neither a mere defense of things as they are nor a diluted kind of socialism, but truly liberal radicalism which does not spare the susceptibilities of the mighty" (ibid.).[3]

From our viewpoint of the present time in the twenty-first century when capitalism has gained a great triumph over socialism, everything seems diametrically opposite to those days. At present, disillusionment with a socialist Utopia prevailed and still remains strong. Market fundamentalism and globalization, instead of socialism and planning, has gained popularity among many intellectuals. Accordingly, we have to think of the modern trend of economic thinking as diffusion of the world view of the market described in popular neoclassical microeconomics that is fundamentally different from Hayek's own image of the market in many ways.

[3]Since Hayek strongly felt after WWII that socialism had completely defeated liberalism and it was necessary to form a liberal Utopia, he must have taken an initiative to hold a conference with 39 liberal scholars and urged foundation of The Mont Pelerin Society in 1947.

The modern trend of economic thinking is probably composed of the following three propositions with respect to the market.

1. The market is the mechanism for efficiently allocating scarce resources to economic agents by free contract and transaction under the given condition of property relation of goods and services at the initial point in time unless we can assume a paradise where limitless kinds and amounts of goods exist and satisfy all the wants of people.
2. In order for the market to work well, we endeavor to fulfill the condition for "perfect competition" as much as possible by deregulating all industries, clarifying property rights, minimizing governments, and increasing the number of and decreasing the size of agents.
3. If the perfect competition condition is fulfilled so that the parametric function of prices can work, the efficient market mechanism is universally and fully usable for the formation of socioeconomic order and mutual coordination of agents' actions.

We name each proposition as follows: (1) "the Definition of the Market by Scarcity," (2) "the Condition for Perfect Competition," and (3) "the Proposition on Market Universality." Such a parametric function or signaling function of prices requires the satisfaction of such conditions for perfect competition as: (a) one-price to one-good law holds because prices in a market are transmitted instantly and with no cost to each economic agent; (b) each economic agent behaves as a price taker because a large number of small-sized agents are assumed; (c) there is freedom for firms of entry to and exit from industries and no institutional obstacles for that; and (d) all goods are homogeneous in quality.

In short, the trend of economic thinking composed of (1)–(3) defines and explains the market as an ideal type of pure price mechanism precisely in the same way as orthodox microeconomics in modern economics does. It regards the market as a highly efficient mechanistic tool that can function more smoothly if we make it approach the condition of perfect competition as close as possible. It is notable that perfect competition that enables the parametric function of prices to be workable could be regarded as a normative criterion for evaluating the condition of the market economy in order to determine whether to execute anti-monopolistic competition policy and deregulation. Since the intellectuals as market fundamentalists stick to the world view that the "free" market is always desirable because it should function well, while forgetting such highly hypothetical conditions as (2) "the Condition for Perfect Competition" and (3) "the Proposition on Market Universality" that specialists and economists never forget, they can be strongly motivated to advocate those policies by depending upon such a world view of the market.

When Hayek talks about his own profession as an economist to his students, because he is fully aware of the peculiar characteristics of economics apart from natural sciences, his remarks sound quite pessimistic and describe an economist being full of sorrow as follows:

> The progress of the natural sciences often leads to unbounded confidence in the future prospects of the human race and provides the natural scientist with the certainty that any important contribution to knowledge which he makes will be used to improve the lot of men.

> The economist's lot, however, is to study a field in which, almost more than any other, human folly displays itself. The scientist has no doubt that the world is moving on to better and finer things and that the progress he makes today will tomorrow be recognized and used. (...) I want to consider the more serious cause for sorrow to the economist, the fact that he cannot trust that the progress of his knowledge will necessarily be followed by a more intelligent handling of social affairs, or even that we shall advance in this field at all and there will not be retrograde movements. The economist knows that a single error in his field may do more harm than almost all the sciences taken together can do good—even more—that a mistake in the choice of a social order, quite apart from the immediate effect, may profoundly affect the prospects for generations (Hayek 1944a, b, pp. 35–36).

The reason why Hayek was so pessimistic to be an economist is concerned with the nature of knowledge created and obtained in economics. While the discovery and accumulation of new knowledge in natural sciences directly means progress and prosperity for human civilization, on the other side, more knowledge cannot necessarily ensure advancement but might lead to retrograde movements in economics. A single error in the choice of a social order may affect the prospects for generations. It can thus do more harm than almost all sciences can do. This is why economists cannot be confident and hopeful, but rather fearful, of the future.

This connotation is completely different from that of "dismal science" that Carlyle puts to economics as a nickname when he describes the character of the correlation between population and starvation in Malthus' population principle as "dismal." In that case, the expression was only used for a particular type of propositions and prospects related to misery in economics. But such pessimism and fear as Hayek attributes to economics arises from the general character of economics, i.e., its inclusion of self-evaluation of scientific statements and proposition of social affairs in economics and its validity and applicability depending on public perception or popularity of the theory. It is evident that Hayek's sorrow and fear of being an economist is much deeper. We should be fully aware of the unique nature of economics and social sciences in general.

5 Hayek's Position on Vision and World View of the Market

It should be reconfirmed that Hayek's vision of the market after 1946 is largely different from the conventional vision of the market in modern microeconomics.

Hayek has made it clear that the knowledge to be discovered through competition in the market is the individual's "capacity to find out particular circumstances" that cannot be regarded as "given data." Hayek has already abandoned the view that a market economy accomplishes efficiency as the result of competition as general equilibrium theory claims. We require "competition as a discovery procedure" precisely because we do not know data in the economy nor the results of competition, and competition in the market is the only available procedure to find them out by utilizing the guidance of prices. The results of a discovery procedure are unpredictable in respect of particular outcomes neither the attainment of efficient allocation of scarce resources nor efficient utilization of knowledge is in a state of equilibrium. What we can expect from competition is to improve the chances of unknown people and to form the general kind of pattern or the abstract character of the self-organizing order (Hayek 1968).

Hayek argues that we must evade the confusion between "order" that the market produces and "economy" in Hayek's term that corresponds to a single organization or arrangement in which someone deliberately allocates resources to a unitary order of ends. Spontaneous order produced by the market is completely different from the "economy" because all the members of such an economy must be guided in their actions by the unitary hierarchy of ends that it serves. The spontaneous order of the market, or the catallaxy, cannot legitimately be said to *have* particular ends. It is also not possible to express the value of the results as a sum of its particular individual products. The concept of an "order" is preferable to that of equilibrium for the discussion of problems of economic policy. While an economic equilibrium never really exists, there is some justification for asserting that the kind of order that our theory describes as an ideal type is approached to a higher degree. This competitive game is not a zero-sum game but a plus-sum game where the income of each member is determined partly by skill and partly by chance.

It is quite clear that, while the purpose of "competitive order" is to make competition work, as Hayek would want, the purpose of "ordered competition" is always to restrict the effectiveness of competition. Therefore, any government policy designed to make competition as effective and beneficent as possible by adopting competition, the market, and prices as its ordering principle, rather than absence of state activity, is necessary.

> The interpretation of the fundamental principle of liberalism as absence of state activity rather than as a policy which deliberately adopts competition, the market, and prices as its ordering principle and uses the legal framework enforced by the state in order to make competition as effective and beneficial as possible (...) is as much responsible for the decline of competition as the active support which governments have given directly and indirectly to the growth of monopoly. It is the first general thesis which we shall have to consider that competition can be made more effective and more beneficent by certain activities of government than it would be without them (Hayek 1947 [1948], p. 110).

Hayek also admits that we have to consider that services such as sanitary and health measures should be provided by the government outside the market and to consider what kind of institutional design of the desirable market economy is necessary. This includes the market policy; the monetary and financial policies; the law of property and contracts and of corporations and associations, including trade unions; the problems of monopolies, taxation, international trade, patent for inventions, copyright, trademarks, labor law, and trade union policies (Hayek 1947).

We thus observed that Hayek's position on the issue of the vision of the market has gradually departed from the general equilibrium theory and reached the point where he recognized the comprehensive institutional design of the competitive order of market economy supplemented by such necessary government policies as we have seen above.

6 Hayek's Position on Vision and World View of Money

During the course of Hayek's transformation of his vision of the market, he also shifted his vision of money: (a) monetary theory of the business cycle and neutral theory of money (Hayek 1931, 1933b), (b) fixed exchange rates (Hayek 1937b), (c) commodity reserve money (Hayek 1943a, b), and (d) competing currencies (Hayek 1976).

Hayek's notion of the neutrality of money was defined as the equality of the natural rate of interest and the money rate of interest. The natural rate is the equilibrium rate to ensure intertemporal equilibrium of consumption and production, viz. the equality of saving and investment. Since deviation from neutrality of money as disequilibrium between the natural rate of interest and the money rate of interest that is initiated by low money rate of interest and expansion of bank lending by credit creation causes forced saving and cyclical fluctuation, a neutral money economy is free from business cycles. Accordingly, making money neutral can prevent booms and depressions (Hayek 1931, 1933b). After the breakdown of the gold standard of the international monetary system, he proposed commodity reserve money backed by stored commodities that is redeemable to a constant combination of commodities, instead of bullion, for stabilizing the value of money (Hayek 1943a, b).

The free market order periodically suffers from fluctuations, in particular, depression, and unemployment in the course of business cycles. Hayek, in order to overcome such shortcomings of the capitalistic market economy, proposed that government or the central bank should be deprived of its monopoly of the issue of money in order to let private banks and enterprises to freely issue their peculiar moneys that compete with each other so that the public can choose good moneys among them (Hayek 1976).

Hayek believes that such liberalization or denationalization of the issue of money will be able to neutralize money and stabilize the value of money so as to prevent excessive inflation and deflation that are the main defects of the present market economy. This is because discrete monetary and fiscal policies of the government and central bank that often bring about huge deficit of finance will be prohibited or restricted under such a situation. Hayek tackled the fundamental problems of markets and money and presented a new evolutionalist institutional design of money by a "gardener," different from a constructivist one by a "planner" that he continues to criticize. Even though Hayek's proposition of denationalization of money is somewhat astonishing to people with a usual world view, it is conceivable that his proposal for the institutional design of the market and money and his vision of the markets and money is theoretically consistent. This is because the platform institutions of both the markets and money in view of media design, not mechanism design, are thought to be self-organizing and evolutionary spontaneous order via the principles of variation (innovation), transmission (learning knowledge), and selection (competition).

7 The Relation of Vision and World View for Hayek and Keynes

Hayek has been, even if unknowingly or tacitly, concerned in many writings with both vision as what the economists use to create economics and world view as what the intellectuals use to diffuse it. In fact, he at the outset mentioned on the topic in his inaugural lecture at LSE in 1933 as follows:

> Yet, in large measure, this knowledge [of the economist] is disregarded and in many respects public opinion even seems to move in a contrary direction. (. . .) [T]here is strong reason to believe that it must be the result of a particular historical situation. For the views at present held by the public can clearly be traced to the economist of a generation or so ago. So that the fact is, not that the teaching of the economist has no influence at all; on the contrary, it may be very powerful. But it takes a long time to make its influence felt, so that if there is change, the new ideas tend to be swamped by the domination of ideas which, in fact, have become obsolete. (Hayek 1933a [1991], pp. 17–18)

Hayek's idea here is that the economist has a strong influence on the public through his vision and theory, but it takes a long time to take effect, so that the old dominant theories tend to form the public's world view or public opinions, and, as a result, the present theory is often neglected or unaccepted by the public. I presume that the idea that Hayek expressed in 1933 was transferred by Keynes to the famous passage at the end of his *General Theory* in 1936. It is because we can see a close similarity between their main ideas, and Hayek's idea was clearly precedent to Keynes' one.

> At the present moment people are unusually expectant of a more fundamental diagnosis; more particularly ready to receive it; eager to try it out, if it should be even plausible. But apart from this contemporary mood, the ideas of economists and political philosophers, both when they are right and when they are wrong, are more powerful than is commonly understood. Indeed the world is ruled by little else. Practical men, who believe themselves to be quite exempt from any intellectual influences, are usually the slaves of some defunct economist. Madmen in authority, who hear voices in the air, are distilling their frenzy from some academic scribbler of a few years back. I am sure that the power of vested interests is vastly exaggerated compared with the gradual encroachment of ideas. Not, indeed, immediately, but after a certain interval; for in the field of economic and political philosophy there are not many who are influenced by new theories after they are 25 or 30 years of age, so that the ideas which civil servants and politicians and even agitators apply to current events are not likely to be the newest. But, sooner or later, it is ideas, not vested interests, which are dangerous for good or evil (Keynes 1936, pp. 383–384).

Although the contents of their ideas are almost the same, the contexts in which they use such ideas are different. While Hayek used it to condemn the dominance of socialism and negligence of liberalism in pessimistic tones, Keynes used it to cautiously but optimistically predict the fate of his own ideas of *The General Theory* as in "at the present moment people are unusually expectant of a more fundamental diagnosis; more particularly ready to receive it; eager to try it out, if it should be even plausible" (Keynes, ibid.).

Hayek had clearly realized the dual aspects of economics as investigation of the "facts" and persuasion of the public since his early days even before Keynes did.

> I shall not argue that the economist has no influence. On the contrary, I agree with Lord Keynes that "the ideas of economists and political philosophers, both when they are right and when they are wrong, are more powerful than is commonly understood. Indeed the world is ruled by little else." The only qualification I want to add, and with which Lord Keynes would probably agree, is that economists have this great influence only in the long run and only indirectly, and that when their ideas begin to have effect, they have usually changed their form to such an extent that their fathers can scarcely recognize them (Hayek 1944a [1991], pp. 36–37).

Here Hayek could have claimed his precedence of such an idea without just saying "I agree with Lord Keynes." Nevertheless, he was more interested in warning Keynes and the readers by adding such an important qualification as "they [economists' ideas] have usually changed their form to such an extent that their fathers can scarcely recognize them," namely, Keynesian distortion of Keynes. The propositions in the passage are true of both Hayek and Keynes, especially after their death. Whether we see their vision and world view as the source of sorrow/fear or that of joy/hope might depend on how we conceive and visualize the evolution of both the economy and economics (Nishibe 2006).

8 A Comprehensive System of Economics for the Economist and the Public

I have presented the provisional hypothesis that once vision is axiomatized/systematized, it becomes theory and that generalization of theory generates methodology which, once it is created, regulates theory (Nishibe 2010).

In order to compare with Hayek/Keynes's case, we present the other cases in the following figures that show the whole picture of economics.

In Hutchison's case where the relations between theory and methodology are focused only for the economists, theory is viewed as properly reflecting reality while it is regulated by methodology (Fig. 1). Methodology is considered to regulate the types of theory (induction/ deduction) or the relation between reality and theory (verification/falsification). Theory reflects/describes reality, but reality is mostly independent of theory.

Caldwell (1982, 1985) criticizes Hutchison's type of monism of empirical positivism or falsificationism that regards methodology as a criterion of demarcation to distinguish science from non-science and admits methodological pluralism as a

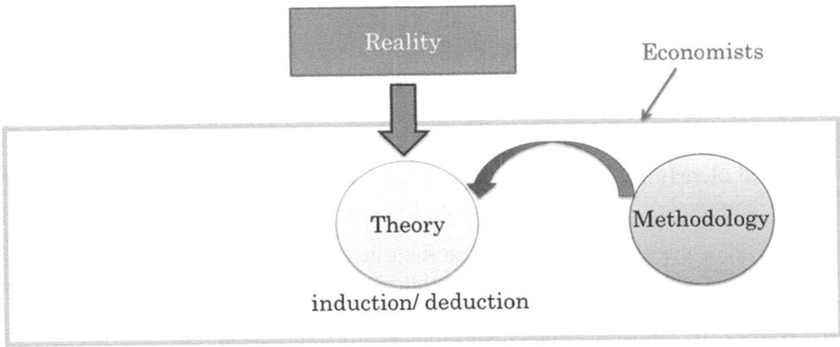

Fig. 1 Hutchison/Caldwell's case

"meta-methodological position" (Caldwell 1985, p. 240) where various theories (scientific programs) coexist competing with each other through "critical" mutual evaluation in order to improve the understanding of economics. It seems to him that different scientific programs depend on such distinctive epistemological and problem-dependent positions from which they view reality. His main interest is in how economists do in practice as mutual critical evaluators and how methodologists make economists understand what economics really is. While Caldwell partially admitted the causal relation from theory to methodology, he neither recognized any causal relation from theory to reality, nor introduced the concept of vision acting as a catalyst to form theory. Then he is classified into the same category as Hutchison in the broad sense as in Fig. 1.

On the contrary, in the case of Lawson and Fleetwood's critical realism, the main focus is on the transformations from empirical realism into transcendental (critical) realism in methodology for economists, in particular, as to ontological positions. They contend that methodology as a primary cause determines whether the relations between reality and theory are deductionist or abductionist as in Fig. 2 (Lawson 1994; Fleetwood 1995).

Schumpeter, on the other hand, emphasizes the role of vision as a "pre-analytic cognitive framework" in order to view reality from a particular angle of problem and interest. Vision thus works as a catalyst to enable the economist to create a new theory that is equipped with some universal analytical toolbox called "economic analysis" as in Fig. 3 (Schumpeter 1954).[4]

Finally, we introduce the concept of world view or public opinion in addition to those of vision, theory, methodology, and reality and examine the relations between

[4]Schumpeter (1954) in Chap. 4 "'The Sociology of Economics" explains "ideology." Truly, the concept might seem to be that of world view or public opinion, but in fact it is completely different. For Schumpeter regards it only as rationalization or political bias of class interests of the public according to conventional Marxist interpretation and as something to be detached from "economic analysis" that is what he regards as scientific contents, not as something that can affect or change reality. On the other hand, "economic thought" is defined as normative statements for economic policies for the economists.

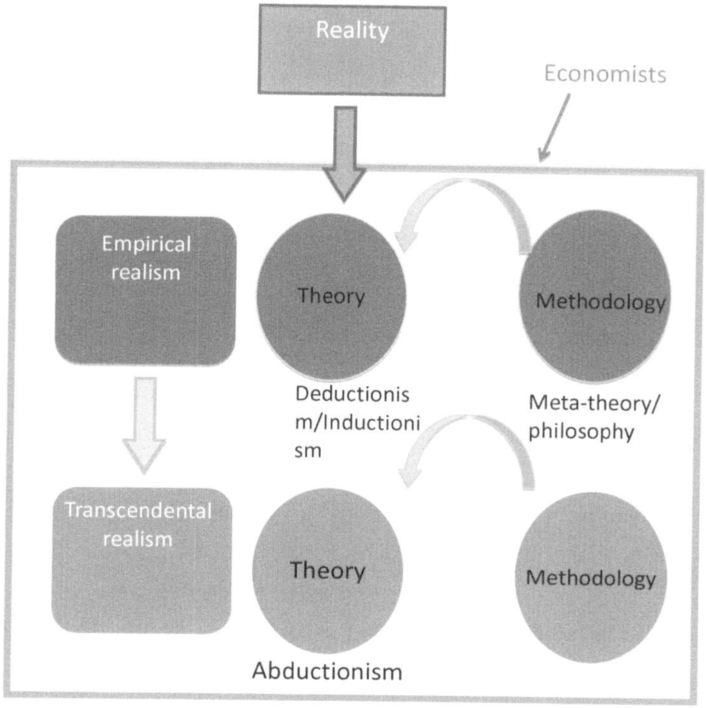

Fig. 2 Lawson/Fleetwood's case

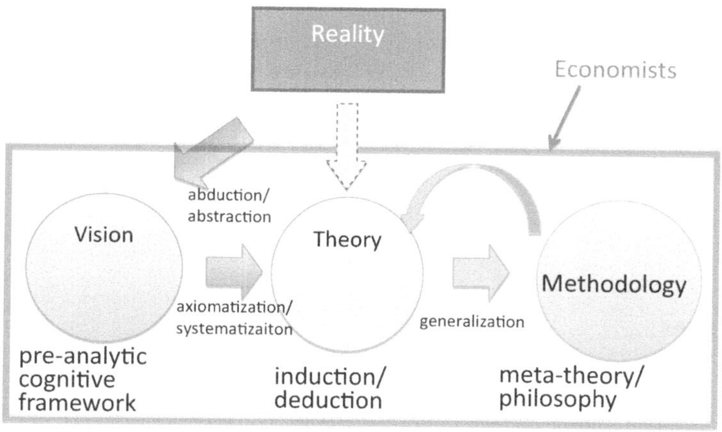

Fig. 3 Schumpeter's case

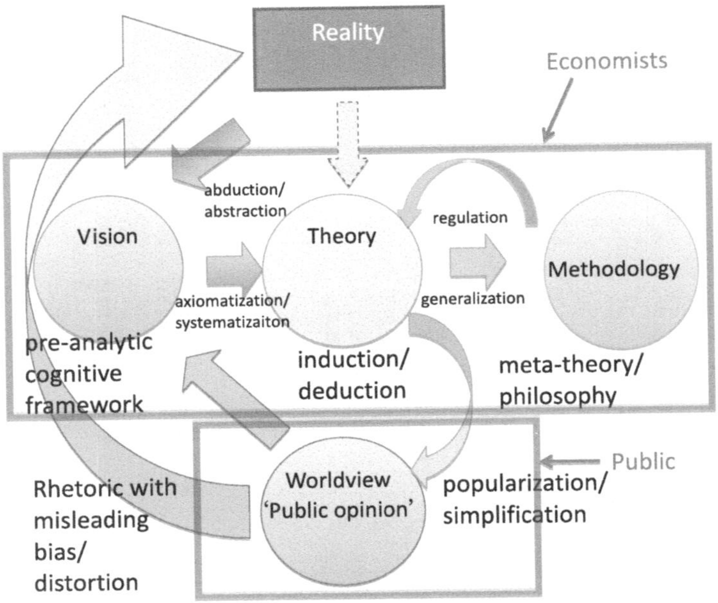

Fig. 4 The relation between vision, theory, methodology, and world view: Hayek/Keynes' case with world view or "public opinion"

those components. Figure 4 describes a dynamic picture of economics as a whole not only for the economists but also for the public. According to Hayek, world view is the old, previous, dominant, popular, amateurish, simplified, and distorted pseudo-theory formed and diffused by the intellectuals and firmly held by the public. It is largely different from the new, present, frontier, professional, complex, and sophisticated theory created by the economist. World view affects reality as it functions for the public as a fixed and stereotyped cognitive framework for decision-making and actions as in policies and activities of governments. Accordingly, the formation of vision of the economist is more or less influenced by reality as well as world view or public opinion.

References

Caldwell, B. J. (1982). *Beyond positivism: Economic methodology in the twentieth century*. London: Allen & Unwin.

Caldwell, B. J. (1985). The case for pluralism. In N. De Marchi (Ed.), *The Popperian legacy in economics*. Cambridge: Cambridge University Press.

Caldwell, B. J. (1988a). Hayek's transformation. *History of Political Economy, 20*, 4.

Caldwell, B. J. (1988b). Hayek's 'trend of economic thinking'. *Review of Austrian Economics, 2*, 175–178.

Caldwell, B. J. (2004). *Hayek's challenge: An intellectual biography of F.A. Hayek*. Chicago, IL: University of Chicago Press.
Fleetwood, S. (1995). *Hayek's political economy*. London: Routledge.
Foss, N. J. (1995). More on "Hayek's transformation". *History of Political Economy, 27*(2), 345–364.
Hayek, F. A. (1931). *Prices and production* (1st ed.). London: Routledge.
Hayek, F. A. (1933a [1991]). The trend of economic thinking. *Economica, 13*, 121–137.
Hayek, F. A. (1933b). *Monetary theory and the trade cycle*. London: Routledge.
Hayek, F. A. (Ed.). (1935). *Collectivist economic planning*. London: George Routledge.
Hayek, F. A. (1937a [1948]) Economics and knowledge. *Economica, 4*(new series), 33–54.
Hayek, F. A. (1937b [1999]). *Monetary nationalism and international stability*. Publication No. 18, The Graduate Institute of International Studies.
Hayek, F. A. (1943a [1948]). The facts of the social sciences. *Ethics, 54*(1), 1–13.
Hayek, F. A. (1943b [1999]). A commodity reserve currency. *Economic Journal, 53*, 176–84.
Hayek, F. A. (1944a [1991]). *On being an economist.*
Hayek, F. A. (1944b). *The road to Serfdom*. London: George Routledge.
Hayek, F. A. (1945 [1948]). The use of knowledge in society. *American Economic Review, 35*(4), 519–529.
Hayek, F. A. (1946 [1948]). *The meaning of competition.*
Hayek, F. A. (1947 [1948]). *"Free" enterprise and competitive order.*
Hayek, F. A. (1948). *Individualism and the economic order*. Chicago, IL: University of Chicago Press.
Hayek, F. A. (1949 [1997]). The intellectuals and socialism. *University of Chicago Law Review, 16*, 417–433.
Hayek, F. A. (1954 [1991]). *History and politics.*
Hayek, F. A. (1960). *The constitution of liberty*. Chicago, IL: University of Chicago Press.
Hayek, F. A. (1968 [1978]). *Competition as a discovery procedure.*
Hayek, F. A. (1976). *Denationalization of money*. London: The Institute of Economic Affairs.
Hayek, F. A. (1978). *New studies in philosophy, politics and economics*. Chicago, IL: University of Chicago Press.
Hayek, F. A. (1991). *The trend of economic thinking*. In W. W. Bartley & S. Kresge (Eds.). *The trend of economic thinking: Essays on political economists and economic history*. Chicago, IL: University of Chicago Press.
Hayek, F. A. (1997). *Socialism and war* (B. Caldwell, Ed.). Chicago, IL: University of Chicago Press.
Hayek, F. A. (1999). *Good money, Part I, II* (S. Kresge, Ed.). Chicago, IL: University of Chicago Press.
Hurwicz, L. (1960). Optimality and informational efficiency in resource allocation process. In K. J. Arrow, et al. (Eds.), *Mathematical methods in social sciences*. Stanford: Stanford University Press.
Hurwicz, L. (1971). Centralization and decentralization in economic process. In C. B. McGuire (Ed.), *Decision and organization*. Amsterdam: North-Holland.
Hutchison, T. W. (1981). *The politics and philosophy of economics*. Oxford: Basil Blackwell.
Keynes, J. M. (1936). *The general theory of employment, interest and money*. London: Macmillan.
Lawson, T. (1994). *Realism and Hayek: A case of continuous transformation* (in Colona and Hageman 1994).
Maki, U. (2001). *The economic world view: Studies in the ontology of economics*. Cambridge: Cambridge University Press.
Mises, L. V. (1920). *Economic calculation in the socialist commonwealth* (in Hayek 1935).
Nishibe, M. (2006). Redefining evolutionary economics. *Evolutionary and Institutional Economic Review, 3*(1), 3–25.
Nishibe, M. (2010). Hayek's transformation of market-images in the 1930-40s. In H. Hagemann, T. Nishizawa, & Y. Ikeda (Eds.), *Austrian economics in transition*. London: Palgrave Macmillan.
Schumpeter, J. A. (1954). *History of economic analysis*. Oxford: Oxford University Press.

Part II
The Measures Taken by the ECB Considered in the Light of the Ideas of Mises and Hayek

What Is Wrong with the 2% Inflation Target?

Brendan Brown

The fable of the Emperor's new clothes describes aptly the situation of central bankers today. They claim that their box of nonconventional tools enables them to strongly influence long-term interest rates. And more fundamentally they boast of having the ability to steer the overall inflation rate so as to achieve with remarkable precision a given target (2% p.a.) for this variable over say 2-year intervals. Their patchy successes in both endeavours have won them some acclaim. And yet on closer examination, they have little power if any on either score—except as derives from public gullibility. There are unfortunately many who would not dare to challenge the existence of such power for fear of revealing their own lack of understanding.

It would have been far better if the emperor (the central banker in chief) had not assumed those robes. Inflation targeting and the tools used in its pursuance are in in fact harmful to economic prosperity and more narrowly financial stability. It is a principal purpose of this paper to demonstrate that conclusion.

How can we be so sure that the vaunted powers of the central bank to fix the inflation rate and strongly influence long-term interest rates are at best make-believe and at worst destructive?

When we consider the power to influence long-term interest rates we might start with the observation of Paul Volcker in the 1980s that he could not outsmart the markets. And even when as today the Fed holds maybe as much as 20% of the total stock of long-term dollar interest rate exposure, shifts in rational-sober expectations regarding inflation and the future neutral level of interest rates are surely decisive to

B. Brown (✉)
Mises Institute, Auburn, AL, USA

Hudson Institute, Washington, DC, USA

MUFG, London, UK
e-mail: Brendan.Brown@mufgsecurities.com

A. Godart-van der Kroon, P. Vonlanthen (eds.), *Banking and Monetary Policy from the Perspective of Austrian Economics*,
https://doi.org/10.1007/978-3-319-75817-6_5

market pricing. That is unless some type of flawed mental processes have become dominant (as may be the case under episodes of 2% inflation targeting as described below where yield-hungry investors become overconfident in dubious hypotheses such as secular stagnation in their pursuance of illusory term premiums).

1 Power to Target Inflation in Doubt

As regards the power to stabilize the inflation rate at 2% p.a. over 2-year periods, how could this be possible?

Central banks under a fiat money regime control absolutely the supply of high-powered money (defined in this system as currency in circulation plus bank reserves). And they may choose to peg a short-term official interest rate. But there is no reliable simple predictive relationship between either the path of high-powered money or of the official short-term interest rate and measured inflation outcomes at least over the normal range of recent experience (say the past three decades).

If high-powered money were solidly at the pivot of the monetary system—meaning that there is a large stable demand for this aggregate (influenced in predictable ways by short-term interest rates, prices, and incomes in particular)—then indeed we could hypothesize a reliable relationship between its path and prices. This power of the pivot is demonstrable if we move outside the fiat universe and imagine instead a gold money system where bullion and coin are in effect high-powered money (and any paper money components are 100% backed by gold bullion or coin). The movement of prices (for goods and services on average) there is bounded from below and above by the growth of the above ground gold stock and demand for this in all its forms. Within those bounds there is considerable flexibility especially over short and medium-term periods.

In the short run money interest rates move around to equalize supply and demand of high-powered money, in this case gold, which is itself noninterest bearing. At higher money market rates, there is less demand for high-powered money as its opportunity cost rises (and this applies also to monetary assets against which the provider must hold large cash reserves, e.g. sight deposits). These money rates are likely to fluctuate in a highly volatile fashion. Long-term rates largely ignore the volatility except in so far as there is new information to be gained (with focus on the mean over a considerable period of time) that is relevant to the setting of long-term interest rates. For example, the mean of the money rates may be somewhat low by previous standards, reflecting a continued tendency towards excess supply of high-powered money. Changes in long-term rates as induced by estimation of money market conditions over the medium-term (there are many other influences on long-term rates of course) and wealth changes stemming from fluctuations in the real price of bullion influence the dynamics of price and income formation. These are ways in which well-pivoted high-powered money exerts its influence and fosters a strong relationship with prices of goods and services.

No one could sensibly vouch that under such a well-pivoted monetary system price indices as calculated by the official statisticians will record a zero, negative or positive change, over short or medium periods of time. And indeed in Austrian school economic tradition, there is an aversion to defining inflation in terms of movements of the "price level" and a preference for a monetary interpretation not itself based on pseudoscience (see Bagus 2003; Salerno 2003). Such economists would have balked at a strict definition of inflation in terms of monetary data as the path of money demand over time is unpredictable.

Yes historical experience and theory suggests that under a fully gold money regime goods and services prices revert to the mean in the long run but there is no assurance of this, given lack of knowledge about mining conditions and in particular the elasticity of supply of metal with respect to changes in the real price of gold (see Meltzer and Robinson 1989). The advocates of sound money point out that though there is no guarantee of stable prices on average over the long run, the amount of inflation and more generally monetary turmoil (what J.S. Mill described as the money monkey wrench getting into all the other machinery of the economy—see Friedman 2006) should be less than in any alternative monetary regime, including that where the official aim is stable prices or stable inflation (see Salerno 2010). In any case, swings in prices over several years related to changed conditions in the mining industry which are surely detectable and influence thereby informed expectations are not such a serious matter as the hazards of the wild and unpredictable forces determining prices which can gain power under a fiat money regime.

2 Natural Rhythm of Prices Defies Targeting

Under a system where high-powered money is at the pivot, as in a gold money regime, there is considerable scope for prices to fluctuate under real influences, and in a way, which aids the invisible hands in their job of steering the capitalist economy in an efficient manner. Indeed stable prices over the short and medium-term would indicate a defect in the price-signalling mechanisms of a capitalist economy under sound money.

For example, during a business cycle downturn, prices (under a sound money regime) would tend to fall to a lower level (reflecting the micro-decisions of firms confronting a weakening of demand for their output); widespread perceptions that these prices are below the norm for the cycle on average cause consumers and businesses to bring forward spending (so contributing to a business recovery). The high-powered money pivot as described does not get in the way.

Yes, in principle a rise in the real price of gold (as goods and services prices fall generally) would lead to increased gold production—but this is a long-run reaction and in any case helps offset any tightness in the gold market emanating from a lower level of interest rates during the recession. Forecasts of higher gold production would sustain expectations of a rise in goods and services prices (fall back in real gold price) further ahead.

Similarly, a bout of rapid productivity growth would bring many prices down and there would be no immediate monetary force to resist this (under a sound money regime). Widespread price falls in such circumstances are indicative of economic prosperity (with real incomes rising), not so-called deflationary distress. A fall in real cost of mining gold (consistent with a productivity spurt throughout the economy including the mining sector) could mean increased monetary base growth in the longer term, but there would also be a more rapid growth in demand for bullion in line with accelerated real income growth. So there may well not be any push-back even beyond the short run from monetary forces against this natural rhythm of prices downwards during a productivity spurt and that is indeed desirable, as any such push-back tends to generate asset price inflation (to be further discussed below).

Nor would the high-powered money pivot get in the way of price fluctuations reflecting variations in resource scarcity. For example, famine, disruption in energy supplies, or wartime destruction all go along with shortages that at a microeconomic level would lead firms to increase prices. There would be an expectation that these would drop in the future—and this expectation would alleviate shortages in the present (as consumers would choose to delay expenditures where possible). This natural rhythm would not be disturbed by the forces emanating from high-powered money well pivoted as described. Transitory higher prices might mean more demand for high-powered money related to transactions, but real incomes would have fallen and so would many nominal incomes (negative for demand for high-powered money).

3 Monetarism and Ersatz Gold

Under monetarist regimes such as practised by the Deutsche Bundesbank and Swiss National Bank in the 1970s and early 1980s, high-powered fiat money was put at the pivot of the monetary system which operated in some respects as an ersatz gold standard system (see Brown 2013). But the ersatz was far from perfect.

The natural demand for high-powered money under this ersatz gold regime is light, though it can be fortified by high legal reserve requirements on the banks (which they seek to avoid by creating "near money" not subject to the requirements and apply growing amounts of funds in lobbying against). Banknotes and central bank reserves do not enjoy the breadth and distinctiveness of demand as enjoyed by gold in all its forms. Deposit insurance, too big to fail, credit card monopoly power, and the war on cash all take their toll (on a potential broad and stable demand for high-powered money).

In technical terms under a monetarist regime, the public will feel less disequilibrium pain from being a given percentage away from its optimal holding of high-powered money than under a gold regime, meaning less urgent rearrangement of portfolios is triggered in response. Hence the relationships between money and nominal income or prices are looser.

Central bankers administer the supply of high-powered money under these ersatz gold standards. There is no counterpart to the automatic mechanisms of the gold standard (where variations in supply would be brought about by mining industry responses to changes in the real price of gold). Some empirical research on Bundesbank monetarism suggests that in fact high-powered money was steered largely so as to manipulate short-term interest rates in accordance with the neo-Keynesian Taylor rule—though this account has been disputed by Bundesbank researchers (Geberding et al. 2004).

Applying a Friedman style rule (constant $x\%$ expansion p.a. of the monetary base) would not cope well with an increased real demand for cash related to changes in payment or liquidity preferences. These could trigger monetary tightness which in a gold system would be relieved by increased mining of gold. On the other hand, central bank administered high-powered money should avoid the autonomous changes in supply under a gold standard reflecting the discovery of new mines or technological improvements. The importance of these so-called autonomous factors in potentially destabilizing a gold regime should not be exaggerated given evidence that technological changes in the mining industry or new discoveries came in response to changes in the real price of gold (see Meltzer and Robinson 1989).

In a monetary system with high-powered money solidly at its pivot (with trend growth of this aggregate set at a very low level) and no targeting of "the price level" or "inflation" by the monetary authorities which would affect the climate of expectations in the economy at the micro-level, one would indeed anticipate considerable fluctuations in prices. If averages of these (prices) were calculated, they would rise and fall in reflection of factors mentioned above (productivity, business cycles, resource shortages) and indeed variations in high-powered money supply relative to (unknown) demand.

Yes, there would be some tendency for prices to revert to mean over the very long run, but there would be little grounds for confidence in price level or inflation stability over short or medium periods of time. Firms in their individual pricing decisions would be less susceptible to taking forecasts of inflation as a general starting point for their analysis, formulating instead their own estimates of price elasticity of demand taking account of individual knowledge (mass of micro-information including state of competition).

4 A Dislodged Monetary Pivot Means Price Inertia and Institutionalism

By contrast monetary regimes in which price level or inflation stabilization is the dominant prescription tend to encourage an important role for "inflation inertia" and contrived price formation, to be rudely interrupted on occasion.

In such regimes, where powerful forces do not emanate from the pivot, a zone of inertia exists where inflation today is where it is because dominant expectations are in line with that. These dominant expectations can evolve, either gradually or due to shock. And in the evolution process, institutional factors play a role. [Arthur Burns, e.g. was described as an "institutional economist", explaining variations in inflation by a range of observations about how trade unions and monopolists, e.g. were behaving—see Wells (1994) and Hodgson (2000).]

There is no strong monetary narrative to compete with the combination of inertia and institutionalism because the link between money and prices or nominal incomes under a non- or mal-pivoted monetary regime is so loose and unpredictable. Firms when they price long-term delivery contracts and labour when it enters into wage contracts set prices based on expectations about the future—and central bank policy as expressed in targets for the price level or inflation can reinforce inertia in this process.

It is true that prices must move over time in a way which is consistent with monetary trends, so the force of inertia is ultimately subservient to monetary forces. But in a monetary system without high-powered money firmly at its pivot, the power of these forces to overturn inertia or institutionalism is often weak.

For example, if the central bank is operating policy by pegging and re-pegging a short-term official rate, then an inflationary momentum could develop with the central bank effectively allowing (very likely unwittingly) high-powered money and other monetary aggregates to move in such a way (unknown in advance) to accommodate this. And where the monetary base is only weakly at the pivot of the monetary system even with rates market determined monetary forces might not emerge in any strength to break the inertia and related institutional patterns.

5 How Money Breaks Inertia

Nonetheless admitting the role of inertia and institutionalism is not the same as denying monetary influence on price outcomes or embracing Keynesian notions of frictions and rigidities in the price mechanism which would persist even under sound money. And there are break-outs from inertia possible including decisions by the monetary authorities to fight inertia by mobilizing the monetary forces at their command. Attempts to model the causes and extent of break-outs (from inertia) are notoriously unreliable. Some potential catalysts are one-offs and could include in present circumstances (2017) policies of economic nationalism in the USA which might boost upward pressure on wages (e.g. tax changes which favour production in the USA rather than abroad).

The trigger factors which the economic forecasters monitor include labour market tightness (the Phillips curve), prospective budget deficits, exchange rate depreciation, central bank commentaries (about how sound or unsound money may become in the future), and bouts of rapid demand growth reflected in wage and price pressure. In turn these could emanate from undetected monetary disequilibrium where interest rates are well below the unknown neutral level for example.

Central bankers now claim to be able to model the neutral or natural interest rate. An extensive literature has grown on empirical estimation of this—see, for example, Williams (2017). The basis of these estimations is to look at inflation outcomes over a period of year, and if these are below target, then actual market rates on average must have been below neutral. But this procedure begs the question of whether the targeted rate was out of line with the natural rhythm of prices; for example, rapid productivity growth, a business cycle downturn, or perhaps a negative price shock from globalization and falling price of imports may have set off a downward rhythm in prices consistent with sound money. The estimators of the natural or neutral rate do not take into account evidence of asset price inflation which might suggest that indeed the present rhythm is below the inflation target.

Once inertia has been broken, what is the path ahead, including a possible formation of a new inertia?

The history of the Great Inflation in the USA (the mid-1960s to the start of the 1980s) reveals all the problems of forecasting and even recognizing inflation breakouts in real time (see Meltzer 2005). These difficulties were so much greater in the actual weakly pivoted system than in a hypothetical well-pivoted monetary system where automatic forces of discipline can be counted on asserting themselves. But in a poorly pivoted or unpivoted monetary system (such as was the case under the Great Inflation, especially once any effective free market gold link was broken in 1968), the dangers of instability loom larger.

The Great Inflation did not come about as inflations historically because of government greed for revenues and inability or unwillingness to raise taxes from nonmonetary sources (specifically freely functioning capital markets). Some role was played, however, early in the mid-1960s by the Federal Reserve's aim to contain the rising (nominal) cost of long-term borrowing as inflation expectations rose influenced in part by the Vietnam War. Historically high inflation or hyperinflations have usually emanated from government inability or unwillingness to tap savings via capital markets at a going market rate consistent with a sound money regime.

The most blatant example is where a central bank fixes the long-term rate at well below any reasonable estimate of neutral level and in effect standing ready to buy as much bonds in the market as necessary to prevent a fall in their price below the floor. The central bank at the same time is ready to buy bonds from the government at new issue at that price to finance current operations; but this means losing complete control of the money base and so ultimately of the price level. Long-term bonds in effect become virtually indistinguishable from money except for the risk of sudden price drop at some unknown point should there be a return to a sound money path (and the yield is compensation for this); in effect the central bank sells on demand at a fixed price this quasi-money asset.

6 From Great Inflation to New Episodes of Inflation Inertia

The Great Inflation was marked by considerable spells of inertia evolving from one to the next (higher inflation) amongst a host of institutional explanations. The breakout triggers included super-tight labour markets populated by powerful unions, rapid growth in demand in fact propelled by interest rates well below neutral (though this was not understood by monetary officials in the USA and many other countries at the time), a general understanding in markets and amongst the public that economic policy-makers were following a theory that unemployment could be reduced via a once and for all permanent rise in inflation, and eventually a collapse of the global monetary system and with it the gold-dollar peg, and from there to a bubble in commodity prices including crucially oil.

All of this produced a new climate of high inflation expectations. To reverse this climate change, it required the resolve in the White House to bring in a Fed Chair who would administer a normalization programme including a brief monetarist experiment albeit with highly unknown parameters (president Carter's appointment of Paul Volcker) and to allow that Chair to continue his programme despite the arrival of severe recession (President Reagan through 1981–1982).

A new inflation inertia formed in the aftermath of that monetarist experiment as the monetary base was effectively dislodged from the pivot of the monetary system and policy making gradually gravitated in stages towards an inflation-targeting system. Such a regime rests on a starting point of inflation inertia plus a contingency plan to fight serious prospective deviations ahead (whether too little inflation or too much inflation). These fights—actual and perspective—could mean considerable turbulence along the way.

That danger could be reduced potentially with good forecasting, but no one should count on that—and policy course correction could be brittle. Moreover, recent experience has reiterated that course correction comes with huge potential side-effects in form of financial instability. Even then the course correction may not be very effective at least in the short or medium-term. Longer term the course correction may potentially bring a very big swing of inflation.

Under the Great Monetary Experiment (launched by Fed Chief Bernanke at the start of the 2010s) inflation inertia played a role in dogging the central bankers in their attempt to get inflation up from a lower level to a 2% target. In particular, the Federal Reserve despite massive injections of monetary base and long-term interest rate manipulation was not able to swiftly raise inflation to target. Even so, it was "successful" in combatting the natural rythm of prices downwards in the weak phase of the business cycle, with dollar depreciation and commodity price rises playing a key role here. "Success" impeded a strong economic rebound from emerging. Note that a parallel loss of power for high-powered money can exist under well-pivoted monetary regimes though such spells should be short-lived (in comparison to a non-pivoted regime). The problem emerges where the unknown neutral level of interest rates (in nominal terms) is most likely below zero.

This is indeed an unusual situation, likely reflecting deeply depressed investment sentiment in the aftermath of financial panic and/or severe recession. In principle, flexible procyclical prices come to the rescue. As prices fall to a below normal level amidst expectations of an eventual recovery in the next business cycle upturn, households and businesses bring forward their spending. And note under the gold standard regime this happened without nominal short-term rates (or long-term rates) ever approaching zero. The expectation of a rise in prices means that low nominal interest rates are in fact substantially negative in real terms.

Under the 2% inflation-targeting regime, prices have not played this role.

The 2% announced target and the non-standard policy tools used have encouraged inflation inertia albeit sometimes at a level below target. Why cut prices even in a weak economy when the central bank is announcing to everyone that its new tools will prevent deflation? The use of non-standard tools instead might fan asset price inflation (a condition of this sufficient good news around for speculative stories to form and be chased and for investors to have sufficient confidence to follow hunt for yield strategies). But this asset price inflation might itself be an obstacle to a rise in the neutral rate level to above zero. Everyone and their dog realize that there is a likelihood further ahead that there will be big price falls in some speculative asset classes and there is correspondingly a reluctance to make long-gestation investments (outside some lead sectors with particularly compelling speculative stories) matched by a preference to engage in financial engineering (in particular boosting returns by increasing leverage). The reluctance described means that the neutral level of interest rates (unobserved) may fall even further below zero.

7 How Did We Get to the 2% Inflation Standard?: Origins

The intellectual and historical origins can be dated back to the 1920s. The collapse of the international gold standard in 1914 was followed (in the aftermath of the First World War) by an effective gold-dollar based "system". The newly created Federal Reserve determined the growth of high-powered money in the USA (and no longer as in a gold standard world was this determined wholly or mainly by gold movements) and in doing so became influenced by a hotchpotch of considerations—including fine-tuning the business cycle (fighting severe recessions, as that of 1920–1921); giving a helping hand to the British in their efforts to put Sterling back on a truncated gold standard, in fact nearer a dollar standard; and stabilizing the price level (fighting tendencies of prices to fall). The latter objective was not universally approved by all Federal Reserve members at the time—with Benjamin Strong in particular voicing some disapproval though it seems from the record that he implicitly went along with the prescription (as advocated by Professor Miller in the Board and outside by Irving Fisher)—see Brown (2013).

Benjamin Strong's discomfort was based on its inconsistency with the rules of a gold standard system—where the first and only operating rule was sustaining gold convertibility. But in practical terms that operating rule was no longer sufficient in a world where the USA was the only major power on a full gold standard.

Under the Bretton Woods system, there was no price level or inflation targeting.

The rules of the game were essentially sustaining a global dollar standard built on the unspecified assumption (in the founding treaty) that the USA would follow a "stable monetary policy"—and a partial guarantee of this was that the USA would convert dollars on demand (by non-US residents) into gold at the fixed price of US $35 per ounce. In fact the US inflation rate in the 1950s and early 1960s varied between 0% and 2% in broad terms (if measured as today taking account of hedonic price adjustments that would be between −2% p.a. and 0). Then there was the Great Inflation lasting from the mid-late 1960s through into the 1970s.

In the aftermath of the brief monetarist experiment (1978–1982), the Federal Reserve under Chairman Volcker continued to make one or more monetary variables its intermediate target—not taken by any means literally—with the overall aim for monetary policy as set by Congress (see Pollock 2013) including price stability along with high employment. In fact the inflation rate during this period 1983–1990 varied between 2% and 4% p.a. Subsequently in the wake of the 1990–1992 recession, as productivity rose sharply (mid and late 1990s) alongside the blossoming IT revolution, inflation edged down towards 2% p.a. on average over the business cycle as a whole, but above that rate near the peak of the cycle (as, e.g. in 2000).

8 A Fateful FOMC Meeting on 2% Inflation

It was around mid-way in the long cyclical expansion of the 1990s (July 2–3, 1996) that then Fed Chair Greenspan invited the FOMC to discuss whether inflation already now down to 2–3% should be halted in its decline at that level or whether the aim of price stability should mean that the Fed should pursue policy such as to bring the inflation rate down further (see transcript of the meeting). Janet Yellen, then a Fed Governor, gave a paper in favour of calling a halt, fundamentally arguing that a little inflation was pro-growth given a whole list of inflexibilities in the wage-price mechanisms (including the hoary Keynesian topic of money illusion) and also making reference to biases in inflation calculation (even though in fact if this were estimated the same way as in the 1950s or earlier it would have been near 4% p.a. at this time). She cited the Congressional mandate of price stability and maximum employment and suggests there is a trade-off between these as inflation falls into a low range. Incidentally she did not use what later became a key point of the inflation targeters—the avoidance of zero-rate bound problems which could be the catalyst to deflation.

There was no formal decision taken by the FOMC on Yellen's advocacy, and some objections were raised by fellow members (e.g. shouldn't Congress be consulted, and one member, Larry Lindsey, focussed on the issues of tax frictions and disincentives under a regime of permanently low inflation). Greenspan summarized the sense of the meeting as to proceed with considerable care and trial and error in pursuing the objective of price stability once inflation came down to low levels.

Some unfavourable discussion took place concerning the Canadian experience of pursuing a "very low inflation target" (introduced in 1991 and with the objective of 1–3% by the end of 1995). In fact that range was achieved by 1993, after which the Bank of Canada and Government rolled over the unchanged target. The target was introduced initially as a way of motivating the central bank to continue lowering the inflation rate but then became an emblem of the status quo. There was no mention at the FOMC of the New Zealand launch of inflation targeting in 1989. Again, as in

Canada that launch was not of a permanent inflation-targeting regime, although it subsequently became that (see Gonzalez-Hermosillo and Ito 1997), but rather a device for lowering the inflation rate from a present higher level and motivating the central bank to act in that way (see Shewin 1999).

These targets in effect for lowering inflation did subsequently undergo metamorphosis into regimes of permanent unchanged "low" inflation targets, in some cases already by the time of this FOMC meeting. And of course there was already a growing economics literature on the purported benefits of monetary frameworks build around the target of a permanent low inflation rate (see Bernanke 2002).

A key issue not raised at the July FOMC meeting was the natural rhythm of prices (e.g. price falls during recession and bouts of productivity growth—see above) and how defiance of this (by in effect driving interest rates well below the unknown neutral level) could precipitate asset price inflation. This is strange given that the USA was already in an economic miracle period in which productivity surged. Rapid globalization spurred by the entry of China into the WTO and by the revolution in communications technology was adding to the natural downward rhythm of prices. (The nearest parallel was the telegraphy revolution and the US economic take-off fuelled by massive waves of immigration in the 1880s). It is precisely at such times that under sound money prices in general would in fact fall (as occurred in the 1880s episode under the so-called Great Deflation—in fact a time of great prosperity, see Rothbard 2005). There should have been even less reason than usual for reticence in allowing inflation to fall to very low levels or even negative levels at such a time. The failure of Greenspan and his colleagues to take this point on board explains the subsequent fuelling by the Fed of a powerful asset price inflation which culminated in the Asian credit bubble and burst and ultimately the IT bubble and burst (see Brown 2015).

9 The 2% Inflation Standard Goes Global

Fast forward and we have a series of decisive steps in the launch of the global 2% inflation standard.

First, in late 1998 just prior to the launch of EMU, the ECB effectively adopts a 2% inflation standard, though denying that this was in fact the case and the Maastricht Treaty in fact mandated stable prices as the aim (see Brown 2014). Then in autumn 2002 President Bush appointed the leading advocate of inflation targeting—Professor Ben Bernanke—to the Board of the Federal Reserve, subsequently promoting him to chair 3 years later. In spring 2003 central bankers in both Washington and Frankfurt gave new precision to their objectives of permanent low inflation in the context of a perceived "deflation threat". Eventually in 2014, Japan, long a standout against permanent inflation targeting, joined the 2% standard (see Brown 2015).

In broad brush, we could describe the almost finished first two decades of the twenty-first century as hosting a global 2% inflation standard. And to match there have been two great asset price inflations, both of which fit the description of type B (depression) rather than type A (boom). These are two types of asset price inflation identified by the present author in another paper (see Brown 2017). All asset price inflations have their origins in monetary disequilibrium. When this occurs during an economic boom, positive feedback loops from rising asset prices generate irrational exuberance (type A). When this occurs during periods of weak economic performance amidst very low or negative rates of return on safe assets (money and short maturity government bonds) then a frantic hunt for yield can occur (provided there are some pockets of apparent great investment opportunity), in which investors prefer to take on unfavourable bets (disguised often in speculative narratives about which they would be sceptical if acting rationally) to the certainty of loss (type B).

Both the asset price inflations so far in this century (both type B) were started by the Federal Reserve leading the way to "breathe inflation" back into the economy in the aftermath of a recession and market crash.

The first was in the aftermath of the IT crash and 2000–2002 economic downturn. In April 2003 President Bush had reappointed Greenspan to Fed Chair (through to early 2006), and it is plausible that towards gaining that extension there was understanding that he would work constructively with the new academic force on the board, Professor Bernanke (appointed the previous year). And indeed in that spring, the Chair gave his notorious speech about inflation being too low (at around 1% p.a.). The efforts to hold down rates and only raise them gradually despite an emerging economic upturn surely played a key role in powering the types of irrationality which characterize asset price inflation, and in this case "type B".

Fortified by similar action in Europe and Japan (though the latter was not on a 2% standard as yet but struggling to prevent prices falling), the symptoms of asset price inflation emerged across a range of asset classes (not all at the same time) along with the carry trades which are so typical of this monetary disease. In this instance the survey would include the carry trade into high-yield credits—especially sub-prime mortgages and Spanish mortgages—and into high-yielding currencies out of yen; the growing residential real estate boom in the US; in Europe there was the carry trade into the weak sovereign debt; there was the rising speculative temperature in financial equities and much else (see Brown 2015).

Similarly in the aftermath of the 2008–2010 recession and panic, the Fed led the way in a campaign to boost the inflation rate up to its 2% inflation target and to do so designed and opened a box of nonconventional tools not previously used (though some antecedents can be found in the 1934–1936 years—see Brown). As the hunt for yield got underway, huge carry trade activity gathered, whether in currencies (into emerging market and commodity currencies), credits (corporate investment grade and high-yield debts), illiquidity (especially private equity), or long-maturity government debt. Speculative temperature rises again occurred (not simultaneously) across a range of asset classes including equity (especially Silicon Valley and so-called dividend yielders), real estate (both in emerging markets and some advanced—including residential and commercial), and commodities amongst others (including oil).

The speculative stories to match included China and other emerging markets having high growth forever, insatiable demand for energy, exponential rising monopoly rents of Big Tech and their non-assailability and of course "nowhere else to go". Arguably the biggest carry trade and related speculative frenzy of all, typified by peak leverage, was China (a counterpart to the Weimar Republic in the great asset price inflation of the 1920s).

It is too early at the time of writing to say how the second great asset price inflation (type B) under the inflation-targeting regime ended up (this has not stopped the architects and directors of the regime from praising its success!). But it is not too early to put forward the counterfactual hypothesis that if the Federal Reserve (and foreign central banks) had accommodated rather than fought the tendency of prices to fall in deep recession the outcome would have been a journey to economic prosperity without the burden of another asset price inflation disease and all the malinvestment and other woes (including the monstrosities of Big Tech) which accompany that.

10 Europe's Fateful Entry to 2% Inflation Standard

As mentioned above Europe joined the 2% inflation standard originally in 1999 at the start of EMU. Entry was strengthened when in early 2003 Professor Issing announced that the ECB would be as zealous in preventing inflation from falling below 2% as rising above (see Brown 2014).

A special argument applied by both Issing and subsequent ECB officials for a 2% inflation target in the context of EMU has been the need for relative price adjustment between member countries over time. A 2% inflation target allows these to take place without pervasive nominal wage cuts having to be made anywhere or even without any widespread price cutting. For Keynesian economists concerned about money illusion and wage rigidities that has been an important consideration. Alongside such concerns has been a culture of political correctness at the ECB where policy is never made explicitly with the current German situation in mind. All action is justified in terms of euro area average indices—present and forecast—and what these signal about the economic and monetary path.

This fixation of ECB officials on price inflexibility, wage rigidities, and political correctness has led the ECB far away from a sound money path. In a well-functioning capitalist economy under conditions of sound money, some prices and wages will sometimes be falling, and there may be some geographic clustering present. The avoidance of this does not merit a journey into permanent inflation (at 2%) and related monetary instability (the thwarting of natural rhythm in prices, e.g. brings about spells of asset price inflation). And in any case, the pursuance of sound money should mean the occurrence of periodic bouts of downward pressure on prices or wages in a member economy should be less than where money has been unsound. The political correctness of not focusing on Germany is at odds with Robert Mundell's historical observation that central banks of federal states with a dominant (economically) member do focus on that state where symptoms of monetary instability might very well show up first or most strikingly. Washing all data up into union averages mean the alert systems work less well.

Take the actual experience of EMU to date. The targeting of 2% inflation at the level of the euro area as a whole despite a natural rhythm of prices which was much lower (explained by rapid globalization including the collapse of the Berlin Wall which created downward pressures on prices and wages especially in Germany during the early years of EMU) led to asset price inflation. One factor in the easy policies of the ECBs at that time was the weakness of the US dollar (with the Greenspan-Bernanke Fed pursuing a policy of breathing in inflation) and the intention of moderating the rise of the euro (and so in fact the ECB imported US monetary instability). Asset price inflation in Europe showed up as huge speculative froth in the weak sovereign bond markets (Italy, Spain, Greece), in financial equities, in Spanish real estate, in a range of credit products (including mortgage-backed debt), and elsewhere. Along with these features, wages boomed in Spain, and in Italy wages and prices glided higher though the economy was losing competitiveness especially vis-à-vis key emerging markets and of course Germany. In the subsequent denouement including the panic and recession of 2008–2009 reality struck, but the adjustment downwards of prices and wages occurred in slow motion if at all, perhaps in part due to an overall climate of inflation inertia as created by the central bank (see above).

As the ECB finally implemented its own version of the Great Monetary Experiment with the added feature of negative interest rates and massive transfers via its balance sheet of Northern savings into the South, symptoms of inflationary malaise appeared. Notably several of these were concentrated in Germany. The super cheap euro went along with the world's largest trade surplus, real estate prices boomed across the major cities, and prices and wages showed a rising momentum with the labour market tight despite large immigration. Yet the ECB Chief, senior officials, and the Bundesbank all repeated the mantra that policy was made for the euro area as a whole not for Germany. The fact that there were still stale high prices in some countries which had yet to adjust downwards should not have taken away from the live symptoms of goods and services inflation and asset price inflation in Germany. And of course there were symptoms of asset price inflation more broadly than in Germany (and including Germany)—including buoyant carry trades in currencies, credit, and term premiums.

11 The Journey Away from 2% Inflation

The argument here has been that 2% inflation is a deeply flawed standard. It conflicts with the natural rhythm of prices in a capitalist economy, and the conflict shows up as bouts of eventually painful asset price inflation (booms and bust). It strengthens forces of inertia which can cripple the invisible hand and hinder the path to prosperity. Moreover it is an emperor's new clothes story—there is no reliable way in which central banks can deliver 2% inflation given the lack of knowledge about monetary influences in a system where monetary base has been removed from the pivot of the system. And even when still at the pivot, the relationships between money and economic outcomes are not strong enough to form a reliable basis for inflation targeting. The way forward put here is to ditch inflation targeting and put monetary base back at the pivot of the monetary system.

But how can we do this in the context of our present fiat monies?

Gold bullion has unique properties as a candidate for high-powered money for which there is no equivalent under a fiat money system. It enjoys a large natural and stable demand, and there are no close ersatz substitutes. Yes, under a gold standard, banks could hold short-dated Treasury Bills as a reserve to back sudden surges in demand for gold coin—in the expectations that they could liquidate the bills and present banknotes for bullion at the issuing authority—but there are costs and uncertainties in this procedure; and for households gold coin and bullion are distinct assets from paper even under a gold standard regime.

So in the world of the second best, how could we hope to re-create any of these attributes of the monetary base?

Here are a few suggestions.

Reserves at the central bank, like gold, must not pay interest. Obstacles to a vibrant use of cash in the economy should be demolished (anti-trust action against credit card companies, e.g. which use their power to force retailers to accept their cards without charging fees, issuance of high denomination notes to satisfy demand for these as medium of exchange). Bank demand for reserves (which would be held voluntarily not as a legal reserve requirement) would be boosted by the curtailing and ideally abolition of too big to fail, lender of last resort, and deposit insurance (as above).

Yes, Treasury bills would be a very close substitute for cash and reserves at the central bank from the viewpoint of banks. And so a tightness of reserves supply could be alleviated by small changes in T-bill rates—meaning that high short-term interest rate volatility (which shelters long-term interest rates from official manipulation) and ultimately signalling effect of the average (over a period of time) for estimates of neutral rates (as described early in this paper for the gold standard) would be missing. Second best is not first best.

Setting the supply of high-powered money is a deeply challenging aspect of a monetary regime which has high-powered money at the pivot of the system. As discussed above an $x\%$ p.a. target expansion is much less supple in providing stability than the forces which regulate high-powered money growth under a gold standard system. And in any case the $x\%$ p.a. is not set in stone but can be adjusted whether by whim of the monetary authority or according to a set of rules set in legislation or constitutional law. In principle these would guide the monetary authorities to setting a path for monetary base growth over the long run that was consistent with sound money. And so if indications suggested that sticking to a given monetary base path was creating serious downward pressure on prices amidst monetary disequilibrium, then the path would be adjusted upwards.

All of this is very messy and subject to wide discretion and inevitably politics. And indeed whether such a monetary regime would persist is essentially decided in the arena of politics. That was true also of the gold standard whose survival or resuscitation depended on supportive political forces (e.g. consider the history of the gold standard's introduction in the USA following the civil war—see Rothbard 2005). That standard had a long record and body of theory to support it, and there was widespread public affection for such a system. A fiat monetary base system would similarly become more stable if it won public affection—the nearest example being the esteem which the hard DM won amongst the German public.

12 Public Esteem for Sound Money

How could the architects of a new monetary regime to succeed the 2% inflation standard hope to gain this public esteem, so essential to the success ultimately of the project?

There has to be a clear statement of aims, and these have to be understood and desired by a broad section of public opinion. The aims would include stable prices as defined over the very long run, keeping the monetary monkey wrench out of all the other machinery in the economy (in layman's terms avoiding the sequence of bubbles and busts and promoting thereby economic prosperity), free financial markets meaning interest rates not subject to price control (rate fixing) and prey to crony capitalism (such as occurs in highly regulated and non-competitive markets), no more interest income famines, no panics about unaffordable housing due to soaring speculative temperatures there amidst monetary-induced waves of desperation, and the reigning in of abuse of monetary powers by the central bankers who would face vigorous vetting by the legislature.

The vast balance sheets of the central banks which accumulated during the Grand Monetary Experiment would have to be shrunk such that the monetary base subsisting would be freely demanded at zero interest rates at the start. Judging that size is of course a matter of trial and error—meaning that evidence of the base being too large or small at the beginning by a wide margin (as would come from strong inflationary or deflationary pressure) would have to be corrected. And the actual shrinking would necessitate some type of accord between the central bank and finance ministry so that the former can swap its holdings of say long-maturity bonds with the latter and obtain short-term bills instead (which are then sold into the market so as to influence the amount of high-powered money outstanding). The accord would allow the maturity of net government debt (aggregated across government as a whole including the central bank) to increase gradually (rather than suddenly, as would be the case if the central bank had to dispose of its bonds directly in its programme of monetary normalization).

In sum the journey away from the 2% inflation standard to sound money can be driven only by a strong political momentum in its favour. There lies the challenge. It is plausible that the political momentum would be greatest after an episode of deep monetary failure. But where this failure has had as most visible consequence asset market boom and bust rather than high goods and services inflation, it is notoriously difficult for advocates of sound money to put together a winning coalition. There are so many potential scapegoats against which popular rage can be directed by parties with an alternative agenda (to sound money)—and it is not at all obvious through all the fog that unsound money was enemy no. 1.

References

Bagus, P. (2003, Winter). Deflation: When Austrians become interventionist. *Quarterly Journal of Austrian Economics, 6*(4), 19–35.

Bernanke, B. (2002, November 21). Deflation: Making sure it does not happen here. Speech before the National Economists Club, Washington, DC.

Brown, B. (2013). *The global curse of the federal reserve* (2nd ed.). London: Palgrave.

Brown, B. (2014). *Euro crash* (3rd ed.). London: Palgrave.

Brown, B. (2015). *A global monetary plague*. London: Palgrave.

Brown, B. (2017, Spring). Asset price inflation – Type A(boom) vs type B (depression). *Quarterly Journal of Austrian Economics 20*(1), 29–60.

Friedman, M. (2006). *The optimum quantity of money*. London: Aldine Transaction.

Geberding, C., Worms, A., & Seitz, F. (2004). *How the Bundesbank really conducted monetary policy: An analysis based on real-time data*. Deutsche Bundesbank Discussion Paper, Series 1: Studies of the Economic Research Centre, No. 25/2004.

Gonzalez-Hermosillo, B., & Ito, T. (1997, December). *The Bank of Canada's monetary policy framework: Have recent changes enhanced central bank credibility* (IMF Working Paper).

Hodgson, G. M. (2000). What is the essence of institutional economics? *Journal of Economic Issues, 34*(2), 317–329.

Meltzer, A. (2005). Origins of the great inflation. *Federal Reserve Bank of St. Louis Review, 87*, 145–175.

Meltzer, A. H., & Robinson, S. (1989). Stability under the gold standard in practice. In M. D. Bordo (Ed.), *Money, history and international finance: Essays in Honor of Anna J. Shwartz*. Chicago, IL: University of Chicago Press.

Pollock, A. J. (2013). "Rethinking the Federal Reserve's Many Mandates on its 100-year anniversary" a hearing before the Committee on Financial Services, US House of Representatives, December 12, 2013, Serial no. 113-56.

Rothbard, M. (2005). *A history of money and banking in the United States*. Auburn, AL: Mises Institute.

Salerno, J. (2003, Winter). An Austrian taxonomy of deflation – With application to the US. *Quarterly Journal of Austrian Economics, 6*(4), 81–103.

Salerno, J. (2010). *Money, sound and unsound*. Auburn, AL: Mises Institute.

Shewin, M. (1999). Speech to New Zealand Association of Economists Conference, July 1, 1999.

Wells, W. (1994). *Economist in an uncertain world: Arthur Burns and the Federal Reserve 1970–1978*. New York: Columbia University Press.

Williams, J. C. (2017, February 21). Three Questions on R Star. *Federal Reserve Bank of San Francisco, Economic Letter*.

Unintended Consequences of ECB Policies in Europe

Andreas Hoffmann and Nicolas Cachanosky

1 Introduction

Despite great advances in macroeconomics since the 1980s, the financial crisis of 2007/2008 has caught most of the world as well as most economists by surprise. In search for an explanation, Austrian ideas have seen a comeback *beyond* Austrian circles.[1] In reference to Hayek's famous Nobel Prize Lecture, Caballero (2010), for instance, suggests that macroeconomic theorists should worry about the knowledge problem in macroeconomics and take limits of macroeconomic analysis more seriously than they did before the crisis in order to prevent deriving false conclusions and making false predictions. Once regarded useless, in discussions on the causes of the 2007/2008 financial crisis as well as consequences of the policy responses, in particular the Mises–Hayek or Austrian business cycle theory (ABCT) has been rediscovered to explain what went wrong.

Economists at the Bank for International Settlements were among the first to warn central bankers about global credit booms and worrisome financial imbalances in the 2000s, suggesting that—in line with Hayek's work—holding inflation at bay alone does not guarantee long-term macroeconomic stability. Compatible with Austrian ideas, Taylor's monetary policy view on the financial crisis emphasizes that the US Federal Reserve (Fed) held interest rates below natural rates prior to the boom,

[1]Ferguson (2009) places the Austrians among the winners of the financial crisis. For an overview on recent Austrian(-inspired) macroeconomics literature, see Cachanosky and Salter (2016).

A. Hoffmann (✉)
Institute for Economic Policy, Leipzig University, Leipzig, Germany
e-mail: ahoffmann@wifa.uni-leipzig.de

N. Cachanosky
Department of Economics, Metropolitan State University of Denver, Denver, CO, USA
e-mail: ncachano@msudenver.edu

A. Godart-van der Kroon, P. Vonlanthen (eds.), *Banking and Monetary Policy from the Perspective of Austrian Economics*,
https://doi.org/10.1007/978-3-319-75817-6_6

sowing the seeds of crisis. Explicitly motivated by the Austrian-BIS view, Bordo and Landon-Lane (2013) provide evidence that expansionary monetary policy is a regular trigger of asset price booms. Finally, discussing the policy responses to the crisis, White (2012) outlines unintended consequences of too-low interest rates consistent with Austrian ideas.

In the spirit of this research, we shall revisit the unintended consequences of the European Central Bank's (ECB) low interest rate policies with a focus on the periphery countries of the European Union (EU) since the 2000s from a modern Austrian perspective.

In the first part of the chapter, we argue that the adoption of EU institutions in the periphery countries of the euro area as well as in the New Member States of the EU signaled some credibility to markets for further integration. Convergence expectations and the ECB's expansionary monetary policy were conducive to credit booms that turned bust in 2007/2008. The subsequent European debt crisis revealed that the money-induced credit boom also incentivized governments to increase borrowing at relatively low rates. We show that the credit and debt booms in Europe are consistent with the ABCT and summarize the main findings in the Austrian literature on the unintended monetary policy effects during the boom. To this end, we will draw heavily upon our own empirical and theoretical work in which we augmented the Mises–Hayek theory to consider risk and explain (recurring) international credit cycles as well as resource misallocations.[2]

The second part of the chapter sheds some light on *adverse effects* of the ECB crisis management through an Austrian lens. As the European Monetary Union had little experience and tools to deal with a broader European financial and debt crisis, the ECB's accommodative policies were the (only) means readily available to prevent a shutdown in financial markets and to support governments. We show, however, that ECB policies were not successful in stimulating bank lending and investment. The main beneficiaries of holding rates at low levels are governments, who use the financial leeway to delay painful reforms. We suggest that the ECB's policy has unintentionally slowed down the recovery in the crisis economies and worsened Europe's growth prospects since 2009.

2 Convergence Expectations cum Monetary Expansion: The Boom of the 2000s

For an Austrian-style credit boom to get started, we need two basic ingredients: (1) positive expectations about future returns and (2) easy credit conditions.

[2]See Cachanosky (2014a, b, 2015b), Hoffmann (2010, 2014), Hoffmann and Schnabl (2011, 2013, 2016b), Schnabl and Hoffmann (2008), and Cachanosky and Hoffmann (2016).

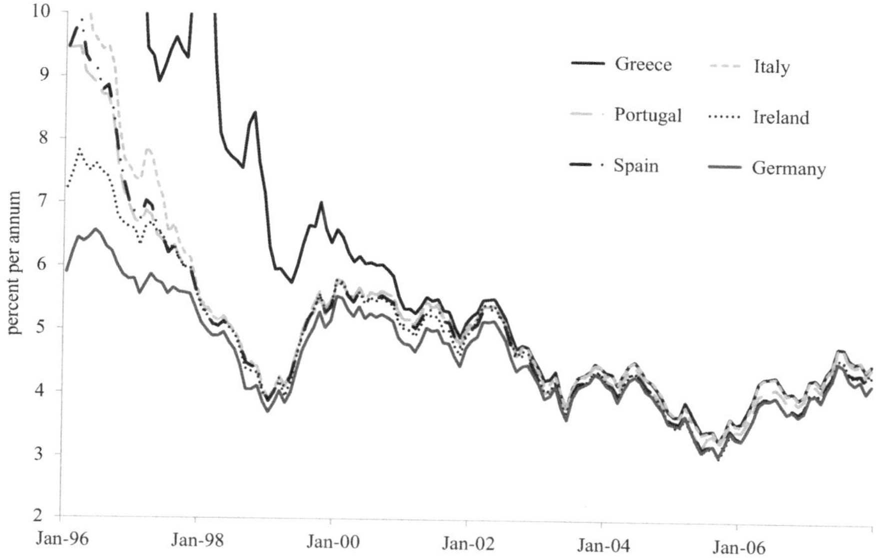

Fig. 1 Government bond yields in the euro area periphery and Germany (Data: IMF, International Financial Statistics)

1. EMU and Expectations

First, expectations and investment prospects in Europe were up following the start of European Monetary Union (EMU) because political integration was supposed to improve macroeconomic stability in large parts of the union. The EU set up a number of institutions in the 1990s to allow for a credible and irreversible introduction of the euro that were supposed to guarantee (1) free trade, (2) stable money, and (3) balanced budgets. The Single Market Act was supposed to establish the free movement of production factors within the euro area. The ECB committed itself to adhere to a near 2% inflation rule, providing the currency area with more monetary stability than most members historically had. The Maastricht treaty and its stability and growth pact were supposed to contribute to balanced budgets and sustainable government finances.

Figure 1 shows that with the introduction of the euro and the abandonment of the national currencies, European sovereign bond yields converged toward the German bund. Investors and banks did not discriminate much anymore between holding bunds and other bonds until 2007. It is not clear, however, to which extent the stability and growth pact and the no-bailout clauses in the Maastricht treaty indicated fiscal policy responsibility of individual governments. Monetary unions may also lower the default risks if investors believe other members or the central bank (Bernoth et al. 2004) would bail out troubled members in case of emergency. However, the fall in yields toward the bund yield suggests that EMU triggered expectations of real and nominal convergence. The introduction of the euro was considered irreversible. Codogno et al. (2003) provide quantitative evidence that

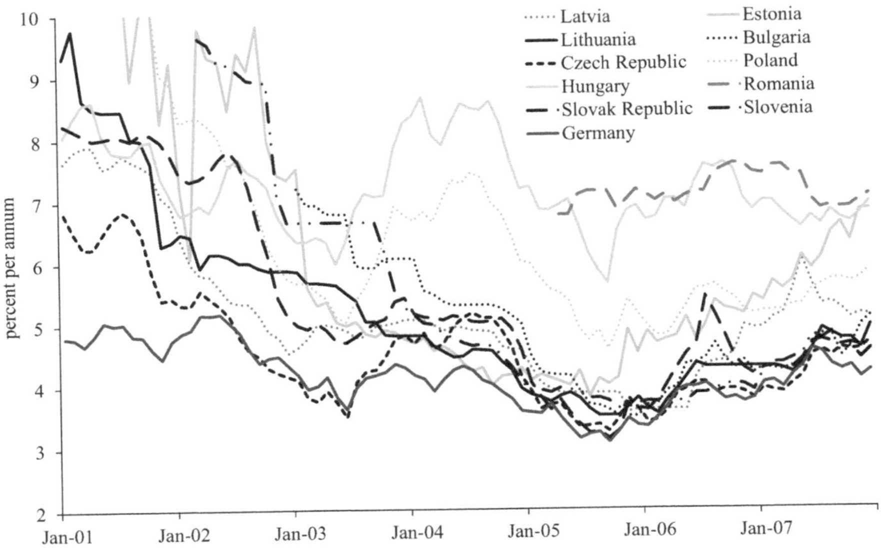

Fig. 2 Government bond yields in the new member states and Germany (Data: IMF, International Financial Statistics)

bond yield differentials mostly hinged on factors such as international risk, which may affect default risks in the euro area depending on debt-to-GDP ratios.

In Central and Eastern Europe (CEE), EU enlargement seems to have provided hopes for economic convergence. As joining the EU meant adopting its institutional framework and subsequently participating in the EMU, in the so-called New Member States of the EU government-borrowing costs fell substantially when EU accession was decided. Luengnaruemitchai and Schadler (2007) wrote of an "EU halo effect" in CEE as fundamentals alone did not justify the fall in bond yields after 2003. In line with this, Ebner (2009) shows that factors such as ECB interest rates had a larger impact on bond yields than fundamentals in the New Member States of the EU until the 2007/2008 financial crisis. However, we want to emphasize that fundamentals and the state of fiscal policy continued to matter. Although three of the VISEGRAD countries (Poland, Slovak Republic, and the Czech Republic) saw government borrowing costs fall substantially, Hungary's government did not benefit from falling borrowing costs. Hungary went through strong election cycles. Policy credibility was rather low (Hoffmann 2013b) (see Fig. 2).

2. Low Interest Rates, Credit Booms, and Structural Distortions

Second, according to the Mises–Hayek credit cycle theory, a distortion of relative prices and an unsustainable credit boom are *unintended consequences* of holding market interest rates "too low for too long" when a rise in expectations increases investment demand. To keep the economy in equilibrium, banks have to set capital market rates according to the natural rate of interest which balances saving and investment plans over time. If banks hold capital market rates below equilibrium, the economy may enter a credit boom as too low interest rates depress saving incentives (and hence incentivize future consumption). Given low interest rates, however, current consumption, investment in capital-intensive industries (Hayek 1931), or investments with a high financial duration (Cachanosky and Lewin 2014, 2016a, b) pick up as they *seem* more lucrative.[3] In an environment of positive expectations, lower capital market rates may falsely signal to a share of investors that saving and therefore future consumption increased (Cachanosky 2015a), bringing about malinvestment due to an information problem. Therefore, the credit boom, originating from a deviation of the market from the natural rate of interest, goes along with changes in the structure of production that are not sustainable.

The Austrian theory of the credit cycle suggests that banks have incentives to expand credit too far at unchanged rates, due to competition for the greatest market share (Hayek 1929). Hayek (1937) refers to the banks' possibility to do this as the *perverse elasticity* of credit money. A central bank can restrict such a credit expansion, for instance, by increasing refinancing costs for banks. Banks then need to tighten credit and increase interest rates for investment projects in accordance to the higher demand. Saving would become more attractive.

However, such *leaning against the wind* policies is unlikely to happen at the right time and to the correct extent due to the possibility of *type I errors*. Rather than leaning against the wind and smoothing the credit cycle, central banks may welcome the developments as they are in line with secondary central bank targets, for instance, they may help close the output gap. Central banks (with strong employment mandates) may even aim to increase the amplitude of cycles as long as consumer price inflation does not pick up rather than working to smoothen out the naturally recurring cycles due to the *perverse elasticity* of bank credit.

Indeed, following the bursting of the US dot-com bubble, the Federal Reserve (Fed) cut interest rates decisively to a (then) unprecedented low of 1%. Although growth had picked up by 2003, the Fed hesitated in raising policy interest rates as inflation remained in bounds. The Fed may have been misled by increases in productivity during this period (Selgin et al. 2015). In the presence of productivity gains, a stable price-level policy may be expansionary in the sense that money supply exceeds money demand. As long as this excess of money is injected into economy through the financial market, we may get a rise in the supply of *credit* and a reduction of interest rates below their equilibrium or natural levels.[4] The ECB seems to have followed a similar policy as the Fed in the aftermath of the dot-com crash (Hoffmann 2013a).

---

[3]Cachanosky and Lewin argue that elusive Böhm-Bawerk's *roundaboutness* or average period of production can be understood as the financial duration of the expected cash flow of an investment project. For the history of the problem of the average period of production, see Lewin and Cachanosky (2018).

[4]Leijonhufvud (2009) argues that the price-level behavior was also misleading for the Fed due to countries in the periphery of the USA to keep their exchange rates undervalued with respect to the US dollar.

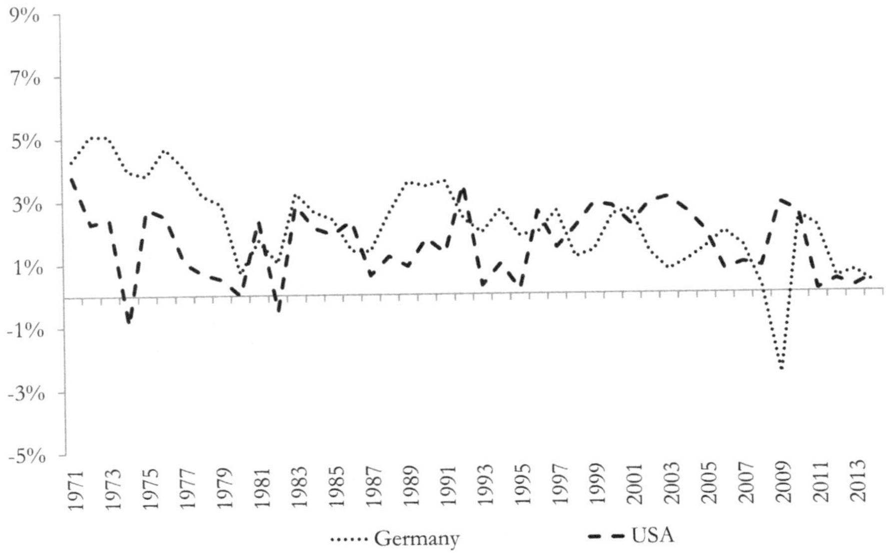

Fig. 3 Productivity growth. Source: Datastream

The corresponding drop in interest rates in Europe and the USA is sustainable only if the natural rate of interest declined over the same period. However, there was no evidence that the growth potential of the advanced economies, which may be seen as a proxy for the long-term natural interest rate, had declined as much in the 2000s (Laubach and Williams 2003). Productivity growth in the USA and Europe (Germany) remained, by and large, constant from 1995 to 2007 (Fig. 3). In a recent empirical study, Juselius et al. (2016) show that the natural interest rate had *not* declined much during this period. Policy interest rates remained below natural interest rates.

In Europe, catch-up expectations *met* low interest rate policies between 2002 and 2007. Because expected returns were higher in the European periphery, banks mainly increased leverage and extended credit to firms in Southern and Central and Eastern Europe.

Figure 4 illustrates the intra-European transmission of an Austrian-style credit boom from the creditor countries of Europe, like Germany to the periphery.[5] The creditor economies tend to have saving surpluses, planned savings exceed investment ($S_1^c > I_1^c$). Capital is exported to the (CX_1^c) periphery, which has higher investment demand than savings supply at euro area-wide interest rate ($I_1^d > S_1^d$). The international capital market is cleared at the euro area capital market interest rate

[5]This following part follows Hoffmann and Schnabl (2016b).

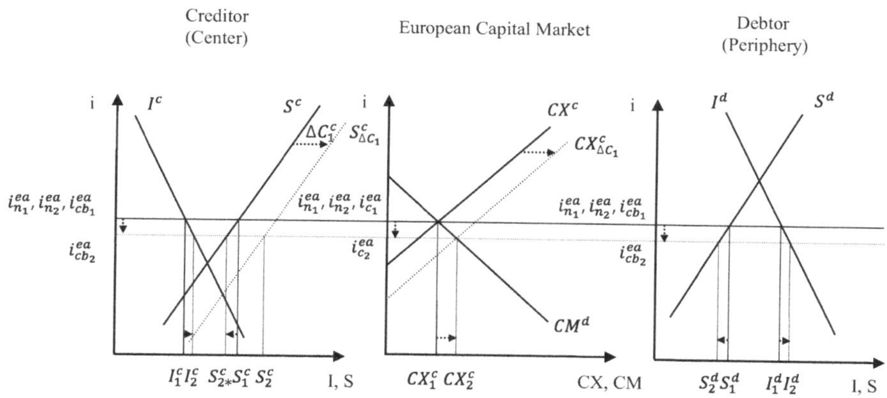

Fig. 4 Credit boom: center-periphery model. Source: Based on Hoffmann and Schnabl (2016b)

$i^{ea}_{c_1}$, which—assuming no special frictions in the common market—is equivalent to the national capital market interest rate ($i^{ea}_{c_1} = i^{c}_{c_1} = i^{d}_{c_1}$, with $CX_1^c = CM_1^d$).[6] We further assume an equilibrium in international capital markets, with the capital market interest rate being equal to the global natural interest rate ($i^{ea}_{c_1} = i^{ea}_{n_1}$). We first assume that the ECB interest rate matches the capital market interest rates, as well as the euro area natural interest rate ($i^{ea}_{cb_1} = i^{c}_{c_1} = i^{ea}_{n_1} = i^{ea}_{c_1} = i^{d}_{c_1}$).

When the ECB lowers the policy rate (below the natural interest rate) to $i^{ea}_{cb_2}$, the financial sector creates additional credit ΔC_1^c. The credit expansion mimics an increase in planned savings, modeled by a shift of the savings curve to the right. The euro area capital market interest rate falls from $i^{ea}_{c_1}$ to $i^{ea}_{c_2}$. Capital exports (imports) of the creditor (debtor) increase to CX_2^c.

At the fallen interest rate, investment increases from I_1^c to I_2^c in the creditor economy (e.g. Germany) and from I_1^d to I_2^d in the periphery economies. Planned savings fall to S_2^C* in the creditor economy and to S_2^d in the debtor (periphery) economies. S_2^c represents the credit supply in the creditor economy ($S_2^c = S_2^c* + \Delta C_1^c$) at $i^{ea}_{c_2}$. A rise in capital flows reflects the increasing gap between savings and investment in the creditor economy as well as in the debtor periphery economies.

However, planned savings have not increased with the credit expansion but have fallen to $S_2^c* + S_2^d$. Therefore, the euro area capital market interest rate is below its natural interest rate, $i^{ea}_{c_2} < i^{ea}_{n_2} = i^{ea}_{n_1}$, constituting a global disequilibrium between savings and investment. The decline of market interest rates below the natural rate

---

[6]Note that in line with the balance of payments identity, capital exports and capital imports are equivalent to current account positions with inverse signs, reflecting national preferences for intertemporal savings and consumption.

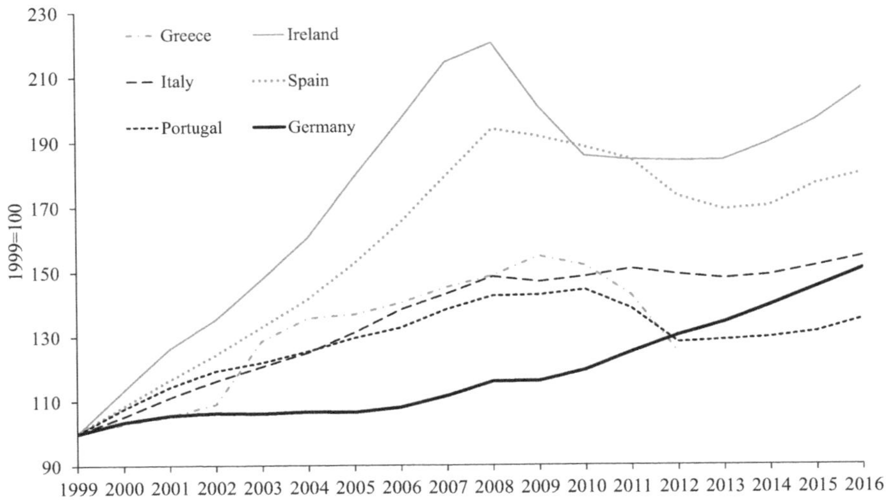

Fig. 5 Wages in Germany and Europe's periphery. Source: IMF, International Financial Statistics

triggers an unsustainable credit boom as well as production distortions in the booming economies. The default risk of investment increases if (given resource constraints) the euro area capital market rate should return to its natural rate.

In the European periphery economies, capital markets are less developed than in its core. Therefore, the absorption capacity of capital markets following an increase in domestic lending is limited. Consumer and asset prices are more sensitive to a monetary expansion than in countries with well-developed consumer goods and capital markets.

Indeed, given the rise in investment in Southern Europe until 2006, GDP and wages grew much faster in the periphery economies of the euro area than in, e.g., Germany (see Fig. 5). Cross-border credit flows from Northern European banks to the EU periphery were reflected in large intra-European trade and investment imbalances until 2008, i.e., current account deficits in the Southern European countries and current account surpluses in Germany and some other Northern European countries (Schnabl and Zemanek 2011), which were later considered a symptom of the crisis (Fig. 6).

Similarly, in CEE, positive expectations related to EMU membership attracted investments from international investors. Capital inflows surged because the interest rate spread between the euro area and CEE was high and CEE improved its macroeconomic stability as a prerequisite for EU accession. Importantly, many

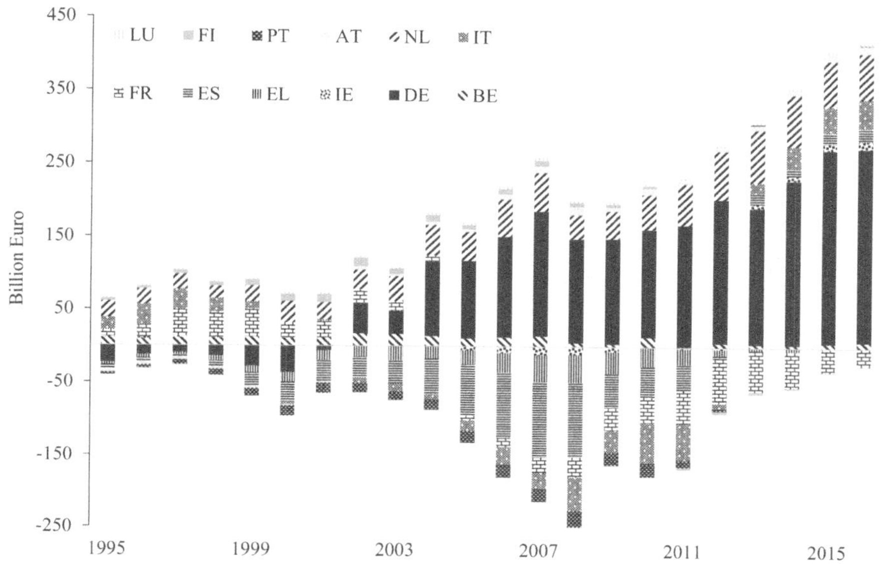

Fig. 6 Current account imbalances in the EMU. Source: IMF, International Financial Statistics. Since 2012 the EMU is a net exporter to the world. Intra-European current account imbalances declined when capital left the periphery countries. In the following, e.g., German exports to third countries increased, while exports to Europe's periphery fell

CEE banks are subsidiaries of European banks. Therefore, they had easy access to EMU financing. Cross-border lending became closely linked to domestic credit growth, which led to an increase in the dependence on foreign financing and low interest rates (Hoffmann 2016).

Although the transmission of monetary policy from the center to the periphery economy depends on the exchange rate policy followed in the non-euro area periphery, flexible exchange rates may not have helped the small periphery countries to isolate themselves from EMU monetary policy. Indeed, Cachanosky (2014a, 2015b) shows that Latin American countries experienced Austrian-type business cycles, regardless of their exchange rate regime during the credit boom of the 2000s. Like a small boat sailing through a storm, a small economy has *some* control on *how* the cycle is going to play out domestically, but it *cannot* avoid a cycle that is triggered by the largest economies.

In most NMS of the EU, credit growth and new investment contributed to a higher growth of output, employment, and rising incomes during the boom. Since interest rates were relatively low, saving was depressed, and consumption was fueled. Current account deficits accumulated in particular in countries that stabilized exchange rates against the euro as hard pegs seem to have provided additional credibility (Égert et al. 2006; Hoffmann 2010). For instance, the Romanian and Estonian current account deficits grew from 5% of GDP in 2001 to 13 and 17% of GDP in 2007. Countries with flexible exchange rates as Poland did not see such a dramatic increase in the saving-investment imbalance. In Poland, the current account deficit rose from 3% of GDP in 2001 to 5% of GDP in 2007 (Hoffmann 2010).

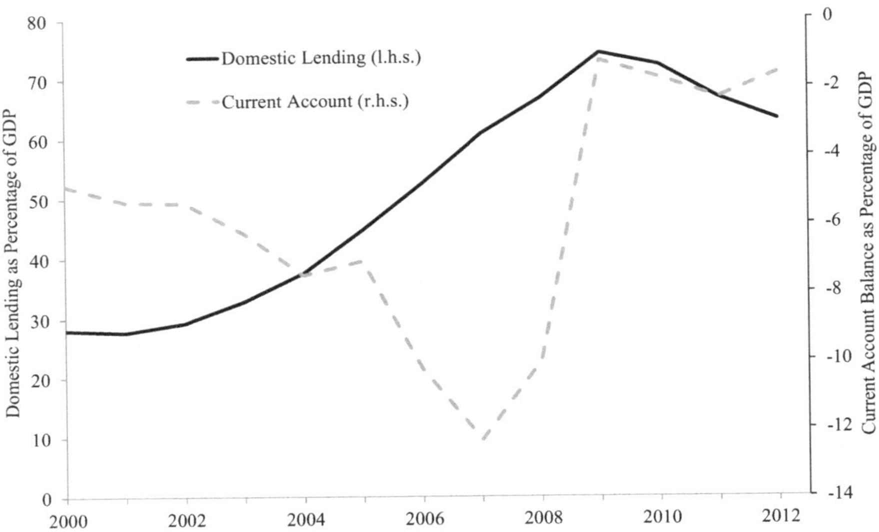

Fig. 7 Domestic lending and current accounts in the new member states. Source: World Development Indicators, 2016, Arithmetic averages

Figure 7 illustrates the rise in domestic lending and current account deficits until the financial crisis of 2007/2008.

In an international Austrian business cycle framework, Cachanosky (2014b) shows that a reduction in market interest rates of a center county will affect how resources are allocated in *time*, namely, it will incentivize investors to invest in projects with expected cash flows that have higher *modified durations*.[7] Cachanosky (2014a, 2015b) further finds that those economic sectors that in relative terms are more capital intensive should be particularly affected by easy monetary policy. For the NMS of the EU, the models would suggest that the non-tradeable goods sectors may have benefitted at the expense of the export sector when the low interest rate policies of the ECB led to substantial real appreciation of the currencies in the NMS.

Cachanosky and Hoffmann (2016) provide quantitative evidence of such production distortions in Europe. Studying the effects of monetary policy at the industrial level in ten European countries, they show that monetary policy changes affected gross value added unevenly across industries and countries. The low interest rate environment of the 2000s seems to have caused substantial microeconomic distortions in Europe during the buildup of the bubble—which is in line with the Austrian credit boom theory.

Moreover, the low interest rate environment contributed to a *perception of convergence* and fiscal policy credibility, allowing governments to borrow at lower costs. As the credit boom artificially elevated growth rates, it put a downward bias on estimated debt-to-GDP ratios, hiding increases in government expenditure (Fig. 8).

[7]See also the discussion in Cachanosky and Lewin (2016b, pp. 31–33).

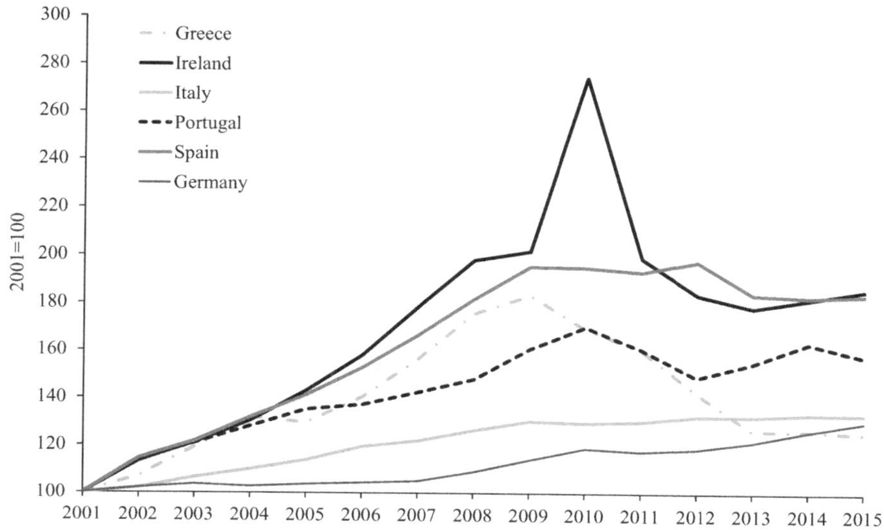

Fig. 8 Government expenditure (Relative to 2001). Source: World Economic Outlook

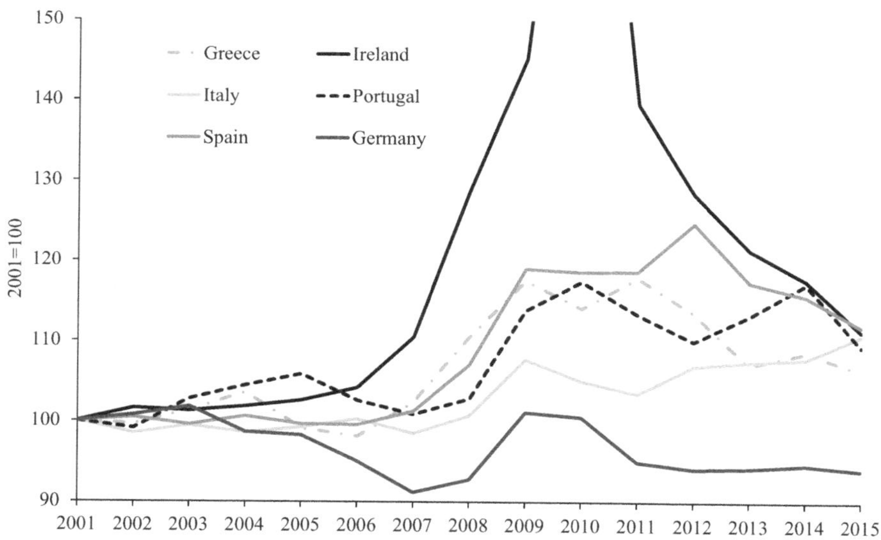

Fig. 9 Government expenditure as percent of GDP (Relative to 2001). Source: World Economic Outlook

Falling social security payments and rising revenues due to high employment rates allowed governments to stock up benefits and promise, e.g., higher pensions. Figure 9 shows that government finances looked better than they really were as government expenditure as percentage of GDP did not grow substantially until 2008 despite the dramatic rise in expenditure (relative to 2001). When GDP dropped, unemployment rose, and fiscal stimuli were perceived necessary, government expenditure as percentage of GDP rose rapidly. Due to the expansion in the boom, government expenditure as percentage of GDP remained at an approximately 10% higher plateau in the crisis economies.

3 The Crisis and the ECB

In 2006, the economies of the euro area periphery (Spain, Portugal, Ireland, Greece, and Italy) as well as those of the NMS of the EU started to show signs of overheating. Consequently, the ECB raised its refinancing rates to rein in inflation. The interest rate increases dampened the macroeconomic outlook and thereby the stability of the markets in both the periphery of the euro area and the new member states. Asset prices and credit growth stagnated.

The US subprime market crisis of 2007–2008 contributed to an increase in risk aversion around the world. When liquidity in the large capital markets dried up, the NMS faced substantial capital outflows and depreciation pressure. The sudden stop after the Lehman collapse and the following "Great Recession" paralyzed European markets. In the periphery economies of the euro area as well as in the NMS, credit and asset (housing) booms went bust.

The financial crisis evolved into a European sovereign debt crisis as investors started to doubt the sustainability of government debt in euro area periphery countries. Capital left Greece, Ireland, Portugal, and later Spain and Italy. The capital flight from South to North sharply increased government bond yields in the euro area crisis economies. Discrimination between bonds did not only depend on debt-to-GDP ratios. Instead, investors revised expectations about future developments, tax revenues, or the sustainability of current account balances, pushing up government borrowing costs (Aßmann and Boysen-Hogrefe 2012; Barrios et al. 2009).

Like the Fed, the ECB cut policy interest rates to an all-time low when the financial crisis arrived to Europe and fully accommodated financing needs at a rate which stabilized the inter-banking market. Interest rate cuts were accompanied by Emergency Liquidity Assistance (ELA-credit) of national central banks to (officially) illiquid financial institutions. Fiscal support was granted via public capital injections to euro area commercial banks and bilateral credit lines as well as IMF credit to struggling governments (which were later institutionalized). Thus, the no-bailout clause was immediately ignored. From May 2010 to September 2012, the ECB further bought (government) securities on secondary markets via its Security Markets Program (SMP). The ECB's so-called Big Bertha—named in reference to Germany's famous Krupp-manufactured super-howitzer in World War I— the long-term refinancing operations (LTRO), which lasted from late 2011 to February 2012, belongs to one of the largest liquidity injections of a central bank to this date (Crosignani et al. 2016).

Absent the presence of effective bailout institutions in the young and diverging monetary union, the ECB was pushed further and further into the role of a government financier—(officially) to stabilize financial markets. When pressure on governments grew, the ECB started to purchase government bonds from periphery countries in secondary markets to bring down bond yields, help make government financing "sustainable," calm down financial markets, and encourage bank lending (ECB 2012a). A main reason for purchasing government debt is the close link between sovereign and bank risks. European banks hold substantial amounts of euro area sovereign debt in their portfolios. To contain rising government bond yields in the South of Europe, the ECB famously *announced* an unlimited government bond purchasing scheme—the Outright Monetary Transactions (OMT) program (ECB 2012b) in July 2012, which was often interpreted as an implicit government yield cap (Reuters 2012). At the same time, restrictions on financial markets were supposed to mitigate the capital flight to the North (Reinhart 2012).

In the meantime, EU governments also started to tighten financial regulation (e.g., prudential measures like capital regulation) in order to promote financial stability and gradually agreed on establishing so-called stability (bailout and supervisory) mechanisms to more effectively supervise the banking system and provide fiscal help for crisis economies via guarantees. For instance, in hope of shielding taxpayers from losses in the future, in 2014 the EMU installed the Single Resolution Board as a second pillar of the banking union to complement its Single Supervisory Mechanism (SSM). Whereas the SSM supervises banks, the Resolution Board handles the restructuring of banks and shall make sure, for instance, that creditors of troubled financial institutions are bailed-in in the future. When it comes to bailout institutions, the European Stability Mechanism (ESM), ratified in late 2012, permanently provides up to 500 billion euros in assistance to euro area countries. In exchange for ESM funds, EU institutions demand structural reforms that shall help signal a return to sustainable fiscal policies and growth.

Within a currency union, such credible reforms, for instance, on labor markets, may help countries regain the confidence of financial markets. Increasing economic freedom may further lighten up growth prospects. Especially in Greece, negative growth rates and declining tax revenues put a drag on fiscal sustainability after the bursting of the bubble revealed that growth during the 2000s was unsustainable. Borrowing costs rose dramatically. Because problems of tax evasion and rigid labor markets have limited the scope of action for governments to mitigate the fiscal crisis and encourage a rebound of the Greek economy, public spending cuts were the only solution. Although spending cuts tend to be the less harmful form of austerity (Alesina and Ardagna 2010), they may not be conducive to lowering deficits when growth is negative and a downward spiral sets in (DeGrauwe and Ji 2013). As the level of debt to GDP continued to increase, fiscal policy credibility was lost. Until today, euro area governments via their bailout institutions and the ECB continue to fill the void and prevent defaults of EMU member states or a breakup of the monetary union.

Whereas the Fed was able to orchestrate an exit from quantitative easing, the ECB has decided to further increase quantitative easing measures from 60 to 80 billion euros a month in 2016. As QE alone bypassed the overall mark of 1 trillion euros, the ECB will increase its asset holdings to above 30% of nominal GDP. Still, domestic lending, growth, and inflation rates remain below target. To bring about a turnaround in domestic lending, the ECB regularly considers new measures such as corporate bond purchases.

4 (Unintended) Consequences of ECB Stabilization Policies?

4.1 An Austrian View on ECB Policies

Based on the Austrian theory, a dramatic monetary accommodation is reasonable as long as mistrust among banks dramatically raised banks' lending and borrowing rates in the inter-banking market (Hayek 1967 [1931], pp. 108–109)[8] and the natural interest rate has fallen. Indeed, productivity growth remains below its pre-crisis level since 2009. However, the expansion of the ECB crisis policies since 2015 via bond purchases that contributed to a prolonged period of very low nominal and real interest rates along various maturities seems to reflect a rather more aggressive than usual ECB policy (Sachverständigenrat 2015, p. 171).

Mises' *law of unintended consequences*, indeed, taught us that the ECB's well-intended monetary interventions might help prevent unemployment and boost output temporarily. However, such interventions inhibit a rapid readjustment of distorted relative prices during crisis periods, which may hamper a true takeoff of the economy in the medium and long run. Salerno (2012, p. 23) argues, "It is precisely the rise of the natural interest rate implicit in the relative decline of factor prices that restores the entrepreneurs' natural optimism and venturesomeness." Moreover, monetary interventions may have even worse *unintended* consequences in some other parts of the market as new distortions feed themselves through the price system (Mises 1929). Therefore, stabilization policies may backfire and necessitate additional interventions to deal with the unintended consequences.[9]

Juselius et al. (2016) suggest that central banks *failing* to lean against financial boom and bust cycles but instead aiming to clean up after crises have contributed to a fall in the natural interest rate in the post-crisis period, which triggered additional

[8]This is usually referred to as Hayek's *secondary deflation. The first deflation is the one caused by the crisis. The second* deflation is the one caused by an increase in money demand that is not accommodated by an increase in money supply. In the analytical context of the equation of exchange ($MV = Py$), M should increase to accommodate changes in V, not to stimulate the economy (by aiming to increasing y). This monetary rule is referred to as *Hayek's rule* (Gustavson 2010). Similarly, NGDP targeting is proposed by *market monetarists* since the 2008/2009 crisis (Cachanosky 2014c; Sumner 2012).

[9]See White (2012) for an extensive account on unintended side effects of zero interest rate policy in the US economy.

stimulus. Borio et al. (2015) provide empirical evidence that the financial boom led to a substantial reallocation of resources that lowered productivity growth since 2009. They suggest that the recent history of financial excesses may further increase uncertainty about investment prospects if no visible market cleansing and restructuring of the economy is allowed for. From an Austrian perspective, without such a market cleansing that restores confidence, the monetary easing-elasticity of expectations will fall such that additional stimulus is likely not to have the intended consequences and the natural rate of interest remains depressed. Market participants "will avoid using for an expansion of their operations the easy money available, because they will keep in mind the inevitable end of the boom" (Mises 1943, p. 251).

The Austrian analysis suggests that aggressive ECB policies may fail to restore confidence necessary to bolster a takeoff of investment and lending—at least in the short run as malinvestment is not undone during the recession. The fear of outstanding structural adjustments may result in a lower innovation and growth potential of the crisis economies and lead to a further decline in natural interest rates (Hoffmann 2014).

4.2 *Evidence of Adverse Effects of ECB Policies on Bank Lending and Investment*

The ECB's monetary stimulus was indeed not able to bring about the results the ECB had hoped for. The ECB's very own bank lending survey suggests that the impact of QE on lending was limited until April 2016, although lending rates have come down since 2012. Only in the second half of 2016, loan demand to firms increased at the margin (ECB 2016). As the low interest rate policy has compressed the lending-deposit rate spread, traditional banking has become less attractive. Given the number of struggling financial institutions and the uncertainty about the value of sovereign debt held by the banking system (and the ECB), a decline in cross-border banking in the euro area as well as to NMS of the EU depresses domestic lending (Hoffmann 2016). Not surprisingly, corporate borrowing dropped substantially since 2009 (Fig. 10).

Instead, banks started to engage in additional risk-taking. At first, betting on the survival of the euro area, banks bought additional government bonds of periphery economies in the midst of the debt crisis when spreads between the German bund and the periphery bonds widened, refinanced via the ECB. The additional bond holdings add to the problem of interdependence of sovereign and bank risk in Europe. Therefore, the costs of defaults were further raised, which may benefit both banks and governments as higher costs may increase the likelihood of further bailouts.

Moreover, EU regulation considers these high-yielding government bonds as being risk-free. Therefore, banks did not have to issue additional capital to fulfill capital regulation (Acharya and Steffen 2016).

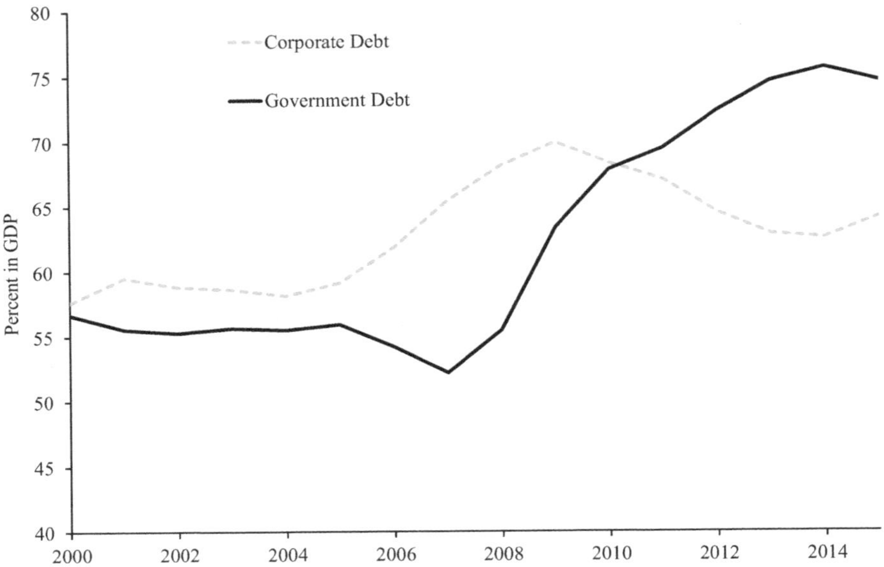

Fig. 10 Borrowing of corporate sector and central governments (euro area). Source: ECB, Oxford Economics

The ECB programs further provided incentives to hold risky government assets of shorter horizons. In particular, following the ECB's announcement of its 3-year long-term refinancing operations, an unprecedented program of collateralized lending, in December 2011, Spanish, Italian, and Portuguese banks have increased the holding of domestic short-term government debt for use as collateral in refinancing operations (Acharya and Steffen 2016; Crosignani et al. 2016).

The ECB's aim was of course to support bank lending and trigger some inflationary expectations that would increase spending and growth. However, Acharya et al. (2016) have shown that, for instance, the OMT program did not help adding loans to sound businesses. The announcement of the OMT program recapitalized financial institutions with large shares of sovereign debt via increases in bond prices. Low capital ratios have provided an incentive to roll over loans of bad quality firms in order to prevent losses such that otherwise undercapitalized banks increased lending to so-called zombie firms, firms that cannot service the debt, in order to prevent loan write-downs as well as increases in nonperforming loans (see Hoffmann and Schnabl, 2016a). According to the Austrian theory, these unprofitable firms should fail during a crisis. Freeing resources would allow factor prices to adjust and bring about a rise in the natural rate of interest, which might allow for a takeoff of the economy.

Policies in the USA differed as the Troubled Asset Relief Program (TARP) ensured the recapitalization of banks. Like in Japan during the 1990s (Hoshi and Kashyap 2010), TARP forced banks to increase capital cushions and write-down of bad assets. However, in contrast to the intentions, there is evidence of increased risk-

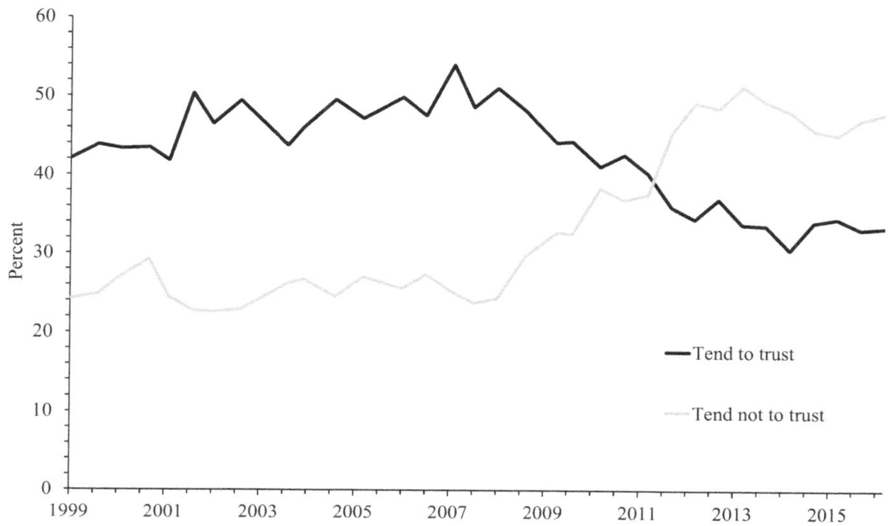

Fig. 11 Trust in ECB (in percent of population) (Source: European Commission, Eurobarometer, Public Opinion on ECB in European Union)

taking of large TARP banks, stemming from moral hazard (Black and Hazelwood 2013). In sum, it seems hard to encourage higher capital ratios and bank lending during periods of financial instability when profits in the real economy remain clouded.

The failure of monetary policy to reach its announced targets has become a problem for central bank credibility. The ECB seems unable to commit to its goals. The so-called Eurobarometer shows that trust in the ECB has fallen in the EU (Fig. 11).

4.3 The Return of State Banking

As the private financial sector of the euro area continues to struggle and bank balance sheets stagnate, the role of government in banking increased substantially. On the one hand, this is a result of capital injections or bailouts of private banks (for instance, Dexia in Belgium, Royal Bank of Scotland, Hypo Real Estate and Commerzbank in Germany, Fortis in the Benelux, ABN Amro in the Netherlands, Allied Irish Bank in Ireland). On the other hand, so-called development banks are flourishing in Europe.

Backed by bailout guarantees and outside the standard regulatory framework, public development banks like KfW (Kreditanstalt für Wiederaufbau, Germany) or ICO (Instituto de Crédito Oficial, Spain) have aggressively expanded their activity to fill the gaps in financing of small- and medium-sized businesses or the export business (e.g., the KfW's subsidiary called Ipex). The German development bank KfW, initially founded to allocate marshal funds after the war, is now close to tying Commerzbank in terms of assets—Germany's second largest private bank (Monnet et al. 2014).[10] To copy KfW's success, many euro area countries that did not have such a public development bank founded one.

State development banks *ought* to finance businesses that would otherwise not find financing to heal *perceived* market failures or support industries that are thought to make a difference in the future. The growth of these bureaucracies is worrisome from an Austrian perspective. First, public guarantees seem to help bid away customers from private banks, undermining competition in the banking sector. For instance, Ipex's export financing business seems to be highly profitable for KfW. It is not clear why a development bank subsidiary has to engage in such activities. Second, although, for instance, KfW loans are typically subsidized loans handed out via commercial banks, there are distributional effects as to who are the partner banks that hand out loans. Moreover, these programs subsidize certain industries (green energy) or sectors (housing), mitigating risks in private banking and skewing incentives to increase portfolios in certain areas. Third, when politicians decide on future industries based on a political agenda, they may heavily interfere with the market process and provide substantial mal-incentives to finance bad projects. Even the most benign social planner tends to have trouble determining promising industries. False judgments can lead to ever-increasing subsidies in the future or major corrections in markets. As the size of public development banks has already expanded dramatically in recent years, there may well be substantial risks accumulated (outside fiscal balances) in the name of public improvements.

4.4 Evidence of Adverse Effects on Reform Process

ECB president Draghi repeatedly emphasized that ECB stimuli can only work in tandem with sensible structural reforms that encourage innovation and growth, addressing directly the national governments (Draghi 2016). However, while the ECB prevented a rapid shutdown of the public sector in the crisis economies as well as the resulting losses in financial markets that would bring about an even greater financial crisis, the bond purchases also dampened the immediate adjustment pressure for the governments of the euro area. Since 2012 bond prices do not reflect fundamentals anymore. Governments do not have to face the market anymore. The disciplining effect is gone. In fact, the OECD finds that the reform process in the periphery of the euro area slowed down at the time when Draghi expanded policies (OECD 2016).

In contrast to these euro area countries, the NMS of the EU were forced to adjust much faster during the crisis following the decline in cross-border banking. Given

[10] In contrast to our assessment, the authors of the cited article welcome the return to state banking.

the capital flight, for instance, the Baltics went through a process of internal devaluation to be able to hold the peg to the euro. Decisive spending cuts and labor market reforms were credible signals. Borrowing costs in the Baltics declined below those of Greece or Spain and the economies rebounded quickly. When less flexible countries were close to abandon the euro in 2011 to be able to regain competitiveness by devaluing the currency in nominal terms, Estonia introduced the common currency. Latvia and Lithuania followed in 2014 and 2015, respectively (Hoffmann 2013b).

4.5 Government Benefits

It comes as no surprise that the effect of the ECB's easing policy is substantial in the periphery economies of the euro area and led to a re-convergence of government bond yields following Draghi's famous "Whatever it takes" speech (July 26, 2012). However, the combination of ECB policy and the increasing demand for safe securities also benefited the stronger countries of the EMU such as Germany (Hoffmann and Zemanek, 2012). Germany's borrowing costs for newly issued government securities fell by 2–4% (depending on maturity) relative to the average yields from 1999 to 2008, allowing the Ministry of Finance to roll over outstanding debt at lower yields and longer maturities. Considering all newly issued securities from 2009 to December 2016, the cumulative savings to the German government until maturity will be approximately 300 billion euros (Hoffmann, 2017).

Lower refinancing costs provided leeway to the German government. Figure 12 illustrates the corresponding fall of Germany's annual debt-servicing costs from about 14% in 2009 to 6% of total government expenditure in 2016. Overall government spending (including debt service) remained constant at around 300 billion euros during this period, implying an increase in government consumption. The effective benefits to the government are rising every year as additional low-yield securities are issued and more high-yielding debt securities are replaced by lower-yielding securities. In 2011, before Draghi's bond-buying offensive, the German government effectively saved 7 billion euros in interest rate payments relative to the pre-crisis costs. In 2016, the effective savings will be approximately 24 billion euros. On the one hand, yields for newly issued debt securities have fallen since 2011. On the other hand, by now, the government has rolled over most outstanding debt since 2009. If bond yields remain at about 0.5% for 10-year bunds (the real return is negative), the effective savings to the German state will continue to rise.

The increase in government spending, however, means that the German government bids additional resources away from the private sector, which can make investment less profitable and may be detrimental to growth. Although government finances are currently balanced due to the rather benign economic development in Germany, it will be hard to reverse the government's expansion in times when tax revenues decline, bond prices fall or bailout risks in the euro area materialize. Therefore, the long-term sustainability of government debt is at risk. Indeed,

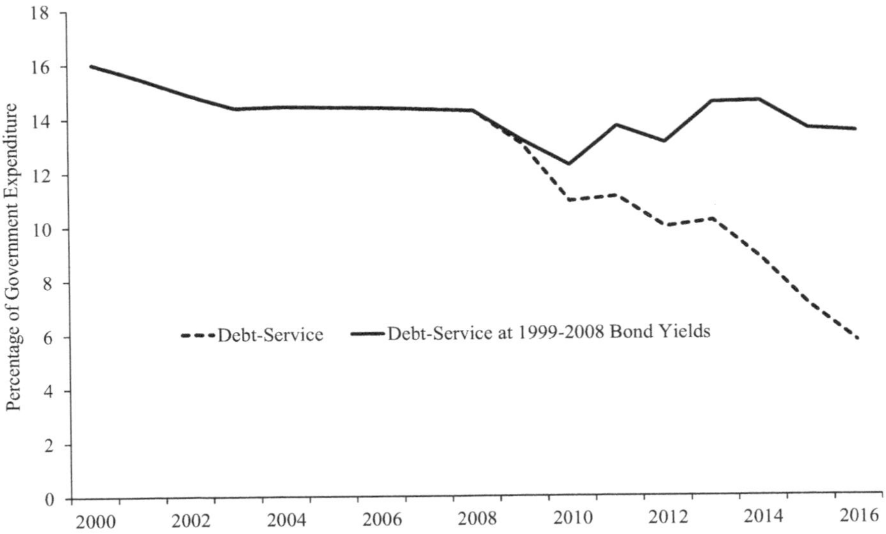

Fig. 12 German debt service (Source: Hoffmann, 2017)

Germany's government finances look similar to those of Spain before the crisis (Hoffmann, 2017).

5 Summary

The 2007/2008 financial crisis and its far-reaching consequences have not left macroeconomics unaffected. More than before, researchers explain periods of economic distress and crisis with a focus on underlying financial distortions. Financial frictions have become a central element in most macroeconomic models, as problems in the financial sector are widely perceived to have promulgated and accelerated the economic downturn. Consistent with the new focus on the role of financial markets, also the credit boom view of financial crises, which stresses the importance of overborrowing of banks during boom periods in triggering the subsequent bust, has seen renewed interest. Among these credit boom theories, the Austrian theory emphasizes how monetary policy mistakes may trigger unsustainable credit booms and increase the depth and duration of the subsequent crisis.

In this chapter, we build on older and newer Austrian contributions to provide an understanding of how well-intended ECB policy contributed to and prolonged the crisis in the euro area. In particular, we apply the Austrian, or Mises–Hayek, business cycle theory and the *law of unintended consequences*. The ABCT helps explain the building of the bubbles and distortions in the periphery countries of Europe that ended when the global financial crisis unfolded in 2007/2008. We are aware that the ABCT cannot explain all factors that contributed to the crisis. The chapter remains silent on issues as important as the role of innovations, rating agencies, housing policies, financial regulation, or inequality in explaining the boom period. We believe, however, that the ABCT lens provides a sound understanding of the dynamics of the credit boom as well as a convincing explanation of how monetary policy contributed to the financial crisis, i.e., the core theme of this chapter.

The *law of unintended consequences* allows contextualizing how policy decisions result in unexpected outcomes that tend to trigger new policies with their own unintended consequences. Absent established bailout institutions, the ECB had become the main player in dealing with the complex evolution of the crisis. Providing an overview of short-term effects of actual ECB crisis policies, we have suggested that outcomes differed substantially from what policy makers originally desired. To this date fragile banking sectors, weak lending, the rise of state banking, and sluggish average growth in many periphery countries cast doubts on the success of ECB measures.

The ECB is certainly not to blame for all problems Europe currently faces. ECB policies may be less effective than they otherwise would be because it was not clearly spelled out what the ECB was allowed to do in times of crisis, which led to uncertainty and lawsuits whenever new programs were announced. Moreover, ECB policies coincide, for instance, with new regulatory initiatives that may be counterproductive as well as governments that are unwilling to reform. However, we have provided evidence that, in contrast to its objectives, the main beneficiaries of ECB policies seem to be governments. As governments find it easier to refinance, the ECB provides them with leeway to delay unpopular reforms. Rather than successfully combating the crisis, ECB policy, thereby, unintentionally increases crisis duration and (indirectly) prevents a sustainable takeoff of the European economy.

Acknowledgment We thank Lukas Fuss for excellent research assistance.

References

Acharya, V., & Steffen, S. (2016). The "greatest" carry trade ever? Understanding eurozone bank risks. *Journal of Financial Economics, 115*(2), 215–236.

Acharya, V., Eisert, T., Eufinger, C., & Hirsch, C. (2016). *Whatever it takes: The real effects of unconventional monetary policy* (SAFE Working Paper No. 152).

Alesina, A., & Ardagna, S. (2010). Large changes in fiscal policy: Taxes versus spending. *NBER Chapters in Tax Policy and the Economy, 24*, 35–68.

Aßmann, C., & Boysen-Hogrefe, J. (2012). Determinants of government bond spreads in the euro area: In good times as in bad. *Empirica, 39*(3), 341–356.

Barrios, S., Iverson, P., Lewandowska, M., & Setzer, R. (2009). *Determinants of intra-euro area government bond spreads during the financial crisis* (European Economy, Economic Papers 388).

Bernoth, K., von Hagen, J., & Schuknecht, L. (2004). *Sovereign risk Premia in the European government bond market* (ECB Working Paper Series No. 369).

Black, L., & Hazelwood, L. (2013, December). The effect of TARP on bank risk-taking. *Journal of Financial Stability*, 790–803.

Bordo, M., & Landon-Lane, J. (2013). *Does expansionary monetary policy cause asset price booms; Some historical and empirical evidence* (NBER Working Paper No 19585).

Borio, C., Kharroubi, E., Upper, C., & Zampolli, F. (2015, December). *Labour reallocation and productivity dynamics: Financial causes, real consequences* (BIS Working Paper No 534).

Caballero, R. (2010). Macroeconomics after the crisis: Time to deal with the pretense-of-knowledge syndrome. *Journal of Economic Perspectives, 24*(4), 85–102.

Cachanosky, N. (2014a). The effects of US monetary policy on Colombia and Panama (2002–2007). *The Quarterly Review of Economics and Finance, 54*(3), 428–436.

Cachanosky, N. (2014b). The Mises-Hayek business cycle theory, fiat currencies and open economies. *The Review of Austrian Economics, 27*(3), 381–299.

Cachanosky, N. (2014c). Hayek's rule, NGDP targeting, and the productivity norm: Theory and application. *Journal of Stock & Forex Trading, 3*(2), 1–9.

Cachanosky, N. (2015a). Expectations in Austrian business cycle theory: Market share matters. *The Review of Austrian Economics, 28*(2), 151–165.

Cachanosky, N. (2015b). U.S. monetary policy's impact on Latin America's structure of production (1960–2010). *Latin American Journal of Economics, 51*(2), 95–116.

Cachanosky, N., & Hoffmann, A. (2016). Monetary policy, the composition of GDP and crisis duration in Europe. *Global Economic Review, 45*(2), 206–219.

Cachanosky, N., & Lewin, P. (2014). Roundaboutness is not a mysterious concept: A financial application to capital theory. *Review of Political Economy, 26*(4), 648–665.

Cachanosky, N., & Lewin, P. (2016a). An empirical application of the EVA® framework to business cycles. *Review of Financial Economics, 30*, 60–67.

Cachanosky, N., & Lewin, P. (2016b). Financial foundations of Austrian business cycle theory. *Advances in Austrian Economics, 20*, 15–44.

Cachanosky, N., & Salter, A. (2016). The view from Vienna: An analysis of the renewed interest in the Mises-Hayek theory of the business cycle. *The Review of Austrian Economics, 30*, 169–192.

Codogno, L., Favero, C., & Missale, A. (2003). Yield spreads on the EMU government bonds. *Economic Policy, 18*(37), 503–532.

Crosignani, M., Faria-e-Castro, M., & Fonseca, L. (2016). *The (Unintended?) consequences of the largest liquidity injection ever* (Working Paper).

DeGrauwe, P., & Ji, Y. (2013). *Panic-driven austerity in the Eurozone and its implications*. VOXEU.ORG Blog.

Draghi, M. (2016). ECB forum. The Future of the International Monetary and Financial Architecture. Sintra, Portugal.

Ebner, A. (2009). An empirical analysis on the determinants of CEE government bond spreads. *Emerging Markets Review, 10*(2), 97–121.

ECB. (2012a). *Annual report 2011*. Frankfurt: European Central Bank.

ECB. (2012b). *Technical features of outright monetary transactions*. Press Release. Frankfurt: European Central Bank.

ECB. (2016, October). *Bank lending survey*.

Égert, B., Backé, P., & Zumer, T. (2006). *Credit growth in Central and Eastern Europe – New (over)shooting stars?* (European Central Bank Working Paper No. 687).

Ferguson, N. (2009, December). Dead men walking. *Foreign Policy*.

Gustavson, M. (2010). The Hayek rule: A new monetary policy framework for the 21st century. *Reason Foundation, Policy Study, 389*, 1–50.

Hayek, F. A. (1929). *Geldtheorie und Konjunkturtheorie* (2nd ed.). Salzburg: Wolfgang Neugebauer (1976).
Hayek, F. A. (1931). *Prices and production* (2nd ed.). New York: Augustus M. Kelley (1967).
Hayek, F. A. (1937). *Monetary nationalism and international stability*. Fairfield: Augustus M. Kelley (1989).
Hoffmann, A. (2010). An overinvestment cycle in Central and Eastern Europe? *Metroeconomica, 61*(4), 711–734.
Hoffmann, A. (2013a). Did the Fed and ECB react asymmetrically with respect to asset market developments? *Journal of Policy Modeling, 35*(2), 197–211.
Hoffmann, A. (2013b). The euro as a proxy for the classical gold standard? Government Debt financing and political commitment in historical perspective. *Journal des Économistes et des Études Humaines, 19*(1), 41–61.
Hoffmann, A. (2014). Zero-interest rate policy and unintended consequences in emerging markets. *The World Economy, 37*(10), 1367–1387.
Hoffmann, A. (2016). The collateral effects of political integration on credit growth in the New Member States of the EU. *Economic Systems, 40*, 658–669.
Hoffmann, A. (2017, February 27). *The Germans have learned nothing*. ThinkMarkets blog.
Hoffmann, A., & Schnabl, G. (2011). A vicious cycle of manias, crises and asymmetric policy responses – An overinvestment view. *The World Economy, 34*(3), 382–403.
Hoffmann, A., & Schnabl, G. (2013). Monetary nationalism and international economic instability. *The Quarterly Journal of Austrian Economics, 16*(2), 135–164.
Hoffmann, A., & Schnabl, G. (2016a). Adverse effects of unconventional monetary policy. *The Cato Journal, 36*(3), 449–484.
Hoffmann, A., & Schnabl, G. (2016b). Monetary policy in large industrialized economies, emerging market credit cycles, and feedback effects. *Journal of Policy Modeling, 38*(5), 855–873.
Hoffmann, A., & Zemanek, H. (2012). Financial repression and debt liquidation in the USA and the Euro Area. *Intereconomics: Review of European Economic Policy, 47*(6), 344–351.
Hoshi, T., & Kashyap, A. (2010). Will the U.S. Bank recapitalization succeed? Eight Lessons from Japan. *Journal of Financial Economics, 97*, 398–417.
Juselius, M., Borio, C., Disyatat, P., & Drehmann, M. (2016). *Monetary policy, the financial cycle and ultra-low interest rates* (BIS Working Paper No 569, July).
Laubach, T., & Williams, J. (2003). Measuring the natural rate of interest. *The Review of Economics and Statistics, 85*(4), 1063–1070.
Leijonhufvud, A. (2009). *Two systemic problems*. CEPR Policy Insight No. 29, pp. 1–5.
Lewin, P., & Cachanosky, N. (2018). The average period of production: History of an idea. *Journal of the History of Economic Thought, 40*(1), 81–98.
Luengnaruemitchai, P., & Schadler, S. (2007). *Do economists' and financial markets' perspectives on the new members of the EU Differ?* (IMF Working Paper No. 07/65).
Mises, L. (1929). *Kritik des Interventionismus*. Jena: Gustav Fischer.
Mises, L. (1943). "Elastic expectations" and the Austrian theory of the trade cycle. *Economica, 10* (39), 251–252.
Monnet, E., Pagliari, S., & Vallee, S. (2014). *Europe between financial repression and regulatory capture* (Bruegel Working Paper, 9 July).
OECD. (2016). *Economic policy reforms: Going for growth interim report*. Paris: OECD.
Reinhart, C. (2012). The return of financial repression. *Financial Stability Review, 16*, 37–48.
Reuters. (2012). ECB may set bond yield target, but keep it quiet. *Reuters online*, Issue August 23, 2012.
Sachverständigenrat. (2015). *Zukunftsfähigkeit in den Mittelpunkt, Jahresgutachten 15/16*. Wiesbaden: Sachverständigenrat zur Begutachtung der gesamtwirtschaftlichen Entwicklung, Statistisches Bundesamt.
Salerno, J. (2012). A reformulation of Austrian business cycle theory in light of the financial crisis. *The Quarterly Journal of Austrian Economics, 15*(1), 3–44.

Schnabl, G., & Hoffmann, A. (2008). Monetary policy, vagabonding liquidity and bursting bubbles in new and emerging markets – An overinvestment view. *The World Economy, 31*(9), 1226–1252.

Schnabl, G., & Zemanek, H. (2011). Inter-temporal savings, current account trends and asymmetric shocks in a heterogeneous European Monetary Union. *Intereconomics: Review of European Economic Policy, 46*(3), 153–160.

Selgin, G., Beckworth, D., & Bahadir, B. (2015). The productivity gap: Monetary policy, the subprime boom, and the post-2001 productivity surge. *Journal of Policy Modeling, 37*(2), 189–207.

Sumner, S. (2012). The case for nominal GDP targeting. Mercatus Research.

White, W. (2012). *Ultra easy monetary policy and the law of unintended consequences* (Federal Reserve Bank of Dallas Working Paper No. 126).

The Failure of ECB Monetary Policy from a Mises-Hayek Perspective

Gunther Schnabl

1 Introduction

Since the early years, the European Monetary Union is encumbered by large imbalances. Up to the outbreak of the European financial and debt crisis in the year 2008, the countries in the southern and western part of the European Monetary Union experienced extraordinary boom phases, which were first understood as economic catch-up process and then turned out as unsustainable overinvestment and speculation booms. The economic development in Germany remained sluggish at first and seems to have turned into exuberance since the outbreak of the crisis in the periphery of the monetary union.

The paper analyzes the causes and consequences of cyclical and structural imbalances within the European Monetary Union based on the monetary overinvestment theory by Mises (1912) and Hayek (1929). The overinvestment theory allows us to identify an overly loose monetary policy as a reason for unsustainable overinvestment and speculation booms. To understand the heterogeneous economic development within the monetary union, the overinvestment theory is combined with the theory on optimum currency areas (Mundell 1961). In addition, the literature on the role of fiscal policies to cope with asymmetric shocks within a monetary union (De Grauwe 2016) is incorporated.

By doing so, the paper extends the literature, which regards financial exuberance and crisis as the outcome of overly loose monetary policies (Adrian and Shin 2008; Brunnermeier and Schnabel 2014; Hoffmann and Schnabl 2008, 2011, 2014, 2016) to the context of the European Monetary Union. It is a counter hypothesis to views, which see—based on Keynes (1936)—the European financial and debt

G. Schnabl (✉)
Universität Leipzig, Leipzig, Germany
e-mail: schnabl@wifa.uni-leipzig.de

A. Godart-van der Kroon, P. Vonlanthen (eds.), *Banking and Monetary Policy from the Perspective of Austrian Economics*,
https://doi.org/10.1007/978-3-319-75817-6_7

crisis (euro crisis) as the outcome of a random shock (De Grauwe 2011). It also contradicts views that the gradual decline of growth rates in the industrialized countries including the member states of the European Monetary Union is due to a savings glut originating in aging societies and an exogenous gradual fall of the marginal efficiency of investment (Bernanke 2005; Summers 2014).

By challenging the view that the crisis in the European Monetary Union can be resolved with the help of very expansionary monetary policy (Draghi 2014), a timely exit of the European Central Bank from zero and negative interest rate policy and comprehensive asset purchases is recommended.

2 Monetary Overinvestment Theories and Boom-and-Bust Cycles

Based on the overinvestment theories of Mises (1912) and Hayek (1929), four types of interest rates can be distinguished (see Hoffmann and Schnabl 2011): First, the internal interest rate i_i reflects the (expected) returns of (planned) investment projects. Second, the natural interest rate i_n is the interest rate that balances supply of (saving) and demand for capital (investment).[1] Third, the central bank sets the central bank interest rate i_{cb}. Fourth, the capital market rate i_c is defined as the interest rate set by the private banking (financial) sector for credit provided to private enterprises. For simplicity we assume that the capital market rate equals the central bank rate.

2.1 *Boom and Bust in the Overinvestment Framework*

In the monetary overinvestment theory, an economy is in equilibrium when the central bank rate equals the natural rate of interest. Then, planned savings are equal to investment. An economic upswing starts when—for instance—an important innovation raises the internal interest rate of investment, bringing about a rise in

[1]Hayek (1929) and Wicksell (1898) had different concepts of the natural interest rate. According to Wicksell (1898), the deviation of the central bank and capital market interest rates from the natural rate of interest disturbs the equilibrium between ex ante savings (S) and investment (I) plans. This leads to inflationary ($I > S$) or deflationary pressure ($S > I$). During a credit boom the supply of goods cannot satisfy the additional demand for goods at given prices, which leads to inflation. Mises (1912) and Hayek (1929) explained business cycles by the deviation of the central bank (capital market) interest rate from the natural rate of interest. Hayek emphasized the importance of the intertemporal alignments of plans of producers and consumers to explain overinvestment as a mismatch between the production structure and consumer preferences. The natural interest rate is the interest rate which aligns saving and consumption preferences with the production structure over time.

investment at given interest rates. In the left panel of Fig. 1, the investment curve shifts from $I_{i_{i_1}}$ to $I_{i_{i_2}}$, with the natural rate of interest rising from i_{n_1} to i_{n_2}. If the central bank would lift the policy rate from i_{cb_1} to i_{n_2}, assuming a perfect interest rate transmission to credit markets, planned savings and investment in the economy would stay in equilibrium ($S_2 = I_2$). If, in contrast, as in the left panel of Fig. 1, the central bank does not raise the central bank rate ($i_{n_1} = i_{cb_1} = i_{cb_2} < i_{n_2}$), too low interest rates will give rise to an unsustainable overinvestment boom. Holding policy rates too low (for too long) can be defined as type 1 monetary policy mistake.

To market participants, a rise in credit to the private sector at constant interest rates signals that the saving activity of households has increased. Additional credit-financed investment projects aim to satisfy the expected rise in future consumption. As planned household savings did not increase, an unsustainable disequilibrium between ex ante saving and investment $S_2 < I_2$ at $i_{c_2} < i_{n_2}$ is created. Additional investments of some enterprises lead to further investments of other enterprises, which accelerates the cumulative upward process. As soon as capacity limits are reached and free capacities in labor markets are fully used, wages and prices rise.

Price increases signal to enterprises additional profits and therefore trigger further investments. There are spillover effects to financial markets. Stocks are attractive because of low interest rates on bank deposits. Stock prices increase, also encouraged by higher (expected) profits of enterprises. When stock prices move upward, speculation may set in, providing extra momentum such that "the symptoms of prosperity themselves finally become [. . .] a factor of prosperity" (Schumpeter 1912: 226). As the owners of stock and real estate feel richer, consumption is stimulated via the wealth channel, which adds to inflationary pressure.

The turnaround occurs when the central bank increases the central bank rate to contain inflationary pressure (Mises 1912; Hayek 1929, 1937). The benchmark for the profitability of past and future investment projects is lifted. Investment projects with an internal interest rate below the risen central bank and capital market interest

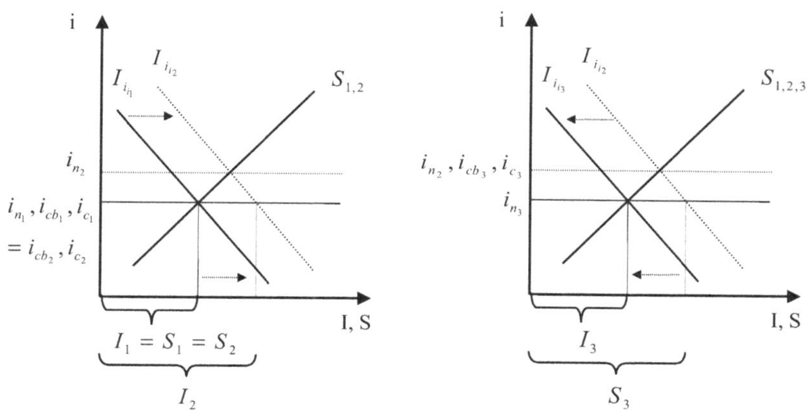

Fig. 1 Overinvestment boom and crisis

rates turn out to be unprofitable. As first enterprises are forced to dismantle investment projects, the investment activity of other enterprises will stagger. The investment curve shifts back from $I_{i_{i_2}}$ to $I_{i_{i_3}}$ (see right panel of Fig. 1). As stock (and other asset) prices start to fall, the equity of banks and enterprises falls, bringing about a credit crunch and further disinvestment. A cumulative downward process sets in. Wages fall and unemployment grows.

The monetary overinvestment theories assumed that during the downturn the central bank holds the interest rates above the natural interest which can be labeled monetary policy mistake of type 2. The high central bank interest rate comes along with a high capital market interest rate and thus a tightening of credit during the crisis. The right panel of Fig. 1 shows that when the policy interest rate is held above the natural interest rate ($i_{cb_3} = i_{c_3} > i_{n_3}$), ex ante saving is higher than investment ($S_3 > I_3$). The recession is aggravated.

2.2 Asymmetric Central Bank Crisis Management

Hoffmann and Schnabl (2008, 2011, 2014, 2016) stress with respect to the monetary policymaking of the large central banks since the mid-1980s that central bank monetary policy mistakes were not made symmetrically as assumed by Mises (1912) and Hayek (1929). Instead, since the mid-1980s, the large central banks have set policy interest rates low during periods of economic upswing, thereby fueling overinvestment and unsustainable booms in financial markets. This corresponds to type 1 monetary policy mistakes. In contrast, during (financial) crises, interest rates were cut decisively to prevent type 2 monetary policy mistakes. With the so-called Jackson Hole consensus, central bankers claimed that central banks do not have sufficient information to recognize bubbles, but should react decisively to financial turmoil (Blinder and Reis 2005). The consequence of such asymmetric monetary policy crisis management patterns has been a cyclical downward trend in nominal and real interest rates in the large economies as shown in Fig. 2.

With interest rates approaching the zero bound (in Japan since 1999 and the US and euro area since 2008), large-scale asset purchases have gradually expanded central bank balance sheets (Fig. 3). Government bond purchases of central banks (i.e., unconventional monetary policies) have pushed down the interest rate at the long end of the yield curve. Up to the present the gradual exit from very expansionary monetary policies (tapering) has remained limited to the Federal Reserve, which has reduced asset purchases to zero and is only slowly lifting interest rates.

As national monetary policy decisions are interconnected via the exchange rates (Hayek 1937), the global interest rate path can be assumed to have been an important side condition for the monetary policy decisions of the European Central Bank. A tight monetary policy of the European Central Bank relative to other large central banks would have been costly, because the resulting euro appreciation would have slowed down growth, in particularly in countries with historically weak currencies.

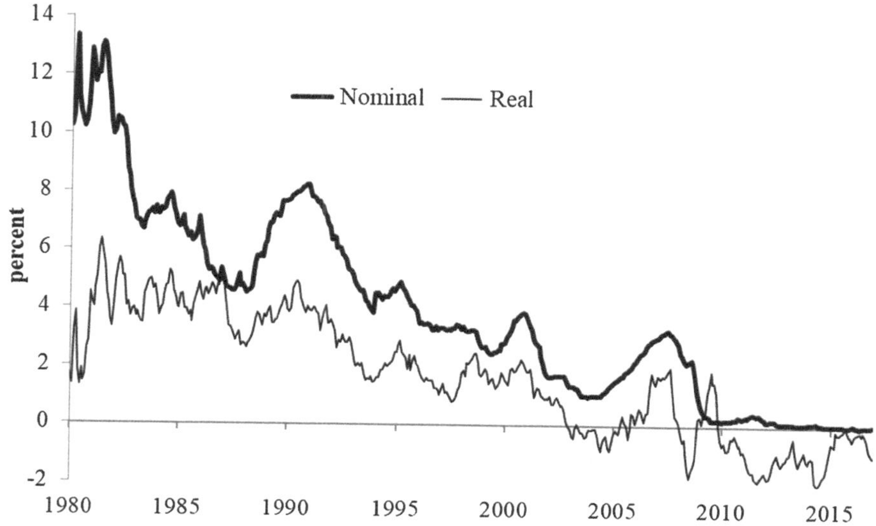

Fig. 2 Short-term interest rates: US, Japan, and Germany/euro area. Source: International Monetary Fund (IMF). Arithmetic averages. Money market rates: Germany up to 1998

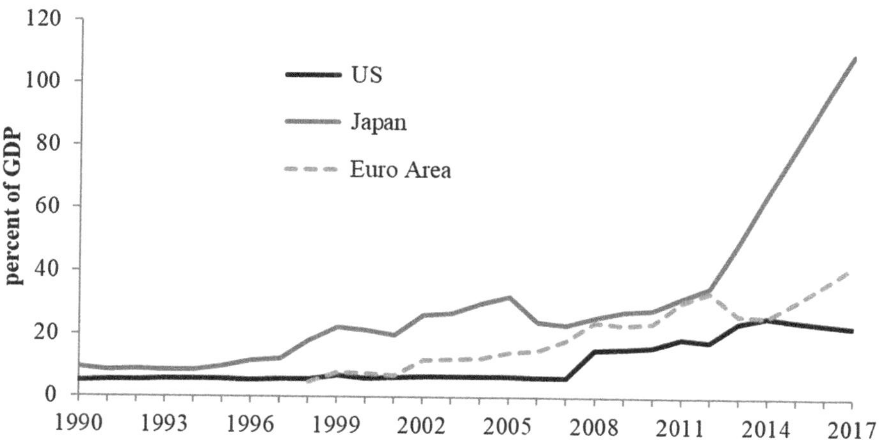

Fig. 3 Central bank assets (percent of GDP): Japan, US, euro area. Sources: World Economic Outlook (WEO), European Central Bank and Eurostat. 2016 und 2017 are projections

3 Reasons for the European Financial and Debt Crisis

Although the institutional framework of the European Central Bank was modeled after the price stability-oriented German central bank (Deutsche Bundesbank), in the course of time, the way of monetary policymaking in the EMU gradually diverged toward the model as it prevailed in the southern and western European countries prior to the European Monetary Union. This caused boom and bust in different parts of the monetary union in different periods of time.

3.1 The Institutional Framework of Common European Monetary Policymaking

Prior to the European Monetary Union, two different (and intertwined) growth and central bank models in Europe prevailed. Germany and some smaller northern European countries such as Austria and the Netherlands had comparatively high saving rates, high investment, and export-driven growth. The northern European growth model depended on price stability-oriented central banks, which ensured low real interest rates as a prerequisite for buoyant investment. Central bank independence (as in the case of the Deutsche Bundesbank) went along with fiscal discipline. Governments had to finance expenditures via tax revenues. As the smaller northern European countries pegged their exchange rates more or less tightly to the German mark, the German central bank was in the center of the northern European growth model.

In contrast, in the southern and western part of Europe, the growth models were oriented toward consumption and government expenditure. An important source of public financing were the central banks, which were subject to guidance by the governments. This implied higher inflation rates than in the northern part of Europe. The resulting depreciations of the currencies of the southern and western European countries against the German mark provided additional aggregate demand stimulus. For Germany and its smaller neighboring countries, these beggar-thy-neighbor policies were economically and politically acceptable,[2] because they got access to the southern and western European markets. This helped to realize economies of scale in industrial production.

The upshot is that the pre-EMU European growth was based on buoyant industrial production in the northern part of Europe, which generated sufficient productivity gains to realize real wage increases in all parts of the European (Economic) Community. The real income gains for citizens in all western European countries enhanced the political acceptability for the deepening of the European integration process. The resulting gradual implementation of the four freedoms—i.e., free movement of goods, services, capital, and labor—created additional growth and welfare gains (see Freytag and Schnabl 2017).

As the high inflation experience of the 1970s had proven to deliver high unemployment and low growth, in the early 1990s, the German central bank model along with the Maastricht Treaty got implemented for the whole European Union. According to Art. 127 TFEU "*the primary objective of the ESCB shall be to maintain*

[2]As Deutsche Bundesbank did not depreciate the German mark in response to the depreciation of the southern European currencies, destabilizing competitive depreciations were prevented.

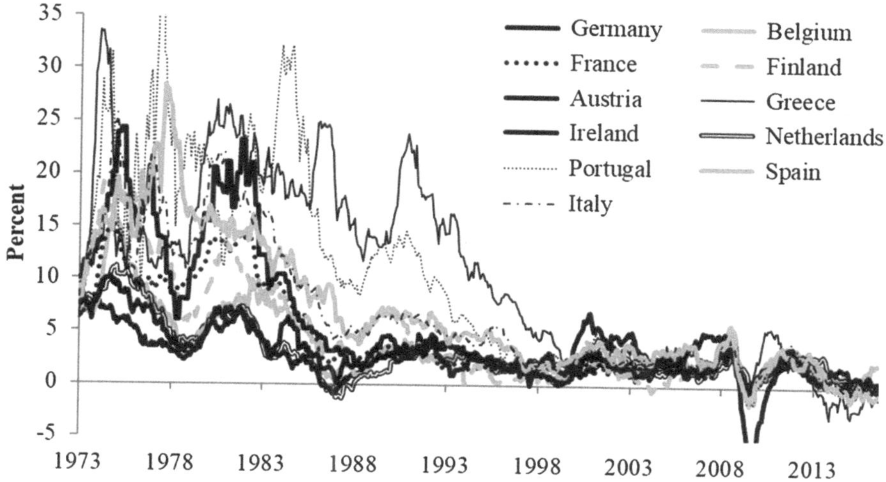

Fig. 4 Inflation convergence in western Europe. Source: IMF

price stability. *Without prejudice to the objective of price stability, the ESCB shall support the general economic policies in the Union with a view to contributing to the achievement of the objectives of the Union as laid down in Article 3 of the Treaty on European Union.*" At first glance, the provisions on macroeconomic convergence in the European (Monetary) Union led to an unprecedented degree of low inflation in Europe, as inflation rates in all EMU member states converged toward the German benchmark (see Fig. 4).

The Achilles heel of the monetary union became the high degree of heterogeneity of the member states. Mundell (1961) had argued that an optimum currency area had to consist of homogenous countries with a low likelihood of asymmetric shocks, i.e., with synchronized business cycles. A high likelihood of asymmetric shocks within a monetary union—as it seemed to be given the differences between the southern and northern European countries—would necessitate a high degree of wage flexibility and/or labor mobility. As tight labor market regulations prevent wage flexibility in most European countries,[3] fiscal policies could be seen as a mechanism to cope with asymmetric shocks and idiosyncratic business cycles.

De Grauwe (2016) shows that idiosyncratic business cycles can be addressed either by a centralized fiscal policy or by coordinated anticyclical fiscal policies on a national level. For instance, if France is in a boom and Germany in a recession, a one-size-fits-all monetary policy (which targets the average inflation of France and Germany) would set a too low interest rate for France. This would contribute to even higher inflation. The interest rate would be too high for Germany, which would further aggravate the recession. The one-size-fits-all monetary policy would be inefficient for both parts of the monetary union.

[3]The Baltic countries have, however, achieved a high degree of labor market and fiscal flexibility.

A common centralized fiscal policy would help to automatically absorb the asymmetric shock, as higher tax revenues (lower spending for unemployment) in France would be equilibrated by lower tax revenues (higher spending for unemployment) in Germany. Alternatively, with fiscal policymaking remaining organized on a national level, fiscal policies could ensure the efficiency of monetary policy, if they would be restrictive in France and expansionary in Germany to synchronize the business cycles in the monetary union (De Grauwe 2016).[4] Yet, the institutional setting of the European Monetary Union did not stipulate a specific role of fiscal policies to cope with asymmetric shocks. The Maastricht criteria put a limit on general government budget deficits (3% of GDP) and the stock of general government debt (60%),[5] but did not install a mechanism to prevent or balance heterogeneous economic development.

3.2 A Mises-Hayek-Based Explanation of the European Financial and Debt Crisis

This set the stage for the European financial and debt crisis, as the combination of the ECB's expansive monetary policy since the year 2000 and uncoordinated fiscal policies on a national level created the breeding ground for an overinvestment boom on the periphery of the European Monetary Union. The European Central Bank cut the main refinancing rate strongly in response to the bursting of the dotcom bubble (starting from March 2000) from 3.75% in May 2001 to 1% in June 2003 (see Fig. 5). Given that the key interest rate fell to a historical low, the likelihood increased that the central bank rate was cut below Hayek's natural interest rate as in the left panel of Fig. 1.[6]

This is suggested by Fig. 6, which uses the Taylor (1993) rule to define a target value for the main refinancing rate of the European Central Bank in consideration of the consumer price inflation and the output gap.[7] Negative values indicate a too low central bank interest rate, which generates inflationary pressure. Positive values indicate a too high central bank interest rate, which leads to deflationary pressure.

[4]With the business cycle being inversed at a later point of time, the mechanism is inversed as well.

[5]According to Art. 126 TFEU "(1) Member States shall avoid excessive government deficits. (2) The Commission shall monitor the development of the budgetary situation and of the stock of government debt in the Member States with a view to identifying gross errors. In particular it shall examine compliance with budgetary discipline..."

[6]In the United States, similar interest rate cuts nurtured a speculation boom in the real estate market, which led into the subprime crisis.

[7]The Taylor rule as a tool to provide an appropriate benchmark for central bank interest rate setting should be treated with caution, because the transmission of monetary policymaking toward consumer price inflation has become increasingly disturbed since the mid-1980s. Incorporating the effects of monetary policy on asset prices would deliver even higher Taylor rule target rates.

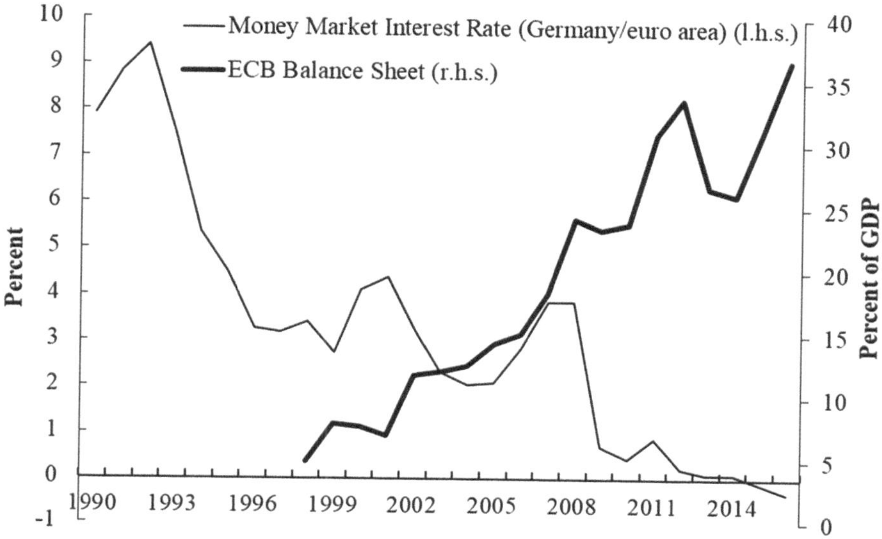

Fig. 5 Germany/euro area money market rate and size of ECB balance sheet. Sources: World Economic Outlook (WEO), European Central Bank and Eurostat. Money market rate: Germany up to 1998

According to this Taylor benchmark, the short-term interest rate set by the European Central Bank was below target for the euro area as a whole at the start of the European Monetary Union and became increasingly too low afterwards. For the subsequent euro area crisis countries (Greece, Ireland, Italy, Portugal, Spain), which experienced a boom since the turn of the millennium, the interest rate set by the ECB was much too low up to the crisis. In contrast, for Germany the monetary conditions set by the ECB were slightly too tight up to the year 2004 and then became slightly too loose.

The asymmetric effect of the one-size monetary policy in different parts of the EMU as indicated by the Taylor rule has been widely attributed to the interest rate convergence process in Southern and Western Europe (see, for instance, Sinn and Wollmershäuser 2012): Because the southern and western European countries had entered the European Monetary Union, financing conditions at all maturities converged from high levels toward Germany's low level. As this convergence process went along with a macroeconomic stabilization process, the high growth rates of the EMU periphery countries were regarded to be fundamentally justified. The resulting sharp decline of the interest rate is assumed to have boosted growth.

The EMU convergence scenario hypothesis neglects, however, the fact that at the same time similar credit booms took place in non-EMU countries such as Iceland and many central and eastern European countries. Therefore, to explain different inflation rates and growth rates in different parts of the European Monetary Union and beyond, the role of fiscal policies in counter-steering or amplifying the (potential) credit booms in different parts of the European Monetary Union has to be considered (Schnabl and Wollmershäuser 2013). In Germany, the expansionary

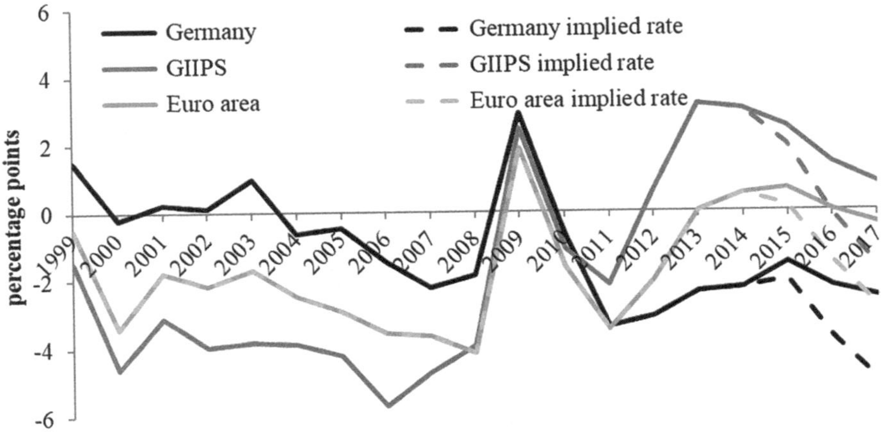

Fig. 6 Euro area money market rate relative to Taylor target rate. Source: OECD Economic Outlook, ECB and National Statistics Offices. The target interest rates are calculated following Taylor (1993) rule based on national inflation rates and output gaps. The lines indicate the deviations of the ECB main financing rate from the Taylor target rates calculated for the euro area and single countries. Positive values indicate the ECB main refinancing rate to be above the national optimal target rate (too tight). Negative values indicate the ECB main refinancing rate to be below the national optimal target rate (too loose). For the GIIPS (Greece, Ireland, Italy, Portugal, and Spain) countries, an arithmetic average is calculated. After the main refinancing rate has reached the zero bound, the ECB embarked on extensive unconventional monetary policy measures including large government bond purchases. The implied rates represent an ECB main refinancing rate which is augmented by the unconventional monetary policy measures taken after the main refinancing rate had reached the zero bound in 2014. For this purpose, it is assumed that the semi-interest rate elasticity of a balance sheet expansion is about 8, i.e., a balance sheet expansion by about 8% leads to a decline in the main refinancing rate by 1 percentage point (this corresponds to the semi-average balance sheet elasticity of the interest rate between 1999 and 2013). The values for 2016 and 2017 are based on forecasts

monetary policy of the ECB after the turn of the millennium was combined with a tight fiscal policy stance. In the late 1990s, the high costs of the German unification had brought the sustainability of the generous German welfare state to its limits. Unemployment had increased strongly during the 1990s.

Given that by 1999 the general government debt had reached the Maastricht limit of 60% of GDP,[8] the government felt forced to implement fundamental reforms. The German government curtailed government expenditure (see Fig. 7), in particular by restraining wage increases in the public sector. As labor markets were deregulated and social security benefits were streamlined, the wage austerity spilled over to the private sector. Investment declined as domestic business perspectives turned gloomy. The tight fiscal policy stance kept inflation low and the real interest rate

[8]After the introduction of the euro, the general government budget deficit fell below the −3% of GDP Maastricht limit. This was partially due to the reforms, which slowed down growth and thereby reduced tax revenues.

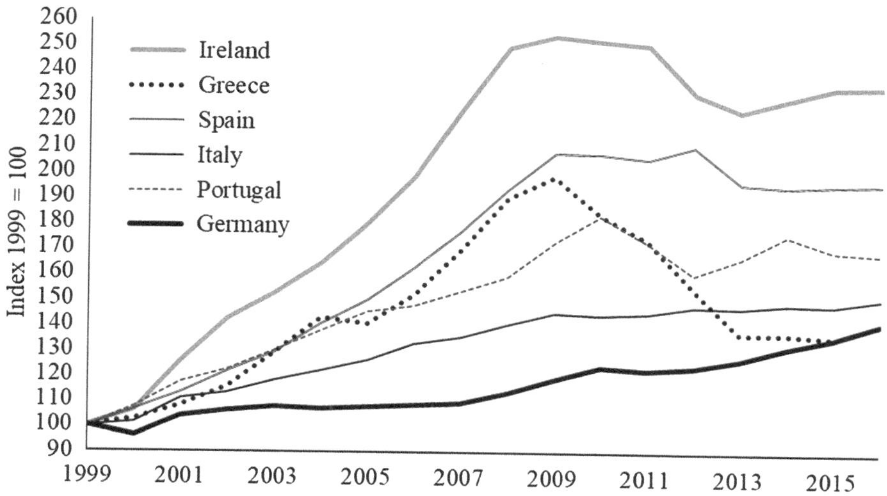

Fig. 7 Diverging spending paths of Germany and EMU crisis countries. Source: IMF: WEO. General government expenditure in euros indexed to 100 in 1999

relatively high, thereby preventing an overinvestment boom despite monetary expansion.

By dampening domestic economic activity, the combination of a loose monetary policy with a tight fiscal policy instead boosted capital outflows from Germany[9] from the year 2001 onward. In the periphery countries inside and outside the euro area, the capital inflows boosted investment, growth, and inflation. Declining real interest rates triggered an overinvestment boom as seen in the left panel of Fig. 1, which came along with speculation in real estate and stock markets. The resulting increase of tax revenues induced a dramatic increase in government expenditures, which added further momentum to the exuberance. Figure 7 shows that the expenditure paths of the subsequent euro area crisis countries were much more expansionary than in Germany.

In short, the divergence of fiscal policy stances in the euro area caused in the face of an overly loose monetary policy a kind of "waterbed effect": the liquidity issued by the European Central Bank as a crisis therapy for the whole euro area was one-sidedly pushed to the periphery causing there overinvestment and speculation booms. The growing imbalances within the European Monetary Union became reflected in growing current account imbalances as shown in Fig. 8. Real wage increases far beyond productivity gains led to a real appreciation of the euros of the subsequent crisis countries and thereby growing current account deficits. This

[9] As the reduction of future pensions was paired with incentives for private provisions for retirement, savings of the private sector increased. The resulting dramatic rise of aggregate savings over investment contributed to the significant rise in capital outflows.

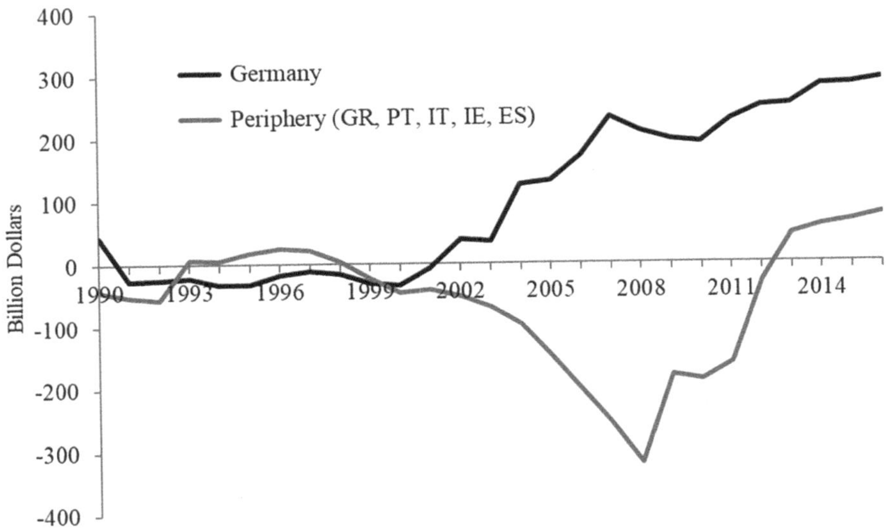

Fig. 8 Intra-EMU current account imbalances. Source: IMF: WEO

process was matched by a real depreciation of the German euro and thereby a growing current account surplus of Germany.[10]

The exuberance was tilted either toward stock and real estate bubbles (Spain and Ireland) and/or toward public consumption booms (Greece, Portugal). As the overinvestment/speculation booms inflated the tax revenues of the southern and western euro area countries, the Maastricht fiscal criteria failed to indicate unsustainable government expenditure. Public spending in the subsequent crisis countries could strongly increase without increasing the public debt levels (Ireland and Spain) or with budget deficits remaining below the Maastricht benchmark (Greece and Portugal). With sharply increasing tax revenues being mainly driven by the ECB's low interest rate policy and large credit provision from Germany, the unsustainable increases of government expenditures became only visible after the economic turnaround in form of sharply increasing public debt levels.

The booms peaked in the year 2008, when after the breakout of the US subprime crisis the mood in international financial markets changed. Since the year 2005—as in the overinvestment theory—both the European Central Bank and the Federal Reserve had stepwise increased interest rates. With German commercial banks having realized substantial losses in the US subprime market, they stopped exporting capital to the periphery countries inside and outside the euro area. This constituted an additional credit tightening beyond the tightening of the ECB monetary policy. With

[10]In Germany, real wage increases were lagging behind productivity increases in the respective time period.

credit financing for the overinvestment booms drying out, the European periphery countries were pushed into a severe crisis as seen in the right panel of Fig. 2.

4 Implications of Monetary Policy Crisis Management

With real wage levels having risen above productivity levels, the resulting European financial and debt crisis necessitated the ad hoc buildup of comprehensive rescue mechanisms such as multilateral rescue packages, the European Financial Stability Facility (EFSF), the European Stability Mechanism (ESM), and an unprecedented monetary expansion of the ECB balance sheet. Within a heterogeneous European Monetary Union, the monetary policy rescue measures of the European Central Bank had different effects in the euro area crisis countries and Germany. Whereas the southern European crisis countries remain stuck in crisis, now Germany is experiencing an overinvestment and speculation boom. Both developments are amplified in both parts of the EMU by pro-cyclical fiscal policies.

4.1 Lasting Stagnation and Zombification in the Crisis Countries

In response to the crisis, the European Central Bank cut interest rates to zero and is strongly expanding its balance sheet by extensive—mainly government—bond purchases (see Fig. 5). Hayek (1933: 20) argued that "to combat the depression by a forced credit expansion is to attempt to cure the evil by the very means which brought it about." The low-cost liquidity provisions via the European Central Bank to the European crisis countries can be assumed to have paralyzed growth in the southern European crisis countries, because Schumpeter's (1912) creative destruction is prevented and distorted economic structures are conserved. As Hayek puts it (1931: 98): "If voluntary decisions of individuals are distorted by the creation of artificial demand, it must mean that part of the available resources is again led into a wrong direction and a definite and lasting adjustment is again postponed."

The negative impact of monetary policy crisis management on investment and growth in the crisis countries comes via the banking sectors, which are bailed out by credit provision of the national central banks at eased collateral requirements.[11] Within the Eurosystem, the resulting additional liquidity requirements of the national central banks are provided by the European Central Bank. The national banking sectors are in addition stabilized by the large-scale government bond

[11] As, for instance, made possible by the so-called emergency liquidity assistance (ELA).

purchases of the European Central Bank,[12] as euro area banks are holding increasing amounts of government bonds. Furthermore, the Agreement on Net Financial Assets (ANFA) allowed since November 2014 for regional monetary policy rescue measures, as national central banks of the Eurosystem were allowed to purchase bonds of their own governments. The structure of the ANFA purchases is strongly tilted toward government bond purchases of southern euro area countries. The volume had risen to 560 billion euros by February 2015.[13]

With the national central banks being part of the Eurosystem, the intra-euro area rescue measures became reflected in the TARGET2 balances of the European Central Bank. TARGET2 (Trans-European Automated Real-time Gross Settlement Express Transfer System) is a real-time gross settlement system for payments within the euro zone, which is used to clear cross-border transfers in the euro area. Before the European financial and debt crisis, the national central banks' positions in the TARGET2 system were widely balanced, because private capital flows were matched by respective payment flows resulting from goods markets transactions.[14] For instance, German (Greek) capital exports[15] (capital imports) corresponded to payments receipts (payments) for German goods sales (Greek goods purchases).

With the outbreak of the crisis, current account deficits of the periphery countries persisted (Fig. 8), whereas German banks stopped providing credit to the commercial banks in the periphery countries. As banks in the crisis countries continued to finance the payments flows for goods transactions, they had to refinance at their national central banks, which themselves refinanced at the European Central Bank. At the same time, the payments received by German export enterprises were deposited via German commercial banks at the German central bank. The upshot

[12]After the European Central Bank had cut interest rates toward zero, it embarked on several bond purchase programs such as the Securities Markets Program (SMP, May 2010 to September 2012, 211 billion euros) and the Outright Monetary Transactions Program (OMT, from July 2012), which was up to today not activated, but included the promise to undertake "whatever it takes" to keep the euro area together. Two Covered Bond Purchase Programs (CBPP1, 60 billion euros from July 2009 to June 2010; CBPP2, 16.4 billion euros from November 2011 to October 2012) expanded the ECB balance sheet. In January 2015, the Asset Purchase Program (APP) was announced, which included the previously launched Covered Bond Purchase Program 3, the Asset-Backed Securities Purchase Program (ABSPP), and the Public Sector Purchase Program (PSPP). The APP allowed purchases of government and corporate sector bonds of up to 80 billion euros per month. Up to March 2017 the aggregated purchase volume was 1740 billion euros. The purchase program was extended with a smaller scale of 60 billion euros per month to December 2017 bringing the overall volume of (government) bond purchases to 2250 billion euros. The purchase programs not only held the money market rate at zero, they also depressed the interest rates at the longer end of the yield curve. This significantly reduced the interest rate burden for over-indebted governments in the euro area, which can be seen to be against Art. 127 of TFEU.

[13]ANFA is equivalent to a regional monetary policy within a one-size monetary policy framework.

[14]Note that according to the balance of payment identity, in the absence of public capital flows, the current account is equivalent to the financial account with inversed sign. Given public capital flows, the sum of private and public capital flows has to match the current account balance with inversed sign.

[15]That is, credit provided by a German bank to a Greek bank.

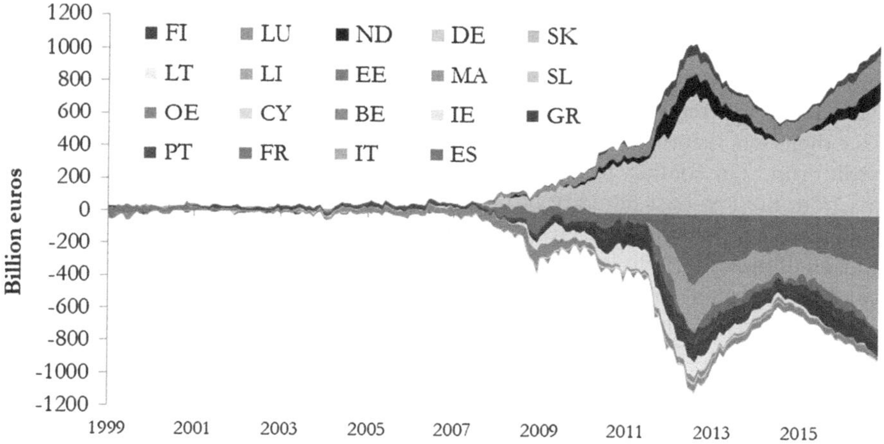

Fig. 9 TARGET2 imbalances within the European Monetary Union. Source: ECB

is that the central banks of the crisis countries became a debtor versus the European Central Bank and the German central bank became a creditor to the European Central Bank. This is reflected in a divergence of the TARGET2 balances of the national central banks at the European Central Bank (Fig. 9). The yearly changes of these balances are equivalent to the public capital flows across intra-EMU borders.

When current account deficits declined and capital flight from the crisis countries increased, this led to capital shortages of the commercial banks of the crisis countries, which were compensated by credit from the national central banks at eased collateral conditions. With this capital being deposited in German banks, the deposits of German commercial banks at Deutsche Bundesbank increased. Thus, the growing divergence of the TARGET2 balances became increasingly driven by capital flight from the euro area crisis countries to Germany. As shown in Fig. 9, a small number of northern European countries—i.e., Germany, the Netherlands, Luxemburg and Finland—provide credit within the TARGET2 system. Most other euro area countries, in particular the crisis countries, are recipients of this public quasi-credit system.

The liquidity provision for the crisis countries prevented on the peak of the crisis a type 2 monetary policy mistake, i.e., a too tight monetary policy stance for the crisis countries. However, as the public liquidity provision via the TARGET2 system persists and ECB government bond purchases holdings to be further extended, the central bank seems to have pushed the capital market interest rate again below the natural interest rate. In Fig. 7 this is indicated by the implied interest rate being below benchmark for the crisis countries recently. The transmission of these monetary policy rescue measures to negative growth effects is via the banking sectors, which suffer from declining profits for three main reasons (Schnabl 2015).

Firstly, the end of the overinvestment boom and the necessary dismantling of low return investment projects create bad loans. The stock of these (potential) bad loans is reduced by monetary policy rescue measures, but the monetary policy rescue measures depress the spread between lending and deposit rates as the traditional source of income of banks.[16] Secondly, the credit volume shrinks, because supply and demand for credit are contracting. In particular, for large companies—which can issue their own securities and stocks—financing costs and thereby the need for bank credit drop.[17] In contrast to large enterprises, small and medium enterprises profit less from the low-cost liquidity provision, as they remain dependent on the ailing banking sector. Although the creeping stagnation beclouds their profit opportunities, banks will prolong credit lines to shaky small and medium enterprises, because they fear their (potential) bad loan problem to worsen or to become visible.

As enterprises can expect that low-cost liquidity provision will persist independent from the profitability, the efforts to strive for innovation and productivity increases are subdued. For Japan—where the (close to) zero interest rate period continues since the mid-1990s—Sekine et al. (2003) find forbearance lending: Banks continue to provide irrecoverable loans to keep themselves and (potentially) insolvent enterprises alive. Peek and Rosengren (2005) associate Japan's central bank crisis management with a misallocation of capital, which makes companies with poor profit prospects survive (which they call "evergreening"). Caballero et al. (2008) show that—given the central bank's low-cost credit provision via *zombie banks*—*zombie enterprises* become dependent on cheap liquidity provision, with productivity increases declining.[18]

In the monetary overinvestment theories by Mises (1912) and Hayek (1929), overly favorable refinancing conditions during the upswing trigger additional investment projects with lower expected returns. The marginal and average efficiency of investments decreases. During the downturn and crisis, investment projects with low internal interest rates are dismantled. The marginal and average efficiency of investments increases. Therefore, in the long term, the average efficiency of investment is

[16]In addition, the low interest rate and the unconventional monetary policy measures depress the margin between long-term and short-term interest rates (transformation margin). Furthermore, the margin between the money market rate and the deposit rate is pushed toward zero.

[17]The declining financing costs of enterprises become visible in growing enterprise savings, which has for instance turned positive in Japan and Germany. The rise in enterprise savings corresponds to a decline in household savings. It is difficult to provide empirical evidence for the hypothesis of a global liquidity glut as launched by Bernanke (2005), because the assumed structural increase in net household savings of aging societies cannot be observed in any of the aging countries with surplus savings such as Germany, Japan, and China. Instead of fixed capital formation, large enterprises tend to invest in financial or real estate markets, where central banks provide a quasi-insurance mechanism against losses. Increasingly, own shares are bought back, because alternative investment categories (bank deposits, government bonds) render low yields due to the asymmetric monetary policy crisis management.

[18]Kornai (1986) characterized the situation in the central and eastern European economies before 1990 as soft budget constraints: unprofitable enterprises were kept alive by credit provision of the state-owned banking sector to avoid unemployment. As savings at state-owned banks were not large enough to cover the financing needs of enterprises, the funds were created by the central bank via the printing press.

mainly constant. With the asymmetric monetary policy crisis management of the European Central Bank, however, the average marginal efficiency of investments declines during the boom and remains low, because enterprises with low expected returns are kept alive.[19]

Because resources remain bound in investment projects with low productivity, private investment is affected negatively. The financing of new (i.e., risky) investment is discouraged because monetary policy crisis management damages the banking sector (see above). Furthermore, as the European Central Bank's crisis management prevents asset prices in crisis countries from further falling and drives up other asset prices (such as German stock and real estate prices), there is an incentive to substitute fixed capital investment by speculation in the financial markets. As shown in the upper panel of Fig. 10, since the outbreak of the European financial and crisis in the crisis countries, investment as a share of GDP has dramatically declined. As currently asset prices are rising higher in Germany than in the crisis countries, capital flight from the crisis countries to Germany is the logical consequence. As the ample low-cost liquidity provision transforms the financial crisis into a structural crisis in which there is no limit to the central bank's government bond purchases, private investments tend to be gradually substituted by public investments and/or government consumption. Persistently high or even growing government expenditure (as share of GDP) is financed by government bond purchases of the European Central Bank.

Long-term growth declines, because the ECB's monetary policy rescue measures slow down productivity gains. In the neoclassical growth theory, growth is dependent on the accumulation of capital. There is a long-term equilibrium between investment and depreciation (steady-state economy). The steady state is derived from the assumption that the marginal efficiency of capital declines with a growing capital stock (Solow 1956).[20] Long-term growth is generated by innovation and technological progress—i.e., increasing productivity (Solow 1957).

Leibenstein (1966) saw motivation and incentives as important determinants of a concept of efficiency which goes beyond allocative efficiency.[21] If the degree of competition declines (for instance, in a monopoly compared to perfect competition), the motivation to strive for efficiency gains declines as well (X-inefficiency). In this sense, enterprises do not realize maximum efficiency gains when the European Central Bank subdues competitive pressure with low-cost liquidity provision.[22] Competition as a discovery procedure (Hayek 1968) is undermined.

---

[19]This interpretation is in line with Borio (2014), who identifies capital overhang as a major determinant of post-bubble crisis.

[20]This assumption is also made by Summers (2014), who argues that the structural decline of growth is due to a global savings glut combined with a declining marginal efficiency of investment. See also Laubach and Williams (2015) for a demand-driven definition of the natural interest rate.

[21]Which assumes constant production costs in different types of markets.

[22]Borio et al. (2016) show the negative impact of credit booms on the allocation of labor and productivity gains.

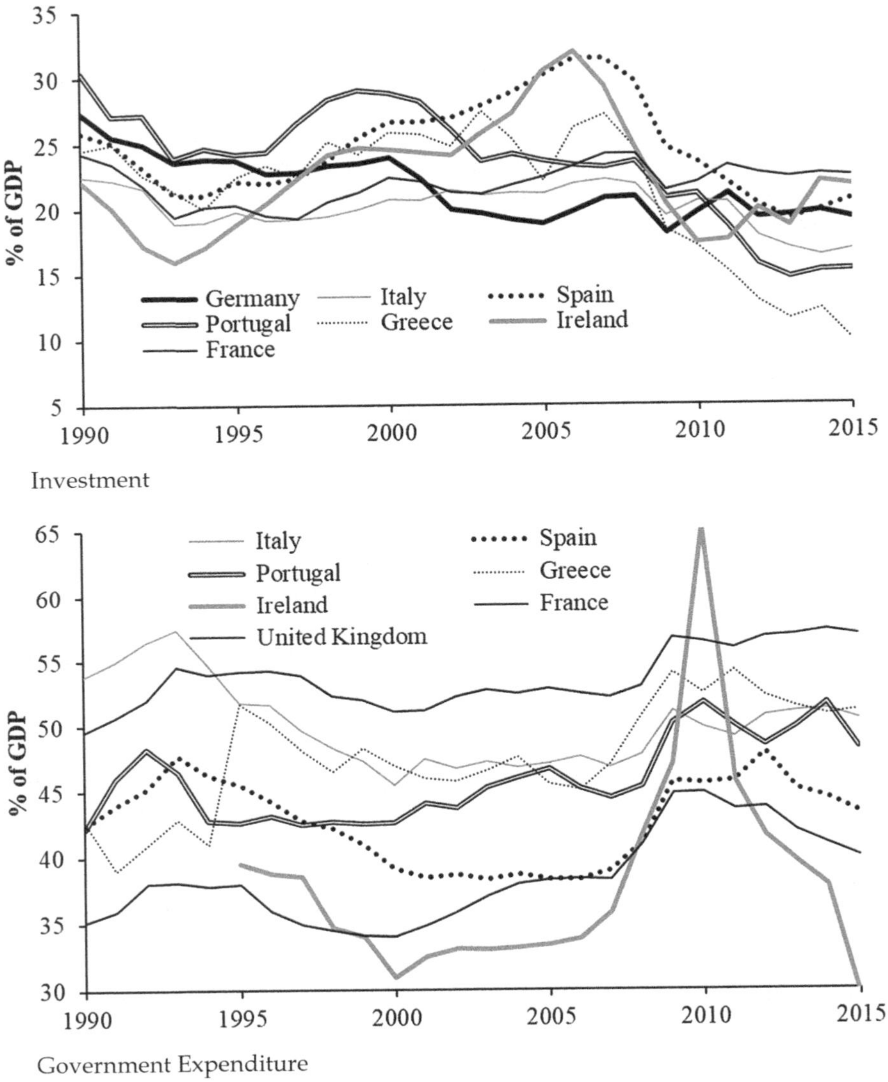

Fig. 10 Investment and government expenditure in the euro area. Source: IMF

By tying resources to sectors with low or negative productivity gains, in the context of the Solow model, the monetary policy rescue measures create a negative allocative effect which results from declining average productivity (defined as output per unit of labor). At the macroeconomic level, with a constant amount of labor, fewer goods and services are produced. Declining or even negative productivity growth implies declining real wage increases or even declining real wage levels, which signal lower consumption in the future. If enterprises anticipate declining demand in the future, they reduce investment. A downward spiral of declining investment, growth, and consumption sets in.

The upshot is that the low-cost liquidity provision of the European Central Bank to the crisis countries via unconventional monetary policy, emergency liquidity assistance, rescue packages, and government bond purchases (which are all reflected in TARGET2 balances) conserves inefficient economic structures in the European crisis countries. Extensive purchases of government bonds allow governments to maintain inefficient expenditure patterns by postponing structural reforms. Gopinath et al. (2015) show empirically that the southern European crisis countries have experienced a significant drop in productivity growth since the outbreak of the European debt and financial crisis. As growth in these crisis countries does not pick up, this further necessitates the extension of the central bank-centered rescue measures.

4.2 *Speculative Upswing Inside Germany and Overinvestment Outside Germany*

With monetary policy paralyzing growth perspectives in the crisis countries, capital outflows have accelerated as indicated by growing current account surpluses (Fig. 8). One target destination of these capital outflows is Germany where growth perspectives have improved because the reform process after the turn of the millennium has strengthened the international competitiveness of the German industry. Furthermore, as German real estate prices did not increase during the precrisis boom, they are regarded to have catch-up potential.

With the ECB's monetary policy rescue measures becoming increasingly focused on the southern European crisis countries, this implies a large likelihood that the European Central Bank has pushed the interest rate level in Germany below the natural interest rate. As shown in Fig. 6, the Taylor rule implies that since the year 2010, the main refinancing rate has been substantially too low. The monetary policy stance looks even much looser if the unconventional monetary policy measures are considered. The implied interest rate is 5 percentage points below the target level, which would be justified by the current levels of inflation (which is close to 2%) and growth in Germany. This suggests that an overinvestment boom as modeled in the right panel of Fig. 1 has set in.

Yet, in contrast to the monetary overinvestment theory, investment in Germany remains sluggish (Fig. 10). The boom mainly takes place in the real estate and stock markets as shown in Fig. 11 in comparison to Spain. Whereas precrisis German real estate prices were stable with Spanish real estate prices increasing strongly, now the trend is reversed: Spanish real estate prices remain sluggish, whereas German real estate prices hike. The monetary policy crisis response of the European Central Bank

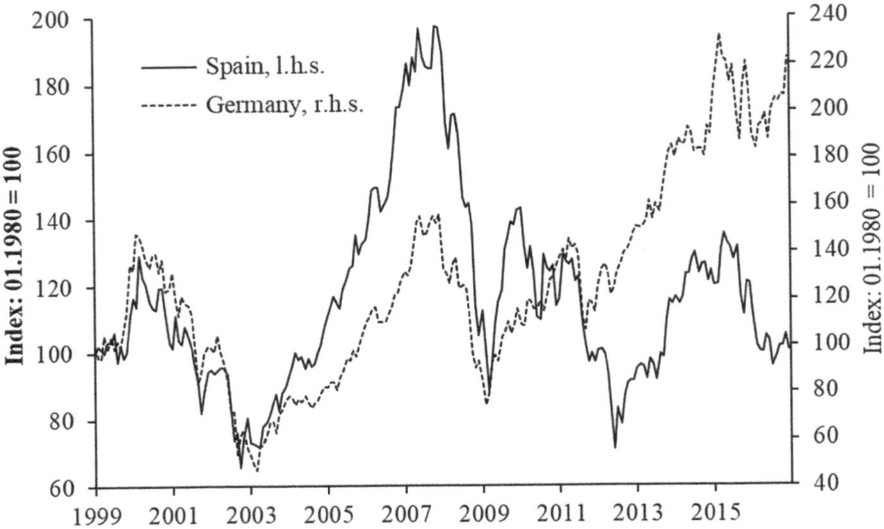

Stock prices (DAX, Madrid SE General)

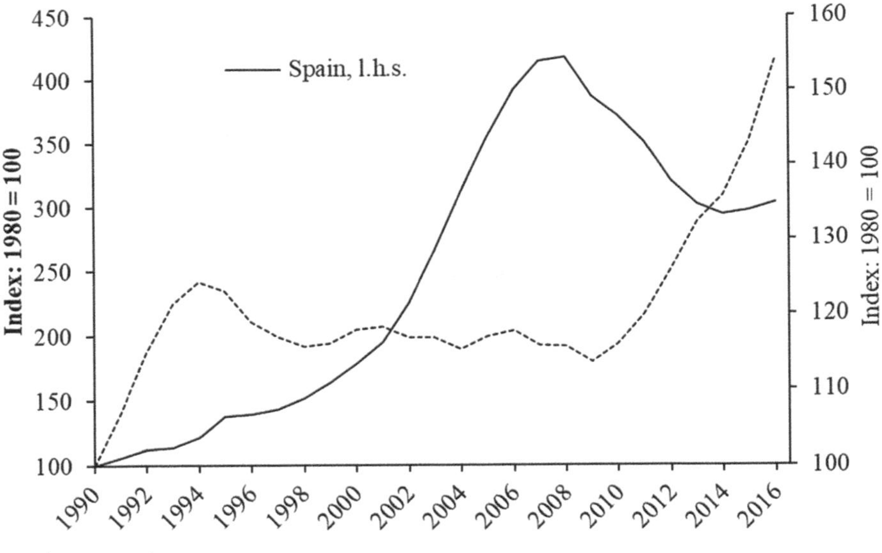

Real estate prices

Fig. 11 Stock and real estate markets compared in Spain and Germany. Source: Thompson Reuters Datastream (stock prices), Oxford Economics (real estate prices)

has boosted German real estate prices for three reasons. Firstly, financing conditions for German real estate credit have considerably improved, as the European Central Bank has not only pushed money market interest rates toward zero but has also nudged long-term interest rates to historically low levels.

Secondly, bank deposits have been historically the preferred form of saving in Germany, because inflation has been low.[23] Given the substantial expansion of the ECB balance sheet, the trust in the stability of money is gradually undermined. With the European Central Bank's monetary policy rescue measures pushing the interest rates of bank deposits toward zero and into negative territory, the inclination to invest in real assets such as real estate has increased. Rising price expectations for real estate in Germany's economic centers have pushed up the expected returns despite fast growing prices.

German stock prices are boosted mainly via the export channel. While German industrial enterprises still profit from the past reforms, monetary policy rescue measures of the European Central Bank have created additional windfall profits by depreciating the euro. While the current account surplus still continues to grow (Fig. 8), the structure has changed. Because of the tightening of fiscal controls[24] in the southern and western euro area countries, current account deficits have disappeared or even turned positive. The German trade surplus versus the crisis countries has substantially declined (Fig. 12). The postcrisis German fiscal expansion (see Fig. 7), which is triggered by growing tax revenues,[25] is, however, not sufficiently large to reduce the German current account surplus. Therefore, the trade surplus is redirected toward third countries outside the European Monetary Union.

Because the German stock index DAX is dominated by large export-oriented enterprises, the index has pointed strongly upward (upper panel of Fig. 11). German overinvestment is taking place on the back of capital exports to other parts of the world, in particular to the United States and the United Kingdom. The bilateral trade balances of Germany, which can be seen as a proxy for bilateral capital flows,[26] as shown in Fig. 12, provide respective evidence. The main determinants of growing net capital exports against the United States and the United Kingdom are the relatively loose (tight) monetary policy of the ECB (Fed, Bank of England) combined with the relatively tight fiscal policy stance of Germany (versus the United States and United Kingdom).[27] One important capital export channel seems to be mergers and acquisitions.

---

[23]Therefore, the share of Germans living in their own flat or house is small compared to southern European countries, where inflation has been traditionally high.

[24]On details see Belke et al. (2016).

[25]Like in the current crisis countries prior to the crisis, the bubble in Germany currently inflates tax revenues.

[26]Positive trade balances are seen as proxy for net capital exports.

[27]Because fiscal policies have a direct impact on investment activity, relative fiscal policies stances—in particular in interaction with loose monetary policy stances—constitute an important determinant of current account balances. See Wollmershäuser and Schnabl (2013) for Europe and Duarte and Schnabl (2015) for larger sample of 86 emerging markets and industrialized countries.

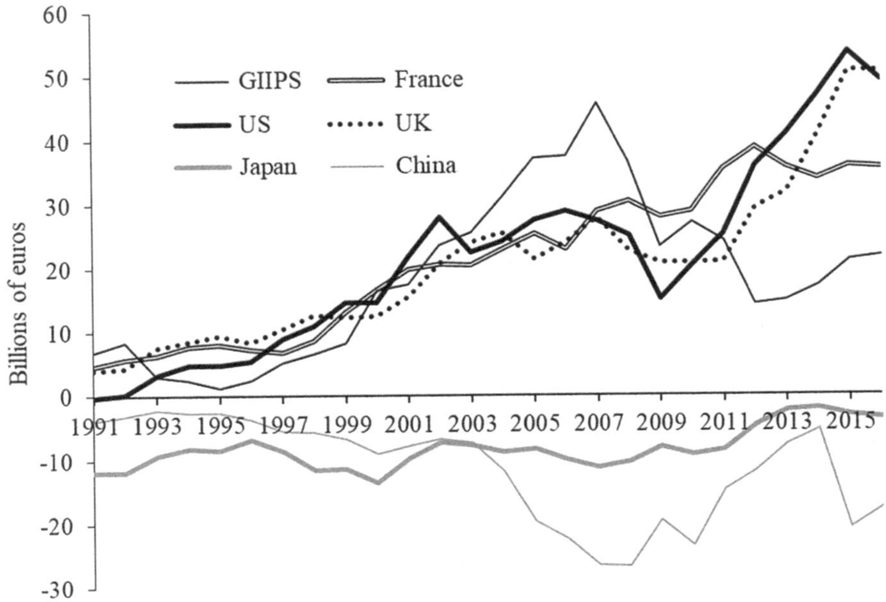

Fig. 12 Bilateral trade balances of Germany. Source: Germany, Statistisches Bundesamt

It remains to be seen if German investment abroad will turn out as over- or malinvestment in the future (as in many cases in the past[28]). The monetary overinvestment theories suggest that the likelihood of overinvestment and speculative bubbles has dramatically increased, as central banks around the world have depressed interest rates below the natural interest rate level. This has disturbed the allocation function of the interest rate (which separates investment with high expected returns from investment with low expected returns) and the signaling function of the interest rate (which indicates the risk of default, for instance, of over-indebted countries).

5 Outlook: Monetary Policy Failure as a Threat to the European Integration Process

The monetary policy of the European Central Bank is from a Mises-Hayek perspective a failure in several regards. First, the ECB's overly loose monetary policy stance is at the roots of the unsustainable investment, real estate and consumption booms in the southern and western euro area countries (and beyond), which have triggered the

[28]For instance, German credit provision to the southern and western European countries and to the US subprime boom has turned sour.

still lingering European financial and debt crisis (euro crisis). Currently, the ECB's monetary policy rescue measures, which are fitted to the crisis countries, nurture the buildup of a stock and real estate bubble in Germany. It therefore sets the stage for a future overinvestment and/or financial crisis in the Germany, which will remain the growth engine of Europe only up to the turning point of the cycle.

Secondly, the time-varying emergence of crisis in the different parts of the European Monetary Union is due to a constructional flaw of a heterogeneous monetary union with decentralized fiscal policies. Whereas labor markets in most member states remained rigid, the organization of fiscal policies at a national level has undermined the effectiveness of the common monetary policy. Fiscal policies have not only missed to cure asymmetric shocks in the monetary union; they have even caused asymmetric economic development! In the face of an overly loose monetary policy, economic upswings have taken the form of unsustainable overinvestment booms and (have) thereby become the precursor for a severe crisis. The Maastricht fiscal criteria have failed and are failing to indicate excessive spending during the speculative upswings as unsustainable tax revenues were/are produced. During the inevitable crisis, hiking government debt levels in the crisis countries are simply a catch-up process for proliferating spending during the precrisis exuberance.

Thirdly, the attempts of the European Central Bank to cure the European financial and debt crisis with zero and negative interest rates as well as with extensive government bond purchases has paralyzed investment and growth in all parts of the European Monetary Union. In the southern European crisis countries, distorted economic structures with a low marginal efficiency of investment are conserved, which constitutes an impediment for a sustainable economic recovery. Also in Germany investment activity has not picked up domestically, but has become tilted away from the European Monetary Union, in particular to the United States and the United Kingdom. The reason is that the ECB's monetary policy rescue measures in combination with relatively tight fiscal policies stimulate capital outflows, i.e., capital flight. Given the global low interest rate environment, foreign investment has a large likelihood to become malinvestment and therefore to become a quasi-transfer in favor of the debtor countries.

Fourth, because the low-cost liquidity provision of the European Central Bank paralyzes productivity gains and growth in the European Monetary Union, while at the same time having redistribution effects, redistribution conflicts within the euro area have emerged and are likely to further intensify. This is the case within every single euro area member state, because the monetary policy rescue measures redistribute via asset markets in favor of the rich (at the cost of the middle class) and in favor of the older generations (at the cost of the younger generations).[29] Furthermore, at a supranational level, the TARGET2 system redistributes from Germany, Luxemburg, Finland, and the Netherlands to a larger number of euro area countries, which are more or less strongly in crisis mode. The large number of the recipient

[29]For details see Hoffmann and Schnabl (2016).

countries of the TARGET2 quasi-transfer mechanism explains the political acceptability of the monetary policy rescue measures in the board of the ECB.

The negative growth and redistribution effects of the monetary policy rescue measures are likely to become in the long term the stepping stone for the European Monetary Union and the European integration process as a whole. As the TARGET2 balances are equivalent to a transfer of wealth from the donor to the recipient countries, an exit of the donor countries from the European Monetary Union is getting more likely in the course of time. The likelihood will strongly increase, after the overinvestment/speculation boom in Germany has ended. Because the monetary policy rescue measures paralyze growth and lead to growing inequality, euro-critical parties questioning the European integration process are already growing in almost all European countries.

The logical political reflex to declining growth and spreading frustration among the population is economic nationalism (see Hayek 1944), which endangers the four freedoms as the fundament of wealth and political cohesion in Europe. This should be reason enough to terminate the ultra-loose monetary policy rescue measures soon. Government bond purchases of the European Central Bank should be ended at once. The main refinancing rate should be lifted slowly, but decisively, to prompt a gradual adjustment of banks, enterprises, and governments to the reconstitution of the allocation and signaling function of the interest rate. Only a tightening of monetary policy will lead to a revival of productivity gains and thereby a recovery of growth, which is the basis for real wage increases all over Europe. Only if market principles are restored, the fundament for integration, wealth, cohesion, and peace in Europe will be reconstituted.

Acknowledgments I thank Raphael Fischer und Taiki Murai for excellent research assistance. I thank the Friedrich August von Hayek Foundation and Jackstädt Foundation for financial support.

References

Adrian, T., & Shin, H. S. (2008). Liquidity, monetary policy and financial cycles. *Current Issues in Economics and Finance, 14*, 1.

Belke, A., Gros, D., & Schnabl, G. (2016). Das europäische Verfahren zur Vermeidung und Korrektur makroökonomischer Ungleichgewichte – Eine Forschungsagenda zu Reformansätzen. *Wirtschaftsdienst, 96*(8), 548–556.

Bernanke, B. (2005). The Global Saving Glut and the U.S. Current Account Deficit. Remarks at the Sandridge Lecture, Virginia Association of Economists, Richmond, VA.

Blinder, A., & Reis, R. (2005). Understanding the Greenspan Standard. Princeton University Department of Economics Working Papers 88.

Borio, C. (2014). The financial cycle and macroeconomics: What have we learnt? *Journal of Banking and Finance, 45*, 182–198.

Borio, C., Kharroubi, E., Upper, C., & Zampolli, F. (2016). Labour reallocation and productivity dynamics: Financial causes, real consequences. BIS Working Papers 534.

Brunnermeier, M., & Schnabel, I. (2014). Bubbles and central banks: Historical perspectives. Mimeo.

Caballero, R., Hoshi, T., & Kashyap, A. (2008). Zombie lending and depressed restructuring in Japan. *American Economic Review, 98*(5), 1943–1977.
De Grauwe, P. (2011). Monetary policy and animal spirits. *Economic Theory, 47*(2–3), 423–457.
De Grauwe, P. (2016). *The economic of monetary union*. Oxford: Oxford University Press.
Draghi, M. (2014, February). The path to recovery and the ECB's Role. Speech by Mario Draghi, President of the ECB, at the Symposium on Financial Stability and the Role of Central Banks organised by the Deutsche Bundesbank, Frankfurt am Main, 27.
Duarte, P., & Schnabl, G. (2015). Macroeconomic policy making, exchange rate adjustment and current accounts in emerging markets. *Review of Development Economics, 19*(3), 531–544.
Freytag, A., & Schnabl, G. (2017). Monetary policy crisis management as a threat to economic order. Forthcoming as CESifo Working Paper.
Gopinath, G., Kalemli-Özkan, Ş., Karabarbounis, L., & Villegas-Sanchez, C. (2015). Capital allocation and productivity in South Europe, Mimeo.
Hoffmann, A., & Schnabl, G. (2008). Monetary policy, vagabonding liquidity and bursting bubbles in new and emerging markets: An overinvestment view. *The World Economy, 31*, 1226–1252.
Hoffmann, A., & Schnabl, G. (2011). A vicious cycle of manias, crises and asymmetric policy responses: An overinvestment view. *The World Economy, 34*, 382–403.
Hoffmann, A., & Schnabl, G. (2014). Monetary policy in large industrialized countries, emerging market credit cycles, and feedback effects. CESifo Working Paper 4723.
Hoffmann, A., & Schnabl, G. (2016). The adverse effects of unconventional monetary policy. *Cato Journal, 36*(3), 449–484.
Keynes, J. M. (1936). *The general theory of employment, interest, and money*. Cambridge: Macmillan Cambridge University Press.
Kornai, J. (1986). The soft budget constraint. *Kyklos, 39*(1), 3–30.
Laubach, T., & Williams, J. (2015). Measuring the natural rate of interest redux. Federal Reserve Bank of San Francisco Working Paper 2015–2016.
Leibenstein, H. (1966). Allocative efficiency vs. X-efficiency. *American Economic Review, 56*(3), 392–415.
Mundell, R. (1961). A theory of optimum currency areas. *American Economic Review, 51*(4), 657–665.
Peek, J., & Rosengren, E. (2005). Unnatural selection: Perverse incentives and the misallocation of credit in Japan. *American Economic Review, 95*(4), 1144–1166.
Schnabl, G., & Wollermershäuser, T. (2013). *Fiscal divergence and current account imbalances in Europe* (CESifo Working Paper 4108).
Schnabl, G. (2015). Monetary policy and structural decline: Lessons from Japan for the European crisis. *Asian Economic Papers, 14*(1), 124–150.
Schumpeter, J. (1912). *The theory of economic development*. Cambridge, MA: Harvard University Press.
Sekine, T., Kobayashi, K., & Saita, Y. (2003). Forbearance lending: The case of Japanese firms. *Bank of Japan Institute for Monetary and Economic Studies, 21*(2), 69–92.
Sinn, H.-W., & Wollmershäuser, T. (2012). Target loans, current account balances and capital flows: The ECB's rescue facility. *International Tax and Public Finance, 19*(4), 468–508.
Solow, R. (1956). A contribution to the theory of economic growth. *Quarterly Journal of Economics, 70*(1), 65–94.
Solow, R. (1957). Technical change and the aggregate production function. *Review of Economics and Statistics, 39*(2), 312–320.
Summers, L. (2014). U.S. economic prospects: Secular stagnation, hysteresis, and the zero lower bound. *Business Economics, 49*(2), 65–73.
Taylor, J. (1993). Discretion versus policy rules in practice. *Carnegie-Rochester Conference Series on Public Policy, 39*, 195–214.
von Hayek, F. A. (1929). *Geldtheorie und Konjunkturtheorie*. Salzburg: Philosophia Verlag.
von Hayek, F. A. (1931). *Prices and production*. New York: August M Kelly Publishers.
von Hayek, F. A. (1933). *Monetary theory and the trade cycle*. London: Jonathan Cape.

von Hayek, F. A. (1937[1989]). *Monetary nationalism and international stability*. Fairfield, NJ: Augustus Kelley Publishers.
von Hayek, F. A. (1944). *The Road to Serfdom*. London: Routledge.
von Hayek, F. A. (1968). Der Wettbewerb als Entdeckungsverfahren. In Internationales Institut, Österreichische Schule der Nationalökonomie" (Hrsg.): Die Österreichische Schule der Nationalökonomie. Texte - Band II von Hayek bis White (pp. 119–137). Wien: Manz'sche Verlags- und Universitätsbuchhandlung.
von Mises, L. (1912). *Die Theorie des Geldes und der Umlaufmittel*. Leipzig: Duncker und Humblot.
Wicksell, K. (1898). *Geldzins und Güterpreise*. München: FinanzBuch Verlag.
Wollmershäuser, T., & Schnabl, G. (2013). Fiscal divergence and current account imbalances in Europe. CESifo Working Paper 4108.

Hayek and Mises on Neutrality of Money: Implications for Monetary Policy

Arkadiusz Sieroń

1 Introduction

The neutrality (or non-neutrality) of money is the key issue of monetary economics addressed by each school of economic thought. From the very beginning of economics, there has been a debate about the role of monetary policy in the economy. Since the so-called monetarist counter-revolution, economists have been much more interested in examining monetary phenomena and have linked them to cyclical fluctuations. Each school of economics emphasizes different causes of the non-neutrality of money, such as price rigidity (new Keynesians) or incomplete information (new classical economists).[1] However, there is a consensus that money is non-neutral in the short term: the real effects caused by the monetary impulses are only transitory, and the economy inevitably returns to the previous steady-state path. In contrast, the Austrian school focuses on the Cantillon effect as the main reason for the non-neutrality of money, and disagrees with the idea that real changes occurring in response to monetary impulses dissipate in the long run.

The aim of this article is to examine the concept of neutral money in light of the Austrian school's ideas. We focus on Hayek's and Mises's writings, as these two authors presented the most far-reaching criticism of the neutrality of money,

---

The article is partially based on the author's doctoral dissertation, entitled "The Effects of Money Supply Growth from the Perspective of the Cantillon Effect."

[1]However, real business cycle theory inverts the analyzed relationship and assumes that changes in the money supply are a response to real disturbances. Hence, it believes not only in neutrality of money but also in superneutrality (Plosser 1990).

A. Sieroń (✉)
Institute of Economic Sciences, University of Wroclaw, Wrocław, Poland

A. Godart-van der Kroon, P. Vonlanthen (eds.), *Banking and Monetary Policy from the Perspective of Austrian Economics*,
https://doi.org/10.1007/978-3-319-75817-6_8

showing that changes in the money supply are never neutral, even in the long term.[2] Based on our analysis, we claim that the writings of Austrian economists on non-neutrality of money significantly developed monetary economics and contributed to the debate on the benefits and costs of the expansionary monetary policy. In particular, central banks' not taking into account the Cantillon effect leads to overly loose monetary policy.

The remainder of the paper is organized as follows. Section 2 presents the concept of neutral money. Section 3 analyzes the Cantillon effect. Section 4 examines the Austrian arguments against money neutrality. Section 5 concludes and provides the implications for monetary policy, including the actions of the European Central Bank (ECB).

2 Neutrality of Money

The neutrality of money means the lack of effects of monetary phenomena on real variables.[3] There are a few different notions of neutrality of money, depending on how one defines "monetary phenomena".[4] Probably the most important notion, which we call "dynamic neutrality," implies that changes in the supply of money only affect nominal variables, while real variables, such as relative prices, production, or employment, remain unaffected. Conversely, the non-neutrality of money means changes in the money supply have an impact on real phenomena.

The concept of neutrality of money is a central economic issue widely discussed from the very beginning of economics as a science. It is sufficient to mention the quantity theory of money formulated at first by Locke, which basically states that the level of prices is always in proportion to the quantity of money. It was probably formulated and believed by classical economists as a reaction against mercantilists' inflationism, but that reaction was exaggerated and hampered the genuine development of monetary economics (Blaug 1985). The quantity theory of money is true but only from the point of view of comparative statics. One economy with twice the money supply of another but with no other differences should have twice as high a general price level. However, it does not follow that doubling the money supply only leads to doubling all prices. For the neutrality of money to hold from the dynamic perspective, several conditions must be fulfilled.[5]

---

[2]On other Austrian economists' views on the neutrality of money, see Chaloupek (2010) or Salerno (2016).

[3]The term "neutral money" gained recognition in the English language literature through Hayek's publications. However, it was in use earlier among Continental economists (Hayek 2008a [1935]; Visser 2002).

[4]On the typology of the neutrality of money, see Sieroń (2014).

[5]According to Hayek (2008a [1935]), there are three conditions for the neutrality of money: constant total money stream, perfectly flexible prices, and long-term contracts based on a correct anticipation of future price movements.

First of all, new money should simultaneously and proportionally increase cash balances of all individuals. It means the lack of a Cantillon effect—called also the first-round effect or the injection effect—which is the distributional effect resulting from uneven changes in the money supply, where "uneven changes in the money supply" means changes that do not affect all cash balances in the same proportion and at the same time.[6]

Second, all prices should be perfectly flexible and change at the same time, as is assumed in Walrasian general equilibrium theory. Otherwise, the increase in money supply would influence the structure of relative prices, affecting the allocation of resources and production. The requirement of perfect flexibility of prices implies the lack of long-term contracts or menu costs.

Third, for money neutrality to hold, agents have to be able to distinguish real from monetary shocks. This condition implies that money surprises have to be ruled out. People should form rational expectations under complete information. Otherwise, individuals may adjust their output in response to mere monetary fluctuations, if they mistakenly consider them to be real disturbances.

These three conditions do not exhaust the list, but they are the most important ones and are thoroughly analyzed by various contemporary economic schools.[7] The new classical economists examine incomplete information (Lucas 1972), new Keynesians focus on price rigidity (Fischer 1977; Mankiw 1985), and the Austrians emphasize the first-round effect.[8] Mainstream economists are generally not interested in studying the Cantillon effect, probably due to unrealistic assumptions they make about such things as the tâtonnement process and the representative agent. The focus on large aggregates and their lack of a sophisticated theory of capital also makes the study of the first-round effect difficult for mainstream economists, especially given all the problems associated with mathematical formalization.

However, the differences between the Austrian school and mainstream economics related to the non-neutrality of money go far beyond the major cause of it. Indeed, Austrian economists offer the most far-reaching critique of the concept of neutral money.[9] They argue that money is non-neutral not only in the short run but also in the long term. Meanwhile mainstream economists believe that non-neutral effects are temporary and vanish after the economy adjusts to the monetary impulse. Last

---

[6]The Cantillon effect is analyzed in detail in the next section.

[7]Other conditions include lack of non-fiat money, lack of government interventions (such as price controls, trade restrictions, or taxes levied on nominal incomes), lack of transaction costs, or constant proportion between cash and bank deposits. See Visser (2002) or Sieroń (2014).

[8]Actually, the Cantillon effect is the basis of the Austrian business cycle theory. Some researchers even suggest that taking the first-round effect into account is the distinguishing feature of the Austrian school and its theory of money and the business cycle. See Horwitz (1994), Zijp and Visser (1994), or O'Driscoll and Rizzo (1996).

[9]Post-Keynesians also criticize the concept of neutral money, but they focus on institutional or qualitative neutrality related to the very existence of the money in the economy, not to the change in the money supply, arguing that "one cannot first analyze the economy in purely 'real' terms and then add on one's monetary theory 'afterwards'" (Cottrel 1994, p. 4).

but not least, the Austrian school believes that the very concept of neutral money is at odds with methodological individualism and the modern subjective theory of value. The next section explains the significance of the Cantillon effect in economics and monetary policy, while the Austrian arguments in favor of the non-neutrality of money are presented in detail in the fourth section.

3 The Significance of the Cantillon Effect in Economics and Monetary Policy

According to Hayek (2008a [1935], pp. 202–203), Cantillon (1959 [1755]) provided the first attempt to "trace the actual chain of cause and effect between the amount of money and prices," pointing out that the impact of a monetary injection depends on the nature of the injection. This phenomenon—which Blaug (1985) calls the Cantillon effect—makes money non-neutral, both in the short and long runs. This is because new money is introduced into the economy only through specific channels and is distributed through the economy unevenly and sequentially, lifting prices gradually and in different proportions. Hence, the increase in money supply leads to the distribution of income from the late to the early recipients of additional money, as the latter have boosted cash balances before prices adjust, while the former get money when prices have already adjusted. Subsequently, there are changes in the structure of relative prices and production because prices increase earlier and/or more in those sectors where the new money first flows. The changes in relative prices then affect the attractiveness of production in different sectors, leading to adjustments in the structure of production.

The first-round effect—which has always been the focus of Austrian economists in their critique of money neutrality (Hayek 2008a [1935]; Mises 1990)—significantly contributes to economic theory, in particular to the theory of money, the theory of business cycles and price bubbles, and the theory of income distribution, contributing to the debate about the role of monetary factors in the economy and the effectiveness of monetary policy.

First, the first-round effect is the basis of Austrian business cycle theory, which examines the effects of the increase in money supply through the credit channel on interest rates and the structure of capital. A detailed discussion of that theory is beyond the scope of this paper. It can be found in O'Driscoll and Rizzo (1996), Hayek (2008a [1935]), Mises (1949 [1998]), Garrison (2001), or Huerta de Soto (2006). The essence is that according to Austrian economists, the business cycle results from the fact that new money is introduced into the economy through the credit market, which reduces the market interest rate and leads to intertemporal disequilibrium in the form of an unsustainable boom and to a subsequently inevitable crisis. Importantly, in the Austrian approach, the economy does not return to the earlier steady-state path after the boom phase. Although Austrians consider the economic boom as unstable and temporary, the boom lowers the rate of interest and leads to malinvestments, entailing lasting effects on the structure of production and the economy. If this theory is correct, then the business cycle is non-ergodic[10] and money is not neutral in the long term.

This theory also offers an important recommendation for monetary policy: central banks should not set interest rates and provide liquidity to commercial banks, because doing so strengthens their ability to expand inflationary credit and leads to an artificial and harmful boom. The theory also applies to the ECB,[11] whose expansionary monetary policy at the beginning of the 2000s led to an economic boom, setting the stage for the financial crisis in the second half of the decade (Benedyk 2013).

Moreover, in the contemporary global economy, the Cantillon effect occurs on the international scale. It means that growth in the money supply in one area—for example, in the euro area—may entail significant economic effects also in other countries. The impact occurs through a few distinct channels, but I would like to point out that the increase in money supply through the credit market lowers interest rates, which may lead to the outflow of capital to other economies due to interest rate arbitrage and the search for yield by accepting investments in riskier countries. Therefore, not taking into account global factors (the international Cantillon effect) can prompt the central bank to adopt an overly expansionary monetary policy.[12]

For example, the interest rate cuts and the subsequent policy of ultralow interest rates conducted by the ECB in the first half of the 2000s led to the outflow of capital from Germany into the peripheral countries of the euro area, which contributed to the unstable booms in these countries and to relatively slow growth in Germany (Sinn 2011). Similarly, there was also an outflow of capital from the euro area as a whole to Central and Eastern Europe, which contributed to business cycles and asset-price bubbles in many countries of that region (Hoffmann 2009).

The first-round effect may also explain the formation of asset-price bubbles since they are the best evidence that prices do not rise evenly and proportionally, as in Friedman's notion of helicopter money (Friedman 1969), but rather unevenly and disproportionately, as described by Cantillon and Austrian economists. Indeed, if money was neutral and the quantity theory of money held, asset-price bubbles—meaning the relative overvaluation of particular asset prices—would not exist. They occur due to the expansion of credit and its continuous inflow to a given asset market, in line with the Cantillon effect. Importantly, there are strong arguments that asset-price bubbles threaten financial stability and that they can lead to a

[10]It means that boom-and-bust cycles cause lasting damage due to resource misallocations that cannot be easily and quickly undone. Consequently, economic growth "may return to its precrisis long-term trend, but output remains below its precrisis long-term trend" (Borio 2015).

[11]Actually, we should refer to the Eurosystem—which consists of the ECB and the national central banks of the member states—as the official monetary authority of the euro area, but we write about the ECB for the sake of simplicity.

[12]Similarly, a country can suffer from inflation and the business cycle even if the central bank conducts a relatively restrictive monetary policy. In other words, national fiat currencies cannot be isolated from global inflation and international business cycles (Hayek 2008b [1935]).

deeper recession in comparison to a business cycle not accompanied by a financial bubble (Borio and Lowe 2002). Meanwhile, central banks, including the ECB, do not take into account asset-price inflation, instead focusing on price stability narrowly defined as stability of the CPI. Hence, it seems that central banks should change their stance on this matter and also monitor asset prices (Bordo and Wheelock 2004)—otherwise, there is a risk of conducting an overly loose monetary policy, leading to imbalances in the economy and financial instability despite stable consumer prices and thus an apparent neutrality of money (as the proposals for price stabilization are based on the notion of neutrality of money).

This is exactly what happened in the euro area in the 2000s. Although the CPI rate did not significantly exceed the ECB's target in the first half of the decade, the loose monetary policy of the central bank (interest rates too low for too long, at least for some countries of the euro area) led to a business cycle, and real estate booms in countries of the euro area where the growth in the money supply was the highest (or where the new money mainly went), in particular Spain and Ireland (Ahrend et al. 2008; Hott and Jokipii 2012).

The Cantillon effect also helps us to understand the relationship between monetary policy and income inequality. As a reminder, the first-round effect implies the distribution of income from late to first recipients of new money, which strengthens the redistributive effects of inflation. The Austrian economists always recognized the redistributive nature of monetary inflation,[13] but until recently they did not analyze its impact on income inequality (Hülsmann 2013). However, it turns out that the relatively poor may suffer from an increase in the money supply, being relatively late recipients of new money (the first recipients of additional money are mainly in the financial sector) and asset holders (as they hold fewer financial assets) (Sieroń 2017).

In particular, it can be argued that quantitative easing—purchases of financial assets by central banks—entails important redistributive effects, which may lead to an increase in income and wealth inequality. Importantly, Mersch, a member of the executive board of the European Central Bank, admits that unconventional monetary policy may increase inequality, although the exact impact is difficult to determine (Mersch 2014). Indeed, Adam and Tzamourani (2015) note that the rise in share prices in the euro area primarily benefits the top 5% of the net wealth distribution.[14] Therefore, they point out the distributional effects of unconventional monetary policy conducted by the ECB after the financial crisis of 2007–2008, as the policy was accompanied by an increase in a number of financial asset prices. In other words, one of the unintended consequences of monetary policy is the redistribution of income and wealth, which may increase inequality, despite the lack of any legitimacy for interfering with the income and wealth distribution in a society.

[13]"As the changes in purchasing power do not affect all prices and wages at the same moment and to the same extent, there is a shift of wealth and income between different social groups" (Mises 1990, p. 73).

[14]Claeys et al. (2015).

To sum up this section, the Cantillon effect is an overlooked but significant concept in economics. Taking it into account enriches the debate about the role of monetary factors and monetary policy, strengthening the Austrian arguments against the neutrality of money, which are presented in the next section in more detail.

4 The Austrian Arguments for Non-neutrality of Money

What are the main arguments of the Austrian economists against the postulate of neutral money? Hayek criticizes the assumption made by mainstream monetary economists that changes in the quantity of money only affect the general price level. His criticism is twofold.

First, Hayek rejects the mainstream's attempts to "establish *direct* casual connection between the *total* quantity of money, the *general* level of all prices and, perhaps, also the *total* amount of production" (Hayek 2008a [1935], p. 199, emphasis in original) as at odds with methodological individualism and the development of economics after the marginal revolution. He states:

> If, therefore, monetary theory still attempts to establish causal relations between aggregates or general averages, this means that monetary theory lags behind the development of economics in general. In fact, neither aggregates nor averages do act upon one another, and it will never be possible to establish necessary connections of cause and effect between them as we can between individual phenomena, individual prices, etc. (Hayek 2008a [1935], pp. 199–200)

Second, Hayek criticizes the assumption that shifts in the money supply affect only the general price level, while the changes in relative prices result from some frictions or disturbances. Such an approach fails to explain, according to him, how the monetary impulses affect the general price level, if not through individual prices. This deficiency of the concept of neutral money embedded in the mechanistic quantity theory of money was noted already by Cantillon in the eighteenth century. His criticism of Locke, taken by Hayek as the epigraph for his first lecture of *Prices and Production*, is as follows:

> He has clearly seen that the abundance of money makes everything dear, but he has not considered how it does so. The great difficulty of this question consists in knowing in what way and in what proportion the increase of money raises prices. (Cantillon 1959 [1755], II. VI.5)

For Hayek, changes in relative prices in response to monetary disturbances are not frictions, lags, or market failures occurring due to price rigidity, incomplete information, or irrational expectations, but the natural and inevitable consequence of monetary impulses. This is because new money enters circulation only through specific channels and some people receive the additional money earlier than others. In consequence, they reduce their enlarged cash balances and increase their spending. Hence there is no simultaneous and proportional rise in all prices, but some of them rise earlier or to a larger extent. In other words, new money is distributed sequentially in the economy, leading to changes in income distribution (some people have more money, but the prices have not yet increased) and the structure of relative prices (prices of goods and services bought by the beneficiaries of monetary inflation are altered the most or the fastest) and, in turn, the structure of production (modification of the relative prices affects the price signals), according to the Cantillon effect.

Importantly, Hayek's methodological individualism leads him to notice that monetary policy does not necessarily have to neutralize changes in money demand, even if it affects the general price level. Instead, the alterations in money supply may merely add new disturbances since the effects of monetary inflation depend on the channel through which the new money enters the economy:

> In order to eliminate all monetary influences on the formation of prices and the structure of production, it would not be sufficient merely quantitatively to adapt the supply of money to these changes in demand, it would be necessary also to see that it came into the hands of those who actually require it, i.e., to that part of the system where that change in business organization or the habits of payment had taken place. (Hayek 2008a [1935], p. 297)

Mises also believes that the quantity theory of money, which is based on the idea of the neutrality of money, is at odds with methodological individualism since it is based on holistic concepts such as the general price level of the velocity of money and does not refer to individuals' subjective valuations, which determine all market phenomena. As early as 1912, he writes:

> The mistake in the argument of those who suppose that a variation in the quantity of money results in an inversely proportionate variation in its purchasing power lies in its starting-point. If we wish to arrive at a correct conclusion, we must start with the valuations of separate individuals; we must examine the way in which an increase or decrease in the quantity of money affects the value-scales of individuals, for it is from these alone that variations in the exchange-ratios of goods proceed. The initial assumption in the arguments of those who maintain the theory that changes in the quantity of money have a proportionate effect on the purchasing power of money is the proposition that if the value of the monetary unit were doubled, half of the stock of money at the disposal of the community would yield the same utility as that previously yielded by the whole stock. The correctness of this proposition is not disputed; nevertheless it does not prove what it is meant to prove.... Half of the money at the disposal of the community would yield the same utility as the whole stock, even if the variation in the value of the monetary unit was not proportioned to the variation in the stock of money. But it is important to note that it by no means follows from this that doubling the quantity of money means halving the objective exchange-value of money. It would have to be shown that forces emanate from the valuations of individual economic agents which are able to bring about such a proportionate variation (Mises 1953 [1912], p. 142).

Mises (1953 [1912]) also points out that a rise in the money supply always means an increase in the amount of money held by particular individuals, not by all members of a society. In consequence, the Cantillon effect operates, leading to the distribution of income among members of the society and changes in the structure of prices and production.

However, Mises's critique of neutral money goes much further than Hayek's.[15] He not only points out that new money spreads through the economy only gradually and unevenly, preventing money from being neutral, but that money would be non-neutral even when cash balances of all members of the society increase in the same proportion. This is because:

> even in this quite impossible case, every increase in the quantity of money would necessarily cause an alteration in the conditions of demand, which would lead to a disparate increase in the prices of the individual economic goods. Not all commodities would be demanded more intensively, and not all of those that were demanded more intensively would be affected in the same degree (Mises 1953 [1912], p. 141).

Therefore, Mises completely rejects the concept of neutrality, arguing that "in a living world there is no room for neutrality of money" (Mises 1990, p. 75) and that "money is non-neutral or it does not exist" (Mises 1990, p. 77). This is because the concept of neutrality is fundamentally inconsistent with the subjective nature of utility:

> If the possessor of a units of money receives h additional units, then it is not at all true to say that he will value the total stock $a + h$ exactly as highly as he had previously valued the stock a alone. Because he now has disposal over a larger stock, he will now value each unit less than he did before; but how much less will depend upon a whole series of individual circumstances, upon subjective valuations that will be different for each individual. Two individuals who are equally wealthy and who each possess a stock of money *a*, will not by any means arrive at the same variation in their estimation of money after an increase of *h* units in each of their stocks of money. It is nothing short of absurdity to assume that, say, doubling the amount of money at the disposal of an individual must lead to a halving of the exchange-value that he ascribes to each monetary unit. (Mises 1953 [1912], pp. 141–142)

Summing up, Hayek's and Mises's arguments against money neutrality maintain that an increase in money supply always affects relative prices. This is mainly because the additional money is distributed unevenly, which leads to a disproportionate increase in prices, as the prices of goods purchased by the first receivers of new money rise earlier or to a larger extent than other prices. It is true that when the adjustment process is completed, the general level of prices increases, but not all prices rise in the same proportion. Hence, the expansion in the money supply leads to

---

[15]Mises rejects the very notion of neutral money as contradictory. Although Hayek also believes that neutral money should not be the purpose of monetary policy, he argues that the concept of neutral money may be a useful instrument for theoretical analysis, or a benchmark for evaluating different monetary policies or regimes (Horwitz 2016). However, Hayek refers to money neutrality in this context to a "set of conditions, under which it would be *conceivable* that events in a monetary economy would take place, and particularly under which, in such an economy, relative prices would be formed, as if they were influenced only by the 'real' factors which are taken into account in equilibrium economics" (Hayek 2008a [1935], p. 302). As neutral money is impossible, Hayek opts for keeping nominal income (MV) constant (Hayek 2008a [1935]). Thus, Salerno (2016) dehomogenizes the views of Mises and Hayek on the neutrality of money. Although we agree that Mises's critique of the concept of neutral money is more decisive than that formulated by Hayek, Salerno fails to notice that the issue of constancy of MV is something different than the concept of "dynamic neutrality"—the two Austrian economists differ on the former issue, while both reject the latter.

an alteration in the structure of prices, which leaves a lasting imprint on the real economy. The concept of neutral money is thus unrealistic, and it results from the flawed holistic methodology that ignores the microeconomic responses to changes in the money supply and from the erroneous application of the conclusions from the comparative statics to the analysis of a dynamic process.[16]

To put it another way, money, unlike other goods, does not have its own market, or what boils down to the same thing, it is traded in all markets. It means that everyone is a dealer in money and holds a certain stock of money (Salerno 1994). Hence, monetary impulses necessarily affect all other markets. As Mises put it emphatically: "Nothing can happen in the orbit of vendible goods without affecting the orbit of money, and all that happens in the orbit of money affects the orbit of commodities" (Mises 1998 [1949], p. 415).

5 Conclusions

The Austrian economists formulate strong arguments against the concept of neutral money. They argue that the neutrality of money not only violates methodological individualism but also cannot be actually achieved in the real world, partially due to the Cantillon effect, which mainstream economists overlook. The non-neutrality of money should be taken into account in the transmission mechanism of monetary policy conducted by central banks, including the ECB, as its primary objective is to maintain price stability (Treaty on the Functioning of the European Union, Art. 127, 1), which was chosen partially due to the belief in the long-run neutrality of money. Indeed, as one can read on the ECB's official website, this purpose is considered to be the natural role of monetary policy, since "monetary policy can affect real activity only in the shorter term. But ultimately it can only influence the price level in the economy" (ECB, n.d.).

There are three main implications of the above analysis for monetary policy, in particular for the ECB's actions. First, the Austrians' arguments for the non-neutrality of money enrich the literature about the limits of monetary policy and strengthen the case against the overly loose monetary policy conducted by the central banks, including the ECB. From the Austrian perspective, the increase in money supply does not lead to merely temporary changes but permanently affects the real side of the economy.

Hence, the non-neutrality of money is a strong argument against the view that central banks should respond to real disturbances or changes in money demand, as monetary inflation does not neutralize monetary deflation and undo its social consequences but "simply add[s] to it the social consequences of a new change" (Mises 1990, p. 76). Therefore, "the only practical maxim for monetary policy to be derived

[16]It is worth pointing out that the Austrian school was always more interested in the study of the dynamic market process rather than static equilibrium (Kirzner 1976; Huerta de Soto 1998).

from our considerations is probably the negative one that the simple fact of an increase of production and trade forms no justification for an expansion of credit, and that—save in an acute crisis—bankers need not be afraid to harm production by overcaution" (Hayek 2008a [1935], p. 298).

Second, central banks' not taking into account the Cantillon effect leads to an underestimation of the negative effects of monetary inflation, including quantitative easing. The first-round effect contributes to business cycles, asset-price bubbles, international spillovers of the increase in money supply, and income and wealth redistribution, which may widen income and wealth inequality. Therefore, the central banks, including the ECB, should pay more attention to asset prices and the redistributive effects of their monetary policy.

Third, the non-neutrality of money postulated by the Austrian economists is a strong argument against price stability as the aim of monetary policy. According to mainstream economics, money is neutral, and the increase in money supply does not affect the economy, as long as the price level remains stable (Hayek 2008a [1935]).[17] However, if money is not neutral, monetary impulses always affect the economy. Hence, inflationary monetary policy may entail negative consequences for the economy—such as business cycles or asset-price bubbles—even when the general price level remains stable.

To sum up, if money is not neutral and affects relative prices, as the Austrian economists argue, then the central banks should either be abolished or at least significantly reconsider how they conduct monetary policy. They should not only adopt a more cautious and conservative stance but also examine how the increase in the money supply is distributed through the economy and how it affects different ratios of exchange between various goods, including the rate of interest, and the structure of capital. This is because what matters for the economy is not a mere increase in the money supply but also the channel of monetary inflation: the effects of monetary policies on the real economy differ depending on the channels of monetary injections. Such a disaggregated analysis of monetary policy and credit expansion in the spirit of Cantillon's seminal work (Cantillon 1959 [1755])—going beyond the large aggregates (such as the general price level) and the focus on narrowly defined price stability—would be a real boon to the development of monetary theory and monetary policy conducted by the ECB and other central banks (Morgenstern 1972; Hayek 2008a [1935]).

References

Adam, K., & Tzamourani, P. (2015). *Distributional consequences of asset price inflation in the euro area* (pp. 1–17) (Deutsche Bank Discussion Paper 27).

Ahrend, R., Cournede, B., & Price, R. (2008). *Monetary policy, market excesses and financial turmoil* (OECD Economics Department Working Paper 597).

[17]The concept of neutrality of money implying constancy of the price level originates from Wicksell (1978).

Benedyk, M. (2013). Polityka pieniężna Europejskiego Banku Centralnego 1999–2013. *Ekonomia–Wrocław Economic Review, 19*(4).
Blaug, M. (1985). *Economic theory in retrospect* (4th ed.). Cambridge: Cambridge University Press.
Bordo, M. D., & Wheelock, D. C. (2004). *Monetary policy and asset prices: A look back at past US stock market booms* (NBER working paper 10704).
Borio, C. (2015). *Revisiting three intellectual pillars of monetary policy received wisdom. Luncheon address*. Washington, DC: Cato Institute.
Borio, C., & Lowe, P. (2002). *Asset prices, financial and monetary stability: Exploring the nexus* (pp. 1–35) (BIS Working Papers 114).
Cantillon, R. (1959 [1755]). *Essay on the nature of trade in general*. London: Frank Cass.
Chaloupek, G. (2010). "Neutrality of money" versus "stability of the price level"—Issues of monetary theory within the Austrian School of economics. *14th ESHET Conference*, Amsterdam, March 25–27, 2010.
Claeys, G., Darvas, Z., & Leandro, Á., & Walsh, T. (2015, June 9). The effects of ultra-loose monetary policies on inequality. *Bruegel, Policy Contribution*.
Cottrel, A. (1994). Post Keynesian monetary economics: A critical survey. *Cambridge Journal of Economics, 18*(6), 587–605.
ECB. (n.d.). *Objective of monetary policy*. https://www.ecb.europa.eu/mopo/intro/objective/html/index.en.html
Fischer, S. (1977). Long term contracts, rational expectations, and the optimal money supply rule. *Journal of Political Economy, 85*(1), 191–205.
Friedman, M. (1969). The optimum quantity of money. In M. Friedman (Ed.), *The optimum quantity of money and other essays*. Chicago, IL: Aldine Publishing Company.
Garrison, R. W. (2001). *Time and money. The macroeconomics of capital structure*. London: Routledge.
Hayek, F. (2008a [1935]). Prices and production. In J. Salerno (Ed.), *Prices and production and other works: F.A. Hayek on money, the business cycle, and the gold standard* (pp. 189–329). Auburn AL: Ludwig von Mises Institute.
Hayek, F. (2008b [1935]). Monetary nationalism and international stability. In J. Salerno (Ed.), *Prices and production and other works: F.A. Hayek on money, the business cycle, and the gold standard* (pp. 331–422). Auburn, AL: Ludwig von Mises Institute.
Hoffmann, A. (2009). *An overinvestment cycle in Central and Eastern Europe* (MPRA paper 15668).
Horwitz, S. (1994). Inflation. In P. Boettke (Ed.), *The Elgar companion to Austrian economics*. Aldershot: Edward Elgar.
Horwitz, S. (2016). Hayek on the neutrality of money. In S. Horwitz (Ed.), *Studies in Austrian macroeconomics. Advances in Austrian economics* (Vol. 20, pp. 61–78). Bingley: Emerald Group Publishing.
Hott, C., & Jokipii, T. (2012). *Housing bubbles and interest rates* (Swiss National Bank working paper 2012–07).
Huerta de Soto, J. (1998). The ongoing methodenstreit of the Austrian school. *J des Économistes et des Études Humaines, 8*(1), 75–113.
Huerta de Soto, J. (2006). *Money, bank credit, and economic cycles*. Auburn, AL: Ludwig von Mises Institute.
Hülsmann, J. G. (2013). Fiat money and the distribution of incomes and wealth. Document de travail du GRANEM2013–02–039.
Kirzner, I. (1976). Equilibrium versus market process. In E. G. Dolan (Ed.), *The foundations of modern Austrian economics*. Kansas City: Sheed and Ward.
Lucas, R. E., Jr. (1972). Expectations and the neutrality of money. *J Economic Theory, 4*(20), 103–124.
Mankiw, G. (1985). Small menu costs and large business cycles: A macroeconomic model of monopoly. *Quarterly J Economics, 100*(2).

Mersch, Y. (2014, October 17). *Monetary policy and economic inequality*. Speech at Corporate Credit Conference. Zurich. https://www.ecb.europa.eu/press/key/date/2014/html/sp141017_1.en.html

Mises, L. (1953 [1912]). *Theory of money and credit*. New Haven: Yale University Press.

Mises, L. (1990). The non-neutrality of money. In R. Ebeling (Ed.), *Money, method, and the market process: Essays by Ludwig von Mises* (pp. 69–77). Norwell, MA: Kluwer Academic Publishers.

Mises, L. (1998 [1949]). Human action: A treatise on economics (scholar's edn.). Auburn AL: Ludwig von Mises Institute.

Morgenstern, O. (1972). Thirteen critical points in contemporary economic theory: An interpretation. *J Economic Literature, 10*(4), 1163–1189.

O'Driscoll, G., Jr., & Rizzo, M. (1996). *The economics of time and ignorance*. London: Routledge.

Plosser, C. I. (1990). *Money and business cycles: A real business cycle interpretation* (NBER working paper series 3221).

Salerno, J. T. (1994). Ludwig von Mises' monetary theory in light of modern monetary thought. *Review of Austrian Economics, 8*(1), 71–115.

Salerno, J. T. (2016). The development of the neutral money concept: The Austrian school further dehomogenized. https://ssrn.com/abstract=2738140

Sieroń, A. (2014). Nieutralność pieniądza. *Studia Ekonomiczne, LXXX*(1), 88–107.

Sieroń, A. (2017). *Inflation and income inequality*. Prague Economic Papers.

Sinn, H.-W. (2011). Germany's capital exports under the euro, August 2, 2011. http://www.voxeu.org/article/germany-s-capital-exports-under-euro

Treaty on the functioning of the European Union. (2012). C326/102. http://eur-lex.europa.eu/legal-content/EN/TXT/PDF/?uri=CELEX:12012E/TXT&from=EN

Visser, H. (2002). Neutrality of money. In B. Snowdon & H. R. Vane (Eds.), *An encyclopedia of macroeconomics*. Cheltenham: Edward Elgar Publishing.

Wicksell, K. (1978). *Lectures on political economy* (Vol. 2). Fairfield, NJ: Augustus M Kelley Publishers.

Zijp, R., & Visser, H. (1994). Mathematical formalization and the domain of economics: The case of Hayek and new classical economics. In R. Zijp & J. Birner (Eds.), *Hayek, co-ordination and evolution*. London: Routledge.

Managing Decline by Expanding Government: The Case of Germany

Erich Weede

1 Introduction: Human Fallibility Necessitates Limited Government and Economic Freedom

Philosophy as well as all the social sciences, economics included, should start from the insight of human fallibility (Popper 1959; Albert 1988). What economists call rationality is merely the *attempt* to maximize benefits and to minimize costs. In my view, one could go a step further: Rationality is the attempt to cope with human fallibility. As Hayek (1960) pointed out, it presupposes individual freedom and responsibility. Responsibility includes suffering the consequences of one's errors. If humans are fallible, then one of the most important characteristics of a social order is whether or not it provides mechanisms for eliminating and correcting errors. This applies to the economy, to academia (or science), and to politics. Within academia or science, rationality requires humans to give up the utopian quest for certainty but nevertheless to continue to rely on logic and experience to make theories ever more consistent as well as compatible with observable facts.

In different spheres of life, there are different mechanisms to overcome error or poor solutions to problems. Competition on price and quality in the market serves a similar function as do scientific debates or competition between parties in politics. It is easiest to institutionalize rationality in a competitive economy (Alchian 1950). Contestable markets and the threat of bankruptcy establish rationality and punish error. Whoever supplies shoddy goods at high prices to the market is unlikely to survive competition. Such suppliers are likely to be eliminated by bankruptcy. Whoever proposes an empty or false theory or who always relies on inadequate designs to test

E. Weede (✉)
University of Bonn, Bonn, Germany
e-mail: e.weede@uni-bonn.de

A. Godart-van der Kroon, P. Vonlanthen (eds.), *Banking and Monetary Policy from the Perspective of Austrian Economics*,
https://doi.org/10.1007/978-3-319-75817-6_9

propositions is likely to lose reputation in science. Politicians who misinterpret or neglect the interests of voters are more likely to lose office than to win elections.

Nevertheless, it is most difficult to achieve a minimum of rationality in the field of politics. Since politics deals with power and since states claim a monopoly of legitimate physical violence,[1] it is obvious that power holders and governments can violently interfere with people's attempts to manage and improve their lives. The Nobel laureate Hayek (1978a) admitted that his opinion about government deteriorated persistently. Few people dare to challenge the errors of autocrats. One of the worst examples of government damage is the "great leap forward" under Mao Zedong in China between 1959 and 1962. Small agricultural collectives were combined to huge communes. There were no longer any private property rights in fields or tools. Therefore, there could no longer be any scarcity prices, nor could there be a rational allocation of resources.[2] Centralized decision-making by cadres educated in Marxism instead of agriculture led to a waste of peasant knowledge and a misallocation of labor in China.[3] Since the material standard of living of Chinese peasants depended on the people's commune instead of their own productivity, there were few incentives to work other than escaping punishment by cadres. As Austrian economists, like Mises or Hayek, would have known, the "great leap forward" turned into a great disaster. More than 40 million people starved to death (Dikötter 2010).

Governments may be challenged and even voted out of office in democracies, but voters are rationally ignorant or worse. In the latter case, they emotionally favor false theories and vote accordingly. That is "why democracies choose bad policies" (Caplan 2007). Given the negligible weight of a single vote in mass democracies, there are no incentives to correct false ideas. Unless one is a dictator, it remains a fact that in politics, one suffers from the errors of others even more than from one's own errors. According to Deutsch (1963, p. 247), one of the main characteristics of powerful people, government officials included, is their ability "not to learn." Being powerful, they are able to resist overcoming false views. Similarly, the German sociologist Dahrendorf (1968, p. 14, my translation)[4] claimed: "Where there is rule or authority, there is error, too."

Overcoming error presupposes that nobody has the power to resist criticism. The opportunity to recognize errors is promoted by decentralized and independent decision-making. If different people work independently and propose how to solve problems, we may find out which solution works best. This is true in academia where competing theoretical ideas are proposed or in the economy where different

---

[1]According to Weber (1922/1964: 1043) in the German original, ein "Monopol legitimer physischer Gewaltsamkeit."

[2]Shortly after Lenin's usurpation of power in Russia, Mises (1920) had already recognized the links between private property in the means of production, scarcity prices, and a rational allocation of resources.

[3]At the end of World War II, Hayek (1945) had built on Mises' insight and declared that a planned economy cannot mobilize the knowledge which is scattered across thousands or millions of heads.

[4]In German, Dahrendorf's statement is: "Wo es Herrschaft gibt, gibt es auch Irrtum."

ways to produce something are the issue. In both cases, decentralized decision-making—whether by academic peers or by consumers and producers in the market—works best. Expanding public decision-making or government has the following effects. As outlined by Hayek (1945, 1960), it makes the mobilization of individual knowledge much less likely. Moreover, collective decision-making is a powerful impediment to innovation. The economic historians Rosenberg and Birdzell (1986, p. 310) made the point very well: "A society which delayed innovations by the amount of time required to reach a political consensus would fall further and further behind a society which did not. . . .It implies the substantive criterion that the benefits of innovation are sufficiently understood and predictable that they can be persuasively verbalized in advance of its adoption—that is that everything is too clear to need the test of experiment." This is a general warning against collective or public decision-making which loses none of its force in democracies. If wrong decisions are legitimized by general acceptance or popularity, correction of errors becomes even more difficult than elsewhere. Then critics need more courage. Then contradiction becomes less likely.

Economic freedom and a capitalist market economy are synonyms. Following Hayek (1961, p. 103) one may justify individual freedom by the insight in the limitation of human knowledge and by hopes for unpredictable progress. It is important that free societies concede to everyone the right to use one's knowledge to one's own benefit or to develop new and conceivably better ideas. As Hayek (1960, p. 71) has pointed out: "Liberty not only means that the individual has both the opportunity and the burden of choice; it also means that he must bear the consequences of his actions and will receive praise or blame for them. Liberty and responsibility are inseparable." A free economy minimizes the need for coercion and consent (Buchanan 1988; Friedman 1962). Although few people are likely to approve of a lot of coercion, there are illusions about the beneficial character of consent. Consent presupposes the necessity to agree with each other and thereby implies some cost. The requirement of consent may repress individualism, innovation, and progress. One should remember Mises' (1944/2007) insights on bureaucracies as enemies of progress, his skepticism about the benefits of rules and regulations. Did they ever contribute to discoveries or inventions?

The basic principle of a capitalist society is that everyone produces whatever she wants. Liberty and entrepreneurship imply the opportunity to mobilize the knowledge which is scattered across thousands or millions of heads (Hayek 1945, 1960). Since knowledge cannot be centralized, capitalist societies are superior to planned economies. By trade one gets from others what one needs. If there are no negative externalities, third persons must not be asked whether they agree or disagree with the trade. A free economy is valuable because it is consistent with human liberty. In principle politics is less valuable, because at best it replaces individual decision-making with political participation. At best, one gets a voice instead of self-determination. Any deviation from the unanimity principle implies that collective decisions may be bad for those individuals who disagree.

2 Econometric Evidence on Economic Freedom

Free market institutes from many counties have collaborated to produce an index of economic freedom which permits quantitative cross-country comparisons between 150 countries (Gwartney et al. 2013). According to the index, an economy is freer, where government revenue and expenditure, including social transfers, are lower, where property rights of individuals and enterprises are safer from government, where markets for goods and labor are less regulated, where governments and central banks do not expropriate citizens by high inflation, and where governments interfere little with free trade across borders. The effects of economic freedom are beneficial. The freer the economy is, the more prosperous a country is, the better the growth rates are, and the higher are the incomes of even the poorest 10% of the population (Gwartney et al. 2013, p. 22). But more economic freedom does *not* imply more inequality of income (Mehlkop 2002; Gwartney et al. 2013, p. 22). One might object against bivariate relationships (like this one) that considering additional determinants of prosperity or growth might affect findings. But the positive impact of economic freedom persists in multivariate analyses (Chauffour 2011; de Haan and Sturm 2000, 2009; Doucouliagos and Ulubasoglu 2006; Farr et al. 1998; Gwartney et al. 2006; Liu 2007; Norton and Gwartney 2008; Vega-Gordillo and Alvarez-Arce 2003; Weede 2006, 2014).

What remains debatable is only whether the level of economic freedom or its improvement has a stronger impact on growth rates and whether the size of government has as strong a negative impact as other deficits in economic freedom. But there are many econometric studies which report negative relationships between government revenues or expenditures or transfer payments on the one hand and prosperity and growth on the other hand, for example, Bergh and Karlsson (2010), Bernholz (1986), Connolly and Li (2014), Poulson and Kaplan (2008), Romer and Romer (2010), Vedder and Robe (2009), and Weede (1986, 1991). The Economist (2013a, p. 16) summarized the relationship by the subsequent rule of thumb: "An increase in tax revenues as a share of GDP of 10 percentage points is usually associated with a drop in annual growth of half to 1 percentage point."[5] It is easy to find reasons why government revenue, expenditure, or welfare payments reduce growth rates. Incentive effects matter. High and progressive taxes undermine incentives. Generous welfare payments reduce the supply of labor. One may rely on welfare instead of work. Even the incentive to teach children to work hard suffers (Lindbeck and Nyberg 2006). Besides, one must not forget that education and social transfers are rivals for limited government budgets. When Germany looked like being in poor shape some years ago, Sinn (2004, p. 43, my translation) made the following comment: "In any case, educational deficits and the economic crises result from a false focus of policies which in the last 30 years expanded social transfers. The welfare state has devoured the means which one might have invested in education, and it has damaged the labor market by producing comfortable alternatives to the job

[5]Of course, there are dissenting views, for example, Lindert (2004).

market." Where economic freedom is weak or absent, structural change or creative destruction (Schumpeter 1942; Gordon 2016; McCloskey 2010, 2016) is slowed down. Economic freedom does not only affect incomes and their growth rate but also individual satisfaction. According to Rode et al. (2013, p. 230), one may summarize: "Economic freedom...not only makes people richer, but it also makes them happier." Astonishingly, this remains true even after controlling for the positive impact of freedom on incomes per capita.

Better still: Economic freedom does not only benefit those who enjoy it but even those who still miss it because of government repression. This also applies in a comparison between rich and poor countries. If rich advanced countries did not exist, then poor countries would not be able to acquire technologies from them and to export their products to rich markets, as East Asians who were still poor 50 years ago have done so successfully. The economic freedom and prosperity of the West turned into the advantages of backwardness for developing countries (Weede 2006, 2012b). These advantages, as assessed by the level of economic development, are among the strongest and most robust determinants of growth rates in cross-national research (Bleaney and Nishiyama 2002; Sala-i-Martin et al. 2004).[6] It is good for poor countries that rich countries exist, even if cross-national income differences are as huge as they are. Otherwise there could be no advantages of backwardness. Globally, there is "trickle down." Actually, one might even refer to a double advantage of backwardness. The first of these advantages refers to the potential for higher growth rates in poor countries than in rich countries. The second one of these advantages refers to the fact that the same real income today buys much lower infant mortalities, better nutrition or cleaner water, and higher life expectancies than it did for the West at an earlier stage of economic development (Becker et al. 2005; Goklany 2007, Chaps. 2 and 3, 409; Kenny 2011). The observable catch-up of the poor in longevity has happened because even the poor in poor countries live longer (Becker et al. 2005). There are even some indications that income inequality between individuals on the globe has been reduced during the last decades.[7]

But there is a definite answer to the question of trends in poverty. Nobel laureate Deaton (2013, p. 1) summarizes his research with these words:

> Life is better now than at almost any time in history. More people are richer and fewer people live in dire poverty. Lives are longer and parents no longer routinely watch a quarter of their children die. Yet millions still experience the horrors of destitution and of premature death.

---

[6]By contrast, the effects of development aid remain questionable (Deaton 2013, p. 15).

[7]It is still debated how the global distribution of income changed in recent decades. If one wants to arrive at some provisional judgment, one may depart from Anand and Segal's (2008, pp. 63–64) compilation and discussion of previous studies. Among those analyses which rely on purchase power corrected data and at least three decades before 2000, six report some decrease but only three some increase in inequality. Empirical research does not support the idea that the poor get poorer, whereas the rich get richer. Instead there are some cues to an egalitarian trend in the global distribution of income, because cross-national differences in average incomes decrease—if nations are weighted by population—even while income inequality within nations increases. Moreover, there is some trend toward the eradication of mass poverty.

> The world is hugely unequal. Inequality is often the consequence of progress. Not everyone gets rich at the same time, and not everyone gets immediate access to the latest life-saving measures. . ..

According to Bourguignon (2015, p. 28ff.), at the beginning of the twentieth century, about 70% of mankind had to survive on 1.25 dollars (2005 purchase power) or less, and at the beginning of the twenty-first century, less than 20% still fall below this poverty threshold. Even Piketty (2015, p. 17), a famous critic of capitalism and capital accumulation in few hands, arrives at the following conclusion about the relative weight of productivity and attendant income growth on the one hand and inequality on the other hand: "Inequality between the top 10% and bottom 10%, as measured by the P90/P10 ratio, is on the order of 3–4, and this is two to three times smaller than the gap in the standard of living between the end of the nineteenth century and the end of the twentieth century and than the gap between the richest and the poorest counties." Or, in between 1870 and 1990, the living standard of the poor (operationally P10) in now rich countries improved much beyond what the living standard of fairly rich people (operationally P90) was at the beginning of the period of observation. In the long run, the speed of productivity growth matters much more for the poor than redistribution does.

3 German Climate Policy

Since the beginning of her government, Angela Merkel felt a special responsibility for global energy and climate policies. In burdening the economy, Merkel is generally supported by the socialist and green parties. Germany intends to simultaneously give up nuclear energy and to become a pioneer in climate protection. Assuming that Merkel and mainstream climate researchers are right in their assumptions that mankind is responsible for climate change and that climate change beyond two degrees will have a strong negative impact on the environment—for a lack of knowledge about the natural sciences, my judgment on this issue should be mistrusted, but as a sociologist, I think that the interdependence between climate scientists and politicians in the Intergovernmental Panel on Climate Change is a threat to the objectivity of the scientific enterprise (Varenholt und Lüning 2012; Weede 2012a)—there still are the following problems. Germans are about 1% of the global population, produce in between 3% and 4% of the global output, and contribute 2.3% to global CO_2 emissions (FAZ 2016c, p. 1). All of these percentages will be falling rather than increasing over time. The capability of such a small country to save the global climate is quite limited. It is more plausible to assume that German restraint in energy consumption and emissions might permit others to emit more. According to Sinn (2012a), this is part of the green paradox. There shall be almost no effect on the global climate. At best a small country like Germany might make other countries imitate a successful energy and climate policy.

To elicit imitation, German energy policy is needed to be so cost-effective that profit-oriented American businesses would follow the German example and that still comparatively poor Asians could afford to follow our example. So far, German policies put a burden of 24 billion euros per year on consumers (FAZ 2016b, p. 17). Even before the cost reached current heights, Lomborg (2013, p. 18, my translation) had summarized the effects under the headline "little effect on the climate for a lot of money." Until 2022 the total cost might sum up to 1 trillion euros (Limburg und Mueller 2015, p. 154). In order to become cost-effective, German energy and climate policy would need to give up its faith in the benefits of planning (Sinn 2012a; Weimann 2014). The most expensive renewable energies should no longer get the highest subsidies. Stability of electrical nets should become a major concern because the intermittent availability of wind or solar energy is already raising big problems (Limburg and Mueller 2015). The trade in emission certificates or a unitary tax on emissions should not be neutralized by a multiplicity of special policies and subsidies. Germany energy policies should not become a disadvantage for German industry compared to America with its shale oil or France with its nuclear energy. If the world is to be saved from climate change, there is no alternative to American and Chinese leadership because these nations emit a lot more than we do. This remains true even after the election of Donald Trump as American president. Better insight on part of the German chancellor who had been trained as a physicist does not change this reality. Without some economic insights and some cost awareness, German climate policy cannot avoid failure. Politics needs to remain the art of the possible. Wishful thinking is to be resisted.

4 Rescuing the Euro

The establishment of the Euro was a political project. The Bundesbank (German central bank), many German economists (e.g., Starbatty 2013), and some Anglo-Saxon economists, too (Feldstein 1997, 2012; Niskanen 2008), remained skeptical about the details and the execution of the plan to introduce a common European currency. Long before the project was even planned, there were prescient warnings. Whereas many contemporary politicians talk as if "more Europe" were always a good idea, Röpke (1979) warned against a bureaucratic greater Europe. Röpke (1979, p. 155) insisted that the limitation of government power or sovereignty was much more important than its transfer from European nation-states to a higher or union level. Hayek (1978b/2006, p. 133) did not believe in the 1970s that a European currency union might come into existence, but he had pointed out the risks coming with such a move. Some countries would get worse money than they had before. One might object that the Euro suffers no higher inflation rates than the Deutsche Mark (DM) before. This is true. But the DM also performed well when the Anglo-Saxon economies suffered significantly higher inflation rates. Whether the Euro will outperform the Anglo-Saxons in difficult times remains to be seen. According to Hayek, countries with a common currency might suffer from the "crude prejudices" or "follies" of others. Since the Euro was firmly based on mostly implicit illusions, this is what happened. The first illusion was that the weaker economies could live without devaluations against the German currency and remain competitive. There was an expectation of convergence instead of divergence within the common currency zone. The second illusion was that differences in the economic philosophies of nations did not matter, not even the fundamentally divergent views of the French and the Germans (Brunnermeier et al. 2016).[8] A third illusion was that treaties are self-enforcing or, at least, honored. Remember that the treaties include provisions about maximum budget deficits and debt burdens as well as prohibitions of monetary financing and bailing out other countries.

Since 2010, saving the Euro, or keeping every country which currently is part of the Eurozone in it, became one of the main items on Angela Merkel's policy agenda. Greece is not the only country which finds it hard to live with the Euro, but the most extreme case. Countries which had weak currencies and multiple devaluations for decades should never have entered a currency union with stronger economies like Germany that boasted a hard currency and experienced upward revaluations. For some years Greece enjoyed low interest rates and a credit binge. Possibly, even the government did no longer know the size of the deficit and the debt burden. In the long run, however, it proved impossible for a country with a relatively less advanced economy to enjoy the standard of living of advanced countries. Greece had lost its competitiveness. Since Greece was part of the Eurozone, it could not regain it by devaluation.

Without an external devaluation one has to regain competitiveness by a cruel process of internal devaluation, i.e., cuts in prices, wages, and employment. Despite having received billions of Euros, the Greek debt mountain grows. Including promised, but not yet paid out credits, the support for Greece amounts to 400 billion euros or 230% of Greek GDP (Sarrazin 2016, p. 238). Comparing this to aid for Germany after the war by the European Recovery Program and taking the different sizes of the countries and their economies into account Sinn (2016, p. 243) estimates that the country has received 36 times as much aid as Germany did after the war. Nevertheless, the Greek economy has suffered a depression and youth unemployment is close to 50%.

Although the Eurozone at its current unsustainable size has been rescued so far, creditor nations suffer from becoming responsible for other nations' debts. One may regard such a policy as a kind of European welfare policy. But the welfare policy did not improve the Greek economy and devastated the prospects of young Greeks. It benefited those private investors who were either foolhardy enough to believe that Greece can pay back its credits or cynical enough to not believe in the no-bailout clause in Maastricht treaty. Admittedly, some private investors suffered a haircut, i.e., they did not get all of their capital back and the contracted interest rate on top of

[8]Pointing to differences in French and German views about monetary and fiscal policies in no way implies that these views are permanent. There have been periods in history when the French views were more liberal and German views were more statist than they currently are.

it. Nevertheless, the politicians who "saved the Euro" and kept Greece within the Eurozone rescued them from a worse haircut. By now, almost all of the private creditors of Greece have been replaced by public creditors. Experts disagree about the risks for the German taxpayer from bailing out Greece, because the risks are not transparent and scattered over target balances, rescue funds, and the European central bank. Sarrazin (2016, p. 240) estimates that the burden on Germany may approach 750 billion euros for all the policies which benefit Greece and the other debtor economies. This is more than twice the German federal budget. Sinn's (2016, p. 232) estimate of 450 billion euros being at risk for Germany is somewhat lower but still about one and a half times the central government budget.

In order to increase the German readiness to pay, it is argued that Germany benefitted a lot from the Euro (Marsh 2013). Sarrazin (2012), however, points out that the entire Eurozone did not grow faster than EU members with their own currencies outside of the Eurozone. Step by step he looks at criteria—such as trends in employment and unemployment or GDP per capita—and finds no evidence that Germany benefitted from the Euro. He observes that the share of German exports going to Euro countries is receding. The balance sheet looks quite different for the Mediterranean countries. The Greek predicament is merely part of a wider story. The currency union became a trap for these countries. Prices and costs of production rose faster than in Germany. Whereas Germany experienced a real devaluation of 21% between 1995 and 2007, the Mediterranean crisis economies and Ireland revalued upward in between 14% and 27% (Sinn 2012b, p. 107). Since the common currency ruled out devaluations, competitiveness was lost. According to Goldman Sachs, Italy might have needed a devaluation of 10–15%, France and Spain of 20%, Greece of 30%, and Portugal of 35% already half a decade ago (Sinn 2012b, p. 110). In Ireland or in the Baltic countries, internal devaluations worked, but in the Mediterranean countries and France, wages and prices are inflexible downward.[9] Finally, there is the dilemma that falling prices and wages might contribute to reestablishing competitiveness but simultaneously make the accumulated debt burden even less bearable (The Economist 2013c, p. 70).

Given the poor competitiveness of Southern Europe and their inability to restore competitiveness by devaluations, Sarrazin's (2012) book title "*Europe Does Not Need the Euro*" (my translation) might be an understatement. Instead the implication of his analysis should read: "Europe cannot stand the Euro." Mediterranean deficits are financed by dynamically growing Target2 balances, i.e., the German Bundesbank (central bank) has claims against the Euro system, whereas many other central banks have liabilities with it. Nobody seems to know whether when

[9] If Bhalla's (2012) econometrically well-supported proposition is true that overvalued currencies contribute to poor growth rates but undervalued currencies contribute to good growth rates, then the Mediterranean countries did much harm to themselves by entering a currency union with Germany. According to Blinder (2013, p. 419), one may summarize the effect on Greece and similar countries by saying: "Eurozone membership became a one-way ticket to a deep, long-lasting recession." According to Sinn (2012b, p. 123), there is no viable alternative to leaving the Euro, if Greece and Portugal want to regain competitiveness.

and how these imbalances will be corrected. Political visionaries overlook the problem. Experts (most of all: Hans-Werner Sinn 2012b) worry. Whereas Americans, Chinese, and Russian pay for German exports, it is not clear whether Greeks, Spaniards, Italians, and possibly even the French ever deliver an equivalent value to Germany.

I do not want to tell the story of rescuing the Euro in detail but focus on the principles. Before 2010, Europeans who failed to succeed in the market economy could only rely on the support of the fellow citizens because of national welfare states. Since politicians everywhere financed part of the welfare state by debt instead of current taxation, the burden was shared by living taxpayers as well as by the not-yet-voting generation destined to inherit a debt burden. In the future, Europeans in need may also rely on the support of taxpayers in richer or better governed countries. Given the well-grounded fears about the sustainability of national welfare states in aging societies, it is not obvious that building a second or European floor of the welfare state makes sense. Fiscal rectitude is punished, and a lack of it is reinforced—or should one say "rewarded"?—by generating a moral claim for support by others. Perverse incentives prevail. Even Slovakia, a poorer country than Greece, has been asked to contribute to rescuing Greece. European politicians act as if rewarding a lack of achievements and fiscal failure were a valuable principle. European politicians want to enforce fiscal stabilization by this perverse reinforcement schedule. Already at the end of the nineteenth century, the British sociologist Herbert Spencer (1891, p. 354) knew better: "The ultimate result of shielding men from the effects of folly, is to fill the world with fools."

Rescuing the Euro did not only rely on illusions and perverse incentives; it also maximized obscurity or minimized transparency. If nations or their governments want to assist each other, the most transparent way of aid would have been give-aways rather than credits to states that look like poor risks. But governments chose credits. Probably, there would have been too much political resistance against giveaways in the donor countries. Moreover, governments chose to rely on a multiplicity of channels for assistance, including Target2 balances, rescue funds, purchases of government bonds by the European central bank, the Outright Monetary Transactions (OMT) program—which has been compared to a free credit default insurance by an eminent economist (Sinn 2016, p. 149)—and emergency liquidity assistance. For Greece, there have been three programs until fall 2016. From the beginning, politicians always tried to generate the impression that the current program would be the last one needed. When the sustainability of Greek debt was questioned, governments did not rely on a transparent haircut but chose a less transparent way to assist Greece: lower interest rates and much longer payback periods which are less transparent but equivalent. A lack of transparency is an attempt by governments to hide from voters what they are doing.

The Euro has become a negative-sum game where more is lost than won. The Mediterranean crisis economies, even France, have lost the option of devaluation and find it hard or impossible to regain competitiveness. Germany has no problems with the external value of the Euro, but it becomes ever more responsible for other nation's debt burden. Moreover, German savers suffer from the low, or zero, or even negative interest rate policy of the European Central Bank. German savers suffer from a slow process of expropriation. After taxes and inflation, the interest rate on safe assets is negative. According to Sinn's (2016, pp. 182–184) estimate, German losses from the low interest rate policy of the European Central Bank may add up to 326 billion euros up to 2015 and the benefit to the crisis countries to 382 billion. There has to be some difference between these numbers, because countries like the Netherlands shared the burden. Under such conditions middle class people can no longer save for their old age. They have to depend on the government—Röpke (1979, p. 137, my translation) called this the "nationalization of men"—i.e., on a shrinking cohort of young taxpayers who have also been burdened with a lot of national as well as fellow European debt. But the damage done by the Euro is even larger than the Eurozone itself. That is why a former chief economist and later governor of the Bank of England (King 2016) suggested that a German exit from the Eurozone might be a lesser evil than the current policies.

In practice, saving the Euro has turned into a permanent excuse for expanding politics, government, and bureaucratic regulation at the expense of the spontaneous order of the market. Essential incentives to work and to economize—in short, the public interest—are lost. Instead the special interests of those, who receive subsidies or transfers, and of politicians prevails, who want to run the show. Serving special interests necessarily implies ever less transparent laws and regulations. Even in the United States which is lagging Europe in establishing big government and the welfare state, a prominent legal scholar (Epstein 1995, p. IX, 14) bemoaned: "There is too much law and too many lawyers." A few pages later, he continues: "We try to solve more and more problems through legal intervention, and fewer through voluntary accommodation and informal practices." Top-down regulation replaces private contracts enforced by government and the courts.

The problem is neither new nor limited to Anglo-Saxon countries. Röpke (1958/2009, p. 45, my translation), too, warned against "taking refuge to bureaucratic regulation whenever a problem comes up." Why too much legal regulation is a problem in the market economy has been best explained by Mises. Mises (1944/2007, p. 34) sees the difference between officials and entrepreneurs in the bureaucrat's interest "to comply with the rules and regulations, no matter whether they are reasonable or contrary to what was intended." In the economy the purpose is to make a profit. Given competitive markets this is only possible by serving consumers. Innovation is an important means to increase profit. Following Mises (1944/2007, p. 56), one should regard progress as "precisely that which the rules and regulations did not foresee." The less transparent law becomes for non-lawyers, the less it may tell entrepreneurs something about the legal consequences of their actions. Except for patent law and the protection of intellectual property, laws are more likely to prevent than to promote innovation. Opaque law is one of the main obstacles for start-ups and productivity growth. The lack of political interest in the simplification of laws and regulations is nicely illustrated by the contemptuous disregard of all parties represented in parliament of the suggestions to simplify tax laws coming from a tax lawyer and former supreme judge at the constitutional court (Kirchhof 2011).

Obviously, the law is no solution to social or political problems if it is not observed. As far as the European growth and stability pact is concerned, compliance has been rare. According to Sinn (2012b, p. 84, my translation), "Until 2011 the deficit threshold had been passed 120 times, but only in 37 instances this was permitted because of sufficiently bad recessions. In 83 instances there should have been sanctions." But sanctions were never applied. Similarly, the no-bailout principle and the prohibition of central bank financing of government debt were disregarded, too. It is hard to see why European politicians can still believe that legal agreement can help to overcome the current European predicament. Better than new agreements which are unlikely to be respected, as we know from experience, would be a return to the original agreements and a serious determination to respect them in the future.

The future of Western democracies is likely to depend on their capability to find a noninflationary way out for their overregulated and graying welfare states which are overburdened by debt.[10] Without re-implementing the principles of responsibility for oneself and liability for the consequences of one's actions and without giving up rewarding mistakes in the name of solidarity, there is no positive future for Europe. Neither legal formality nor democratic majorities suffice to protect one from the effects of perverse incentives and counterproductive decisions. The most important means for limiting inefficient and superfluous government action as well as preventing serious political errors is competition, including tax competition, between governments at all levels: local, state or canton, national or federal, and global (Blankart 2007; Brauckhoff 2012; Feld et al. 2005; Weede 2012b). Of course, competing governments should avoid reducing the tax burden while simultaneously increasing debt financing. Greece and the other weak economies of the Eurozone demonstrate that such a course of action does not work in the long run. Unfortunately, current policies seem to lead us toward more centralization of political decision-making in Europe rather than competition and "market-preserving federalism" (Weingast 1995).

Current debts tend to result in higher taxes or inflation tomorrow. Attempts to "starve the beast," i.e., pressure for expenditure reduction by previous tax cuts, did not work, at least in the short run (Niskanen 2006). Although one still may stick to the view that "starve the beast" might work with some lag in the long run (Tempelman 2006), in the current government debt crisis, we simply do not have the time to build up pressure for expenditure cuts by increasing deficits. Many Western democracies are close to 100% government debt (relative to GDP). High debt burdens are correlated with reduced growth rates (Reinhart and Rogoff 2011). Since expenditure cuts are more effective in denationalizing the economy, balancing the books, and promoting growth (Alesina and Giavazzi 2006; Schulemann 2012),

[10]Of course, the government debt crisis has also been affected by the previous financial crisis (Reinhart and Rogoff 2009). For the United States, Lazear (2012) estimates that decreasing government revenue and increasing expenditure during the crisis contributed about equally to the growth of debt. On risk of inflation, see Hayek (1978b/2006) and Bernholz (2003).

common European liability for debts is a mistake and a giant step forward on Hayek's (1944/1994) "Road to Serfdom."

5 An Open Door to Migration

In energy policy or rescuing the Euro, the Merkel government was never concerned with pursuing the interests of German voters and taxpayers. Instead the focus was on benefiting a much wider constituency: mankind in energy policy or other Europeans in supporting the euro. The issues of cost or cost-effectiveness were consistently sidelined. Asylum, refugee, and migration policy again was driven by global instead of national concerns, again with little concern for cost and cost-effectiveness. In essence, an open door implies establishing a third floor of the welfare state.[11] Concerning migration from poor into rich societies, widely desired goals—like better living standards for poor people on the one hand and stability, prosperity, and the welfare state in rich societies on the other hand—may be incompatible with each other. On the one hand, the elimination of obstacles to global migration could do *much more* for the poor than eliminating the remaining obstacles to international trade or capital flows (Clemens 2011). On the other hand, multiculturalism and the generosity of the welfare state increase residential segregation and migrant overrepresentation in prisons but reduce labor market participation (Koopmans 2010).

Nearly a million poor migrants claiming asylum or refugee status were accepted by Germany in 2015. In countries close to Europe, millions of people are threatened by civil war, poverty, or even hunger. It is certainly desirable to help them. Nevertheless, one has to raise the issue whether global charity—according to Merkel, without an upper limit—should be a task of governments. I do not want to discuss this issue from a legal point but merely point out that our British or French neighbors who share our humanitarian values and legal commitments confronted the migration crisis of 2015 quite differently. They were defensive and restrictive. Moreover, one could raise the question whether humanitarian obligations go as far as neglecting legitimate national interests. Does Germany have to take lots of people with no or extremely weak qualifications for the labor market, even if this absorption raises the risk of terror attacks and reduces social and political stability? Does Germany have to take more refugees than the much bigger rest of Europe put together, including Britain, France, Italy, and Spain? Should we forget that the British decided to leave the European Union after the Merkel government lost control of German borders in 2015 and thereby demonstrated to the British what risks are inherent in the European Union? The humanitarian refugee policy of the Merkel government might even undermine the cohesion of the West. The new

[11]Remember the first floor is the national welfare state and the second floor is redistribution within the Eurozone.

American president, Donald Trump, has not advocated open borders for Muslim refugees and underlined his duty to serve America first.

European welfare states are aging societies. Because of the depth of its demographic crises, much of the following discussion will focus on Germany. But many other European countries are affected by similar problems. It is almost impossible to prevent the ratio of the elderly to the working age population from doubling in the next few decades in Germany (Birg 2015). Therefore, it looks plausible to close the demographic gap with those mostly young people who clamor for access to European welfare states. The needs of aging European economies and the needs of would-be immigrants knocking at our doors seem to complement each other. There is an abundance of young people in the Muslim world and even more so in Africa. Since income per head in many African countries is about 150 €, whereas it is about 3000 € in the richer European countries (Piketty 2014, p. 64), many young Africans will be attracted, even if European growth rates remain low.

Chain migration is a reason why mass migration to Europe is likely to persist or even to accelerate.[12] The more people from some poor country have already settled in a rich country, the more their relatives, friends, and neighbors are tempted to follow them. Chain migration therefore implies that an open door today leads to more claims for access by other migrants tomorrow. Simultaneously, chain migration retards integration, because immigrants live closely together, even in ethnic ghettoes, for economic reasons, like cheap rents, as well as for reasons of preference, in order to live together with kindred people where at least non-working people do not even need to learn the official language of the host country.

It is easy to imagine how immigration might solve the problems of aging societies. Our immigrants would be mostly highly qualified people who earn a lot and happily pay their taxes and social insurance contributions.[13] So far, the balance sheet of migration to Germany looks quite different. According to an official government report (Beauftragte der Bundesregierung 2014, pp. 16–17, 30, 102–103), only 5.4% of German students, but 11.6% of foreign students, do not finish high school (Hauptschule), 13.5% of young people (20–29 years old) in Germany have insufficient vocational training, but among foreigners, the percentage rises to 30.5%. Whereas among nonmigrants the risk of poverty in Germany has been 12.3%, among migrants the risk was 26.8%. From 2008 to 2013, unemployment ratios

[12]Chain migration and the establishment of ghettoes are related problems. For immigrants the costs of adjustment and adaptation are lowered by chain migration and ghettoes. So is the speed of integration. Large diasporas increase migration flows and reduce language skills, educational level, and integration (Beine et al. 2011; van Tubergen and Kalmijn 2005). Where relatives, acquaintances, and neighbors from Anatolia or Kurdistan live in the same part of the city where one ends up, there is little need to learn German. If Turks had immigrants from China or Brazil as neighbors, i.e., people to whom they are not related by language, religion, customs, or habits, then the pressure for integration might be nearly as strong as if they lived among Germans. So, from the point of view of host societies, chain migration into diasporas is highly undesirable.

[13]Becker and Posner (2009, pp. 37–42) suggested how one might get the immigrants which developed economies need. One of them suggested selling immigration rights and the other one intelligence testing.

among foreigners have been at least twice as high as among Germans. If one focuses on testing instead of schooling data, the result is similar: The cognitive competence of immigrant students is much below the cognitive competence of native students in Germany (Rindermann and Thompson 2016, pp. 72–74).

There have been empirical studies which argued that migration has been good for Germany, but following Sinn (2014, p. 18), it has to be pointed out that these findings depend on attributing general government cost (including administration, justice, the police, or defense) only to the native population but excluding recent immigrants. If these burdens are attributed to the entire population, then migrants before the great wave of 2015 imposed a burden somewhere in between of 700 and 2400 € per year on the German taxpayer or about 79,000 € during their lifetime. There are much higher estimates for recent migrants who are likely to find employment only after years of receiving support from the taxpayer. According to Raffelhüschen and Sinn (FAZ 2016a, p. 15, Sinn 2016, p. 121), lifetime expenses for the one million refugees who came to Germany in 2015 might be as much as 450,000 € per head more than they are likely to pay in taxes and social insurance contributions or a 450 billion euros burden on the German taxpayer for a million new arrivals.[14] Merkel's welcome to refugees and claimants for asylum in 2015 is equivalent to adding 15% of GDP to the German public debt.

It is inconceivable to rescue government finances or social security systems in aging Germany by the type of immigration which we actually had in the recent past. In its discussion of a study published by the OECD, The Economist (2013b, pp. 64–65) has pointed out that the fiscal balance of immigration into Germany is worse than any other place considered there. Whereas every second immigrant into Britain in 2009–2010 had earned an academic degree, the corresponding ratio in Germany was one in five. Whereas 10% of the migrants to Britain in 2008 belonged to the highest income decile, this applied to only about 4% of the migrants in Germany. According to these criteria, immigrants into France were also better qualified than immigrants into Germany (The Economist 2012, p. 50).

It is deplorable that the migrants who actually come to Germany and some other European welfare states do not bring along the cognitive capabilities or knowledge capital to contribute significantly to prosperity and growth in their destination country (Rindermann and Thompson 2016, pp. 72–74, 87). According to econometric research, cognitive or human capital is a major determinant of economic growth rates (Hanushek and Woessmann 2015; Weede 2004).[15] If migrants bring

[14]Sinn (2016, pp. 121–123) also discusses some lower estimates but points out that—in his view—all estimates are likely to target the lower bound rather than the upper bound of costs to the German taxpayer. That is why I chose to represent the highest of these lower bound estimates as a reasonable expectation.

[15]In measuring cognitive or human capital, one should rely on test data instead of information about the duration of schooling. One needs output measures instead of input measures. It is less important whether one applies intelligence tests or tests about mathematical reasoning or natural science knowledge. If one uses IQ measures, this does not necessitate taking any view in the debate about nature and nurture or inheritance and environment. In our context the effects of human capabilities matter, not the debate about the causes of these capabilities.

little human capital along, they must be a burden on host societies. It is hardly conceivable that home countries which suffer from poverty, political instability, civil war, or repression educate their emigrants in such a way that they become easily employable in more highly developed countries. A much more plausible proposition is that the poorer a source country of migration is, the less qualified its migrants are for a job in a more highly developed economy. This suspicion is reinforced if technological change is likely to threaten not only jobs which require little qualification and training but is likely to affect more and more middle-level jobs, too, if "average is over" as has been predicted by some eminent economists (Cowen 2013; Gordon 2016, p. 615). Worse still, migration itself always implies some devaluation of the human capital of migrants, if they do not sufficiently command the language of the host country.

Migration into the social safety net necessarily raises tax burdens for the host society and implies some reduction of economic freedom. As pointed out above, economic freedom is another determinant of economic growth rates. High government revenues and expenditures decrease economic freedom, in particular of high-income earners and taxpayers and thereby economic growth rates. Property rights might become less safe in future. If and when most immigrants find a job, then one should also expect distributional consequences. The affluent are likely to benefit, while the indigenous poor are likely to suffer from immigrant competition (Borjas 1996). A reinforcement of distributional conflict is likely to reduce the security of property rights and economic freedom.

Inspired by a British researcher on Africa, poverty, and migration, Paul Collier (2013), one should ask whether mass immigration affects the institutional basis of Western societies and their prosperity.[16] If there are differences in social expectations, habits, and informal norms of indigenous people and migrants, then one has to face the question how much diversity a society can stand. A characteristic of foreigners is that they simply cannot know the social norms of their host society as well as the natives. Sometimes the norms they bring along even contradict the norms of the host society.[17] Whether and how much immigrants endanger the cohesion of host societies depends on the similarity of social norms between source and target countries of the migration process. The religious heritage of nations influences social norms—possibly even after many people have become agnostics. Therefore, it is plausible to propose that immigration by Christians imposes less of a burden on European host societies than Muslim immigration.

In general, cultural heterogeneity is a burden. Willingness to assimilate matters, too. As the editor of a weekly German paper, Josef Joffe (according to Huntington 2004, p. 191), has pointed out: "People came to America because they wanted to become Americans. The Turks do not come to Germany because they want to

[16]Already in a previous book, Collier (2009, p. 58) had pointed out: "Public services are systematically worse as a result of ethnic diversity among citizens." Whereas ethnic diversity is no barrier to big government, it seems to make effective government less likely.

[17]According to the Economist (2007, p. 63), many young Muslims are more radical in their rejection of Western values than their immigrant parents. Among British Muslims in between 16 and 24, 39% agreed that rejection of Islam deserves the death penalty.

become Germans." A similar skepticism might apply to Syrians or Eritreans who currently come to Germany in large numbers.[18] As Huntington (2004, p. 14) has pointed out in his discussion of waves of immigration into America, previous migrations and current migrations differ in a way which makes assimilation more difficult and slow: "As a result of modern communications and transportation, these migrants have been able to remain part of their original culture and community. Their identity is thus less that of migrants than of diasporans, that is, members of a trans-national, trans-state cultural community." As Putnam (2007) has pointed out, diversity may also reduce the social capital of nations.

Indian and Chinese immigrants to the United States tend to be better educated than other Americans and enjoy better incomes than white Americans. As Huntington (2004, p. 298) recognized, they integrate easily: "Even more dramatically than previous European ethnic groups, Asian Americans are 'becoming white' because they have. . .. brought with them values emphasizing work, discipline, learning, thrift, strong families, and in the case of Filipinos and Indians a knowledge of English." More than half of all natural scientists and engineers with a Ph.D. in America have been born abroad (Kapur and McHale 2005, p. 208). It is possible to benefit from immigration, if the door is widely open for talent, but firmly closed for poor people with little education. In order to benefit from immigration, one needs the courage to choose. In Germany or Sweden, immigrants only choose the host country.[19] Nobody dares to ask how immigrants are likely to affect the host society, its institutions and individual freedom, and its prosperity and growth prospects. As long as more of them are a fiscal burden than big taxpayers, as long as mass immigration by refugees forces politicians to consider infringing private property rights in order to house them, and as long as cultural heterogeneity incites governments to pass anti-discrimination laws which necessarily abridge the freedom of contract, individual liberty and economic freedom of the native population are reduced.

Besides, one has also to consider the impact of cultural—i.e., linguistic, ethnic, and/or religious—heterogeneity on political stability (Collier 2009, p. 130; Fiala and Skaperdas 2011; Gat and Yakobson 2013, p. 290; Gubler and Selway 2012; Leeson and Williamson 2011; Logan and Preble 2011; von der Mehden 1973; Wegenast and Basedau 2014). The impact of cultural cleavages is reinforced if these cleavages overlap with class cleavages. Since "a stagnant or, worse, decreasing population increases the influence of capital accumulated in previous generations" (Piketty 2014, p. 84, 233, 421), this is likely to happen in Europe. Indigenous daughters or sons are likely to inherit a lot from their parents, whereas multiple children from poor immigrants will inherit next to nothing. Cultural heterogeneity is increased by mass

[18]Identification of immigrants with the new home country is important because it affects the inclination to make illegal claims on the welfare state. According to Heinemann (2008), patriotism makes such claims less likely. Unfortunately, it is hardly conceivable that immigrants arrive as patriots of the destination country.

[19]The generosity of state benefits for refugees makes claiming asylum in Germany much more attractive than claiming it elsewhere. Benefits are more than 50% higher in Germany than in Britain or even Sweden, more than four times as high as in Hungary (The Economist 2015b, pp. 21–23).

immigration. Consider the fate of the former Yugoslavia with its Catholic Croats, Orthodox Serbs, and Muslims in Kosovo or Bosnia. Or think of Syria or Iraq with Sunni Muslims, Shias, Alawites, Yazidis, and Christians, Arabs, and Kurds. Or think of Nigeria with its Haussas, Ibos, Yorubas, and many smaller ethnicities, with Muslims in the north and Christians in the south. Or consider Pakistan with its politically dominant Punjabis, but before 1971 Bengalis in the East, or currently rebellious Balochs in the West. Even in the United States, it is hard to overlook persistent tensions between black and white. In Northern Ireland, there still are tensions between Protestants and Catholics. According to Gat (Gat and Yakobson 2013, p. 312) ethnic homogeneity matters, or "hardly any nation exists based solely or even mainly on political allegiance to state and constitution." Does it make sense to increase heterogeneity by permitting mass immigration? In order to evaluate the coming degree of cultural heterogeneity, one should not look at the proportion of immigrants or foreigners in the population but among children. Among children below the age of ten in Germany, already about a third have some migratory background (Beauftragte der Bundesregierung 2014, p. 364).

Even without the currently accelerating mass immigration, it has been obvious for some time that Germany will radically change in the next decades. The Economist (2010, p. 4) characterized the German prospect with these words: "The newcomers are not as well educated as the native Germans, but they have more babies. .... In some towns in the Ruhr region the share of the under-fives with migrant backgrounds tops 60%. Overall, they account for a third of the youngest children. By mid-century half of the population will have non-German origins...By then Germany will be a different sort of place." The problem applies more generally to Western and Central Europe. The prognosis for Britain is similar to the one for Germany. In the middle of the twenty-first century, one third of the British population will no longer be "white" (The Economist 2015a, p. 31). Note that the scenario for Germany was developed without anticipation of the immigration wave in 2015. What this new wave might imply has been pointed out by Sarrazin (2016, p. 214). He assumed that every refugee or other migrants might later bring a spouse or other relatives to Germany and that they might have three children. He further assumed that in future there will only be 200,000 new migrants—this number had already been passed in fall for 2016 and had been proposed by the Bavarian CSU but rejected by chancellor Merkel—and then the new migrant population is likely to be 12 million in 2030 and more than 22 million until 2040. Is it possible to integrate all these people on top of the previously arrived migrants?

One should regard European (or Western) institutions as valuable, because Europe and the West established economic freedom first, because economic freedom was a prerequisite of overcoming mass poverty and multiplying incomes per head anywhere between a factor of 16 (McCloskey 2010) and 30 (McCloskey 2016),[20]

[20]On the rise of the West or the European miracle, see also Acemoglu and Robinson (2012), Jones (1981), Landes (1998), North et al. (2009), Pipes (1999), Rosenberg and Birdzell (1986), and Weede (2012b). Most of the authors underline the importance of economic freedom and safe

and because Western prosperity benefits poor countries by giving them the advantages of backwardness. One may well ask "can Europe be the same with different people in it?" (Caldwell 2009). If humanitarian migration policies endanger political liberty and economic freedom in Europe and if mass immigration makes European countries ripe for political instability, lack of economic growth, or even civil war, then the price might become high, for both natives and their uninvited guests who arrive at Europe's gates and clamor for access. Preventing mass migration from poor and war-ravaged countries becomes ever more difficult because of chain migration.

6 Final Conclusions

At least, if one adds government promises to its officials, pensioners, and the ill and other needy persons, then the German government is already indebted with a multiple of its GDP. One also has to consider that the working population of Germany is destined to decrease. There is little reason to hope that immigration will solve Germany's demographic problems. According to Merz (2004, p. 74), much immigration went into social safety net. This is likely to continue. Therefore, the debt burden per working and income tax paying person has to rise a lot unless payments to the aged and unhealthy are cut dramatically. This has been known for a long time (Merz 2004, 2008; Metzger 2003; Prewo 1996).

Government debt and the potential but dramatic increase of it by taking over liability for debt of other Eurozone countries are burdens and risks. Of course, all estimates about the size of the burden, its distribution on victims, and dates, when liability might become debt, are clouded with uncertainty. Some time ago Goldman Sachs estimated German liabilities for Eurozone debt to be 949 billion euros, whereas the damage from the dissolution of the Eurozone for Germany might be 800 billion euros (FAZ 2013, p. 23). We seem to have a choice between terror without end or an end with terror (see Krämer 2013; Marsh 2013). So far, it is hard to avoid the impression that it might get more expensive over time, that the costly project of saving the Euro may nevertheless fail, and that we still might have to face the costs of a breakdown of the Eurozone. Already now Germany confronts the prospect of slow growth, not only for demographic reasons and because of the existence of a tax and welfare state. Moreover, Germany faces increasing heterogeneity of its population and possibly social, religious, and political tensions resulting from it. Inside the German government as well as outside of Germany, the economic power of Germany is much overestimated. The possibility to improve the fiscal policies of the European crisis states by legal means is also much exaggerated. Here,

property rights. Mc Closkey plays down the role of property rights and refers to "habits of the lip" or equal rights to work on one's material betterment. In my view, these differences should not be exaggerated and may be reconciled under the label of economic freedom. Of course, there are some radically different interpretations of global economic history and the rise of capitalism (Hobson 2004; Pomeranz 2000).

I agree with the Czech central banker Hampl (2010) who treats the Euro itself as a kind of instability pact. Rescuing the Euro is likely to result in a catastrophic overburdening of future generations living in Germany and other donor economies. The two ways of transferring debt—from the voting generation to the next one, from country to country within the Eurozone—will seriously challenge the legitimacy of European democracies. An inefficient climate policy of a comparatively small country with a decreasing demographic and economic weight in the world is more likely to contribute to overburdening the German economy than to save the climate, too.

Exclusive property rights are the basis of civilization, certainly of Western civilization, of economic freedom in the West. Without property rights, there are few incentives to work hard, no scarcity prices on markets, and no mobilization of decentralized knowledge. Property rights are something more than claims or possessions. They are respected by others, by rulers, and by authorities. Property rights and the law are more likely to enjoy general respect, if they fit with the habits and informal norms of a society, with traditions (Hayek 1960). Mass immigration has to endanger traditions—the more culturally distant the immigrants are, the more so. Any society which welcomes masses of people who need protection and claim access endangers itself. Rich societies need fortified boundaries as barriers to entry (Hassner and Wittenberg 2015).

Inspired by Hayek, we have to consider the limits of government. Since Western welfare states appropriated the task of guaranteeing the material welfare of their people, government size as well as government debt has grown rapidly (Tanzi 2013). If Western welfare states, like Germany or Sweden, now take over the task of assisting hungry and homeless refugees from almost everywhere, then government must expand further and economic freedom must become ever more restricted. This process of expanding the duties of government from one's own people to foreigners has begun with development aid. Inspired by Hayek, one should raise the question whether government knowledge ever can be sufficient to take over responsibility for the global mitigation of human suffering (Easterly 2014). No one can seriously argue that government enjoys a comparative advantage over private organizations in the provision of charity.

Some free market economists have always known this and even had a prescient feeling for future challenges. Long before the current mass migration from other civilizations into Europe, Röpke (1979, p. 199, my translation) anticipated its incompatibility with the preservation of our civilization, and he insisted: "Any country needs the right to protect its intellectual and political tradition against immigrants who are incapable of assimilation or might undermine its traditions by their sheer mass." Since Röpke (1979, pp. 207–208) also knew that the welfare state and open borders are incompatible, he asserted the right *and duty* of nations to protect themselves against unwanted mass immigration. He did not advocate the expansion of government duties to include global charity. Already in the nineteenth century, Mill perceived a link between national identity which is ultimately ethnically based and democratic self-government (Mill 1862/1977, p. 547; also Gat and Yakobson 2013, p. 249). Conceivably, open doors to migrants undermine not only prosperity but also democracy. German politicians handle the migration flows irrespective of the needs of the labor market. German climate policies disregard the costs. Although no one has even a plan for rapidly graying Germany to pay back its own debt before a wave of pensioners makes it ever less possible, the German government makes a declining economy assume some liability for other people's debts. One gets the impression that many politicians take the size of the burden they place on taxpayers, consumers, and future generations as an indicator of their own greatness and importance.

References

Acemoglu, D., & Robinson, J. A. (2012). *Why nations fail. The origins of power, prosperity, and poverty*. New York: Crown Business.

Albert, H. (1988). *Kritik der reinen Erkenntnislehre*. Tübingen: Mohr Siebeck.

Alchian, A. A. (1950). Uncertainty, evolution, and economic theory. *Journal of Political Economy, 58*(3), 211–221.

Alesina, A., & Giavazzi, F. (2006). *The future of Europe*. Cambridge, MA: MIT Press.

Anand, S., & Segal, P. (2008). What do we know about global inequality? *Journal of Economic Literature, 46*(1), 57–94.

Beauftragte der Bundesregierung für Migration, Flüchtlinge und Integration. (2014). *Zehnter Bericht über die Lage der Ausländerinnen und Ausländer in Deutschland*. Berlin: Bundesregierung.

Becker, G. S., & Posner, R. (2009). *Uncommon sense*. Chicago, IL: University of Chicago Press.

Becker, G., Philipson, T. J., & Soares, R. R. (2005). The quantity and quality of life and the evolution of world inequality. *American Economic Review, 91*, 277–291.

Beine, M., Docquier, F., & Özden, C. (2011). Diasporas. *Journal of Development Economics, 95* (1), 30–41.

Bergh, A., & Karlsson, M. (2010). Government size and growth: Accounting for economic freedom and globalization. *Public Choice, 142*(1–2), 195–213.

Bernholz, P. (1986). Growth of government, economic growth and individual freedom. *Zeitschrift für die gesamte Staatswissenschaft [Journal of Institutional Economics], 142*, 661–683.

Bernholz, P. (2003). *Monetary regimes and inflation. History, economic and political relationships*. Cheltenham: Edward Elgar.

Bhalla, S. S. (2012). *Devaluing to prosperity. Misaligned currencies and their growth consequences*. Washington, DC: Peterson Institute for International Economics.

Birg, H. (2015). *Die alternde Republik und das Versagen der Politik*. Berlin: Lit.

Blankart, C. B. (2007). *Föderalismus in Deutschland und Europa*. Baden-Baden: Nomos.

Bleaney, M., & Nishiyama, A. (2002). Explaining growth: A contest between models. *Journal of Economic Growth, 7*(1), 41–56.

Blinder, A. S. (2013). *After the music stopped. The financial crisis, the response, and the work ahead*. New York: Penguin.

Borjas, G. J. (1996). Affluent Americans gain, poor Americans lose. *Atlantic Monthly, 278*(5), 72–80.

Bourguignon, F. (2015). *The globalization of inequality*. Princeton: Princeton University Press.

Brauckhoff, K. (2012). *Steuerwettbewerb in der Europäischen Union*. Bruxelles: European Liberal Forum.

Brunnermeier, M. K., James, H., & Landau, J.-P. (2016). *The euro and the battle of ideas*. Princeton: Princeton University Press.

Buchanan, J. M. (1988). Economists and gains from trade. *Managerial and Decision Economics*, special issue (Essays in Honour of W.H. Hutt), 5–12.
Caldwell, C. (2009). *Reflections on the revolution in Europe. Can Europe be the same with different people in it?* London: Allen Lane.
Caplan, B. (2007). *The myth of the rational voter. Why democracies choose bad policies*. Princeton: Princeton University Press.
Chauffour, J.-P. (2011). What matters for development – Freedom or entitlement? In J. Gwartney, J. Hall, & R. A. Lawson (Eds.), *Economic freedom of the world, Annual Report* (pp. 167–178). Vancouver, BC/Potsdam: Fraser Institute/Liberales Institut.
Clemens, M. A. (2011). Economics and emigration. Trillion-dollar bills on the sidewalk? *Journal of Economic Perspectives, 25*(3), 83–106.
Collier, P. (2009). *Wars, guns, and votes*. New York: Harper.
Collier, P. (2013). *Exodus. How migration is changing our world*. Oxford: Oxford University Press.
Connolly, M., & Li, C. (2014). *Government consumption spending inhibits economic growth in OECD countries* (Working Paper). University of Miami.
Cowen, T. (2013). *Average is over. Powering America beyond the age of the great stagnation*. Penguin (Dutton): New York.
Dahrendorf, R. (1968). *Für eine Erneuerung der Demokratie in der Bundesrepublik*. München: Piper.
De Haan, J., & Sturm, J.-E. (2000). On the relationship between economic freedom and economic growth. *European Journal of Political Economy, 16*, 215–241.
De Haan, J., & Sturm, J.-E. (2009). Is the IMF right? How robust is the relationship between market-oriented institutions and policies and economic growth? In P. Graeff & G. Mehlkop (Eds.), *Capitalism, democracy and the prevention of war and poverty* (pp. 108–134). Abingdon.
Deaton, A. (2013). *The great escape. Health, wealth, and the origins of inequality*. Princeton: Princeton University Press.
Deutsch, K. W. (1963). *The nerves of government*. New York: Free Press.
Dikötter, F. (2010). *Mao's great famine. The history of China's most devastating catastrophe, 1958-62*. London: Bloomsbury.
Doucouliagos, H., & Ulubasoglu, M. A. (2006). Economic freedom and economic growth: Does specification make a difference? *European Journal of Political Economy, 22*, 60–81.
Easterly, W. (2014). *The tyranny of experts. Economists, dictators, and the forgotten rights of the poor*. New York: Basic Books.
Epstein, R. A. (1995). *Simple rules for a complex world*. Cambridge, MA: Harvard University Press.
Farr, W. K., Lord, R. A., & Larry Wolfenbarger, J. (1998). Economic freedom, political freedom, and economic well-being. *CATO Journal, 18*(2), 247–262.
FAZ. (2013, Februar 16). Deutschland hängt an der Währungsunion. *Frankfurter Allgemeine Zeitung*, 23.
FAZ. (2016a, März 2). Ifo-Chef Sinn tritt für Grenzkontrollen ein. *Frankfurter Allgemeine Zeitung*, 15.
FAZ. (2016b, November 3). Das Preisschild der Energiewende. *Frankfurter Allgemeine Zeitung*, 17.
FAZ. (2016c, November 4). Weltschicksalsministerium. *Frankfurter Allgemeine Zeitung*, 1.
Feld, L. P., Kirchgässner, G., & Schaltegger, C. (2005). Fiskalischer Föderalismus und wirtschaftliche Entwicklung: Evidenz für Schweizer Kantone. *Jahrbuch für Regionalwissenschaft, 25*(1), 3–25.
Feldstein, M. (1997). EMU and international conflict. *Foreign Affairs, 76*(6), 60–73.
Feldstein, M. (2012). The failure of the euro. *Foreign Affairs, 91*(1), 105–116.
Fiala, N., & Skaperdas, S. (2011). Economic perspectives on civil wars. In C. J. Coyne & R. L. Mathers (Eds.), *The handbook on the political economy of war* (pp. 177–194). Cheltenham: Edward Elgar.
Friedman, M. (1962). *Capitalism and freedom*. Chicago, IL: The University of Chicago Press.

Gat, A., & Yakobson, A. (2013). *Nations. The long history and deep roots of political ethnicity and nationalism*. Cambridge: Cambridge University Press.
Goklany, I. M. (2007). *The improving state of the world. Why we are living longer, healthier, more comfortable lives on a cleaner planet*. Washington, DC: CATO Institute.
Gordon, R. J. (2016). *The rise and fall of American growth. The U.S. standard of living since the Civil War*. Princeton: Princeton University Press.
Gubler, J. R., & Selway, J. S. (2012). Horizontal inequality, crosscutting cleavages, and Civil War. *Journal of Conflict Resolution, 56*(2), 206–232.
Gwartney, J. D., Holcombe, R. D., & Lawson, R. A. (2006). Institutions and the impact of investment on growth. *Kyklos, 59*(2), 255–273.
Gwartney, J. D., Lawson, R. A., & Hall, J. (2013). *Economic freedom of the world*. Vancouver, BC/Potsdam: Fraser Institute/Liberales Institut.
Hampl, M. (2010). The euro's instability pact. *The Wall Street Journal, 29*, 13.
Hanushek, E. A., & Woessmann, L. (2015). *The knowledge capital of nations*. Cambridge, MA: MIT Press.
Hassner, R. E., & Wittenberg, J. (2015). Barriers to entry: Who builds fortified boundaries and why? *International Security, 40*(1), 157–190.
Hayek, F. A. v. (1944/1994). *The road to Serfdom*. Chicago, IL: The University of Chicago Press.
Hayek, F. A. v. (1945). The use of knowledge in society. *American Economic Review, 35*(4), 519–530.
Hayek, F. A. v. (1960). *The constitution of liberty*. Chicago, IL: The University of Chicago Press.
Hayek, F. A. v. (1961). Die Ursachen der ständigen Gefährdung der Freiheit. Ordo, *12*, 103–109.
Hayek, F. A. v. (1978a). *The campaign against Keynesian inflation. New studies in philosophy, politics, economics and the history of ideas* (pp. 191–231). Chicago, IL: The University of Chicago Press.
Hayek, F. A. v. (1978b/2006). *Good money, Part II:* The standard. Indianapolis: Liberty Fund.
Heinemann, F. (2008). Is the Welfare State Self-Destructive? A Study of Government Benefit Morale. *Kyklos, 61*(2), 237–257.
Hobson, J. M. (2004). *The eastern origins of western civilisation*. Cambridge, UK: Cambridge University Press.
Huntington, S. P. (2004). *Who are we? The challenges to America's national identity*. New York: Simon and Schuster.
Jones, E. L. (1981). *The European miracle*. Cambridge: Cambridge University Press.
Kapur, D., & McHale, J. (2005). *Give us your best and your brightest*. Washington, DC: Center for Global Development.
Kenny, C. (2011). *Getting better. Why global development is succeeding – and how we can improve the world even more*. New York: Basic Books.
King, M. (2016). *The end of alchemy. Money, banking, and the future of the global economy*. London: Little, Brown.
Kirchhof, P. (2011). Ein einfaches Bundessteuergesetzbuch – Politische Notwendigkeit oder akademischer Traum? *Zur Debatte [Themen der Katholischen Akademie Bayern], 8*(11), 9–12.
Koopmans, R. (2010). Trade-offs between equality and difference: Immigrant integration, multiculturalism and the welfare state in cross-national perspective. *Journal of Ethnic and Migration Studies, 36*(1), 1–26.
Krämer, W. (2013). *Kalte Enteignung. Wie die Euro-Rettung uns um Wohlstand und Renten bringt*. Frankfurt/Main: Campus.
Landes, D. S. (1998). *The wealth and poverty of nations*. New York: Norton.
Lazear, E. P. (2012). The US fiscal situation: Causes and remedies. *The Economist's Voice, 9*(2), 1–7.
Leeson, P. T., & Williamson, C. R. (2011). Can't we all just get along? Fractionanization, institutions and economic consequences. In C. J. Coyne & R. L. Mathers (Eds.), *The handbook on the political economy of war* (pp. 58–71). Cheltenham, UK: Edward Elgar.
Limburg, M., & Mueller, F. F. (2015). *Strom ist nicht gleich Strom. Warum die Energiewende nicht gelingen kann*. TvR Medienverlag: Jena.

Lindbeck, A., & Nyberg, S. (2006). Raising children to work hard. *Quarterly Journal of Economics, CXXI*, 1473–1503.
Lindert, P. H. (2004). *Growing public. Social spending and economic growth since the eighteenth century*. Cambridge: Cambridge University Press.
Liu, L. (2007). *Wirtschaftliche Freiheit und Wachstum*. Münster: Lit.
Logan, J., & Preble, C. (2011). Fixing failed states: A dissenting view. In C. J. Coyne & R. L. Mathers (Eds.), *The handbook on the political economy of war* (pp. 379–396). Cheltenham, UK: Edward Elgar.
Lomborg, B. (2013, Oktober 7) Extrem viel Geld für wenig Klimaeffekt. *Frankfurter Allgemeine Zeitung, 18*.
Marsh, D. (2013). *Europe's deadlock. How the euro crisis could be solved – and why it won't happen*. New Haven, CT: Yale University Press.
McCloskey, D. N. (2010). *Bourgeois dignity. Why economics can't explain the modern world*. Chicago, IL: University of Chicago Press.
McCloskey, D. N. (2016). *Bourgeois equality. How ideas, not capital or institutions, enriched the world*. Chicago, IL: University of Chicago Press.
von der Mehden, F. R. (1973). *Comparative political violence*. Englewood Cliffs, NJ: Prentice-Hall.
Mehlkop, G. (2002). *Wirtschaftliche Freiheit, Einkommensungleichheit und physische Lebensqualität*. Opladen: Leske und Budrich.
Merz, F. (2004). *Nur wer sich ändert, wird bestehen*. Freiburg: Herder.
Merz, F. (2008). *Mehr Kapitalismus wagen*. München: Piper.
Metzger, O. (2003). *Einspruch! Wider den organisierten Staatsbankrott*. München: Riemann.
Mill, J. S. (1862/1977). The collected works of John Stuart Mill, Vol. XIX. Essays on politics and society. Part II. London: Routledge and Kegan Paul.
Mises, L. v. (1920). Die Wirtschaftsrechnung im sozialistischen Gemeinwesen. *Archiv für Sozialwissenschaft und Sozialpolitik, 47*(1), 86–121.
Mises, L. v. (1944/2007). *Bureaucracy*. Indianapolis: Liberty Fund.
Niskanen, W. A. (2006). Limiting government: The failure of 'Starve the Beast'. *CATO Journal, 26* (3), 553–558.
Niskanen, W. A. (2008). *Reflections of a political economist*. Washington, DC: CATO Institute.
North, D. C., Wallis, J. J., & Weingast, B. R. (2009). *Violence and social orders*. New York: Cambridge University Press.
Norton, S. W., & Gwartney, J. D. (2008). Economic freedom and world poverty. In J. D. Gwartney & R. A. Lawson (Eds.), *Economic freedom of the world. Annual report 2008* (pp. 23–40). Vancouver, BC/Potsdam: Fraser Institute/Liberales Institut.
Piketty, T. (2014). *Capital in the twenty-first century*. Cambridge, MA: Harvard University Press (Belknap).
Piketty, T. (2015). *The economics of inequality*. Cambridge, MA: Harvard University Press (Belknap).
Pipes, R. (1999). *Property and freedom*. New York: A. A. Knopf.
Pomeranz, K. (2000). *The great divergence: China, Europe, and the making of the world economy*. Princeton: Princeton University Press.
Popper, K. R. (1959). *The logic of scientific discovery*. London: Hutchinson.
Poulson, B. W., & Kaplan, J. G. (2008). State income taxes and economic growth. *CATO Journal, 28*(1), 53–71.
Prewo, W. (1996). *From welfare state to social state*. Zellik (Belgium): Centre for the New Europe.
Putnam, R. D. (2007). E Pluribus Unum. Diversity and community in the twenty-first century. *Scandinavian Political Studies, 30*(2), 137–174.
Reinhart, C. M., & Rogoff, K. S. (2009). *This time is different. Eight centuries of financial folly*. Princeton: Princeton University Press.
Reinhart, C. M., & Rogoff, K. S. (2011). *A decade of debt*. Washington, DC: Peterson Institute for International Economics.

Rindermann, H., & Thompson, J. (2016). The cognitive competences of immigrant and native students across the world. *Journal of Biosocial Sciences, 48*, 66–93.
Rode, M., Knoll, B., & Pitlik, H. (2013). Economic freedom, democracy and life satisfaction. In J. D. Gwartney, R. A. Lawson, & J. Hall (Eds.), *Economic freedom of the world* (pp. 215–233). Vancouver, BC/Potsdam: Fraser Institute/Liberales Institut.
Romer, C. D., & Romer, D. H. (2010). The macroeconomic effects of tax changes: Estimates based on a new measure of fiscal shocks. *American Economic Review, 100*, 763–801.
Röpke, W. (1958/2009) Jenseits von Angebot und Nachfrage. Düsseldorf: Verlagsanstalt Handwerk.
Röpke, W. (1979). *Internationale Ordnung heute* (3. Auflage). Bern: Haupt.
Rosenberg, N., & Birdzell, L. E. (1986). *How the West Grew Rich. The economic transformation of the industrial world*. New York: Basic Books.
Sala-i-Martin, X., Doppelhofer, G., & Miller, R. J. (2004). Determinants of long-term growth. *American Economic Review, 94*(4), 613–835.
Sarrazin, T. (2012). *Europa braucht den Euro nicht*. München: DVA.
Sarrazin, T. (2016). *Wunschdenken. Europa, Währung, Bildung, Einwanderung – warum Politik so häufig scheitert*. München: DVA.
Schulemann, O. (2012). *Steuererhöhungen zur Haushaltskonsolidierung – ein Irrweg*. Berlin: Bund der Steuerzahler.
Schumpeter, J. (1942). *Capitalism, socialism and democracy*. New York: Harper and Bothers.
Sinn, H.-W. (2004). *Ist Deutschland noch zu retten?* München: Econ.
Sinn, H.-W. (2012a). *Das grüne Paradoxon Plädoyer für eine illusionsfreie Klimapolitik*. Berlin: Ullstein.
Sinn, H.-W. (2012b). *Die Target Falle*. München: Hanser.
Sinn, H.-W. (2014, December 29). Ökonomische Effekte der Migration. *Frankfurter Allgemeine Zeitung, 18*.
Sinn, H.-W. (2016). *Der schwarze Juni. Brexit, Flüchtlingswelle, Euro-Desaster. Wie die Neugründung Europas gelingt*. Freiburg: Herder.
Spencer, H. (1891). *Essays: Scientific, political and speculative* (Vol. 3). London: Williams and Norgate.
Starbatty, J. (2013). *Tatort Euro. Bürger, schützt das Recht, die Demokratie und euer Vermögen*. Berlin: Europa Verlag.
Tanzi, V. (2013). *Dollars, euros, and debt. How we got into the fiscal crisis and how we get out of it*. Basingstoke: Palgrave Macmillan.
Tempelman, J. H. (2006). Does 'starve the beast' work? *CATO Journal, 26*(3), 559–572.
The Economist. (2007, March 10). Testing Muslim views. If you want my opinion. *The Economist 382*(8519), 62–63.
The Economist. (2010, March 13). Older and wiser. A special report of Germany. *The Economist 394*(8673), after page 50.
The Economist. (2012, December 22). Immigrants. Better than billed. *The Economist 405*(8816), 50.
The Economist. (2013a, February 2). Northern lights. Special report: Nordic countries. *The Economist 406*(8821), after page 40.
The Economist. (2013b, June 15). Immigration and the public finances. *The Economist 407*(8840), 64–65.
The Economist. (2013c, October 26). The euro crisis. Debtor's prison. *The Economist 409*(8859), 69–70.
The Economist. (2015a, February 21). Bagehot. David Cameron's many mansions. *The Economist 414*(8926), 31.
The Economist. (2015b, August 29). Migration in Europe. Looking for a home. *The Economist 416* (8953), 21–23.

Van Tubergen, F., & Kalmijn, M. (2005). Destination-language proficiency in cross-national perspective: A study of immigrant groups in nine Western countries. *American Journal of Sociology, 110*(5), 1412–1457.

Varenholt, F., & Lüning, S. (2012). *Die kalte Sonne. Warum die Klimakatastrophe nicht stattfindet.* Hamburg: Hoffmann und Campe.

Vedder, R., & Robe, J. (2009). *Taxes and economic growth: Implications for German tax reform.* Munich: Taxpayers' Association of Europe.

Vega-Gordillo, M., & Alvarez-Arce, J. L. (2003). Economic growth and freedom. *CATO Journal, 23*(2), 199–215.

Weber, M. (1922/1964). *Wirtschaft und Gesellschaft*. Köln: Kiepenheuer und Witsch.

Weede, E. (1986). Sectoral reallocation, distributional coalitions and the welfare state as determinants of economic growth rates in industrialized democracies. *European Journal of Political Research, 14*, 501–520.

Weede, E. (1991). The impact of state power on economic growth rates in OECD countries. *Quality and Quantity, 25*, 421–438.

Weede, E. (2004). Does human capital strongly affect economic growth rates? Yes, but only if assessed properly. *Comparative Sociology, 3*(2), 115–134.

Weede, E. (2006). Economic freedom and development. *CATO Journal, 26*(3), 511–524.

Weede, E. (2012a). Wahrheit und Gewissheit; Klimaschutz und Politik. *ORDO, 63*, 385–401.

Weede, E. (2012b). Liberty in comparative perspective: China, India, and the West. In F. Macmahon (Ed.), *Towards a worldwide index of human freedom* (pp. 189–241). Vancouver, BC/Potsdam: Fraser Institute/Liberales Institut.

Weede, E. (2014). Wirtschaftliche Freiheit – Hintergrundbedingungen, Auswirkungen und Gefährdungen. *Wirtschaftspolitische Blätter, 61*(3–4), 443–455.

Wegenast, T. C., & Basedau, M. (2014). Ethnic fractionalization, natural resources and armed conflict. *Conflict Management and Peace Science, 31*(4), 432–457.

Weimann, J. (2014, Juni 2). Der verschwiegene Klimapolitik-Skandal. *Frankfurter Allgemeine Zeitung, 16*.

Weingast, B. R. (1995). The economic role of political institutions: Market-preserving federalism and economic development. *Journal of Law, Economics, and Organization, 11*(1), 1–31.

Part III
Proposed Monetary Reforms for the Future

Anti-deflationist Paranoia

Jesús Huerta de Soto

1 Introduction

No one can have failed to hear the widespread outcry that for months has been sounding against deflation. In all the media we are met with a dismal, apocalyptic scene in which deflation is the worst of all worlds. Such is the picture the media are portraying, and there is little use in even mentioning the political sphere. We need only remember the statements of the Spanish prime minister and those of the most prominent European political leaders.

Meanwhile, what is happening in the academic world? The voices most often heard come from an amalgam of New Keynesians, or of neoclassical economists, or of monetarists. Though they believe their views are diametrically opposed from a theoretical standpoint, they nevertheless all agree that deflation is the worst of all worlds. Hence, there is a kind of phobia of deflation, a serious psychological illness which I have termed "anti-deflationist paranoia." What we must do is to study it (if it indeed corresponds to reality, both theoretically and practically speaking), using the analytical tools of Austrian economic theory.

Apart from the sketch I am going to give you here today, I would recommend that you examine both my own work [specifically Chapter 6 of the book *Money, Bank Credit, and Economic Cycles* (Huerta de Soto 2012, pp. 444–456), which largely centers on the analysis we are going to discuss today] as well as the doctoral thesis of my disciple Philipp Bagus (Bagus 2015), which is devoted entirely to the Austrian theoretical analysis of deflation.

Closing speech at the Seventh Spanish Conference on Austrian Economics. These remarks were delivered Thursday, June 12, 2014, in Madrid, and have not been published before.

J. Huerta de Soto (✉)
King Juan Carlos University, Madrid, Spain
e-mail: huertadesoto@dimasoft.es

A. Godart-van der Kroon, P. Vonlanthen (eds.), *Banking and Monetary Policy from the Perspective of Austrian Economics*,
https://doi.org/10.1007/978-3-319-75817-6_10

According to Mises, deflation is a monetary change which consists of a decrease in the money supply (Mises 1966, pp. 422–424) or, to put it another way, an increase in the demand for money (to decrease supply is to increase demand). Any contraction in the supply of any good or service brings about a relative rise in scarcity, and thus also a rise in the price, which is affected by the contraction in the supply. In this case, the contraction is in the money supply, and the effect, other things being equal, is an increase in the price of the monetary unit (the price of money is its purchasing power).

So, the purchasing power of the monetary unit grows, and this growth manifests itself to us visually as a general drop in the monetary prices of the goods and services which are exchanged in the market. It is not really that the prices of goods and services fall: what actually happens is that the purchasing power of the monetary unit, or the price of money, rises as a result of the contraction. In other words, the price of money goes up, and we must hand over more goods for each monetary unit; or rather, we acquire more with each monetary unit because its price or purchasing power has increased. This is the scientific definition of deflation. Colloquially speaking, however, people have simply come to use the word "deflation" for what is actually the typical effect of true deflation: a widespread, greater or lesser decrease in the monetary prices of the different economic goods and services.

Now I would like to follow up this introduction with an analysis of three different types of deflation. It is important to grasp the differences between them, because then we will be able to better comprehend the events that are occurring around us and those that have occurred in the past. So, this explanation will be extremely useful in an analytical sense.

Before we begin, let us consider that in a purely anarchocapitalist society (with a gold standard, no state, etc.), it is still possible to conceive some isolated episodes of deflation, sensu stricto. For example, if the galleon *María de las Mercedes* sinks with x tons of gold coins inside, there is a contraction in the money supply, because this quantity of gold disappears from the market. This is an isolated event and relatively insignificant. We could also imagine a natural catastrophe or a war that could cause a very sharp increase in uncertainty and in turn a substantial rise in the demand for money. These are conceivable but chance situations that do not trigger systematic nor recurrent distortions in market prices.

The three types of deflation I will cover are the following:

First, deflation deliberately provoked by the state.

The second type I will refer to is deflation which results from an error of institutional design with respect to the banking system, an error that has allowed banks to act with a fractional-reserve ratio, against general legal principles. This has been the economy's Achilles' heel for twenty centuries. All recurrent, cyclical economic problems spring from this error of institutional design, from this odious privilege granted to banks, by which they can act outside general legal principles and neglect to maintain a 100% reserve ratio on demand deposits. Consequently, the money supply behaves like an accordion. Just as easily as it expands, due to the generation of "virtual" money, it later contracts. This is especially and invariably true when the market uncovers the investment errors committed during the bubble stage.

There is also a third type of deflation, which is "good" deflation. In fact, it is not really deflation, sensu stricto, because it does not derive from a contraction in the money supply nor from an increase in the demand for money, but rather from an increase in the production of goods and services throughout a prosperous market process in which the government does not intervene, and which grows at a faster rate, in general, than the money supply. This is the healthiest process of economic growth conceivable.

With this overview of the three different types of deflation in mind (the most conceptually useful ones in understanding events around us), let us now briefly analyze each one.

2 The First Type of Deflation

The first type of deflation, as you will recall, is deflation deliberately provoked by governments. There are different historical examples of this first type, such as the deflation induced following the Napoleonic Wars. However, the most talked-about case is the monumental error committed by the Chancellor of the Exchequer of the United Kingdom in 1925, Mr. Winston Churchill. Churchill insisted on reintroducing the gold standard after World War I but at the pound's gold parity prior to World War I, the centenary of which we commemorated in 2014. This was a very grave error, because World War I was financed, as always, by inflation. The market was flooded with sterling notes, which meant that the de facto parity of sterling banknotes with gold fell dramatically.

I must remind you that the whole debate over whether or not to return to the gold standard in the 1920s and 1930s was a false debate from the outset. Many theorists claim it was a great error, but the only error was that their opponents insisted on returning to the gold standard at the pre-World War I parity. Of course, it was key to return to the gold standard, with all the disciplinary restraint it entailed for authorities, but it was vital to take into account the reality of the tremendous expansion of fiduciary media that had been injected to finance the war.

Hence, those historians of economic thought who assess the debate make the mistake of thinking that those who wished to return to the gold standard were wrong. No. They were right. Nevertheless, they committed the grave error, like Winston Churchill, of insisting on returning to the gold parity prior to World War I, and this return involved a monetary contraction and induced deflation, especially in the United Kingdom, and the consequences were quite severe because the economic system was subjected to unnecessary tension. England was a great export power, and as a result of this appreciation of the pound, it ceased to export, which caused problems of adaptation, unemployment, etc. Hayek, in one of his most brilliant articles, maintains that just when the English economy had digested this error, England abandoned the gold standard (Hayek 1984, p. 15).

3 The Second Type of Deflation

The second type of deflation is that which inevitably occurs in a system like ours, which has rested on a fractional reserve ever since Peel's Bank Charter Act of 1844. I will refrain from repeating to you the Austrian theory of the economic cycle, which you already know by heart anyway. The bubble leads to systematic errors of investment and seriously distorts the real structure of the market, which is very dynamically efficient [as I explain in my book *The Theory of Dynamic Efficiency* (Huerta de Soto 2010)] and reveals the investment errors sooner or later. At that moment, a financial crisis erupts, because it becomes clear that a large number of the loans banks granted during the stage of credit expansion were granted for unviable or unsustainable investment projects. Furthermore, since the collateral for those loans from the bubble stage are deposits created from nothing, it is revealed that banks' assets have only a fraction of the value that was thought, while banks' liabilities remain the same, and thus the entire banking system is in a state of failure.

This is where a highly curious phenomenon occurs; I call it "the phenomenon of the pyromaniac firefighter." For one of the most important conclusions to be drawn from the existence of this fractional-reserve system is that its survival depends on a lender of last resort (or central banker) who, as these errors are regularly discovered, heads off the collapse of the entire monetary system and our ultimate return to the very beginning of the process of monetary development. This would be a social tragedy because, as you know, money is the quintessential social institution, and we cannot do without it, not even in a fractional-reserve banking system like the current one.

In the face of this situation, there is relatively little central banks can do. At most, they can keep private banks from failing, by providing them with all sorts of loans and assistance. And that is about it. However, a process of monetary contraction (i.e., a process of deflation) is inevitable. This is the second type of deflation, the type I was referring to when I offered the simile that the current monetary system is like an accordion: just as easily as it expands, it contracts. This is because economic agents discover that many of the investments they so eagerly made during the bubble stage were pointless. To a greater or lesser extent, at all levels, we must get to work and try to salvage what actually can be salvaged: companies are closed down, reorganization takes place, workers are laid off, etc. And everyone tightens their belts to repay loans and to avoid suspending payments or reorganize as painlessly as possible. This process teaches us a lesson, and it comes as no surprise that most loans are repaid to the banking system at a faster rate than new loans are requested. In short, much of the virtual money created during the bubble stage disappears, and the money supply inevitably contracts in the form of deflation.

Here I would like to make an observation, because the Austrians have been accused of being "liquidationists" who are pleased with deflation. This is not the case. It is an unjustified caricature. We as Austrians are not masochists, nor do we wish to inflict unnecessary harm on people. We simply hit a raw nerve when we point out that the origin of the crisis does not lie in deflation (which everyone mistakenly identifies as the cause of the evils), but rather in the previous stage, that of the speculative bubble. For this reason, the entire banking system must be redesigned and a 100% reserve requirement established on demand deposits and their equivalents. These should be treated in the same way as any other deposit of a fungible good, for instance, wheat or oil. Nevertheless, until this goal is achieved, we must ensure the continuance of the current monetary system and then accept as inevitable a certain degree of deflation derived from every process of financial crisis and reorganization (Huerta de Soto 2012).

Rothbard goes so far as to state that we should see a good side to deflation in stages of depression (Rothbard 1993, pp. 863–871). On the one hand, he mentions that this deflation helps to liquidate erroneous projects, to accelerate the process to detect unviable investment projects, and to lay the foundation for the subsequent recovery (which does not earn him the label of "liquidationist"). On the other hand, he indicates that in the stage of unavoidable, relative monetary contraction which follows every bubble, the tables are somehow turned, and the creditors who were at a disadvantage in the bubble stage are now at an advantage with respect to debtors. This is a far cry from the claim that Austrians love deflation per se and that we are "liquidationists." Our actual message, I repeat, in positive analytical terms and without value judgments, is that the origin of the crisis lies in the prior expansion and that in the current monetary system a certain degree of deflation is inevitable following every artificial expansion of credit, regardless of the central bank's course of action.

So far, we have dealt with the first two types of deflation. Incidentally, a strong relationship exists between the two. If you read Rothbard's book, *America's Great Depression* (Rothbard 2000), you will see how Winston Churchill's terrible blunder of needlessly provoking deflation in his country by insisting on ignoring the monetary knowledge accumulated since at least Ricardo and returning to the pre-World War I pound-gold parity subjected the British economic system to such pressure that the English, led by the Governor of the Bank of England, Montagu Norman, turned for help to their cousins from the former colonies namely, the Americans, whose monetary system was under the direction of the relatively young Federal Reserve (created in 1913), with Benjamin Strong Jr. (President of the Federal Reserve Bank of New York) at the de facto helm.

By the way, very similar measures have been demanded by Europe's periphery countries, which did experience necessary domestic deflation. These countries expected Germany to give in and to expand its credit and spend more. This is just more of the same. There is nothing new under the sun: in the presence of self-induced deflation (Winston Churchill's shot in the foot), the English resorted to pressuring the United States to inject money and somehow ease the problem facing English exports, especially in the United States, which was their largest market. Benjamin Strong Jr., who even had a permanent office in the Bank of England, went along with the request and arranged a bubble (that of the Roaring Twenties) in the United States, and upon this bubble rested the credit expansion which would end in the Great Depression of 1929. So here we can see a clear connection between the first and the second types of deflation.

Incidentally, Milton Friedman created a myth about the Great Depression of 1929. As a myth, it has been one of the most destructive to the economy and consists of the claim that the depression sprang from the monetary-policy errors of the Federal Reserve, which did not inject enough money. In fact, this has been the official, academic version ever since the publication of the book, *A Monetary History of the United States*, by Anna J. Schwartz and the late Milton Friedman (Friedman and Schwartz 1971). However, the Great Depression was not "great" due to the errors of the Federal Reserve. There is no doubt that the Fed did what it could; it even injected a massive amount of money and kept the entire American financial system from disappearing. Nevertheless, as we have already pointed out, after every bubble, the deflationary process, which can be more intense or less, is inevitable. Moreover, if deflation was very intense, the cause did not lie in a failure of the Federal Reserve to inject what was needed, but in the monumental errors of economic policy committed by President Hoover and later by President Roosevelt, both of whom focused their efforts on advancing and pushing for higher nominal wages, raising taxes, and public spending, making the economy more rigid, and furthering a protectionist agenda of increased tariffs worldwide as had never been seen before. Hence, it should come as no surprise that, under these circumstances, the following spread: discouragement, economic disruption, and thus, further deflation that turned the recession of 1929 into a Great Depression.

Imagine what would have happened in the last cycle, which has just concluded, and from which we are beginning to emerge, if governments had reacted just as Hoover and Roosevelt did. We would be in a severe depression with much more serious deflation. And it would not be owing to a lack of money injection by central banks, but to errors of specific economic policy. Or, to put it in today's language, a failure to have implemented the necessary economic-liberalization reforms.

We also have the famous Japanese example, which is the one always cited to scare us about deflation. We are told that because of its deflation, Japan has spent years without a recovery, and with very insignificant growth. This is the crude, short-sighted, erroneous argument of many who lack training in economics, or who have received inadequate training, or who simply cheer on the champions of inflation for political reasons (and we will discuss them later). Moreover, if Japan has faced slight deflation (for in today's colloquial terms, the drop in prices has not been drastic) for over a decade, this deflation has not put the country in its decidedly weak economic state (incidentally, the economic weakness is relative, given that Japan has a huge amount of accumulated capital, and any visitor to the country can see how prosperous it is, especially with respect to 20 years ago). The slowness of economic growth in Japan, and the fact that it has been losing ground to a number of nearby geographic competitors, stems entirely from its extraordinary degree of rigidity and, particularly, from continuous intervention in the Japanese economy by the government, which has adopted hardly any effective liberalization measures to date. On the contrary, in Japan, all of the possible interventionist measures have been tried. The Japanese government has applied the whole inventory of Keynesian and monetarist recipes. And all they have managed to achieve is to become one of the most indebted countries in the world and to maintain their rigidity indefinitely.

4 The Third Type of Deflation: In Defense of Good Deflation

We now come to the third type of deflation. When we enter the recessionary stage and deflation appears, i.e., the inevitable monetary contraction I referred to before (the disappearance of "virtual" money in a context of fractional-reserve banking managed by central banks), people gradually begin to discover viable, sustainable opportunities, and because economic agents are not very inclined to request loans, the money supply remains relatively stable, and little by little, an increase in productivity occurs. It is then that the third "deflation" scenario begins to unfold. This is what is referred to as "good" deflation and results from an increase in productivity with a relatively constant monetary supply.

We will now briefly review the arguments the press offers and distinguished economists often repeat concerning the "terrible" nature of deflation. Let us consider them one by one.

We can begin with the claim that deflation is the worst that could happen because it affects debtors unfavorably and creditors favorably. It is time for us to pause and think a moment. If, as a result of a process of productivity growth, particularly in this stage in which the economy begins to recover, the production of goods and services should grow faster than the money supply, which would mean an increase in the purchasing power of the monetary unit, economic agents, who are very nimble negotiators of their borrowing and lending operations, would take these deflation expectations into account and incorporate them when reaching an agreement on the corresponding market interest rate.

Let us recall that a market interest rate has three components: first, the social rate of time preference (let us suppose it is around 2%); second, the component for expected inflation or deflation; and third, the risk component for the specific contract or sector in which the exchange of present goods for future goods takes place. We could go a step further and add, as Mises does, a component for pure entrepreneurial profit (we could even make a concession to the new real-bills doctrine because, sure enough, to the extent that those loans are short-term secondary media of exchange, they will have a negative premium because they are very liquid, but we will set this topic aside now).

What I mean to say is that, in a deflationary environment, economic agents themselves already have the expected deflation in mind, and they reduce or make negative the premium for changes in the purchasing power of money. If secular deflation of around 1% per year is expected in the coming years, and the social rate of time preference is 2%, the nominal market rate in the absence of risk will tend to be 1%. And this is no problem, because it harms no one. Economic agents, both debtors and creditors, negotiate and agree on a nominal interest rate for the corresponding transactions, and thus the first argument has been refuted.

Someone could ask me, "What about credit agreements signed years earlier, in an environment that was not deflationary?" Well, listen, you made a mistake and contracted a debt under different circumstances, and now you have to accept the consequences and repay your loan in monetary units of greater purchasing power: each of us must lie in the bed he or she has made. In this case, a phenomenon does occur in which debtors are placed at a disadvantage and creditors at an advantage, but in a way this compensates for the prior injustice, as Rothbard explained and I mentioned before. And let no one claim that this situation is very grave, because "aggregate demand" contracts. In aggregate terms, nothing contracts, because while it is true that those who took on a debt in the bubble stage are unfavorably affected, and thus their contribution to the aggregate demand is smaller, creditors are favorably affected, and thus their contribution to the aggregate demand is bigger, and aggregately speaking (economists do love aggregates!) the (aggregate) demand does not necessarily change. So, we have unraveled the first argument.

However, another argument runs that deflation is horrible because companies sell less as a result of the drop in prices, and a cumulative contraction process is set in motion. This argument is very unsound as well. In a context of monetary growth under the gold standard, we would generally expect companies' aggregate sales to grow at around 1%. (The world stock of gold has shown secular growth of around 1–2% per year, as indicated by various studies.)

So then, what comprises the turnover, or sales income, of the companies that grow at 1%? The turnover is comprised of a number of units of goods and services, which are produced by each company, and this number grows at a faster rate, 2–3%, which is precisely why the price of each unit tends to fall. Nonetheless, a fall in unit price certainly does not harm companies. On the contrary, it is a sign of the healthiest process of economic growth conceivable, which derives from an accumulation of capital, from innovations, etc. This growth process makes available to economic agents and consumers goods of increasing quality at lower unit prices, though companies' growth is modest or even very slow and follows the trend of growth in the money supply, around 1%. But there is no contraction anywhere.

Besides, remember the entire theory of capital. I could be here for hours, but it is perfectly possible to earn a lot of money even though sales do not increase in monetary terms. Lesson number one in accounting: profit is income less costs. If your income does not grow, or if it grows slowly, you can earn lots of money if you reduce costs by renegotiating them, which is relatively easy if you change your way of thinking as an entrepreneur and accept that you are in a deflationary environment (in colloquial, and not academic, terms) of declining prices. This environment is the setting for the soundest and most prosperous market process of growth imaginable, as I just mentioned. In fact, even if sales fall for certain companies, particularly those in the sectors closest to consumption, this need not be at all detrimental to these firms. How will the entrepreneurs react? They will reduce costs more intensively. This is called the Ricardo Effect. If I have fewer sales, I must let workers go and replace them in the margin with capital equipment. This occurs mainly because the drop in prices means an increase in real wages. Again, this is the Ricardo Effect: at the margin it is better to replace some labor with capital equipment. The laid-off workers are freed from the companies closest to consumption and will end up working in companies in the sectors furthest from consumption, precisely those that are going to produce the new capital equipment the first companies needed to cope with the new deflationary environment. Capital Theory 101: these are fundamental principles that unfortunately very few of my colleagues have studied, and thus they completely overlook them.

Another argument goes that when consumers notice prices are starting to go down, they think to themselves, "Since tomorrow the price will be lower, I won't consume today," and thus the price drops further. Tomorrow comes, and since the expectation of lower prices persists and was confirmed in the past, consumers again hold off consuming (though they get a little thinner), and the day after tomorrow they delay yet again (and get thinner still), and then ... they die of hunger. Deflation appears, and the world collapses. This is the horrific deflation argument. Consumers are idiots, and we quit consuming if prices are expected to fall. Is this true or not?

The prophets of doom issue dramatic warnings about the deflationary catastrophe, but in reality, declining prices do not curtail consumption; they actually stimulate it. And if you do not believe me, there are endless examples. What has happened with iPhones and iPads? Do you know how much the first personal computer I bought cost me? Their price has not stopped falling, nor has their quality stopped rising, and this has not kept demand for them from growing. In fact, to eliminate this feeble argument, we need not even resort to "Pigou's wealth effect" nor to the tendency of the nominal demand for money to decrease as its purchasing power increases. These very strong effects also appear, but in the medium and long term.

There are other even more absurd deflation arguments, like the one I read the other day, which ran that with deflation, in the end there will have to be negative nominal interest rates in the market. It is impossible for there to be a negative nominal rate in the unhampered market (of course not in Draghi's entirely manipulated money markets). Even in the most deflationary environment imaginable, when the market interest rate approaches zero, because the deflation premium is rising, as the interest rate gets closer and closer to zero, and given that the interest rate is the value used to discount the expected flows of rents from each capital good, what happens? Well, the value of capital goods, which are always on entrepreneurs' minds in their processes of innovation and imagination for discovering sustainable investment projects to satisfy the future needs of consumers, approaches infinity, and therefore the entrepreneurial opportunities to undertake sustainable investment projects multiply and become increasingly attractive. Moreover, this happens with greater intensity the closer the nominal interest rate gets to zero; but as is logical, in no case will the nominal interest rate become negative in a true free market for credits.

And you must not say to me, "But Professor Huerta de Soto, who is going to get into an investment project, with all the headaches involved, if he or she is going to receive a very low interest rate?" Because for me, the valid argument is, "Professor Huerta de Soto, who is going to get into an investment project if Papa State is going to pester him, impose regulations on him, send inspectors to visit his company every other day, fine him; and furthermore, if he earns anything, the state is going to wring it out of him, take 52 percent in income taxes, plus another 8 percent in personal wealth tax, plus estate tax, etc." This is an argument I accept. Under these conditions, investing is strictly for the birds. However, here the lack of investment, and the unemployment that accompanies it, does not result from deflation, but from the stream of interventions I have just cited. Nevertheless, in a context free from such assaults on individual liberty, just think what it means to find a sound, sustainable investment project in which your money is returned to you in the future, in 1, 2, 4, or

5 years, in monetary units of a higher purchasing power, because we are in a deflationary environment. And on top of that, you receive, for example, 0.5% more. That project is worth its price in gold. Not only do you recover, with a higher purchasing power, the monetary units you invested, but you receive 0.5% more in the form of interest or profit.

I realize that we must change our mindset, and it takes effort. All of us who are here, and our parents and grandparents, have lived only in an inflationary environment, not in a deflationary one. All economic agents (entrepreneurs, workers, public officials, politicians, etc.) are automatically accustomed to living with inflation, and when inflation is zero or deflation appears, we are disconcerted. We must change our thinking and our habits. Hayek's evolutionary theory is very relevant here. This takes time and work, but it is not impossible. Mises has already made it clear in the different studies and papers which he produced as an advisor to the League of Nations during the interwar period, and which you should reread (Huerta de Soto 2012, pp. 716–723).

Even in the academic sphere, we must admit, as Mises did, that a sound, suitable, and complete theory of deflation is sorely missing. To remedy this academic deficiency, Professor Philipp Bagus and I have devoted our efforts in several writings (Bagus 2015; Huerta de Soto 2012).

We need to change the mindset of economic agents, authorities, leaders, and also academic economists, who have a different worldview, one that since World War II has been exclusively inflationary. There are also historical examples which, although they do not prove anything (because history, though a very valuable art, at most illustrates theories, but cannot prove nor disprove them), perfectly illustrate today's analysis of deflation, my criticism of anti-deflationist paranoia. One of the periods of greatest prosperity in the United States began with the end of the Civil War in 1865 and lasted almost until the beginning of the twentieth century. It was a period of cumulative growth, year after year, of between 2% and 4%, with secular deflation, year after year, of around 1%. Even Milton Friedman recognizes this and examines it in his book, *A Monetary History of the United States*. However, after describing the phenomenon, he observes that it baffles him, because it somehow refutes his whole argument. And then on he goes (Friedman and Schwartz 1971, pp. 15 and 30)! Moreover, Alfred Marshall acknowledges the same evolution in the United Kingdom during a similar period (Marshall 1926). He declares that growth can take place with deflation. In fact, he goes even further and states that the soundest, most sustainable, prosperous, just, and harmonious model of growth is the deflationary one. The reason is that with this model, prosperity spreads to all layers of society, across social classes, in the form of lower and lower prices for the goods and services people consume. Continuous tension and conflict between social agents to renegotiate the different contracts upward in nominal terms are no longer necessary. We no longer need unions nor politicians to act as mediators. They are all unnecessary! Perhaps that is precisely why they like inflation so much: none of them wants to end up unemployed and fully exposed.

There is no more favorable environment for the accumulation of capital and for saving than an environment of monetary stability and zero inflation, or deflation. This encourages people to save and, thus, to finance new investment projects, which, when they mature into consumer goods and services in a more or less distant future, will even further boost the prosperity of all economic agents. Without a doubt, it is the most just, harmonious, efficient, and sustainable process of economic development. It generates the fewest tensions in the market and shows the greatest respect for the environment, which suffers particularly during the bubble stage, when unnecessary strain is placed on it and trees are cut down, mountains are destroyed to make cement to build houses nobody wants, and the atmosphere is filled with carbon dioxide to carry out foolish investment projects. I repeat, the deflationary process is the healthiest process of economic development conceivable.

Oddly enough, in an environment of deflation, or zero inflation, like the one we are in, in terms of national accounts and statistics, economic development becomes apparent mainly when the GDP deflator data is given to the official in charge of the corresponding ministry. That is, the nominal figures do not rise, and all the officials are worried and waiting, and it turns out that there is a drop in prices of between 2% and 3%. Real GDP is up! Contrary to popular opinion, in terms of national accounting, a decrease in prices ultimately takes the shape of an increase in GDP.

5 Conclusion

To wrap up, I would like to finish with the following question. What are the psychological and sociological reasons for the hostility toward deflation? What is the origin of this serious psychological illness I have called "anti-deflationist paranoia"?

I commented before on how difficult it is for us to change our habits, especially when, for several generations, the environment we live in has been inflationary and completely different. Inflation is a drug. It is an extremely dangerous drug, a great and deadly temptation for the whole social body. Politicians love inflation and hate deflation. With deflation, the information they receive from the budget office is that government revenue is not increasing, but flat. Hence, it becomes difficult for them to pay for public spending and continue to buy votes. In addition, they feel pressure, because they no longer wield monetary-policy autonomy. They are obliged to manage public resources faithfully and with effort, something they consider foreign to their profession. Politicians believe their profession consists of buying votes with newly created money (not even the money of others) and then bequeathing the inflation to their successor within a few years. And they can no longer do that.

Why do you think Jesus Christ left quickly after the multiplication of loaves? Because he saw that people were selfish, that they barely cared about his sermon, and that what they wanted was to make him king in order to live for free and never do a lick of work again. Today the manna and the multiplied loaves seem to be inflation. The only way to make the impossible possible is to rely on inflation or to issue debt that is later monetized. Yet all of this disappears like a dissolving sugar cube in a deflationary environment with very slow monetary growth and without monetary-policy autonomy. That is why politicians always hate deflation, especially if they are hoping inflation will help them repay public debt (i.e., by swindling their creditors with a masked haircut). Therefore, the best way to rein in a politician is not to form a political party, nor to debate with him in Parliament. That is all a waste of time. Indeed, the only way to put a stop to the nonsense of politicians is to rely on the discipline imposed by a monetary restraint. The gold standard provided such a restraint in the past, and the closest thing to it we now have is the euro (provided Draghi does not destroy it!). That is the only true way.

Also delighted with inflation are trade unionists. Inflation covers their backs, since the devastating effects of union policies, which tend to make the labor market more rigid (artificial increases in wages, the minimum wage, etc.), are concealed in an inflationary environment. However, in an environment of zero inflation, or of deflation, these effects are fully exposed, and we immediately realize that such policies are harmful.

I repeat, the only way is to lead politicians and trade unionists, like leading steers do at a bullfight, down the corridor of monetary stability. For as my grandfather used to say, people like to be fooled. You explain a serious, sensible product, with guaranteed savings, a low interest rate, etc. (a classic life insurance policy, e.g., like the ones I provide), and then you explain something that looks really good on the surface ("Look, if you put your money into this fund, you're going to get rich; it's going to go up in value every year, etc."), and ten people out of ten take the bait.

In short, entrepreneurs are confronted by countless daily problems in their companies. If you offer them a very cheap and easy short-term loan with flexible repayment options, they all end up falling for it, just like they did during the bubble stage.

That is why inflation is so popular. That is why it is so perverse and does so much damage. That is why it is a drug so lethal to society. And that is why deflation is so necessary.

Thank you all very much for your patience.

References

Bagus, P. (2015). *Defense of deflation*. Heidelberg: Springer.

Friedman, M., & Schwartz, A. J. (1971). *A monetary history of the United States 1867–1960*. Princeton: Princeton University Press.

Hayek, F. A. (1984). *1980's Unemployment and the unions: The distortion of relative prices by monopoly in the labour markets*. London: Institute of Economic Affairs.

Huerta de Soto, J. (2010). *The theory of dynamic efficiency*. London: Routledge.

Huerta de Soto, J. (2012). *Money, bank credit, and economic cycles*. Auburn, AL: Ludwig von Mises Institute.

Marshall, A. (1926). *Official papers*. London: Macmillan.

Rothbard, M. N. (1993). *Man, economy, and state: A treatise on economic principles*. Auburn, AL: Ludwig von Mises Institute.

Rothbard, M. N. (2000). *America's great depression*. Auburn, AL: Ludwig von Mises Institute.

von Mises, L. (1966). *Human action: A treatise on economics*. Chicago, IL: Henry Regnery.

The Reconsideration of Hayek's Idea on the De-nationalization of Money: Taking the Growing Tendency of Digital Currencies in Consideration

Chikako Nakayama

1 Introduction

At the end of the twentieth century in 1999, when there was no influential digital currency yet, Friedman expressed his view in an interview, "I think that the Internet is going to be one of the major forces for reducing the role of government. The one thing that's missing, but that will soon be developed, is a reliable e-cash, a method whereby on the Internet you can transfer funds from A to B, without A knowing B or B knowing A."[1] Some interpret this statement to predict Bitcoin[2] and praised Friedman's foresight. But he might not have expected so much development would take place within less than 20 years that there are several similar attempts to Bitcoin as well as the possible ones issued by big banks and by the central banks for which research projects of their responsible members are making efforts.

On the other hand, the history of economic thoughts and theories has a long tradition of dealing with money and currencies: There have been investigations on the origins and essence of money, the state theory, or the credit theory of money, for example. Here, we investigate some arguments on money, focusing on the relation of money to the market concept of the Austrian School of Economics, taking our contemporary development of digital money in view.

---

[1]Brito and Castillo 2016 quoted this paragraph at the beginning of their book, together with another quotation from Satoshi Nakamoto. This seems to be taken from an interview conducted by John Berthoud at the National Taxpayers Union Foundation (NTU/F) in 1999. (http://youtube/mlwxdyLnMXM).

[2]Following the professionals, we use the word Bitcoin or BTC with the capital letter B to mean its system and the other without the capital letter (bitcoin) to explain some concrete usage of this digital currency.

C. Nakayama (✉)
Institute of Global Studies, Tokyo University of Foreign Studies, Tokyo, Japan
e-mail: nakac@tufs.ac.jp

A. Godart-van der Kroon, P. Vonlanthen (eds.), *Banking and Monetary Policy from the Perspective of Austrian Economics*,
https://doi.org/10.1007/978-3-319-75817-6_11

2 Growing Tendencies of Digital Currencies Including the Birth of Bitcoin

2.1 *The Impact of the Original Idea of Bitcoin*

As is well known, the idea of Bitcoin was originally shown in 2008 in a paper by a Satoshi Nakamoto whose personality, career, affiliation, or profile could not further be detected. His paper was rather brief with nine pages, not published in any journal with peer reviews, but distributed to some mailing list as a kind of design paper.[3] But the idea to make a currency through some computer system immediately stimulated many engineers who strove for making suitable software and circumstances to realize it. And their endeavor bore fruit, the first transaction with Bitcoin, already in the following year of 2009.[4]

In 2012, the European Central Bank published a rough but schematically classifying report on virtual currencies in general, placing Bitcoin in this context as one of the most prominent cases "to compete against real currencies as a medium of exchange.[5] Then Bitcoin gradually began to attract wider attention since early 2013 when the transaction volume and market capitalization had amounted to a considerable level. Here, we first overview several issues of the original paper which are of interest from the standpoint of economic theory of money and credit.

At the very beginning of the paper, Nakamoto threw a critical eye on the weakness of a trust-based normal transaction model for Internet commerce, with financial institutions "exclusively... serving as trusted third parties to process electronic payments" (p. 1). Normally, we are much accustomed to using exclusively national currencies as a unit for most of our shopping and trade including internet commerce and do not think in each transaction how the normal model of trust or what kind of financial institutions intervene and play some role there. But according to Nakamoto, transaction costs tend to increase to avoid mediating disputes and fraud, even though it was still impossible to eliminate such irregularity completely. The problem of high transaction cost might be popular among many people who have a high cost of remittance, especially for payments beyond national boundaries.

Nakamoto hence proposed an electronic payment system based on the cryptographic proof, using a timestamp server for the whole chronological line of transactions to protect both sellers and buyers. He emphasized that it then enables any two willing parties to transact directly without any third party, which means cryptology is the replacement for people's trust in financial institutions.

The references of this paper show that the main motivation for the author might have been the exploration of cryptology and timestamping, taking its security and

---

[3]Saito (2014, p. 3).

[4]*Ibid.*, p. 18.

[5]ECB (2012, p. 19). Even though the ECB admitted that it could at least partly not be "a fully fledged analysis" but rather "a first attempt at providing a basis for discussion on this issue" (*Ibd.*, p. 33), it has certainly played an important role as a basis for discussion.

privacy into consideration.[6] But the paper itself was brimmed with rich ideas for further development in many directions, so that by 2016, the technology of cryptology of block-chain has become independently discussed for its own potential, not necessarily being connected with Bitcoin. Some indicated, after pointing out Bitcoin's complexity, which makes it possible to describe it as a protocol, a currency, a payment system, or a technology platform, that it is open source software at its core.[7]

Another author of an introductory book of Bitcoin and block-chain, Antonopoulos, explains in the preface of his book in 2014, "I still remember the moment I finished reading those nine pages, when I realized that bitcoin was not simply a digital currency, but a network of trust that could also provide the basis for so much more than just currencies." (Antonopoulos 2014, p. xi). Then he continues the next sentence as follows; "the realization that "this isn't money, it's a decentralized trust network,..." (*Ibid.*). Perhaps he was cautious enough to distinguish between currency and money, but it is evident here that his attention was laid more on the decentralized network of trust than on the possible birth of a new digital currency. On the contrary, we rather focus on the point that Nakamoto defined "an electronic coin as a chain of digital signatures" (Nakamoto 2008, p. 2). Nakamoto definitely found some creation of money there.

It might be asked whether this possibility of a new digital currency can provide a solid and sustainable measurement unit for internet commerce as Nakamoto had originally planned, or possibly for other commerce in a society as well, to complement or eventually to replace those with the normal "trust-based" procedure with financial institutions. There have been different forecasts, sometimes with empirical evidence,[8] but to forecast the future is not our theme.

Instead, we deal with a point of argument that our socially embedded system of transactions of money with financial institutions was fundamentally questioned by the idea of Bitcoin. Financial institutions are not only the private banks through whose accounts the seller and the buyer remit or receive their money. Further, the central bank is included, which integrates private banks, issues the currency, and manages and maintains the whole procedure and administration. Besides, the existence of the authority and power of nation-states to set the currency plays an important role there, on which the whole international monetary system is constructed. In order to analyze this point, Hayek's treatise on this theme in 1976 has been the most important reference for those who have treated the theme of Bitcoin.[9] We attempt to clarify the insightful discussions that were deployed already around the 1970s, and that some more progress beyond their vision has been going on.

---

[6]In the references, there were eight papers and articles, most of which were presented ones in some symposium on information, computer, communication, privacy and security, etc.

[7]Athey et al. (2016, p. 2).

[8]The empirical research of Athey et al. (2016), for example, concluded that Bitcoin would not prevail so widely as to replace for legal tenders.

[9]In Japan, Okada (2015), Noguchi (2014), Nishibe (2014) discussed Bitcoin and mentioned to this treatise of Hayek.

2.2 The Problems of Digital Currency Seen in Bitcoin

The ECB (2012) gave a short historical overview of money: from some form of money as early as 2200 BC, then commodity-backed money around the eighteenth century, to fiat money or "any legal tender designated and issued by a central authority". Money had gradually come to be seen to have three functions: as a medium of exchange, unit of account, and store of value. These forms of money were followed by the creation and development of the World Wide Web in the mid-1990s, which engendered virtual communities and their own digital currencies, although other local, unregulated currencies had already existed before that. Then the schemes of definition and categorization were discussed. They picked up the closed (in-game only) virtual currency, the ones with unidirectional and bidirectional flows, vouchers and coupons, and also the electronic money the funds of which could be expressed in the same unit of account as legal tender. Finally, Bitcoin was discussed as the heir of these successions in this overview.

Nakamoto explained how new bitcoins were generated and brought into use by the creator of the block and interpreted that "the steady addition of a constant of amount of new coins is analogous to gold miners expending resources to add gold to circulation. In our case, it is CPU time and electricity that is expended (Nakamoto 2008, p. 4). Some interpreted this analogy as matching to one of the assertions of business cycle theory of the Austrian School of economics to come back to the Gold Standard, and others were skeptical of it.[10] In fact, Hayek mentioned his consistent stance for the gold standard or a fixed rate of exchange in his 1976 treatise, which we are going to deal with later.

The problem was, even though Bitcoin was originally planned only as a medium of exchange, that is, to have only exchange value, it was possible that "the 'mining' activity . . .leads to money creation without the receipt of funds" (ECB 2012, p. 43), and "users of the system actually exchange real currency for computing bits" (Ibid., p. 39). As the ECB reported, this has gradually happened in increasingly large volume, and governments of each country had to decide their stances and possibly take some measures on it. In China where a precursory virtual currency of Q-coin had been circulated or in the EU, the legal framework was already discussed to some extent before the appearance of Bitcoin.

But the Japanese government, for example, seemed to have been so remarkably unfamiliar with this problem, as to issue an official statement in 2014 that they regarded bitcoin neither as a currency nor as a financial commodity, but taxable as a

[10]ECB (2012) thought 'the theoretical roots of Bitcoin can be found in the Austrian school of economics' (p. 22) and raised two points of reference: One was the business cycle theory of the Austrian School and the gold standard as its conclusion, while the other was Hayek's treatise in 1976. But Matonis (2011) emphasized the dislike of Bitcoin by libertarians, and Velde (2013) was skeptical to this analogy. Trautman and Harrell (2016) briefly surveyed this issue as the theoretical foundation of Bitcoin (pp. 24–26).

material under Japanese law.[11] The grasp seemed stranger than the definition of the GAO (Government Accountability Office) and the FinCEN (Financial Crime Enforcement Network) in the USA around 2013 that virtual currencies were those "that operate like a currency in some environments, but do not have legal tender status in any jurisdiction," implying that they depended "upon a general acceptability in voluntary transactions if it is to have any use or value ... entirely within a virtual economy, or in lieu of a government-issued currency to purchase goods and services in the real economy" (quoted in Trautman and Harrell 2016, p. 11). Then in a few years, the Japanese government enacted a bill with some amendment at the end of April to May 2016, with which Bitcoin became defined as an "asset-like value."[12]

Certainly, it has been a big problem for each government how to tax the profit accrued by Bitcoin. It contradicted with the tax system because the transactions with bitcoin easily surpassed national boundaries in its own procedure, as is usual these days also for transactions without bitcoin. But to tax is not the only problem. The fact that Bitcoin does not have any own particular area or country makes regulating it complicated in general, but the citizens who should suffer from any crime concerning it have to be protected within a normal legal and social framework. What Nakamoto originally strove for was to avoid double-spending and the intervening destruction by greedy attackers, on which he calculated the probability that any attacker should catch up to the honest one. He concluded that it was not very probable that the system of Bitcoin could be attacked and destroyed. But this proof did not suffice to cover the extensive areas for regulation. Brito and Castillo 2016 classified several aspects of regulation in the USA in collation to FinCEN, such as the legality as a private currency at all,[13] regulation against possibilities of money laundering, crimes in money transmissions, etc. Böhme et al. 2015 indicated that there were Bitcoin-specific crimes such as theft, attacks on the mining pools, and supplemented the need for consumer protection.

2.3 *The Meaning of Trust in Connection to Bitcoin*

The legal and social aspects of Bitcoin bring us back to the issue of trust. Nakamoto emphasized that the cryptographic proof could be the replacement for people's trust for financial institutions. This terminology of Nakamoto corresponded to Hayek's terminology of people's trust in banks.[14] We know on the other hand, however, in

[11]The statement was issued shortly after an exchange for bitcoin in Tokyo, Mt. Gox, went bankrupt around the end of February in 2014.

[12]The Japan-times, one of popular English newspapers in Japan, reported it on the 25th of May, 2016.

[13]It might also be an issue at all, even though "privately issued currencies are not forbidden, and in fact many local currencies are in circulation" (Brito and Castillo 2016, p. 41).

[14]"People ... trust that a bank, to preserve its business, will arrange its affairs so that it will at all times be able to exchange demand deposits for cash, although they know that banks do not have

some other monetary theory, it has been discussed as people's belief, collective belief, or confidence in money that makes the money valid and effective in a society.[15] If we look closely into the reason why people trust banks, we will come to this belief in money that the banks issue. Still, in Nakamoto's explanation of transactions of Bitcoin, we also find potential problems of trust between two interested parties or transactions without fraud in Nakamoto's usage of the term. Taking these conditions in mind, we set up our hypothetical theme around the concept of trust.

According to Williamson, the concept of trust has been an elusive one for economic theorists, especially those who laid importance on institutions and transaction cost.[16] He warned that it was redundant or misleading to use the term 'trust' easily or its absence where contractual safeguards or their absence were discussed. But he then classified three kinds of trust as the outcome of many different questions and comments he had got from other streams of economic thought. First he discussed the calculative trust to be measured by subjective probability, second he picked up hyphenated trust, and finally he went on to the nearly non-calculative trust. The trust Nakamoto had utilized without naming it partly corresponded to the first one, when he examined the unlikeliness of success of greedy attackers on Bitcoin. But the first type will not be sufficient for analyzing diverse problems of money and transactions, so that the second and the third types are also worthwhile to be considered.

Besides, there is another keyword in connection to trust which Nakamoto attempted to clarify. It is the security of privacy against the general public, or we can append the privacy against the intervention of institutional powers. Institutional powers tend to intervene more than necessary in the noble cause of protection and trust of the public. Nakamoto seemed to be conscious of this problem. The network of Bitcoin was designed to be globally open and did not have restrictions for access to entry or for getting information from it. Nakamoto explained as follows: "The traditional banking model achieves a level of privacy by limiting access to information to the parties involved and the trusted third party. The necessity to announce all transactions publicly precludes this method, but privacy can still be maintained by breaking the flow of information in another place: by keeping public keys anonymous" (Nakamoto 2008, p. 6).

Nakamoto paraphrased that the public on the internet could see someone sending some amount to someone else, but that they could not know who, whom, and how much. Each frame of information constitutes a part of the cryptographic proof and thus has to be open, but the owners of the private key are not open. Hence, we ask

---

enough cash to do so if everyone exercised his right to demand instant payment at the same time" (Hayek 1976/1990/2014, pp. 48–49).

[15]For example, Orlean (2004).

[16]There has been a lineage of economic theories of transaction cost after Ronald H. Coase had discussed this concept in his article on firm in the 1930s. Then it was Oliver Williamson who investigated this lineage in the context of (new) institutional economics. As to the "elusiveness" of trust, see Williamson (1993, p. 453).

whether this kind of semi-security of identity would eventually be contradictory to the principle of a free market system as Hayek had explored.

3 Hayek's Consideration

3.1 The Historical Background of Hayek's 1976 Treatise

In the previous section, we indicated that Hayek's treatise on the denationalization of money in 1976 had almost been the only reference for those who sought for theoretical foundations of a rising tendency of digital currencies. But of course Hayek was not the only economist who had made research on money around the 1970s.[17] It was a time when the international system of fixed exchange rate was suddenly abandoned by the Nixon Shock in 1971, the decisive crisis of the reserve currency of US dollar, which shook the whole international economic system and was the catalyst for it to be reconsidered and reconstructed. It was natural for economists to explore monetary issues fundamentally. Setting the problem in a way to question the apparently evident system of one currency for one nation-state, and to think of the possibility of competing monies or competing supply of money as a result, could naturally be included within view.

As Hayek himself mentioned, it was his consistent position to support fixed rates of exchange since the 1930s, and the crisis of that international system would definitely been his concern. What he had believed was that 'a fixed rate of redemption in terms of gold or other currencies ... prevented monetary authorities from giving in to the demands of the ever-present pressure for cheap money' (Hayek 1976/1990/2014, p. 109). But he saw this preventive effect and pressure of fixed rates to not be strong enough and to not function in the 1970s and felt desperate about it. He mentioned at the very beginning of his treatise in 1976 that his motivation to write it was closely connected to his hopelessness of 'finding a politically feasible solution ... to stop inflation' (Ibid., p.13). In spite of the preventive pressure of fixed rates, governments had taken unsuitable policy measures of money supply and caused inflation. Hence, he gradually went on to reach a somehow surprising idea that governments should be deprived of its monopoly of the issue of money.

He explained that he had been consistent on this for more than 30 years since he wrote one of his books, *The Road to Serfdom*, published in 1944. In this widely read book, he insisted that a small policy measure of economic control by the government would lead in the end to totalitarianism and the suppression of individual liberty. Also in this sense, he kept his stance from the interwar period to the postwar context of the 1970s. The claim for denationalization of money could be seen as Hayek's

[17]Hayek admitted that Klein (1974) was prior to his investigation, which was "until recently unknown to me, (but) had clearly explained the chief advantage of competition among currencies" (Hayek 1976/1990/2014, p. 27). But Hayek mistook Klein's article as being published in 1975.

declaration of political stance of liberalism against the state, with the conviction against totalitarianism.

In the treatise, Hayek conceded that he did not even think of any other possibility than the governmental control of a single uniform kind of money in 1960. Certainly in his book in 1960, he claimed that we could not easily change the system of money and credit arranged and controlled by governments.[18] He listed up three fundamental reasons for this. The first reason was that he saw changes in the relative supply of money to be "much more disturbing than changes in any other circumstances that affect prices and production" (Hayek 1960/2011, p. 452). The second was the relation of the supply of money to credit. Hayek placed much importance on it, stating that all modern economic life rested on this supply of money in relation to credit. And the third was the large volume of government expenditure. Further, he gave some more detailed explanation of the first one there.

In a sense, he might be seen consistent in that he attributed a large role and hence also a large influence of governments on monetary matters. Because of this importance of governments' role and influence, he once refrained from depriving of their monopoly and then later, on the contrary, insisted on it. Writing about Hayek's change of stance, Nikaido (1985) saw his deepening of philosophical thoughts on money and its competition from the 1960s to the 1970s. According to this view, his thought experienced a process of conceptual purification, with which the institution of money was seen to be self-regulating, so that it did not need any force, control, or intervention from outside.

But whether to accept this view or not, Hayek in his treatise in 1976 contrasted such voluntary accepted money with forcible one, looking back on the long "mistrust" against paper money in the history. "Money which is current only because people have been forced to accept it is wholly different from money that has come to be accepted because people trust the issuer to keep it stable" (Hayek 1976/1990/2014, p. 111). Here, his usage of the concept trust is remarkable. Hayek attempted to decompose the constituents of what Nakamoto called as financial institutions and came to separate private banks from the complex of the central power of government (and the central bank, though not mentioned).[19] In his thinking, people's trust in private money would be similar to the one for demand deposits which banks are able to redeem immediately at customer demands and would depend on the competence of new issuers to keep the purchasing power of that money stable.

In this way, Hayek made an observation about people's unconscious acceptance, a visible sign of trust, of the legal tender as the only money, especially as a means of payment. According to him, legal tender only signifies that a creditor cannot refuse the money issued by the government in discharge of a debt due to him. He picked up several historical cases where the value of legal tender saliently declined during and

[18]Hayek (1960/2011, p. 452). This change has been seen as an important turning point of Hayek's thought. For example, Nikaido (1985, p. 307).

[19]Hudson criticized such a view of the individualistic theory, economic liberals and of bankers', in his perspective of the history of debt (Hudson 2004, p. 118).

after the First World War, etc.,[20] and judged conclusively that legal tender was only a legal device to force people to accept the money issued by the government. He, hence, disclosed his position of liberalism to support the competition of private banks with the government.[21]

3.2 *The Problems of Money Creation with Eurodollar*

In our understanding, the birth and development of Eurodollar exerted considerable influence on the thoughts on money and currency as well as on the monetary practice from the 1960s to the 1970s. Hayek was no exception in this connection. Concerning Hayek's change of stance, we discussed in the previous section, we can recognize a considerable influence of the Eurodollar. And discussions with his contemporary economists such as Machlup[22] or Friedman show how clamorous the controversies among economists as well as journalists were on the Eurodollar toward the end of the 1960s. It also gives us a vivid image how the reaction of people to the possible emergence of a new currency would look like.

In 1960, Hayek expressed his skepticism of the Eurodollar and claimed that the governments should keep their monopoly of the issue of money "to prevent anybody else from issuing tokens with the same name," and explicitly mentioning dollars (Hayek 1960/2011, p. 452). But in the 1970s, he admitted that many people in Europe would prefer dollars to their national currencies if they were legally permitted or what was more, that they did use dollars even without such permission, so that the most severe penalties would not be able to prevent this tendency from increasing rapidly. From his statements, the national currencies in Europe were not recognized any more as the only or the most trusted ones by more and more people, opening the possibility to use dollars' accounts there. Hayek seemed to be embarrassed by the size and rapid spread of these "unaccounted-for dollar notes" (Hayek 1976/1990/2014, p. 85) or Eurodollars all over the world.

It might look just as parallel usage and eventual competition of European national currencies with the US dollar. In fact, the literature of competing monies chose similar historical examples; some referred to the situation in China in 1948–1950 where the U S dollar as well as Chinese Nationalist paper currency were used, or in

[20] *Ibid.*, pp. 39–40. By the way, these examples had empirical strength by Hayek's career and his personal experience in Austria in the post-WWI period.

[21] Seen in more long-term history, however, the relationship between the government and private banks has been more complicated. Huerta de Soto mentioned to the custody of the continental European juridical tradition, dated back to the old Roman Law. He discussed that it later bore some cases of open and legal violation when the government gave privilege of fractional reserve to some bankers (Huerta de Soto 1995, pp. 29–31).

[22] Machlup originally stemmed from Austria and belonged to the fourth generation of the Austrian School of Economics together with Hayek, Oskar Morgenstern, etc.. He then immigrated and got the US citizenship already in the 1940s.

Korea in 1952–1953 with the Korean currency and US dollars (Tullock 1975, p. 491), while others mentioned some colonial monetary arrangements of New England colonies in the USA in the eighteenth century (Klein 1974, p. 439). Though these examples would have a character of political temporality in history, they did appeal as real cases of dual and competing currencies.

But on the other hand, it was also possible to define the Eurodollar as "a newly invented currency of the international financial and monetary system which no one can actually feel, touch, or see," dealt in only in large units and only by wholesalers, namely the banks and not by the customers of the banks themselves, as some other economist at the same time (1970s) elaborated.[23] Here, it matters that a new unit of money was born from people's preference for a new possibility.

It is interesting that Hayek, while not explicitly recognizing it as such, but perhaps half-consciously, accepted the emergence of Eurodollar as a new type of monetary phenomena. This aspect of the "creation" of the Eurodollar was explored by Machlup in 1970,[24] which Hayek mentioned briefly in his treatise when he posed the question of what was money. Hayek soon answered this question, proposing to rather use the word currency instead of money or at least to avoid the usage of the noun money. He indicated that the term money could designate many different things with various degrees, so that it would be better to use the adjective. In this way, Hayek sketchily generalized Machlup's more detailed investigations with concrete examples, only quoting Machlup's usage of the term "moneyness" and "near-moneyness" and avoided to mention the Eurodollar itself. But in fact, Machlup assuredly stated there that the criterion of moneyness was immediate availability in discharge of debt and it was "undoubtedly met with respect to the Eurodollar deposits owned by individuals and nonbank corporations" (Machlup 1970, p. 225). He then discussed the stable and volatile elements of the demand for Eurodollar for transactions, for investment and assets, and for speculations.

From the theoretical viewpoint, the difference lay in the degree of their reliance on the concept of market. For Machlup, the concept of market defined as a meeting of people whose interests match with each other was not enough to explain the complex reality at that time. It was his intention to clarify the multifaceted and often confused phenomena around the system of Eurodollar, for example, its transactions, loans, credits, deposits, as well as "the loans outstanding, the assets held, the deposit liabilities owed" (Machlup 1970, pp. 220–221), under the conceptualization of "a creation of money." On the contrary, Hayek attempted to show the importance of money as the loose-joint in the market mechanism itself. For Hayek, "money is not a tool of policy, . . . but it should be part of the self-steering mechanism" (Hayek 1976/1990/2014, p. 102).

---

[23]Strange (1971, p. 14). Strange classified Eurodollar as one of the neutral currencies defined in the sense of political neutrality. But as we discuss here, Eurodollar was surrounded by highly political circumstances of international economy, so that the adjective neutral did not seem very suitable.

[24]As the subtitle of his article, "a mystery story," showed, Machlup might also have been mystified by the phenomena of Eurodollar.

From the viewpoint of real politics, Machlup was certainly not unconscious of the fact that the Eurodollar was conspicuously special within the category of Eurocurrencies.[25] It was certainly because of the special role of US dollar as "the foremost international transactions currency."[26] Besides, he also cast his eyes on the importance of the City of London to have "developed a system providing not only the lowest transactions cost but also payment of interest on all kinds of deposit balances" (Machlup 1970, p. 244). He indicated that dollar transactions in London thus seemed to be the ideal combination of currency and location for many people. In this sense, the Eurodollar as a new currency was certainly not a genuine alternative to legal tenders, in the sense of independence of any institutional authority of nation-states, but rather parasitic on it.

However, Machlup seemed to be more aware of the potential of the Eurodollar to be free from restrictions of the international monetary system among the nation-states, each of which had own national currency. He attributed a considerable, if not the entire, role of the growing preference of American banks for accepting funds through their European branches, and the growing preference for dollar loans and dollar deposits in European banks, to the freedom from regulations and from reserve requirements. There were also cases, he indicated, where lower transaction costs were the result of less or no regulations and conventions for nonresidents might stimulate people's preference. Even though these might be seen as anomalous or pathological (Fratianni and Savona 1971, p. 121), it could not be negated that such preferences let ever more transactions deviate from and beyond the control of a normal monetary system at that time.

In comparison with these considerations by Machlup, Hayek was faithful enough to the theory of the arranging role of competition, which was supposed to work on the very foundation of the market mechanism. The explanation with a table of information list of issued currencies, "For a decision so important for business as which currency to use in contracts and accounts, all possible information would be supplied daily in the financial press, and have to be provided by the issuing banks themselves for the information of the public" (Ibid., p. 53), expressively showed the righteous image of the market process. And also in showing an example of a competing currency—a privately issued Swiss ducat in this case, he just assumed serious efforts of banks to gain the trust of people. He argued that "competition would certainly prove a more effective constraint, forcing the issuing institutions to keep the value of their currency constant" (Ibid., p.48).

[25]Machlup spared the last one paragraph of his article to justify his almost exclusive deal with Eurodollar, comparing the statistical data of deposit liabilities of other six Eurocurrencies amounted less than 20% with the rest of more than 80% of Eurodollar in 1969 (*Ibid.*, p. 260. Other Eurocurrencies were with German mark (Euromark), the Swiss franc, the pound sterling, the Dutch guilder, the French franc, and with the Italian lira.

[26]*Ibid.*, p. 243. Strange (1971) quoted a passage to show this two-sidedness of American position; "...although ... the Eurodollar market can be interpreted as an attack on the monopoly position of American banks, it is also a tribute to the monopoly position of the dollar" (Strange 1971, p. 209).

3.3 Deviation from Hayek's Expectations

On the other hand, in comparison with Milton Friedman, Hayek looked much more positive to this new monetary phenomenon.[27] Friedman announced his stance already in 1969 and held his stance as long as possible that there was nothing special in Eurodollar and that it had two characteristics. First, Eurodollars were short-term obligations to pay dollars, and second, the banking offices of these obligations were located outside the USA. He argued that banks in general had to be subject to the regulations and legally required reserves of the country they were located in, but that for Eurodollar markets there were almost no regulations in practice.

Just as Machlup emphasized the possibility of Eurodollar to be free from such restraints, Friedman also admitted that the rigid regulations such as the Regulation Q, exchange control, or other governmental controls in the USA rather stimulated the development of the Eurodollar. Still, he insisted that the banking institutions for Eurodollar were just a part of normal fractional reserve banking system, so that the development of the Eurodollar was mostly drawn from a bookkeeper's pen, the operation of which "had affected the statistics far more than the realities" (Friedman 1969, p. 20). Seen in his unusual manner to repeat this term of bookkeeping operation several times persistently in his article, he did not want to accept that there should be any substantial influence of the virtual development of the Eurodollar on the international economy.

This stance seemed to influence Friedman's judgement of Hayek's proposal. He expressed his skepticism of its realization despite being in favor of the proposal itself: "we have ample empirical and historical evidence . . . (that) private currencies which offer purchasing power security would not drive out governmental currencies" (Friedman 1977, p. 26). Hayek quoted this critical attitude of Friedman and commented that he was surprised that Friedman had so little faith in competition to make a better institution prevail.

But the discrepancy may come from their different ideas on the relation among the trusted financial institutions which consist of private banks, the central bank, and the government, or in principle the state, instead of the government of the day, which authorizes the whole system. Hayek found it effective to warn the government that banks could possibly take the position of competition and decrease people's demand for governmental currency when the government was failed by malfunctioning or abusing power, while Friedman thought it unlikely to happen. Friedman thought that people's (or possibly also his own) trust for the government would be stronger than Hayek had expected.

In other words, it was Hayek's own despair that politics did not function as he wrote at the beginning of his treatise, that let him dare to argue that his proposal would become practicable only with a "much more far-reaching change in our

[27]Hayek added this part only in the second edition, in order to give a reply mainly to Friedman's criticism on his proposal in an interview in 1977. Friedman's stance to Eurodollar can also be seen in Friedman (1969).

political institutions" (Hayek 1976/1990/2014, p. 84). He believed that allowing private banks to issue their own currencies would be, so to speak, to be on the side of ordinary people in opposition to governmental authority, while Friedman was skeptical of the opinion that such privatization would break the rigid structure of authority complex.

By the way, we might add that the ultimate tradeoff between privately issued and governmental currencies was not exactly what Hayek hoped. Hayek rather thought of the possibility of coexistence of several currencies within the monetary system. At least he showed such a description as the long-run prospect: "...once the system had fully established itself and competition had eliminated a number of unsuccessful ventures, there would remain in the free world several extensively used and very similar currencies. In various large regions one or two of them would be dominant, but these regions would have no sharp or constant boundaries, and the use of the currencies dominant in them would overlap in broad and fluctuating border districts" (Ibid., p. 126.). As this statement shows, Hayek's long-term vision of monetary order was not the cutthroat struggle for the only seat, but rather some peaceful plurality of good currencies with communities using them being flexible and partly overlapping.

We can assume that Hayek had reached such a vision from his theoretical investigation of regional currencies, social credit, or free money of his contemporaries such as Silvio Gesell, Major C. H. Douglas, H. Ritterhausen, or Henry Meulen, as he referred to in his treatise. These authors, though they sometimes became radical with criticism of state theory of money seeking for the revolutionary alternative of legal tender, generally paid attention to the social and communal aspect of money. Hayek might have shared such view to a considerable extent.

But as was experienced in the case of the Eurodollar, history developed far beyond such a harmonious vision of coexistence. Though Hayek elaborated cases of international markets of competing currencies, people's demand for currencies rather deviated toward the niches of such international institutions and toward speculative directions, which gave rise to the whole stories of offshore markets, tax havens, etc. In this sense, Hayek's vision of the open market mechanism for competing currencies was not exactly hitting the mark.

4 The Meaning of Trust in Relation to Market and Transaction Cost

Looking back on the investigation on Hayek's treatise in 1976, we have seen that considerable fundamental questions were posed on the essence, characteristics, and creation of money, currency, liabilities, debt, deposits, etc. For those who got acquainted with such discussions and controversies, it was already imaginable that the national currency would not be the only one and the virtual operations might open up a vast room of possibilities for new currencies. The trusted financial institutions, as Nakamoto mentioned, had been decomposed into the government and private banks, and Hayek discussed that people's trust for possible private money which would rest on the ability of issuers to keep its purchasing power and that it would surpass the legal force of governments to force creditors to accept governmental money. The tradeoff between the new and the old currency is not the only outcome of competition, but some possibility of coexistence in the long run was also drawn as a vision. But there were some cracks in his reasoning.

Beyond the expectation of Hayek, as Nakamoto explicitly stated, banks have to take appropriate measures for avoiding fraud, disputes, conflicts or any kind of troubles, and for keeping the privacy of their customers. These measures are necessary in order to gain people's trust, but inevitably increase the transaction costs, some part of which banks impose on the side of customers as a fee. Hence, there came such attempts as Bitcoin to dispense with such transaction costs once and for all.

It was natural for Hayek, one of the representative economic theorists with the faith in the market mechanism, not to have taken transaction costs into consideration. In the frame of market theory, the environment of markets is assumed to be exogenous in the market theory. But in the frame of institutional economics, it is argued that there are several kinds of institutional trust. What Williamson put up as the second category of hyphenated trust is not very often noticed, because they are embedded. Williamson listed up societal culture, corporate culture, politics, regulation, professionalization, or networks (Williamson 1993, p. 476). These factors have some influence on compliance in the practice of transactions and function as the safeguard and, hence, constitute the substance of trust between the interested parties. In other words, the question Bitcoin has raised was whether the transactions within and beyond such institutional trust could in fact be replaced for by the cryptographic proofs.

Besides, the necessity for banks to keep the privacy of customers is contradictory to the openness of all the information in the market of competing currencies Hayek believed. To gain people's trust, banks make an effort to keep their information secret, which would damage the transparency of markets and possibly induce illegal transactions in some cases. It will not necessarily be a bank that keeps information secret, but it can be the cryptographic mechanism and in a different way. Still, we always have to ask how and how far private information should and could be kept secret. As we have suggested in the second part of this article, the issue of security of privacy and identity of individuals is indispensable and should be elaborated much more in our digital age, departing from the optimism of market theory.

References

Antonopoulos, A. M. (2014). *Mastering Bitcoin*. Sebastopol: Oreilly & Associates Inc.

Athey, S., et al. (2016). *Bitcoin pricing, adoption, and usage: Theory and evidence* (Working Paper No. 3469). Stanford, CA: Stanford Graduate School of Business.

Böhme, R., Christin, N., Edelman, B., & Moore, T. (2015). Bicoin: Economics, technology, and governance. *Journal of Economic Perspectives, 29*(2), 213–238.
Brito, J., & Castillo, A. (2016). *Bitcoin: A primer for policymakers* (2nd ed.). Arlington: Mercatus Center at George Mason University.
European Central Bank. (2012). Virtual currency scheme 21, Frankfurt am Main.
Fratianni, M., & Savona, P. (1971). Eurodollar creation: Comments on Prof. Machlup's propositions and developments. *PSL Quarterly Review, 24*(97), 110–127.
Friedman, M. (1969). *The Euro-dollar market: Some first principles* (Selected Papers No. 34). Chicago: Graduate School of Business, University of Chicago.
Friedman, M. (1977, August). Interview: Milton Friedman. *Reason*, 24–29.
Hudson, M. (2004). The archaeology of money: Debt versus Barter theories of money's origins. In L. Randall Wray (Ed.), *Credit and state theories of money: The contributions of A. Mitchell Innes*. Cheltenham/Northampton: Edward Elgar.
Huerta de Soto, J. (1995). A critical analysis of central banks and fractional-reserve free banking from the Austrian School perspective. *The Review of Austrian Economics, 8*(2), 25–38.
Klein, B. (1974). The competitive supply of money. *Journal of Money, Credit and Banking, 6*(4), 423–453.
Machlup, F. (1970). Euro-dollar creation: A mystery story. *Banca Nationale del Lavoro Quarterly Review, 94*, 219–260.
Matonis, J. (2011, June 26). Why are libertarians against Bitcoin? *The Monetary Future*.
Nakamoto, S. (2008). *Bitcoin: A peer-to-peer electronic cash system*. http://bitcoin.org/bitcoin.pdf
Nikaido, T. (1985). Theory of the "de-nationalization of money": Trust and control in Hayek (in Japanese). *Departmental Bulletin Paper of Kyoto university (Keizai Ronsou), 135*(4), 304–321.
Nishibe, M. (2014). *The Mystery of Money (in Japanese)*. Tokyo: NHK Publishing.
Noguchi, Y. (2014). *The virtual currency revolution (in Japanese)*. Tokyo: Diamond- Sha.
Okada, H. (2015). The influence of the emerging virtual currency on nation, society, and economy (in Japanese). *IEICE Fundamental Review, 8*(3), 183–192.
Orlean, A. (2004). What is collective belief? In P. Bourgine & J.-P. Nadal (Eds.), *Cognitive economics: An interdisciplinary approach* (pp. 199–212). Berlin: Springer.
Saito, K. (2014). *Korede Wakatta Bitcoin (in Japanese)*. Tokyo: Tarojiro-sha Editus.
Strange, S. (1971). *Sterling and British policy: A political study of an international currency in decline*. London/New York/Toronto: Oxford University Press.
Trautman, L. J., & Harrell, A. C. (2016). Bitcoin versus regulated payment systems: What gives? *Cardozo Law Review*. forthcoming.
Tullock, G. (1975). Competing monies. *Journal of Money, Credit and Banking, 7*(4), 491–497.
Velde, F. R. (2013, December). *Bitcoin: A primer* (Chicago Fed Letter No. 317). Chicago, IL: The Federal Reserve Bank of Chicago.
von Hayek, F. A. (1960/2011). In R. Hamowy (Ed.), *The constitution of liberty*. Chicago/London: The University of Chicago Press.
von Hayek, F. A. (1976/1990/2014). *Denationalization of money – The argument refined: An analysis of the theory and practice of concurrent currencies* (3rd ed., reprint). London: Institute of Economic Affairs.
Williamson, O. E. (1993). Calculativeness, trust, and economic organization. *Journal of Law and Economics, 36*(April), 453–486.

Cryptocurrencies from an Austrian Perspective

Alistair Milne

1 Introduction: The Challenge of Restoring Free Markets in Money and Credit

Austrian economics provides fundamental but too often ignored insights into the challenges of monetary and macroeconomic policymaking. The Austrian theory of the business cycle offers a persuasive account of the genesis of the 2007–2008 crisis: it was made possible by the reliance of central banks worldwide on the reduction of short-term rates of interest to promote private sector spending. This encouraged an unsustainable expansion of money and credit. The only substantive difference from previous financial crises, something that allowed the preceding credit boom to proceed for so far and so long, was that instabilities arising from maturity mismatches appeared in new and therefore hidden variants, through money market funding of mortgage-backed securities and other structured credit assets. Austrian economics also provides a valuable explanation of previous episodes of global economic instability, for example the breakdown in the early 1970s of the post-

---

On being invited to write this chapter, I first wrote a lengthier and more technical discussion of cryptocurrency technologies and their use to reduce the role of both the state and banks in money creation. That paper is available on SSRN at https://papers.ssrn.com/sol3/papers.cfm?abstract_id=2946160. My intention is, eventually, to write a book length treatment of the issues raised by this investigation. I am indebted to the support of the Department of Banking and Finance at Monash University Business School during a period of study leave when this chapter was written and for comments from Denys Firth, Charles Goodhart, David Mayes and George Selgin and from a number of seminar presentations.

Citation: Milne, Alistair, Cryptocurrencies from an Austrian Perspective (April 17, 2017). https://ssrn.com/abstract=2946160 or https://doi.org/10.2139/ssrn.2946160

A. Milne (✉)
Loughborough University, Loughborough, UK
e-mail: a.k.l.milne@lboro.ac.uk

A. Godart-van der Kroon, P. Vonlanthen (eds.), *Banking and Monetary Policy from the Perspective of Austrian Economics*,
https://doi.org/10.1007/978-3-319-75817-6_12

war Bretton-Woods fixed exchange rate system based on a gold exchange standard as a consequence of insufficient discipline on US monetary creation.

Austrian economics is also the only free-market orientated school of thought drawing full attention to the deficiencies of the global policy response since 2007–2008.[1,2] Central banks and governments around the world have mitigated the impact of the crisis on output and employment, providing more than $10 trillion dollars of financial support to prevent bank failures, cutting short-term interest rates for all the major currencies close to zero and engaging in a sustained and aggressive fiscal expansion that has more than doubled the ratio of public sector debt to GDP.

These measures may have been effective short-term palliatives, but they have done little to deal with underlying causes. While substantial increases in regulatory capital requirements and a wide range of other regulations have reduced tax-payer exposure to banking risks, investors have been left in little doubt that they will be protected once again should the entire financial system once again be threatened. The resumption of growth in the advanced economies is based as before on credit creation and maturity mismatch. The mispricing of assets and misallocations of capital evident before the crisis have continued, in many cases becoming even more marked. Economic expansion has been much stronger than was generally expected in the 18 months following the collapse of Lehman brothers, but this recovery has not been strong enough to allow a winding down of fiscal expansion. A policy of temporary 'pump priming' has turned into a policy of permanent and unsustainable fiscal deficits.

These deficiencies seem to make a new and potentially even more serious global economic crisis inevitable. The uncertainties are about its timing and form. Perhaps there will be renewed fiscal and monetary expansion in response to the next economic downturn, postponing the inevitable adjustment for a number of years further down the road? Perhaps the crisis will emerge as a collapse of confidence in government liabilities, including central bank money, rather than in banks and secured money market instruments? Another crisis is looming; we just do not know when it will happen or how it will emerge.

As discussed in other chapters of this book, Austrian thinking offers many policy recommendations that can help avoid such an undesirable outcome. There is though a barrier to their adoption: they are still largely perceived as politically unacceptable. To take one example, consider the proposals for 'free banking' with freedom for any entrepreneur to establish a bank and with regulation limited to the same kind of regulatory framework that applies to most other industries—the rigorous application

[1]Some flavour of the reaction of the Austrian economists and their criticisms of government bailouts at the time of the 2008 crisis can be found at https://mises.org/library/bailout-reader.

[2]Heterodox post-Keynsian economics in the Minskian tradition provide another critique of the mainstream policy consensus, agreeing with Austrian school thinking that current policies will lead to an eventual and even more serious global economic crisis. This analysis though is predicated on the assumptions of inherent flaws in the market economy and therefore advocates an even more radical replacement by the state of market mechanisms and market allocations of resources than has already taken place to date.

of the framework of law to enforce contractual agreements, prevent frauds and stop the sale of unsafe or misleading products and services. This leaves banks that are unable to fund themselves facing the same disciplines as other commercial organisations, having to suspend operations and wind themselves down. This can be expected to result in much safer and sounder banking, with limited use of unstable fractional reserving. Nevertheless, in the wake of the crisis and the general blame cast (with some justification) on irresponsible bankers, no political programme can be realistically expected to prioritise such a reform. An outcome of the global financial crisis is instead that money and credit are nowadays seen more than ever, both in the mind of the public and politicians that seek their votes, as a state responsibility.

This chapter offers a novel *technological* perspective on the challenge of restoring public faith in the effectiveness of market mechanisms in the provision of money and credit. The technology concerned is the radical decentralisation of payments, without any need for a state controlled monetary base or centralised settlement, made possible by using distributed ledgers (or 'blockchain'), the shared transaction records that underpin cryptocurrencies such as Bitcoin. It is proposed here that all money—both state supported fiat money and money issued by banks to finance lending—should be placed on a single distributed ledger. This can then support many of the key Austrian proposals for monetary arrangements.

This proposal set out here may be regarded as a rather 'impure' version of Austrian thinking. It is not obviously the arrangement that would emerge from a voluntary agreement amongst citizens and businesses in the absence of state intervention. An important co-ordinating role is still envisaged for the state, sponsoring the establishment of the distributed ledger for both bank and fiat money. Still, even if this proposal does not go as far as many proponents of Austrian policy ideas would like, it has—it will be argued—the key advantage of greater potential political acceptability.

It requires little or no change in the day-to-day experience of payments and borrowing by households and companies. The panoply of bank regulations does not have to be torn down from the outset; they can be removed gradually. Banks cannot object (as they do to proposals for 100% reserving) that the ledger makes it difficult for them to extend credit. It also makes the relationship between banks and customers and banks *much* more transparent than at present. No longer are banks engaged in an arguably illegal contractual engagement by holding customer money as withdrawable deposits rather than risky investments, deposits whose withdrawal they cannot guarantee in all circumstances, hence helping promote the political case for private sector creation of money and credit.

The Austrian perspective as developed in this chapter is not one which views the explosion of competing private sector open-source decentralised digital monies (Bitcoin, Ethereum, Ripple, NEM, Monero and several hundred more) as a practical implementation of Hayek's ideas on the denationalisation of money—i.e. an evolution in which money is supplied by competing private sector providers seeking to establish their credibility with the public rather than by the state. This perspective is endorsed by many working or commenting on the development of new digital currencies[3] and explored by Chikako Nakayama in the preceding chapter of this book.

These two perspectives, as set out in our two chapters, are different but not inconsistent. Should the ideas put forward in this particular chapter be put into effect, with fiat and bank money all placed on a distributed ledger, this does not create any additional barriers to the launch of a private sector cryptocurrency also issued on a distributed ledger which competes with existing state supported fiat money. A competing private sector cryptocurrency might also—as envisaged for the state sponsored cryptocurrency described here—allow banks to create money through a securitisation of loans onto their own ledger. State and private cryptocurrencies could still compete if there is demand for using both from households and companies.

The chapter is organised as follows. Section 2 summarises the proposal and explains how it supports Austrian proposals on money and credit. Changing banking arrangements and payments technologies over the past two centuries have altered perceptions about the nature of money—with the understood and accepted medium of exchange in the modern economy evolving to become transaction balances held with banks. This proposal for shifting these bank transaction balances onto a mutual distributed ledger reverses the resulting encroachment of banks and the state on the supply of money. The next two sections develop the proposal in more detail. Section 3 examines the arrangements for execution and settlement of payments as they have evolved today, requiring central banks to provide reserves as a settlement asset and a permanent commitment to liquidity support to commercial banks and money markets in order to avoid interruption in the flow of money and payments. It then discusses the changes to these arrangements required for placing fiat money and bank money on a single distributed ledger and hence obviating the need for settlement in central bank reserves or unconditional central bank support for the banking system. Section 4 discusses the implications for bank regulation and the provision of money and credit. It also considers the political acceptability of the proposal. Section 5 concludes.

[3]For example (Koenig 2015), an entertaining but rather proselytising introduction to Bitcoin and its supporting Blockchain ledger explicitly invokes the link to Austrian economics in both title and text. His book—as well as describing the technology for non-specialists and documenting some of the viewpoints of those involved in the 'Bitcoin movement'—espouses the radical position that these technologies will prove to be a more profound technological development than even the internet, replacing the malign role of the nation state in both economics and politics. A wealth of websites and internet forums share similar viewpoints.

2 Distributed Ledger Money and Austrian Policy Objectives

This section outlines the proposal of this chapter and explains how it can achieve Austrian monetary policy objectives.

2.1 The Proposal

The proposal itself is simple and can be presented in general terms without reference to cryptography or information technology. It has the following elements:

- Banks create monetary deposits as they already do today, but all commercial bank money and central bank money now takes the form of an electronic equivalent of a central bank note, i.e. a decentralised money transferred directly from one holder to another.
- This decentralisation is achieved by having *both* commercial banks and the central bank issue their money on a 'mutual distributed ledger', a universal but decentralised record of the issuance and transfer of all money used in exchange (including paper notes and token coin whose issue is fully backed against the ledger).[4]
- As a result of this decentralisation, there is no need for subsequent settlement using central bank reserves and no longer any distinction between (in Austrian terminology) the medium of exchange and money substitutes or (in conventional monetary vocabulary) outside and inside money.
- Deposits that are not on the ledger but promise immediate redemption on demand into ledger money are required to state explicitly that they are loans at risk of potential temporary suspension or permanent default, should the issuer not have a sufficient reserve of ledger money to redeem as promised.
- All payment instruments (e.g. cards, credit transfers, automated clearing such as direct debits and standing orders) become mechanisms for instructing transfers of ledger money.
- The difference between commercial bank issue and fiat issue by the central bank is that fiat issue is permanent and cannot be withdrawn; commercial bank issue is only temporary, in the form of a short-term securitisation of future anticipated repayments, on loans of good credit quality over the short to medium term.
- Two mechanisms ensure repayment and prevent an inflationist exploitation of money issue:

[4]'*Mutual* distributed ledger' is a coinage of my co-author Michael Mainelli. Describing distributed ledgers as *mutual* highlights a key feature, the absence of any trusted central authority, which is both a strength (supporting resilience, immutability) and a weaknesses (creating challenges of governance).

(a) Repayment onto the ledger is covered by a 'triple lock'—if the bank customer does not repay the loan to the ledger then the bank that provided the loan repays; if the bank does not repay, then the entire banking industry makes the repayment in proportion to their outstanding money they have issued on the ledger at the time the initial loan is made. The ledger becomes a creditor on the bank, with a claim prior even to the tax authorities, repaying other banks as this claim is recovered.

(b) The bank money so securitised is 'overcollateralised', i.e. for each €100 of loan principal pledged as repayment, the bank must provide € x in upfront money to the ledger (i.e. the new money created is only € $100 - x$ of the principal value of the pledged loan). This 'x-percent reserving' allows an effective partial implementation of the 100-percent reserving advocated by many Austrian thinkers.

- Bank transactions deposits are no longer bank liabilities, rather they are transaction or 'wallet' services providing access to payment instruments and accounting statements for holders of ledger money; a payment instruction for any supported instrument can only be carried out if there is sufficient ledger money to fulfil the instruction when it is made.

This proposed arrangement goes well beyond the discussions of possible central bank issue of cryptocurrency made, at least to date, by a number of central banks worldwide.[5] It is not just the issue of a virtual central bank liability, the internet equivalent of a central bank issued banknote, or the use of distributed ledger to support a virtual currency that is completely backed by central bank money.[6] It is a complete redesign of the arrangements for holding and paying fiat and bank money with profound implications for the relationship between banking and the state.

Most importantly, it allows the banking industry to take final responsibility for repayment of temporary creation of money on the ledger. Hence, authorisation for banks to issue money on the ledger and to monitor the quality of the credit assets pledged can become an industry rather than a state responsibility.

[5]Central banks have naturally been paying close attention to the technologies of virtual money; see, for example, Ali et al. (2014b, a). The central issue in these discussions has been whether there is demand for holding a central bank issued cryptocurrency, i.e. something like the suggested Fedcoin outlined by Koning (2014) and Andolfatto (2015). Demand is uncertain; users may prefer the guaranteed anonymity of notes and coin, and there are already effective means for carrying out most online monetary transfers using bank money. For further discussion, see Fung & Halaburda (2016). Bank of Canada and Bank of England research on this topic can be accessed through their webpages, various postings on http://www.bankofcanada.ca and http://www.bankofengland.co.uk/research/Pages/onebank/cbdc.aspx. Sveriges Riksbank has also announced they are investigating possible issue of digital currency (Skingsley 2016).

[6]Such as the Utility Settlement Coin or Tibado described above, or the Monetary Authority of Singapore project working with R3 and a consortium of banks to develop a fully centrally backed virtual currency on distributed ledger that can be used in securities settlement and cross-border payments (on this see Monetary Authority of Singpore 2017).

What role is played in this schema by information technology and cryptography? The distributed ledger technology developed for cryptocurrencies such as Bitcoin provides the essential decentralised immediate real-time accounting framework that makes this schema workable. In principle, while it could be put into effect with preexisting technologies, this would have required a central agency to maintain records of transactions and money holdings and approve payments only when the holder has money to pay. Before distributed ledger technologies were available there would then have been serious concerns about the confidentiality, operational risks and operating costs of such an arrangement—putting the entire nation's money onto a centralised computer system that might be hacked or go offline is not an attractive prospect.

Utilising distributed ledger technologies deals with these concerns. The supporting cryptography allows secure and fully flexible permissioning for both the making of payments and the observation of transaction records. Having many copies of the transaction record eliminates operational risks (one node can fail but the network is extraordinarily robust). Distributed ledgers are also entirely automated, so this schema can operate at very low cost (fractions of a cent per transaction), costs which can be easily shared by governments, participating banks and holders of money, based on their issuance and holding of money and number of transactions.

Note, finally, that the resulting state sponsored cryptocurrency, unlike the 'unpermissioned' cryptocurrencies such as Bitcoin, cannot be completely anonymous: identity is required for repayment; law enforcement should be able to trace payments with appropriate court permissions; some further limitations on anonymity may be justifiable.

2.2 A Reflection on the Changing Nature of the Medium of Exchange

A central part of Austrian monetary thinking is the distinction between the medium of exchange and fiduciary media (or 'money substitutes') and the social and technological changes in money and banking of the past two centuries. It is argued here that modern monetary arrangements have evolved so that today the medium of exchange is no longer commodity or fiat money but rather bank transaction deposits. Therefore, the implementation of Austrian monetary arrangements requires reducing the role of both the state and of state supported banks in the determination of the volume of bank transaction deposits.

Austrian monetary analysis frequently refers back to the early nineteenth century debates between the banking school and currency school in the UK and the contemporaneous arguments for free banking.[7] The currency school arguments of

[7]See also Schwartz (1989) for a succinct review of these controversies.

McCulloch, Lord Overstone, Torrens and others that stressed the instability resulting from bank money creation won the battle for political opinion but lost the war. The 1844 UK banking act introduced strict limitations on the issue of bank notes on currency school lines, denying the right of issue to new banks established after the act, requiring all additional issue by the Bank of the England and Scottish banks to be backed 100% by gold reserves and preventing any additional issue by other existing banks. But as pointed out by Von Mises (1953) and many other Austrians, the UK legislation did nothing to limit the creation of bank transaction deposits which served as money substitutes through the increasing use of the cheque as a means of payment. The following century saw a massive expansion of chequeable deposits. Cheque payments came to replace gold coins and bank notes as the dominant payment instrument for larger value payments in industry, trade and finance, and the gold sovereign was withdrawn from circulation in 1914.

Austrian thinking argues that the social institution of money is not a *creation* of the state. In the absence of government action, economic incentives still ensure the establishment of a medium of exchange to support trade between strangers. This view seems indisputable. While the historical record is of course open to interpretation, there being few examples of expansion of trade without some accompanying political developments, examples such as the widespread use of silver as a medium of exchange in the earliest international trade between the fertile crescent and the Mediterranean region or of Cowrie shells in trade across much of Africa and Asia, without any accompanying political interaction, attest to the fundamental validity of this Austrian view.

The emergence of money as a social institution without the requirement of state support does not, however, mean that the state has no influence on monetary arrangements; or that the institution of money does not itself evolve over time in response to either social or technological change. This is a particular challenge for the Austrian distinction between the medium of exchange—the socially accepted form of money in exchange—and 'money-substitutes' or fiduciary media, claims which are redeemable on demand in the medium exchange and which are used as a replacement for the medium of exchange for making payments. Examples of fiduciary media include both privately issued bank notes and transferable bank deposits.

Because money is a social institution, there is nothing to prevent a psychological and cultural change in which banking deposits have become transformed, in the minds of those who hold them, from being redeemable claims on money to being money themselves. Nowadays, even when money is withdrawn from bank accounts, it either takes the form of central bank notes or of state issued token coinage. Not only has the past century seen a shift from widespread use of gold as a monetary standard to a fiat money standard, this has been accompanied by an equally fundamental change in the medium of exchange. This arguably is now money in a bank account, in turn leading to the political imperative to provide deposit insurance and the bank safety net so that all privately held bank deposits, whether transaction or savings deposits, are good money.

As the medium of exchange has evolved in the minds of users, no longer taking the form either of gold or state liabilities and instead becoming liabilities of banks, there has been an accompanying blurring of the distinction between money held in a bank, e.g. in a safe deposit and a loan of money to a bank. The public has come to perceive all forms of retail banking deposit alike—whether immediately withdrawable without penalty, withdrawable with some loss of return or term deposits withdrawable only at notice—as money in the care of the bank not as loans to the bank. Similar expectations extended even into wholesale money markets, with expectations that in the event of widespread threat of default on money market obligations the central bank will provide the necessary liquidity to ensure repayment, using the assets financed out of retail deposit taking as collateral.

We have a vicious circle (a 'positive feedback' in engineering terms) of cause and effect in which the perception that bank liabilities are themselves the medium of exchange drives a range of state protections for banking, and these state protections in turn reinforce the perception that bank liabilities are indeed the medium of exchange. This in turn supports the expansion of state support, through state-backed deposit insurance and the implicit bank safety net and the large scale expansion of banking balance sheets. The outcome is an overexpansion of banking assets and liabilities that in turn threatens the viability of the private enterprise economy.

A solution to this incursion of the state into what are naturally private concerns, perhaps the only solution that would appear acceptable politically, is to work with the grain of this newly emerged social institution, to accept that transferable bank deposits function directly as the medium of exchange, but also sharply differentiate these deposits from other bank liabilities whether retail or wholesale that are merely promises to repay the holder in terms of the medium of exchange. The distributed ledger proposal of this chapter utilises the new cryptocurrency technologies to achieve this end.

2.3 *Two Cryptocurrency Myths Dispelled*

Before discussing in detail how distributed ledger money, sponsored by the state, can help achieve Austrian policy objectives, two 'myths' about cryptocurrencies should be dispelled.[8] One is that the suggestion that an unpermissioned open-source cryptocurrency could serve as a monetary standard outside of state control. A second is that current unpermissioned cryptocurrencies could easily compete with established fiat currencies for widespread use in everyday domestic exchange.

Arguments for a cryptocurrency standard circulate frequently in developer communities, with statements along the following lines: a cryptocurrency such as Bitcoin is, by construction, in limited supply and therefore—because it is also durable and divisible—shares many features with gold. This analogy is one reason why the term 'mining' was applied to the cryptocurrency proof of work used in Bitcoin to validate

[8] A fuller discussion of the points made in this subsection can be found in the supporting working paper.

payments, a service rewarded with newly created currency.[9] Because of this analogy with gold, so it is claimed, a cryptocurrency in limited supply can be a trustworthy replacement for unsound state fiat currencies.

This possibility, that the medium of exchange could be a cryptocurrency, is sympathetically but critically discussed by Selgin (2015). He views cryptocurrencies such as Bitcoin as a 'synthetic commodities', i.e. like real commodities such as gold or silver the available stock cannot be increased at will by an issuing authority, but unlike gold or silver cryptocurrencies they have no value in any alternative non-monetary use. There are examples of synthetic commodities which have come to be accepted as media of exchange and successfully avoided the inflationary bias of fiat currency.[10] Still, as Selgin admits, the state adoption of a cryptocurrency whose quantity is outside of state control as a monetary standard seems unlikely, and the possibility of privately created synthetic commodity money supplanting fiat money seems remote—at best it would seem that they might come to be widely accepted in exchange alongside fiat money. He concludes that 'the possibility of monetary stabilisation achieved by means of a synthetic commodity standard remains as hypothetical as it is tantalising'.

Another possibility might be fixing the value of fiat currency against a well-established cryptocurrency, perhaps Bitcoin, requiring the central bank to build up its own reserve of the cryptocurrency, but this could not be seriously considered until the cryptocurrency was already widely used in exchange and from this had achieved comparative stability of value against fiat currency.[11] The record of Bitcoin and of other currencies demonstrates that while cryptocurrency has appeal as a relatively risky financial investment, at least on a modest scale, cruyptocurrency use in exchange is unlikely to achieve any significant traction.

Demand for Bitcoin as a store of value is driven by a number of special factors including: technophile's appreciation of the underlying software and the appeal of

---

[9]The original white paper describing the Bitcoin protocol (Nakamoto 2008) contains a strong statement of the desirability of having money whose supply is not controlled by the state, but instead determined by a peer-to-peer network. This white paper is also the source of the term 'mining' for proof of work rewarded by issue of cryptocurrency.

[10]As an example of a synthetic commodity money, Selgin describes the case of the so-called Kurdish Swiss Dinar, which circulated in Iraqi Kurdistan from 1993 to the US coalition invasion of Iraq in 2003. It had value in exchange even though it was governed by no monetary authority, was not legal tender and was not accepted as payment by Iraqi public institutions. Unlike the official Iraqi dinar, the Kurdish Swiss Dinar proved immune from the large-scale loss of value through inflation under the Saddam Hussein regime; its exchange rate against the dollar was stable and supported by the absolute fixity of its supply (unlike the official Iraqi dinar no new Kurdish Swiss Dinars could be printed).

[11]This relates to the long standing discussion in Austrian monetary economics of difference between the perceived stability of the gold standard proper and the evident instability of the gold-exchange standards established in the 1920s and then again under Bretton-Woods. The stability of gold standard proper is seen by many Austrian economists as resting on the widespread use of gold in direct exchange, e.g. through circulation of gold coin, suggesting that a prerequisite for the use of cryptocurrency as a monetary standard is the widespread use of the cryptocurrency in exchange.

private cryptocurrencies to individuals seeking to counteract the extraordinary growth in the power of the state in the past century, or to those with the more extreme libertarian views of the 'cryptophunk' movement, seeking to exploit cryptography to establish an entire realm of social and economic exchange beyond the reach of the state. There is also a fundamental demand driven by the practical challenges of avoid currency controls and other financial regulations or use in illegal transactions.[12]

Cryptocurrencies have one advantage over previous independent monies which have attracted a hostile reaction from state authorities, closing down many of the most successful examples.[13] The combination of an anonymous peer-to-peer exchange and the protection of identity using cryptography make it relatively difficult to prevent cryptocurrency transactions. The built-in quantity limitations on cryptocurrencies also provide a more credible foundation for competition in currencies than basing these on privately issued commitments to exchange in terms of the value of real commodities.[14] For all these reasons, cryptocurrencies now seem to be permanently established as alternative financial assets.

Despite this initial success, the volatility of pricing and limitations of both technology and governance suggest that no unpermissioned, open-source cryptocurrency can ever capture a major share of payments activity from established fiat currency instruments, whether these are using notes and coins or transferring bank issued fiduciary media. The great fluctuations of Bitcoin pricing mean that it is rather impractical to set prices or write debt contracts in BTC (the Bitcoin unit of account); at best there can be live updating of BTC prices for immediate transactions based on the latest current exchange rate into fiat currency. Where BTC is accepted in payment for goods and services it is almost always rapidly exchanged for conventional nation state currency, so Bitcoin is then serving merely as a payment instrument—like Paypal—not as an alternative medium of exchange.

There are other potential problems with Bitcoin. There are substantial capacity problems in the Bitcoin network that remain far from resolved a year and a half after there were first widely discussed amongst network participants. The totally decentralised Bitcoin governance may prevent a satisfactory resolution ever emerging. It is also far from clear that its relatively costly 'proof of work' can be sustained when the creation of new Bitcoins to reward miners is reduced and eventually ceases.

These practical challenges highlight a more general difficulty of unpermissioned open-source cryptocurrency networks, their lack of governance mechanisms to cope with change. The lack of institutional structure also creates other inherent problems.

---

[12] See (Dowd 2014) for discussion of the demand for holding and using cryptocurrencies and other alternative private currencies.

[13] See (Dowd 2014) for discussion of the closure of both the Liberty dollar and e-gold by US authorities.

[14] See (White 2015) for elaboration of this point and references to earlier work of White and Taub (1985) on the lack of credibility of a private currency pegged to a commodity index.

For example, it is not possible to institutionalise reversal of payments—in contrast to the established payment schemes such as Visa or Mastercard, again substantially limiting use in everyday exchange. This is a consequence of the unpermissioned structure with no real world identity; if identities were known it would be easy to establish mechanisms for payments reversal.

Finally, if contrary to this analysis, widespread adoption of unpermissioned open-source cryptocurrencies was to emerge, this would certainly be accompanied by heavy regulatory intervention to control supporting services such as exchanges and wallets, to prevent their use for illegal purposes or evasion of tax. This would be a further heavy 'headwind' against their widespread use.

All this indicates that the future of cryptocurrencies in the medium to long term will belong to permissioned private sector alternatives—supporting much quicker and more resource efficient processing with more flexible and practical governance that adapts to changing economic and business circumstances.

This though is a quite different model, permissioning means also a need for control of identities and therefore integration into existing banking networks based on fiat currencies; so the outcome is not separate competing currencies but just separate competing means of payments. Such developments may effectively challenge the market power of banks in payment and transaction services but they are not a fundamental change to monetary arrangements.[15] The main exceptions where unpermissioned open-course cryptocurrency may continue to develop are those countries where governments seek to assert control over economic and social activity, through controls on foreign exchange and other regulatory limitations on financial transactions. There unpermissioned cryptocurrency is likely to continue to be attractive as unregulated and unregulatable alternative to repressed domestic and international payments.

2.4 How Placing Deposit Money on a Mutual Distributed Ledger Supports Austrian Ideas

Reading the Austrian contributions to monetary analysis, four policy ideas stand out[16]: (a) an underlying monetary standard in which the supply of the medium of exchange is based on a commodity or other substance in limited supply (the classical gold standard is one possibility, a cryptocurrency standard may be another); (b) 'free banking', with minimal limits on the establishment of banks and market discipline limiting the production of money and fiduciary media, possibly with no central bank

[15] For discussion of the competition implications of new payments technologies, see (Milne 2016).

[16] Appendix B to the supporting working paper https://papers.ssrn.com/sol3/papers.cfm?abstract_id=2946160 provides a fuller review of Austrian views on monetary arrangements.

at all and possibly with competition amongst currencies[17]; (c) limits on the production of fiduciary media (financial claims such as fractionally reserved bank deposits that are readily accepted in payment and immediately redeemable for the medium of exchange); (d) avoidance of all forms of state subsidy and support for banks so their shareholders not taxpayers bear the costs of bank failure. This subsection argues that placing bank transactions and fiat money on a mutual distributed ledger provides a practical means of pursuing all four of these policies.

These policies have remained largely outside mainstream debate not because of disagreement about goals of economic policy but because Austrian policies have been viewed as unrealistic and impractical. The difference of view is though largely about means not about ends. Austrian economists have supported the restoration of the gold standard not as an exercise in nostalgia, but rather because they have seen it as the flawed but only truly effective tool for limiting state creation of money.[18] They propose free banking and avoidance of state subsidy because deposit insurance, central bank liquidity support and 'bail out' of banks encourage risk-taking and neglect of the responsibilities of risk management. They propose limits on the creation of fiduciary media, i.e. bank deposits or other private sector liabilities that serve as money in order to prevent unsustainable private sector credit expansions (nowadays such restriction has become very mainstream, viewed as part of the 'macroprudential' toolkit, though as a form of state intervention this is not endorsed by all Austrian thinkers).

This subsection argues that, with the distributed ledger proposal of this chapter, all four of these policy ideas become more practical and therefore politically acceptable.

(a) An underlying monetary standard in which the supply of the medium of exchange is based on a commodity (more specifically gold).

The case for the restoration of the classical gold standard need not be argued here. The mainstream consensus view is that the costs of such a policy substantially outweigh the benefits. Still it is clear that the mutualised monetary ledger proposed here *could* be the first step towards a full restoration of the classical gold standard, if that was so desired. The ledger would be legally required both to back the state issued money on the ledger with gold *and* to freely buy and sell the state issued money against gold in the open market at a defined price (carefully set at the outset to

---

[17]Hayek (1978, 1979) proposes removing government monopoly on the supply of money and having instead only private produced currencies, competing for the trust of the public and each trading at different market determined values; but this was a relatively late contribution within the Austrian School, a consequence in part of Hayek coming round to the view that restoration of the Gold standard was not possible.

[18]Von Mises and Hayek were not slow to recognise the costs and disadvantages of using gold as a monetary standard. For example, Hayek writes: 'In a securely established world state with a government immune to the temptations of inflation it might be absurd to spend enormous effort in extracting gold out of the earth if cheap tokens would render the same service as gold with equal or greater efficiency'. (Hayek 1937, p 405).

avoid severe misalignment of exchange rates against other countries also on a gold standard). Since all money would then be either gold or commodity backed—or temporarily issued bank supported fiduciary money—this would be a major step towards restoring the use of what would effectively be gold, albeit in a digital certificate form, in day-to-day transactions.

Such a standard could also conceivably, with all money on a distributed ledger, be developed along the lines first proposed by Irving Fisher, backed by a diversified index of commodities rather than a single precious metal. The same commitments would be required, holding the basket as backing of the cryptographic ledger and freely buying and selling to maintain a fixed price against the index.

But the case for the mutualised monetary ledger proposed in this chapter does not rest on such a return to gold or a commodity standard. The goal of avoiding state interference in the money supply could arguably also be achieved by what are now fairly standard institutional safeguards, along much the same lines as those developed over the past four decades to support central bank independence in the setting of interest rates. For example, a politically independent committee could be responsible for determining the quantity of fiat money on the monetary ledger and the extent to which fluctuations in bank money creation should be offset by opposite changes in the stock of fiat money. Therefore, for reasons of political acceptability, any proposed shift to a gold or commodity standard should be sequenced later after the creation of the distributed ledger for money.

(b) 'Free banking', with minimal limits on the establishment of banks and market discipline limiting the production of money and fiduciary media, possibly with no central bank at all

The mutualisation of deposit money allows a substantial reduction in the regulation of banks. It can also be seen as a simpler, lower cost and more practical version of the ring-fencing proposals of the Independent Commission on Banking (Vickers 2011) now partially implemented in the UK or of the controversial 'Volcker rule' in the Dodd–Frank act in the USA. Six years after the Vickers report, the practical challenges are clear; the ring-fencing requires an extensive system of bank monitoring, especially on the funding of bank balance sheets. The Volcker rule is widely regarded as unworkable.

Under the proposal put forward here, obtaining a license for lending, without the accompanying right to issue money on the mutualised ledger, could be made available fairly freely subject only to fairly modest requirements on quality and experience of management. Such initiatives would be like any other investment funds, with some need for protection for investors, especially when offered to unsophisticated retail investors or borrowers, but the extensive panoply of current existing bank regulation is not needed.

The right to issue bank money on the mutual ledger should require meeting higher standards, in particular some assurance that the overall quality of the balance sheet does not substantially threaten failure of repayment onto the ledger. But comparatively simple rules can suffice to accomplish this (in addition to the x-percent reserving). These rules can be the responsibility of the industry to protect other banks. For example, there might be a maximum limit on the ratio of bank monetary deposits to total bank assets, e.g. of 50 or 60%, a ratio that would be easily complied with by existing well-established banks, low enough to prevent start-up banks pursuing a short-term gamble against the protection of the ledger.

The only free-banking proposal that is not directly supported by the mutual distributed ledger is the Hayek proposal for competition amongst commodity-backed currencies, but as already discussed this could conceivably still emerge through alternative private sector ledgers.

(c) Limitations on the production of fiduciary media

This can be achieved imposing an x-percent reserving requirement, with the value of x chosen to achieve an appropriate balance of flexibility in the supply of money that is achieved by allowing market-driven bank creation of money against the instability that arises when banks do not take into account the impact of unsustainable money and credit expansion on the economy as a whole. Initially, x can be chosen to be fairly large, in order to avoid an uncomfortable funding lacuna for banks and an undesired credit contraction. Over time x might be reduced to promote stability.

There are many further issues here about the supply of bank created money that can be explored further beyond the discussion provided in this chapter. One possibility would be treating reserves as tradeable licenses, using a cap and trade to internalise unpriced externalities (Milne 2013; Stein 2012).

(d) Avoidance of all forms of state subsidy and support for banks

This is achieved by ensuring that, after moving all forms of money onto a mutual distributed ledger, state support to banks is denied or strictly limited, even in a systemic financial crisis. A bank that faced difficulties in funding itself would first call on a limited opportunity for collateralised borrowing from the central bank (or perhaps better yet a bank clearing house). Depending on the regulations agreed by the industry for itself, there might be some possibility of suspension of repayment of short-term money market borrowing for a limited period. Once these opportunities—which create time for either an acquisition or an orderly resolution—are exhausted, then the bank would face liquidation.

This in turn means that bank shareholders and behind them holders of bank debt become the sole absorbers of bank risk. State support, beyond very limited provision of money market liquidity, is unnecessary. When banks are liquidated, monetary transfers are not interrupted.

Removal of state support requires that retail depositors, who want to make term deposits in return for interest income, are no longer protected by state-backed deposit insurance. As a consequence, these loans to banks—which is what a bank term deposit is—would likely be secured on individual bank assets, as is the case for the emerging practice of P2P or market place lending. Any deposit insurance would be entirely private sector. Retail investors would of course be well advised to diversify their investments and consider carefully their risk exposure, but this is not different than the situation which arises in any form of retail financial investment, short or long term.

It will though remain politically difficult to entirely avoid state support for banks in an extreme systemic financial crisis. Allowing a large proportion of banks to fail, even when money holdings and payments are not affected by bank failure, would be very disruptive for the provision of credit and hence for economic recovery. For this reason in an extreme crisis, it is likely that only some banks—not all—would be allowed to fail. Even then bank shareholders must not be bailed out.

3 Bank Payment Without Settlement

The previous section has set out the proposal for reform of monetary arrangements of this chapter and discussed how it can achieve the objectives of Austrian monetary thinking. This section examines the operational detail of the proposal, showing how the execution of payments using bank transaction deposits on a mutual distributed ledger no longer requires settlement.

3.1 The Evolution of Bank Payments and Settlement: A Short Historical Review

As a preliminary to this discussion, some historical perspective is in order, in order to make the key point that settlement is *not* an inherent and indivisible aspect of payments. For example, non-bank payments using notes or coin, the physical transfer of money, is final payment. Some bank payment instruments do not require settlement either. Historically, where not prohibited, banks often issued their own private notes which could be presented for redemption in non-bank money, i.e. precious metal or coin. These privately issued bank notes passed from hand to hand and were used in payment without requiring transaction-by-transaction settlement. Similarly bills of exchange—i.e. documents issued by merchants promising to pay a stated sum of money at a stated future date—when ‘accepted’, i.e. the payment guaranteed by a bank, circulated as a form of bank endorsed money. Even today ‘endorsed’ cheques sometimes circulate as bank money without need for transactions settlement.

Interbank settlement emerged as a response to historical circumstance and technological change. Holding money in a bank rather than as precious metal, notes or coin offers advantages of both convenience and security. Even if the money must be withdrawn in order to make payments, fractional reserving by individual banks allows deposit-taking banks to provide monetary services with less opportunity cost from holding the unremunerated medium of exchange. Further convenience and cost reduction can then be achieved through payments that transfer directly from bank to bank, without requiring withdrawal at all. These efficiencies are maximised when the assets used for settlement can be centralised.

From the earliest history of banking, bank-to-bank payments have been possible through one bank holding a bilateral clearing account with another, the balances eventually and as necessary settled by transfer of non-bank money.[19] Something similar to this arrangement continues today in international correspondent banking, where a bank can provide its customers with payment facilities outside its own domestic realm of business by holding a correspondent account with another bank overseas.

In the eighteenth and nineteenth century, such correspondent relationships were also an important part of domestic bank payments, with smaller regional or country banks holding accounts with institutions in financial centres. Examples include English and Welsh country banks holding accounts with clearing banks in London and local banks around the United States holding accounts with money centre banks in New York, Chicago and other 'money centres'.

During the later nineteenth and twentieth century, these bilateral correspondent relationships evolved into the now standard centralised holding of bank reserves as deposits with a central bank used for settlement of bank payments. Under the gold standard as first established in the UK with the restoration of convertibility of Bank of England notes in 1821, these reserves were claims on gold. Holding reserves of gold centrally supported a money market allowing banks to lend reserves amongst each other (in London the 'discount market' which operated by the sale and purchase of discounted bills of exchange) and hence made the most efficient use of limited metallic reserves.

A related parallel development was the growth of centralised cheque clearing. For example, in London, a formal bank cheque clearing organisation was established by 1833, allowing cheques between a group of banks to be periodically collected together and sorted in order that a large number of payment instructions could be settled together with a few interbank payments. From 1854—with the volume of cheques cleared rising rapidly—the London cheque clearing was settled through transfers of deposits at the Bank of England.

This shift to settlement of bank cheque payments using central bank deposits was the first step in the evolution from a pure gold standard in which domestic and international reserves were held as gold specie and coin, to a gold-exchange standard in which reserves were instead claims convertible into gold. A further development was a decline in the use of gold coin in day-to-day payments replaced by token moneys (state issued notes and coins in which the metal content was worth much less than the face value) and bank payments.

---

[19]One early example described by De Roover (1942) is that of the money changers operating in Bruges from the late thirteenth century, whose activities are recorded by the preservation of two of their account books. As De Roober, page 63, describes, oral instructions for bank-to-bank payments could be financed by a corresponding debit or credit to a clearing account held by one bank with the other.

The shift to monetary exchange using token money, paper notes and bank deposit instruments settled in central bank reserves facilitated the replacement of metallic monetary standards by 'fiat' standards in which the reserve assets were no longer even convertible into gold. This final outcome was reached with the eventual final and permanent abandonment of convertibility in the 1971 breakdown of the Bretton-Woods fixed exchange rates amongst the industrial countries (after earlier abandonments of convertibility in 1914 as a consequence of the fiscal pressures of war finance and in 1931 during the international financial crisis of that year).

A further stage in the evolution of bank payments and settlement over the past half century has been the shift from paper-based and manual processing (cheque, giro, manual teller services for deposits and withdrawals) to the automated processing of a wide range of electronic and card payments in use today. This automation has supported another key development: today as already discussed it is bank deposits rather than previous metal or government issued notes and coins which are effectively the medium of exchange; few adult citizens in developed countries are now without bank accounts, even those who rely on state benefits as income are nowadays paid electronically. Associated with this shift has been the widespread provision of bank deposit insurance, with an explicit or implicit state backing. Nowadays, it appears to be a political imperative on government, regardless of where they are on the political spectrum, to protect the money held by citizens as bank deposits. Limiting the exposure of the taxpayer to bank losses then requires close regulation and supervision of banks in order to limit their risk-taking.

The proposal of this chapter for decentralising the medium of exchange by putting all forms of money used in payments, bank transaction deposits together with notes and coins, on a single distributed ledger is a further technological development that can reverse the inexorable shift of responsibility for the provision of money and credit from the private to the state sector. It does so by removing the need for centralised settlement and provision of liquidity. This centralisation was a necessary feature, when bank deposit payments were paper based and took time to execute. Nowadays when payments using deposits are effectively instantaneous, such centralisation is no longer necessary.

Such decentralisation on its own leaves one issue unresolved: if the medium of exchange is not remunerated, then there will always be an incentive for private sector provision of substitutes for the medium of exchange leading to a re-emergence of fractionally reserved banking. Two solutions are available to prevent this. One is to provide required remuneration of ledger money at a similar rate of interest as that on short-term government bonds. Banks would then gain little commercial advantage from fractional reserving because the cost of funding of loans would be similar whether obtained from the ledger or from term deposits and money markets. This though has the disadvantage of undermining the existing business model of banking.

The alternative arrangement developed here, in order to ensure the industry welcomes the new arrangement, is to continue allowing banks to create money, on a temporary basis, in response to market demand. They do this by pledging loans to the ledger in return for the creation of money on the ledger. This is in effect a form of securitisation, and the possibility of abuse can be protected using a variety of methods, many familiar from existing practice in asset-backed securitisation. This arrangement and implications for banking and bank regulation are described in the next section.

3.2 *Settlement of Bank Payments in Central Bank Reserves*

The overwhelming proportion of payments by value in developed countries are transfers of money from one bank account to another. A variety of instruments and payment schemes are available to execute these bank-to-bank payments.[20] These all debit the bank account of the sender of money (the 'payer') and credit the bank account of the recipient of the money (the 'payee'). If the two bank accounts are held at different banks, then the payment also requires a matching interbank settlement, i.e. a transfer of the same value from the payer's to the payee's bank.[21] Nowadays, this settlement is almost always in central bank reserves.

While arrangements for bank payment and settlement are a fundamental part of the institutions of money and banking, they attract little attention either in money and banking textbooks or in the research literature. This section provides a short description of bank payment and settlement and then describes how these arrangements are altered under the proposal of this chapter, i.e. using decentralised cryptocurrency technologies to remove the need for centralised settlement of bank payments and so clearly separating monetary deposits from potentially risky retail investment in banks. The section is completed with a short historical review of the evolution of bank payments and settlement, arguing that present arrangements using settlement in central bank reserves are a historical legacy necessary when providing payment facilities on bank deposits under older paper-based or central server-based technologies, but no longer required when payments are decentralised.

Figures 1 illustrates the operation of our current monetary arrangements, in which bank transaction deposits are used as the medium of exchange and settled in central bank reserves. The right-hand panel is a simplified consolidated balance sheet for the non-bank private sector. Bank deposits include both transaction deposits used for making payments and other term or saving deposits, though the dividing line is not

[20]For example, in the UK, a bank-to-bank payment can be made using the traditional paper instrument the cheque using the cheque and credit clearing scheme (CCCS); through a variety of instructions (direct debit, standing order, bulk payment instructions) via the bank automated clearing system (BACS), a card payment via either the Visa or Mastercard systems; an immediate direct online or telephone instruction via the faster payments scheme (FPS) or using the large value real time scheme (CHAPS).

[21]Settlement can be either at the same time the payment is made, i.e. when the payer's account is debited and the payee's account credited ('gross settlement') or later ('deferred settlement'). If settlement is deferred then until it takes place, the payer's bank has a liability for subsequent settlement to the payee's bank.

General Government/ Central bank	
Assets	*Liabilities*
Real assets	Reserves
C bank repo	Notes
	Bonds

Commercial banks	
Assets	*Liabilities*
Bank Loans	Deposits
Reserves	C bank repo
Money market	Money market
	Bonds/ Equity

Non-Bank private sector	
Assets	*Liabilities*
Real assets	Bank loans
Bonds/ Equity	
Deposits	
Notes	

Fig. 1 Fractional-reserved banking with central bank settlement

clear-cut, for example, savings deposits that allow immediate withdrawals can be regarded as money.

The middle panel shows the balance sheet of commercial banks. There are many competing commercial banks providing monetary deposits and payment facilities to the non-bank private sector. A deposit paid from Bank A to Bank B is settled through a matching transfer of reserves from bank A to Bank B. If Bank A loses reserves from an outflow of deposits, it can replenish them by money market borrowing or by issue of bonds or equity purchased by the non-bank private sector using deposits from other banks.

The left-hand panel is a consolidated balance sheet of general government and the central bank. This presentation highlights the role of central bank reserves (deposits with the central bank) as a source of government funding, something that was a principal reason historically for governments chartering central banks and has again become important with the policies of quantitative easing adopted since the 2007–2008 global financial crisis. There is though a major difference from central bank funding of government in the eighteenth century and today: then the central bank deposits could be withdrawn by conversion into specie; now central bank reserves are inconvertible and can only be transferred to other banks as settlement of bank payments.

Figure 1 highlights a key aspect of our monetary arrangements that block widespread acceptance of Austrian monetary ideas. Central bank reserves are *not* the medium of exchange. They are not held by the private sector and so not used for payments. Central bank issued notes are held by the private sector and are used for payments but notes are supplied on demand as a substitute for bank deposits. The original Misean analysis of the medium of exchange and money substitutes has reversed; it is now bank deposits that are the medium of exchange and central bank issued notes that are the money substitute.

This would not be such a significant change were it not for the accompanying fractional reserving of bank deposits. Were bank transaction deposits backed, one for one, by central bank reserves, i.e. if we had 100 percent reserving, then state-backed fiat currency would still be the ultimate medium of exchange. But bank reserves are fractionally reserved, so it is commercial bank deposit liabilities not central bank liabilities that have evolved today into the medium of exchange.

Fractionally reserved banking requiring, in turn, a central bank that stands ready to provide 'liquidity', i.e. additional central bank reserves, in order that bank payments can be settled and bank customers do not lose access to their holdings of the widespread accepted medium of exchange. This has been reinforced by the introduction of extensive state-backed deposit insurance, first in the USA in the 1930s, then worldwide from the 1970s onward. Thus, Austrian proposals—for removing the support of the state for the banking system and restricting fractional-reserved banking—are perceived not as a strengthening of monetary arrangements but rather as a politically unacceptable undermining of the medium of exchange.

3.3 Settlement no Longer Necessary

The proposal of this chapter for using the technology of cryptocurrencies to put all money on a distributed ledger allows them to function as a medium of exchange without the need for settlement in central bank reserves. An intuition that can help with understanding this point is recognising that demand for liquidity from settling interbank payments is required only by individual banks, not by the monetary system as a whole.[22] Consider in Fig. 1 the hypothetical situation where the monetary system consists of a single bank—which is also the note issuer—instead of several competing banks and a note-issuing central bank. There is then no need for settlement and thus no requirement for liquidity for settling payments between banks and indeed no need for a separate central bank.

While it would never be desirable to have only a single bank—such an institution would have unacceptable market power—it is possible, using the technologies of cryptocurrencies, for all money including monetary deposits to be held on a mutual distributed ledger instead of on bank balance sheets. Moreover, unlike proposals for 100 percent reserving, this need not result in a major loss of funding for bank balance sheets. Figure 2 illustrates how this is possible.

The key difference from current arrangements shown in Fig. 1 is that all money is now placed on a state sponsored mutual distributed ledger, shown as the oval on the lower left of the figure. Note that there is only one type of money, whether issued by the state (fiat) or by banks all money is now held on the ledger. The holder of money has no need to distinguish whether their money holdings were 'originally' created by permanent fiat issue or by temporary bank issue.[23]

An analogy can be made between the arrangements shown in Fig. 2 and the division made by the 1844 Banking Act of the Bank of England into the note issue and banking departments. The state sponsored ledger corresponds to the note issue

[22]What about international transactions? Again, provided the exchange rate is freely floating, there can be no liquidity shortage for the banking system operating within a single currency area.

[23]Technically, it would be possible to trace back the history of transactions on the ledger to determine the proportions of fiat and bank money of any particular holding of cryptocurrency, but there is no economic reason for this making any difference in the acceptability of money in exchange or technical advantage of using this information in payment processing. To fully enforce the equivalence of money on the ledger, a legal prohibition might also be imposed on using information on the proportion of fiat origin as a criteria for acceptance in payment or simply by making all ledger money legal tender.

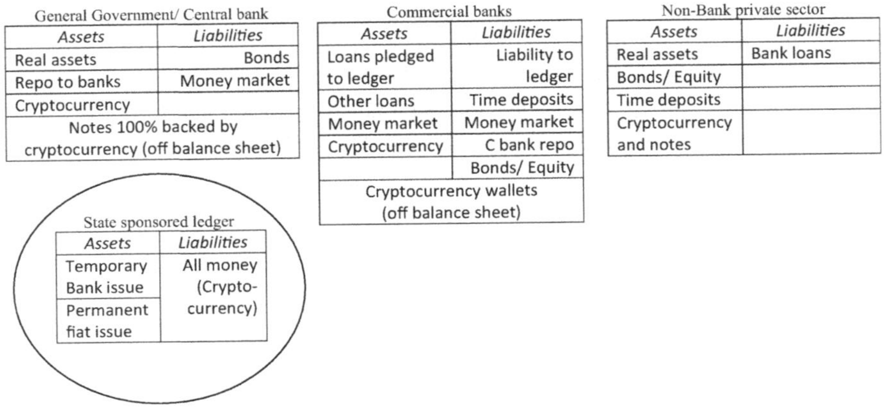

Fig. 2 Fractional-reserved banking without settlement using distributed ledger

department. A banking division of the central bank borrows on money and bond markets, holds cryptocurrency and lends using repo to commercial banks. The analogy is though not exact. Figure 2 is presented on the assumption that there is a state-owned central bank whose balance sheet is then consolidated with that of general government. In 1844, the Bank of England, while state privileged, was privately owned.

Figure 2 deliberately shows the sponsored ledger as separate from the consolidated balance sheet of general government and the central bank. This is done in order to emphasise that if the government or the 'banking' division of the central bank borrows in financial markets and offers collateralised lending to commercial banks and were then to default on their borrowing, this would not affect money and payments.

Some further features of this arrangement as envisaged here are as follows:

- While state money issue is permanent and irrevocable; bank money issue is temporary, backed by a promise of repayment secured through bank loans pledged to the ledger. This provides the necessary elasticity in the supply of money which, historically, has meant that commodity-based monetary standards have in practice tended towards exchange standards with a combination of commodity and bank money.
- The ledger should not be accessible as a source of funding for long-term loan commitments, e.g. mortgages relying on collateral values for repayment. The loans pledged must be amortising loans with a maximum maturity of perhaps 5 years.
- Notes, while still managed and issued by the central bank, are now fully backed by cryptocurrency; the central bank is obliged to purchase or borrow cryptocurrency in order to issue notes. The notes and the cryptocurrency backing are now off-balance sheet.

- Commercial banks no longer hold reserves with the central bank reserves at all. Commercial banks must hold reserves of cryptocurrency, in order to repay maturing liabilities (time deposits, money market borrowing, central bank repos), but these are held directly with the mutual distributed ledger and are no longer part of the infrastructure of payments.
- The non-bank private sector no longer holds or uses bank deposits as money. All money is now on the ledger. To provide customers with payment facilities, commercial banks now provide 'wallet' services, i.e. security, accounting and other money management services for holders of cryptocurrency. From the perspective of the user, little changes; they continue to use their existing banking channels—branch, online, telephone, card payments—exactly as before. The difference though is a transformation of the back office; payment instructions are now instructions for transfer of ledger money.
- Cryptographic security ensures that that the ledger operates as a totally secure and immutable record without any need for a central authority or risk of loss or failure. The supporting distributed software shared by government and private sector ensures its integrity.

4 Implications for Banking and Bank Regulation

This section describes the changes in banking and bank regulation made possible by the decentralisation of money proposed in this chapter. It begins by describing two protections preventing banks from using their authorisation to issue money on the ledger for excessive expansion of money and credit. It then describes how responsibility for bank regulation can shift from the state to the banking industry and the opportunity for withdrawal of state support for banking through scaling back the availability of a lender of last resort and removal of the bank safety net, whether explicit deposit insurance or the implicit bank safety net. Finally, it discusses prospects for adoption.

4.1 The Triple Lock: Ensuring Repayment of Bank Money on the Ledger

The prevention of unsustainable expansions of money and credit requires, with a very high degree of probability, that the commitment to repay bank created money onto the ledger (as illustrated in Fig. 2) is honoured and there is never a call on the permanent creation of money on the ledger to repay loans.

The first obligation of repayment is the same as with existing bank loans; the loan contract agreed between the bank and the borrower obliges repayments that can be made directly onto the ledger, extinguishing the money previously created. The cryptographic coding will automatically take the monetary payment at the agreed time, determined if required to the nearest minute or second. The borrower will default if, at that moment, they have insufficient ledger money associated with their node on the ledger from which the commitment to repay principal has been made.

This leads to an issue not fully pursued in this chapter, which is whether individuals and companies—including both non-bank corporates and banks, can create more than one node on the network. In order to enforce repayment disciplines it would seem appropriate to have only node for every legal entity.

This is a first line of defence against the possibility of the failure to repay money borrowed off the distributed ledger. A second line of defence is the underwriting of the loan obligation by the bank, based on its credit assessment of the borrower. The bank as well as the customer has its own node on the network for its own holdings of cryptocurrency. If the borrower fails to repay principal as agreed, then the algorithm coded on the ledger automatically takes the principal repayment from the bank to pay down the borrowed money on the ledger. Banks would likely have multiple nodes on the ledger, each corresponding to one of the many legal entities within a typical banking organisation, but there should then be an obligation that any call on payment to the ledger, which cannot be completed by a bank subsidiary because it has insufficient money on the ledger, will be fulfilled instead by a payment out of money held by the bank holding company. These bank payment obligations—along with those of the borrower—should all be coded into the distributed ledger and deductions automatically taken by the ledger algorithms, with conditional branching: if not paid by the borrower, then by the bank subsidiary; if not by the bank subsidiary, then by the bank holding company.

If the bank also has insufficient money on the ledger for the required repayment, i.e. if its holding company and subsidiary holdings of money on the distributed ledger has fallen below the required repayment at that point in time, then a third line of defence comes into play. Now the coding of the ledger calls on all other banks to make the repayment onto the ledger, most obviously with an obligation to make payment in proportion to the amount of money they have outstanding on the ledger at the time the money was first created. Once again this is all undertaken automatically, using the algorithms of the ledger ('smart contracts') without the need for any administrative intervention by either banks or regulators. At the same time, the bank that has failed to support its credit underwriting commitment will be entered into resolution. The details of this process are not considered here, but this cannot be undertaken automatically on the monetary ledger without administrative and regulatory intervention, because it involves all the other bank assets and liabilities that remain on a bank's balance sheet. Still one would expect that this resolution process would involve a suspension of various claims, of both debt and equity holders, and a new temporary management with responsibility for determining how to restore the bank to a situation when it can once again command sufficient resources to maintain a sufficient balance of money on the ledger to continue its business and meet any other regulatory requirements.

A further appropriate protection for ensuring confidence that money-financed bank loans are repaid onto the ledger will be to give the claims on the ledger priority over all other creditors in bank liquidation, including even the tax authorities.

4.2 Applying x-Per Cent Reserving to Limit Fractionally Reserved Monetary Deposits

Even with the triple lock, there will be a concern that money-financed bank lending will encourage unsustainable expansion of both money and credit. Bank money on the ledger is still fractionally reserved, providing banks with a low cost source of funding. Moreover, allowing banks to mutualise their monetary funding removes an important current market discipline on bank monetary creation.

Under competitive fractionally reserved banking, banks must allow for the fact that when they create monetary deposits through lending, they will then subsequently lose some of these deposits to other banks and so—if they expand much faster than other banks—will have to shift the balance of their funding from relatively inexpensive monetary deposits to relatively expensive term deposits and money and security market borrowing. Under the proposed mutualisation of monetary deposits of this chapter, this discipline vanishes. To the extent that the costs of overexpansion then fall on other institutions, the result can be excessive expansion of money and money-financed credit.

An additional offsetting discipline can be imposed by requiring banks, when creating money on the ledger as in Fig. 2, to commit x-percent of their own money to the funding of the loan. The actual requirement could lie anywhere between the two extremes of 0-percent reserving (banks need keep not reserves against money created against a loan) to 100-percent reserving (banks can no longer create money at all; all loans must be financed by borrowed money).

This is a form of 'overcollateralisation' of the kind already widely used in asset-backed securitisations. Such overcollateralisation also makes it even less likely there will ever be a call on the ledger to finance bank loan losses on any large scale. Making x too large, however, could limit the supply of credit. Arguably, there are some positive externalities from encouraging bank supply of credit, especially for short-term business lending and in areas such as trade and working-capital finance. Both research and practical experience will have to be taken into account in choosing the appropriate level for x.

Limiting fractional-reserved banking in this way will not just reduce monetary-financed bank lending, it will also restrict the availability of money for the required refinancing of short-term funding, whether on-balance sheet by commercial banks or by shadow banks who are unable to create money on the ledger.

The macroeconomic consequences of the proposal of this chapter—including x-per cent reserving—need a great deal of further study and will benefit from more formal modelling of the externalities arising both in bank lending together with additional externalities from mutualisation of bank liquidity risk. Such externalities—both positive and negative—arise easily in payments networks and are only increased by putting all money on a distributed ledger. Further analysis is needed to help determine an appropriate level of the x-percent requirement for internalising these externalities.[24]

4.3 Prudential Regulation Becomes an Industry Responsibility

The free riding problem arising from the externalities in money creation on the distributed ledger is a key issue on which the practicality of this proposal stands or falls. Two mechanisms for internalising these costs have been described: (1) the triple lock—underwriting by first the borrower, second the bank, third the entire industry and (2) x% reserving requiring banks to put some of their own money as overcollateralisation of money created on the ledger.

Despite these protections, it is conceivable that commercial banks can exploit the opportunity for creating money on the ledger by financing loans with a significant probability of the burden of repayment falling on others. Some form of prudential regulation will be still necessary for banks that issue money on the ledger, in order to 'internalise' this economic externality and prevent free-riding.

Since, under the 'triple-lock', it is industry that is the final line of defence against abuse of the ledger; this in turn suggests that there should be an accompanying move from state to self-regulation, with the industry taking over all responsibility from government for micro-prudential regulation. This is because industry makes repayment of defaulted loans pledged to the ledger and subsequently stands ahead of the taxpayer in exposure to credit risk on the ledger. Therefore, it is the industry not government that should agree rules for loans put on the ledger and for the capital adequacy rules applied to banks that use the ledger for funding their loan.

All elements of state support for the banking industry can be withdrawn. In particular, there is no longer any need for state-backed insurance of bank deposits, which can immediately cease. Transaction deposits are no longer at any risk of loss. Term deposits are credit risky loans to banks, which might be insured by an industry scheme, but should make explicit that this insurance is private sector without state backing, and in extreme situations with widespread bank losses, the compensation fund may be exhausted and not be able to fully protect depositors.

What might industry choose to do? This is their responsibility, but they might, for example, require some form of external rating by a credit rating agency (which would in turn likely require the loans to be packaged as pass-through securitisations) *and* also capital rules for the banks that securitise, since these are securitisations with

---

[24]See (Stein 2012) for discussion of the loan externality, related to the realisation of loan collateral in a crisis.

explicit sponsor support, not balance sheet remote). Since their concern is with the off-balance commitment to repayment of money to the ledger, not the repayment of on-balance sheet bank liabilities, they are likely also to set some maximum ratio of money created on the ledger to total bank assets.

A key point here is though that because the industry is setting these capital rules for themselves, the externality being internalised at industry level, it can be the industry that sets these rules. No longer will they be able to argue that micro-prudential regulation is an unacceptably burdensome constraint on their own business (which is what industry thinks of the current Basel III and Dodd–Frank regulations).[25]

The state steps back entirely from responsibility for micro-prudential regulation. There are in effect two types of banks: banks who issue money on the distributed ledger and those who do not (including all non-bank lending institutions which can be collectively referred to as 'shadow banks'). Prudential regulation is no longer necessary for banks that do not issue money on the ledger: they should be subjected only to rules on customer protection and investor disclosure. In the case of money-issuing banks, all responsibility for additional micro-prudential regulation can be passed in its entirety from the state to the industry. Prudential regulators—e.g. the FDIC and the regulatory divisions of the Federal Reserve in the USA and the PRA in the UK—can be abolished or rather moved from being a government department to become industry governed self-regulatory organisations.

Government will still need to be in the background to ensure that self-regulation does not operate to restrict competition. The FDIC in the USA and the PRA in the UK are privatised, but come under the oversight of the Department of Justice and the Competition and Markets Authority, respectively.

The state could likely also retain a macroprudential responsibility, ensuring that the overall growth of money and credit does not threaten financial stability. The x-per cent reserving described below is the most obvious tool for them to carry out this task, though clearly changes would have to be infrequent and only after extensive consultation.

What about international financial regulation? The Basel committee, the BCBS, can also largely be abolished, but would retain some competition role—making sure that banks from one country do not use their access to the ledger to gain an unfair competitive advantage in other jurisdictions—and perhaps on safety and soundness in foreign exchange markets (merging with the sister committee CPSS would be appropriate).

---

[25]For example, the research and lobbying material of the institute for international finance https://www.iif.com

4.4 Money Markets and the Role of the Central Bank

Not all bank assets and liabilities are recorded on the mutual distributed ledger, far from it. Banks would continue to have debt and equity liabilities on their balance sheet, both short- and long-term borrowing and shareholder funds. Only monetary deposits are moved off-balance sheet onto the ledger. Banks would continue to hold on to their own balance sheet loans that are not funded by money creation, securities and other assets. Only loans pledged to the ledger are moved off-balance sheet, with a conditional liability to repayment.

Banks still need to hold reserves of the cryptographic currency and continue to operate a treasury function, in order to manage their own cash flows, arising from commitments to lend, e.g. lines of credit and any default of loans pledged to the ledger as well as for repaying their own borrowings, whether retail and corporate time deposits or from money and security markets. Banks would participate actively in short-term money markets, taking short-term deposits or issuing tradeable money market instruments such as negotiable certificates of deposit, investing themselves in money market instruments.

What role then for the central bank? Would a central bank be needed under this arrangement at all? It will seem sensible, in order to promote its political acceptability, that when initially established the new arrangement should be as close as possible to what pertains today. The question of the role and operation of the central bank can then be addressed subsequently. In order to minimise the change in institutional arrangements, the sponsored ledger could be set up as a division of the central bank, i.e. in analogy with the 1844 Banking Act.

There would though still be major changes in operation and responsibilities of the central bank:

- The 'banking division' of the central bank, since it would have lost its power of money creation, could potentially default (though since its balance sheet is supported by the state this default would presumably only happen in the context of a general government default). It would be essential that the ledger remained operationally fully separate of the rest of the central bank, in order to ensure that a general government/central bank default did not disrupt money and payments.
- With central bank reserves no longer used for settlement of payments, the central bank, while continuing to be a major if not the most important participant in money markets both as borrower and as lender, would no longer have complete control over short-term money market rates of interest.
- Monetary policy operations, instead of being conducted through control of interest rates, would be conducted by additions to the stock of irredeemable fiat money on the ledger by the ledger department of the central bank. This money would then become a source of funding for general government spending.

As a state owned, not private, entity, considerable thought would have to go into defining the objective and governance of both the ledger division and the banking division of the central bank. Some preliminary thoughts on these can be given here, without claiming to provide a full and final analysis.

The ledger division will initially operate by following as an ultimate monetary target, the rate of inflation as already pursued by central banks worldwide. It will increase or slow down its permanent and irredeemable issue of fiat money on the ledger according to its views on how this will affect the rate of inflation in the short to medium term.

A primary continuing role for the banking division of the central bank will be its historically important role of providing funding for general government expenditure, especially at the short end of the maturity spectrum and in facilitating the marketability of government debt.

A second major role for the banking division of the central bank would be support for short-term markets in money and credit, especially in times of financial stress. The central bank can still hold its own potentially substantial reserve of the cryptocurrency, which it could lend to commercial banks against collateral as appropriate on occasion to help allay difficulties banks might face in refinancing themselves in short-term money markets.

This raises the question of when and how the central bank should conduct such interventions. Monetary policy would be the responsibility of the ledger division of the bank, not of the banking division. The possibility of a 'panic', preventing even sound banks from borrowing in money markets, suggests that the central bank should be prepared, on occasion, to conduct discount window operations—lending at above market rates against good collateral to banks unable to fund themselves. At other times, a desired level of holding of cryptocurrency would have to be determined that bears a large enough ratio to the level of bank money market borrowing to stem any incipient panic.

The central bank might also play some limited role—in effect a market maker—in short-term money markets, lending to the market from its cryptocurrency reserves, in order to limit temporary short-term spikes in money market rates of interest.

The execution of these responsibilities could possibly be supported, in turn, by allowing the central bank to also create money temporarily on the ledger, pledging good quality loans. As a government-owned institution, this would conflict with the proposal put forward here for the triple lock, with private industry providing the ultimate guarantee on repayment to the ledger. Banking division money creation for the purposes of stabilising money and credit markets would have to be on an entirely different basis. Further analysis is needed to determine if any such power is really needed. The outcome of such a mechanism would be to economise on the need for the central bank to hold its own reserve of cryptocurrency. Since there are no real resource costs, the decision of to what extent the central bank creates and then holds cryptocurrency in reserve, or to what extent it is allowed to creating in an emergency, seems immaterial. All that matters is the total reserve, whether created in advance or only at a time of need. To avoid any suggestion that repayment of defaulted loans would become a state responsibility, it would seem best not to allow a state-owned central bank access to the ledger.

Note that these mechanisms are all ultimately concerned with bridging shortages of credit availability; inability to replace credit is still a liquidity risk, but it is a risk that does not interrupt the payments system, at worst it will limit the supply of bank lending (but provided banks have retained some balance sheet capacity, profitable bank lending can still continue to be financed to some degree through money creation on the ledger).

4.5 Resolution of Failing Banks and 'Shadow Banks'

What about the resolution of money-issuing banks or other lending institutions ('shadow banks')? There are really two separate issues to be considered here. The first is the relatively easy challenge of dealing with the isolated failure of an individual institution or of a small number of institutions, whether this occurs as a result of fraud, mismanagement or the materialisation of financial risk.

Such failures should be resolved in just the same way as the failure of a non-financial institution. If no buyer can be found to take over the institution so it can continue as a going concern, then it must be put into resolution, with all credit commitments suspended. If it is a money-issuing bank, then its ledger commitments and wallet services must be maintained (possibly with transfer of wallet services to another provider).

The isolated failure of even a large lender, accounting for say twenty or thirty percent of the provision of loan credit, should also still be perfectly manageable. Lending subsidiaries which continue to be profitable can be sold along with their assets and staff.

More difficult questions arise should failure or the threat of failure affect an even larger proportion of credit markets, something that could arise in the aftermath of an unsustainable expansion of credit. The arrangements proposed in this chapter will go a long way to ensuring that such an unsustainable expansion does not happen, but for this to be credible it must be clear that even in a systemic credit crisis state support will be far from automatic. More discussion is needed, but a sensible and practical response, in such a situation, will be to let the worst institutions with the largest credit losses go under, but provide temporary support through preferred equity investment for the remainder so that the credit market continues to operate in a systemic crisis.

4.6 Prospects for Adoption

The operational rules proposed for the ledger are straightforward, but is adoption realistic? This subsection will argue that the new arrangements will impose minimal disruption on bank customers and be attractive to banks. Hence, they are a politically realistic programme of reform.

Might bank customer resist this proposal? From the perspective of bank customers, this ledger will be operated in the background, with little impact on their day-to-day transactions. With such a scheme, bank monetary deposits would then become 'wallet services', much the same as the wallet services currently provided for holding cryptocurrencies. They would help customers manage and use their cryptographic keys and execute payments. Assuming that the immutable ledger records transactions not balances, then wallet providers, i.e. banks, would also maintain records of account balances for customers. As illustrated in Fig. 1b, it is only the original loan and repayment of principal that would be recorded on the distributed ledger. Associated interest payments would also be agreed in the loan contract, but these obligations do not involve repayment and extinguishing of money on the letter and so would be settled by monetary ledger transfers of the kind shown in Fig. 1a rather than in Fig. 1b.

Tax and other obligations for payment to government would have to be settled in ledger money. While legal tender is no longer a major feature of monetary arrangements, the legal tender status which central bank notes have in many jurisdictions (i.e. the legal obligation to accept bank notes in settlement of debts) could be extended to money on the ledger. This would provide further incentives for bank customers to accept the transition of money onto the ledger.

One possible objection to the ledger is that placing all fiat and bank money on a mutual distributed ledger would require the abolition of cash transfers and their associated anonymity. This is not a valid objection. The use of cash is a quite separate issue unaffected by the transfer of fiat and bank money onto the ledger. Banknotes would continue to be central bank liabilities and would still be issued as of now, on demand, in exchange for money held in transaction deposits, most often through an ATM withdrawal. The only change is that all notes and coins would now be fully backed by money on the ledger.

Banks would continue to provide the full existing range of other banking services to customers. Payment instructions would not be altered (only the subsequent processing of those instructions). Loans could be either money financed or they could be financed directly using the bank's own money. Where banks provide lines of credit, rather than loans with fixed repayment schedules, then they will need to maintain sufficient balances of ledger money, or sufficient loan assets acceptable as collateral on the ledger, to allow customers to draw down on their credit lines.

The major perceived difference for bank customers is the changed status of non-monetary bank deposits without transaction facilities. A fixed term deposit with a bank must be presented and understood as a loan to the bank, money which the bank is not keeping but itself lending on to other customers. From the customers' perspective, such a loan to a bank or an investment in a non-bank alternative lender (a 'shadow bank' or a marketplace lender) will be very much the same. State support of these deposits, in the event of failure of the deposit insurance fund being exhausted, will be forthcoming only in the event of a complete systemic collapse of the banking industry and even then only for some institutions not all.

Banks though will be able to provide some investments that cannot be so easily provided by non-bank lenders ('shadow banks') without ability to create money on the ledger. These are savings deposits with an option for early withdrawal and lines of credit that can be drawn down by the customer as they are needed. They would have some comparative advantage in providing these deposits because of their access to the ledger for money creation.

Might banks resist such a proposal? They will be concerned about the costs of reengineering their payment systems, but their attitudes must depend on the entire package of reform and not just the creation of the ledger. Banks could anticipate a substantially reduced burden of regulatory compliance. They would also obtain a new source of revenue as they take over the role of central banks providing an elastic increase in monetary deposits needed, for example, when there are large demands for means of payment arising for either seasonal reasons or because of large financial market transactions. The ledger would also offer banks new tools for monitoring borrower repayment.

Could banks avoid using the ledger and still provide their customers with payment services? This would require on setting up competing payment schemes with accompanying arrangements for settlement, i.e. setting up a banker's bank or clearing house replacing the existing central bank role of supplying reserves for settlement of payments. Such off-ledger payment arrangements are conceivable and need not necessarily be outlawed, but implementing them would require extensive investment in underlying operational systems—at exactly the same time as substantial investment is also being made in on-ledger operations—as well and agreement on the alternative asset for settlement and arrangement between banks for provision of liquidity. Final judgement must be reserved but it seems unlikely that banks would 'vote with their feet' and en masse withdraw from the ledger.

It would be feasible and desirable to allow banks to substitute loans on the mutual ledger so that loan default and its management can be moved back entirely onto their own balance sheet. This would be recorded in the mutual ledger as two transactions, an existing loan being placed on the ledger at exactly the time when the troubled loan faces a potential default of principal repayment, thus fulfilling the bank's obligation to extinguish an entry on the ledger. The payment arrangements for any loans transferred onto the ledger would have to be set up appropriately at the time the original loan was made, to avoid costly administrative exchange with the borrower to change payment arrangements.

There is though one strong argument against adoption that will have to be given serious consideration. There will be obvious problems for borrowers who have taken on large debts anticipating the continuation of artificially low rates of interest for the foreseeable future. These are not an insignificant group. In the UK, Australia and other countries, many households have taken out large mortgages in relation to their incomes at floating rates of interest and will be exposed to substantial financial stress, following the likely rise of market rates of interest following the ending of central bank control of overnight interest rates. Residential house prices are, in turn, likely to fall sharply. Another likely impact are falls in financial asset prices currently supported at artificially high levels by leveraged finance at low rates of interest.

This is not an argument against adoption, but rather an acknowledgement that the macroeconomic adjustment will be difficult and likely require some *temporary* state action to alleviate some of the worst burdens of repayment. But the alternative, of continuing with state domination of the process of money and credit creation have even greater costs, so this is a nettle that needs to be grasped.

5 Conclusions

Austrian monetary economics draws our attention to fundamental problems caused by state incursion into the provision of money and credit. This incursion not only distorts incentives, it also has resulted in a failure to address the problems of unsustainable credit creation, maturity mismatch and asset mispricing that was behind the last global financial crisis and therefore threatens a future crisis of even greater severity. This could in turn undermine the market-based economic system that has supported the dramatic rise of living standards across the world over the past four centuries.

This chapter proposes a technological solution to this challenge, using cryptocurrency technologies to put all bank transaction deposits and fiat money together on a single 'mutual distributed ledger'. This can achieve Austrian objectives for monetary arrangements, supporting in particular an almost complete withdrawal of the role of the state in banking industry and the provision of money and credit, which will allow a market-based response to our current monetary and macroeconomic economic challenges.

This reform also has several desirable features, including:

- A proper match between customers perceptions ('my money' is kept securely and conveniently by a bank) and actual banking operations (the bank has no permission to use this money for purposes of its own)
- There is no longer a need for a state-backed deposit insurance to protect customer money held in banks (though private sector schemes for insuring returns on investments in banks or alternative non-bank lenders may be provided)
- Complete protection of bank money and payments from any interruption resulting from bank failure. Since all money is on the ledger, not on bank balance sheets, customer access to bank money and payments services can continue uninterrupted even while a failing bank is being resolved.
- No need for settlement of payments using central bank reserves and a substantial scaling back of central bank intervention in money and security markets (though the central bank remains a major participant and may play a role in promoting orderly market conditions).
- Banks continue to engage in *temporary* money creation in order to finance short-term needs for credit, for example, from seasonal fluctuations or substantial financial market transactions, thus providing a private sector (but state supported) solution to the problems of ensuring a sufficient elasticity in the supply of money and credit

- Existing business models and payments arrangements are relatively unaffected, making this proposal more politically acceptable than Austrian policy ideas based on older technologies.

Despite these advantages, the changes proposed here are profound with some substantial economic losers—those who have relied on low cost state distorted finance for investment in real or financial assets. This means that they are unlikely to quickly attract widespread support and may only be taken seriously in policy debate, if this ever happens, only after a further future crisis makes it impossible to deny the shortcomings of current widespread state involvement in our arrangements for money and banking.

References

Ali, R., et al. (2014a). Innovations in payment technologies and the emergence of digital currencies. *Bank of England Quarterly Bulletin*, Q3.

Ali, R., et al. (2014b). The economics of digital currencies. *Bank of England Quarterly Bulletin*, Q3.

Andolfatto, D. (2015). MacroMania: Fedcoin: On the desirability of a government cryptocurrency. In *Macromania Blog*. Available at: http://andolfatto.blogspot.co.uk/2015/02/fedcoin-on-desirability-of-government.html.

De Roover, R. (1942). Money, banking, and credit in medieval Bruges. *The Journal of Economic History, 2*(S1), 52–65.

Dowd, K. (2014). *New private monies: A bit-part player?* London: Institute of Economic Affairs.

Fung, B. S. C. & Halaburda, H. (2016). *Central bank digital currencies: A framework for assessing why and how*. Staff discussion paper 2016–22, Bank of Canada.

Hayek, F. A. (1937). *Monetary nationalism and international stability*. London: Longmans, Green.

Hayek, F. A. (1978). *Denationalisation of money–The argument refined*. London: Institute of Economic Affairs.

Hayek, F. A. (1979). *Free Market Monetary System*, A. Ludwig von Mises Institute.

Koenig, A. (2015). *A beginners guide to Bitcoin and Austrian economics*. Munich: FinanzBuch Verlag.

Koning, J. (2014). Fedcoin. *Moneyness blog*. Available at: http://jpkoning.blogspot.co.uk/2014/10/fedcoin.html.

Milne, A. (2013). Register, cap and trade: A proposal for containing systemic liquidity risk. *Economics: The Open-Access, Open-Assessment E-Journal, 7*(2013–7). https://doi.org/10.5018/economics-ejournal.ja.2013-7.

Milne, A. K. L. (2016). Competition policy and the financial technology revolution in banking. *Digiworld Economic Journal*, (103), 145–161.

Monetary Authority of Singpore. (2017). MAS working with industry to apply Distributed Ledger Technology. *Media Release*. Available at: http://www.mas.gov.sg/News-and-Publications/Media-Releases/2017/MAS-working-with-industry-to-apply-Distributed-Ledger-Technology.aspx.

Nakamoto, S. (2008). *Bitcoin: A peer-to-peer electronic cash system*. https://bitcoin.org/bitcoin.pdf.

Schwartz, A. J. (1989). Banking school, currency school, free banking school. In *The New Palgrave: Money. London and Basingstoke* (pp. 41–49). New York: W.W. Norton.

Selgin, G. (2015). Synthetic commodity money. *Journal of Financial Stability, 17*, 92–99. http://www.sciencedirect.com/science/article/pii/S1572308914000722 [Accessed June 7, 2015.

Skingsley, C., 2016. Should the Riksbank issue e-krona? Speech at *FinTech Stockholm*, 16 Nov 2016, revised 30 Nov 2016. Available at: http://www.riksbank.se/en/Press-and-published/Speeches/2016/Skingsley-Should-the-Riksbank-issue-e-krona/ [Accessed April 15, 2017].

Stein, J. C. (2012). Monetary policy as financial stability regulation. *The Quarterly Journal of Economics, 127*(1), 57–95.

Taub, B. (1985). Private fiat money with many suppliers. *Journal of Monetary Economics, 16*(2), 195–208.

Vickers, J. (2011). *Independent commission on banking: Final report*. Department for Business, Innovation & Skills and HM Treasury. https://www.gov.uk/government/news/independentcommission-on-banking-final-report

Von Mises, L. (1953). *Theory of money and credit, The* Revised., Indianapolis: Ludwig von Mises Institute. Available at: http://cc10.aubg.bg/faculty/kpetrov/Other/Textbook Downloads/von Mises - Theory of Money and Credit.pdf [Accessed July 9, 2014].

White, L.H. (2015, Spring/Summer). The market for cryptocurrencies. *Cato Journal, 35*(2), 357–382.

Blockchain: The New Intellectual Battleground Within Economics

Max Rangeley

Innovations in ledger systems have played a role in the development of mathematics and culture to a degree which remains undervalued even in academic economics circles. The development of ledger systems in Mesopotamia was instrumental in the advancement of early mathematics[1]. In 1494, Luca Pacioli described double-entry bookkeeping; this was an important enzyme for the growth of the Italian banking dynasties of the Renaissance and beyond. Pacioli also taught mathematics to Leonardo da Vinci and understood that, like other areas of mathematics, accounting systems have a logic to them which has a certain aesthetic quality as well as the obvious functional aspects[2]. During the seventeenth and eighteenth centuries, the maturation of stock markets and joint stock companies[3] meant that ledgers now played a key role in allocating ownership of the entities themselves rather than just the underlying assets. What stock markets were to the eighteenth and nineteenth centuries—the first age of globalisation—blockchain technology has the potential to be to the current age of globalisation—the internet age. Writing in Harvard Business Review, Marco Iansiti and Karim R. Lakhani (2017) called blockchain a

[1]For a more detailed analysis of Mesopotamian ledger systems, see Snell's (2007) Ledgers and Prices: Early Mesopotamian Merchant Accounts (Yale Near Eastern Researches).

[2]It was in the *Summa de arithmetica, geometria. Proportioni et proportionalita* (1494) that double entry bookkeeping was first outlined in print along with other areas of mathematics including algebraic theories of the time. Double-entry accounting also possibly developed independently in Korea in the Goryeo dynasty (918-1392) during a time when Kaesong was a regional trading centre.

[3]Although around the middle of the thirteenth century in Toulouse 96, shares of the Société des Moulins du Bazacle (Bazacle Milling Company) traded at a value derived from the profits of the mills the society owned, arguably making it the first company. This concept, however, did not proliferate at the time as it would later in the eighteenth century.

M. Rangeley (✉)
Cobden Centre, London, UK
e-mail: max@cobdencentre.org

A. Godart-van der Kroon, P. Vonlanthen (eds.), *Banking and Monetary Policy from the Perspective of Austrian Economics*,
https://doi.org/10.1007/978-3-319-75817-6_13

"foundational" technology as opposed to, for instance, a "disruptive" technology since it has the potential to affect many different sectors of the economy. As they put it,

> With blockchain, we can imagine a world in which contracts are embedded in digital code and stored in transparent, shared databases, where they are protected from deletion, tampering, and revision. In this world, every agreement, every process, every task, and every payment would have a digital record and signature that could be identified, validated, stored, and shared. Intermediaries like lawyers, brokers, and bankers might no longer be necessary. Individuals, organisations, machines, and algorithms would freely transact and interact with one another with little friction. This is the immense potential of blockchain.

The ledger system that currently forms the basis of our financial and monetary system was well summarised in a Bank of England paper on blockchain (Ali et al. 2014b, p. 263):

> In modern payment systems, payments are made by reducing the balance in a customer's account and increasing the balance in the recipient's account by an equivalent amount—a process that has not changed since the sixteenth century. The difference lies in the technology employed to record the balances and transfer them between different banks. Technological developments over the past 50 years have affected payment systems in two key ways. First, the records and ledgers have been converted from paper to electronic form, which has increased the speed of completing transactions and reduced operational risks. Second, the emergence of low-cost technology has allowed new payment schemes to emerge, such as mobile money schemes.
>
> Despite the application of new technology, the basic structure of centralised payment systems has remained unchanged. At the heart lies a central ledger, with settlement taking place across the books of a central authority, acting as a clearing bank (a service usually undertaken by the central bank of a given economy). Each participant, typically a commercial financial institution, holds a balance at the central bank, recorded in the ledger, but also reflected in the participant bank's own (internal) ledger. Individual customers, branches, or even other (typically smaller) banks would then hold balances at the participant bank, which would again be reflected in their own ledger.

Such pyramidic ledger systems are increasingly impractical in a modern economy. A cheque written in America for a company in Britain, for instance, can take up to four weeks to clear. To put that into perspective, the SS Royal William, the first steamship to cross the Atlantic, did so in 1831 in only 25 days. Blockchain provides a ledger structure for the economy which challenges the nature of modern financial and trading systems at their most fundamental level. The internet as it exists today is good for exchanging information[4]; blockchain allows value to be exchanged with the same ease and without the timocratic elements of the current financial structure.

In his Theory of the Origins of Money, Menger (1892, p. 15) stated "The enigmatic phenomenon of money is even at this day without an explanation that satisfies; nor is there yet agreement on the most fundamental questions of its nature

[4]See Cerf et al. (2012) in "Brief History of the Internet" from the Internet Society.

and functions. Even at this day we have no satisfactory theory of money". When Satoshi Nakamoto, the pseudonymous creator of Bitcoin, wrote his initial paper in late 2008,[5] which outlined how a currency could work and allow the exchange of currency units (and potentially other assets) without the need for a central caretaker, he initiated a cynosure which could affect trade as extensively as the accounting techniques developed during the Renaissance. The method by which Bitcoin maintains its integrity without the need for a controlling party is by using what is known as a blockchain. A blockchain, at least in its initial incarnation, is a ledger system with no central authority[6]—anybody can download the ledger and view all of the transactions which have occurred. As transactions occur, in other words as currency units are transferred between accounts on the blockchain in a peer-to-peer manner, anybody can offer the processing power of their computer to verify the transactions and is then rewarded in bitcoin for doing so. The transactions are then formed into a block and the updates to the ledger are then sent to all computers which have the ledger stored. Consequently, a blockchain can record transactions safely and securely without the need for a central body like a bank or stock market.[7]

In an interview on the future of economics in 1999, Milton Friedman prophetically stated "I think that the Internet is going to be one of the major forces for reducing the role of government. The one thing that's missing, but that will soon be developed, is a reliable e-cash, a method whereby on the Internet you can transfer funds from A to B, without A knowing B or B knowing A".[8] This is of course correct, but the concept could now be expanded a little—what is needed for global commerce and trade to flourish in the internet age is a method whereby assets in general, including money, can be registered and traded reliably without the need for central authorities.

This chapter will look at three key areas of importance to the Austrian School of economics wherein blockchain will have a defining character over the coming years. It is proposed that the most important aspects of blockchain not only support the key tenets of the Austrian School but in fact will make it increasingly difficult to rely on certain tenets of other schools of economics as trading systems become progressively decentralised and distributed.[9]

---

[5]Nakomoto, S (2009) "Bitcoin: A peer-to-peer electronic cash system". (http://bitcoin.org/bitcoin.pdf).

[6]There are now different types of blockchain; some are permissioned (require permission from an authority to access them) while some are permissionless. See the UK Government's Chief Scientific Adviser's report on blockchain (Walport 2016) for more information.

[7]For a more general introduction to blockchain, see Swan (2015).

[8]This is from a 1999 interview with Nobel Laureate Milton Friedman conducted by NTU/F (https://www.youtube.com/watch?v=6MnQJFEVY7s).

[9]In most of the key textbooks of macroeconomics, for instance Mankiw's Principles of Economics (1997, 2014), it is axiomatic to many of the arguments that central banks can "stimulate" the economy through control of the quantity of money.

- First, we shall examine the Austrian School conception of the nature of money. This began with Carl Menger and then following Menger and von Böhm-Bawerk the line of thought continued through twentieth century economic thinkers. The Austrian School places great importance on the nature of money, including in its foundational texts.
- Second, we will look at Hayek's notion of the fatal conceit, both from his 1988 book of the same name and also his related papers and his Nobel Prize acceptance speech *The Pretence of Knowledge*.[10] This essay will make the case that nowhere do these principles hold faster than in the quickly developing world of blockchain technology, especially in how this relates to our very notions of what constitutes money.
- Third, we will look at Austrian business cycle theory and how blockchain will both lead to new thinking in this area and also serve as a natural complement to traditional Austrian thinking with respect to the causes of the business cycle. Business cycle theory is a key aspect in the overall framework[11] and has gained attention in recent years following the financial crisis that threatened, and continues to threaten, the global economy.

These three elements of Austrian School thinking are useful together to understand the current predicament in which the world finds itself and also the ways in which blockchain technology can lead to a revitalisation of the economy based on Austrian principles. Although there are typically a handful of significant innovations which occur each century, few of them have such a broad application within the field of economics as blockchain. Also, few of them have such an importance for the philosophical foundations of our economic system. Blockchain is, thus, a uniquely interesting technology in recent years for both economic theorists and practitioners of finance. There are already a myriad of papers looking at the structure of different types of blockchains and assessing their various merits in particular circumstances (for some interesting examples, see Peters and Panayi 2016); although there will be occasions when specific blockchain types or digital currencies will be mentioned, this chapter will focus on the broader economic considerations rather than individual use cases or abstruse Bitcoin hermeneutics.

[10]Lecture to the memory of Alfred Nobel, December 11, 1974.

[11]See Roger Garrison Time and Money: The Macroeconomics of Capital Structure, Routledge, 2001.

1 Blockchain and the Austrian School Conception of the Nature of Money

The foundational texts of the Austrian School have money at their core.[12] Not only does the Austrian School conception of money define its origins, but it also gives it a central role in how business cycles occur and how these cycles may be mitigated, or indeed prolonged and exacerbated in the case of our current monetary system. Carl Menger's lectures to Crown Prince Rudolf of Austria in the late nineteenth century[13] show that he had an intuitive grasp of how money affects interest rates and the wider economy which is more astute than many of the models used by economists today. Money represents half of every transaction—at least in the absence of barter—and is therefore at the crux of trade theory and microeconomics as well as monetary economics. Mainstream economics generally holds that monopolies are inefficient; the monopoly that constitutes half of every transaction that takes place over an individual's lifetime should be as much open to competition as any other sector of the economy.

In Menger's discourses on the nature of money, he delineates how money arises out of the free market without the need for state intervention. In *On the Origins of Money* (1892), Menger summarised this point as follows:

> Under these circumstances, when anyone has brought goods not highly saleable to market, the idea uppermost in his mind is to exchange them, not only for such as he happens to be in need of, but, if this cannot be effected directly, for other goods also, which, while he did not want them himself, were nevertheless more saleable than his own. By so doing he certainly does not attain at once the final object of his trafficking, to wit, the acquisition of goods needful to himself. Yet he draws nearer to that object. By the devious way of a mediate exchange, he gains the prospect of accomplishing his purpose more surely and economically than if he had confined himself to direct exchange. Now in point of fact this seems everywhere to have been the case. Men have been led, with increasing knowledge of their individual interests, each by his own economic interests, without convention, without legal compulsion, nay, even without any regard to the common interest, to exchange goods destined for exchange (their 'wares') for other goods equally destined for exchange, but more saleable.[14]

Money, of course, generally becomes formalised and acquires through the state its legitimacy (in the most literal sense of the term), but the state is by no means necessary for the development of money to occur. In fact a free market in money is likely to produce something preferable to that which is state-issued, given that if the money produced by the free market does not serve adequately the needs of exchange, then it can be quickly replaced with another form of money. The beauty of Nakamoto's paper and the abstractions therein are that not only does the money

[12]See especially Carl Menger The Origins of Money (1892).

[13]Carl Menger's Lectures to Crown Prince Rudolf of Austria (1994) edited by Erich and Monica Streissler, see p. 171 where Menger also relates interest rates to the "abundance of capital" in the economy.

[14]Carl Menger The Origins of Money (1892, pp. 34).

arise from the free market but it is also maintained by the market itself in the aggregate in that there is no need for a central caretaker. The development of blockchain technology is not only itself the Mengerian money which serves as one of the keystones of Austrian thought, but actually provides the substrate on which these moneys can rise and fall according to the needs of the market.

When analysing the Eurodollar market, Fritz Machlup (1970) used the term *moneyness*,[15] which conveys the idea that many products in a market have certain money-like characteristics and that they can take the form of money in given circumstances, for instance the use of cigarettes as money in prisons (also see the Bank of England's reference to this[16]). Machlup composed his PhD dissertation under Ludwig von Mises and initially wrote on credit creation and capital formation; when he later worked in the USA, he wrote *The Production and Distribution of Knowledge in the United States* (1962) which presciently popularised the notion of the information society, a concept which would later, with the development of blockchain technology, complement his notions of money in ways which he could not have predicted at the time. Hayek's The Denationalisation of Money re-introduced Machlup's idea of moneyness, where Hayek pointed out that it would be preferable if the term "money" were used as an adjective rather than noun so that it could convey the idea that different goods have a "money-like" quality, or "near-moneyness" in Machlup's terminology, to different degrees. Hicks (1935) also pointed out that the liquidity of different goods meant that they could take money-like forms and, as Hayek put it, "shade into each other in the degree to which they function as money". While there have been sound arguments in favour of the basic concept of moneyness in other schools of economics[17] as well as by thinkers including Aristotle and Copernicus,[18] the Austrian School gives it a prominent role in the overall conception of how markets function.

---

[15]See for instance p. 225.

[16]In this vein The Bank of England, in their analysis of digital currencies (Ali et al. 2014a: 278), considered Radford (1945) with respect to the three functions of money—a store of value, a unit of account, and a medium of exchange—who documented "that cigarettes served all three of these roles within prisoner of war camps during the Second World War".

[17]In *The General Theory of Employment, Interest, and Money* Chapter 17, Keynes (1936) noted that "As a footnote to the above, it may be worth emphasising what has been already stated above, namely, that 'liquidity' and 'carrying-costs' are both a matter of degree and that it is only in having the former high relatively to the latter that the peculiarity of 'money' consists....There is, clearly, no absolute standard of 'liquidity' but merely a scale of liquidity—a varying premium of which account has to be taken".

[18]In Aristotle's Politics Book 1:9[1] (c.350 B.C. translated by Sinclair, revised and re-presented by Saunders (2000)) The Philosopher considered money and came to the conclusion that in a market every good has two uses, first it has the use for which it was designed, the second use being as an item to sell or barter—effectively a form of moneyness as value of such goods in the secondary sense rests largely on their liquidity in the market. Copernicus, in his 1526 report on monetary systems to the King of Poland and the Prussian Diet, included a rudimentary form of the quantity theory of money and Gresham's Law as well as an early notion of moneyness.

The Austrian conception of moneyness takes on new features with blockchain technology. Many of the innovations that have occurred thus far on the Bitcoin blockchain have served to expand its functionality beyond money. The development of "coloured coins" began from 2012 as a way to attach other assets or pieces of data to the blockchain.[19] As an example, someone could attach the right to ownership of a bond, stock, copyright title, or other asset to a particular bitcoin (or more generally bitcoin fraction); this can then be traded on the blockchain like any other. The value of the fraction of bitcoin to which the assets are attached does not in any way have to equate to the value of the assets and in fact generally utilises only a nugatory amount of bitcoin so that costs of trading are minimal. The majority of the discussion among central banks thus far with respect to blockchain focuses on the money aspect, and to the extent to which other assets are discussed, it is generally within a context that these are conceptually separate from money and will be traded as such.[20]

Blockchain networks such as Ethereum use a monetary unit to enable Turing-complete distributed computer systems. Increasingly, blockchain networks will integrate a monetary unit, or units, but will not have the monetary system as their core functionality. There is no reason why there must be a defined monetary unit even for a single blockchain and certainly not for the agglomeration of blockchains that will define much of the economy as the technology becomes more widely adopted. On a blockchain with sufficient liquidity what constitutes money could be defined by demand and supply at any moment. Hayek spoke of the desirability of a currency backed by a basket of commodities and why this would likely have several advantages over a currency backed by a single commodity like gold or silver. Among these advantages is that the value of the currency is not as subject to swings in value resulting from the demand and supply of the underlying asset.[21] In an economy in which blockchains are widespread, the types of asset which have a high degree of moneyness could and would be constantly evolving.

[19]See Rosenfeld, Meni (2012). Overview of colored coins. White paper, bitcoil.co.il.

[20]Hayek (1978, p. 57), in The Denationalisation of Money, explained that the roots of this conception of money may lie in the legal convenience of it, "Similarly, the legal fiction that there is one clearly defined thing called 'money' that can be sharply distinguished from other things, a fiction introduced to satisfy the work of the lawyer or judge, was never true so far as things are to be referred to which have the characteristic effects of events on the side of money. Yet it has done much harm through leading to the demand that, for certain purposes, only 'money' issued by government may be used, or that there must always be some single kind of object which can be referred to as the 'money' of the country. It has also, as we shall see, led to the development in economic theory of an explanation of the value of units of money which, though under its simplified assumptions it gives some useful approximations, is of no help for the kind of problems we have to examine here".

[21]One of the key criticisms of Bitcoin has been the volatility, for instance the Bank of England point out that "The standard deviation of daily moves for bitcoin is roughly 17 times greater than that for sterling. The worth of bitcoin as a medium or long-term store of value, however, depends on the strength of demand over time, which will in turn depend on users' evolving beliefs about the ultimate success of the digital currency".

On a blockchain, the money itself becomes programmable so that smart contracts[22] can be written into transactions. The applications for which assets can be used can also be programmed into the blockchain. As Charles Hoskinson, head of blockchain company IOHK, put it:

> You can put all kinds of extremely advanced terms and conditions on a digital account for money: where, when and who can spend it, and how much I can spend. That can happen with a bank account on a digital ledger.[23]

An example from an individual consumer level would be a parent whose child is at university and wishes to send them money but wants to ensure that it will be spent on textbooks; with a blockchain-based currency, this can be programmed into the money itself. Hayek's composite currencies could be continuously evolving depending on the state of the market and could take on a more aleatory nature through the programmable nature of the blockchain.

At the moment, there are several hundred altcoins[24] in existence. Some of the more famous ones include Ether, Dash, and Litecoin, but there is now a rather fascinating ecosystem emerging of different currencies which are not as famous but nevertheless introduce interesting new ideas to the flora and fauna of the new monetary environs. It would not be possible to go through these exhaustively in this chapter, but some of the more interesting currencies include Gridcoin which arose from science departments at the University of California at Berkeley; with Gridcoin by offering spare computational resources from a home computer people are in turn rewarded in newly created coins; the computation donated is used for scientific research in biology, physics, and mathematics. Computation is one of the most important scarce resources in the information age—the others being algorithmic efficiency and information itself—so a currency which can harness a distributed network of computers to aid scientific development is an important step forward. Related to this is Curecoin from Stanford University; Stanford's Folding@home program allows people to offer resources from the processor on their home computer to be used for research into protein folding to find new medicines—by offering computation users can also be paid in newly created Curecoins.

The Neoclassical Synthesis generally views money as a static concept or even seeks to abstract away from it (see, for instance, the Bank for International

---

[22]For one of the pre-Bitcoin analyses of smart contracts, see Szabo, N. 1997. *Formalizing and securing relationships on public networks*—Szabo summarises the concept neatly "The basic idea behind smart contracts is that many kinds of contractual clauses (such as collateral, bonding, delineation of property rights, etc.) can be embedded in the hardware and software we deal with, in such a way as to make breach of contract expensive (if desired, sometimes prohibitively so) for the breacher".

[23]See the Financial Times article "Central banks explore blockchain to create digital currencies" (https://www.ft.com/content/f15d3ab6-750d-11e6-bf48-b372cdb1043a).

[24]Altcoin is the term given to the plethora of digital currencies which arose following the development of Bitcoin, for a list of market capitalisations, see here (https://coinmarketcap.com/).

Settlements writing on this theme[25]). The ways in which money will evolve on the blockchain will be largely in line with traditional Austrian School thinking—we are now entering the first truly global free market in money where what constitutes money will be constantly evolving to meet the needs of the market.

2 The Fatal Conceit: The Use of Blockchain for Monetary Central Planning

In his 1988 book The Fatal Conceit, Hayek commented on the nature of the state and its implicit belief that it can design the future using the tools and knowledge of the present; spontaneous order, on the other hand, means that adaptation can take place organically and can achieve innovations which would not be possible in a designed system:

> Such an order, although far from perfect and often inefficient, can extend farther than any order men could create by deliberately putting countless elements into selected 'appropriate' places. Most defects and inefficiencies of such spontaneous orders result from attempting to interfere with or to prevent their mechanisms from operating, or to improve the details of their results. Such attempts to intervene in spontaneous order rarely result in anything closely corresponding to men's wishes, since these orders are determined by more particular facts than any such intervening agency can know.[26]

At the moment, central banks and other policy makers are looking at how blockchain could be adopted.[27] It did not take long from the inception of Bitcoin for policy makers to understand the potential usefulness of both the currency itself and the underlying protocol used. As well as forming their own ideas of how a central bank issued blockchain could work, policy makers are also looking at how to regulate blockchain technology. The track record of the state in regulating new technologies has not been exemplary. In the late nineteenth century, the first

[25]The Bank for International Settlements (BIS Working Papers No 346) has commented on this, "In the canonical New Keynesian paradigm, rather paradoxically, they are entirely redundant or at least inessential. The canonical model is that of a money-less economy that can do away with the ultimate settlement medium (Woodford's (2003) "cashless economy"). Indeed, paradoxically, when settlement balances (money) are introduced, they act as a "friction", not as the indispensable lubricant in an otherwise inefficient barter-exchange mechanism. It is an economy in which credit is just a vague shadow in the background: since credit does not affect behaviour, its evolution does not need to be tracked. When banks are introduced, credit may have more information content. But, even then, intermediaries do not generate purchasing power; they simply transfer real resources from one sector to the other. The underlying economy is, in this sense, a real economy disguised as a monetary one. Credit is just another real resource that households make available to entrepreneurs. This contrasts sharply with the essence of monetary analysis."

[26]Friedrich Hayek, The Fatal Conceit (1988, Ch. 5 p. 84).

[27]See, for instance, the Bank of England's "multi-year research programme into the implications of a central bank, like the Bank of England, issuing a digital currency" (http://www.bankofengland.co.uk/research/Pages/onebank/cbdc.aspx).

automobiles, or "horseless carriages", were developed more or less simultaneously in Europe and North America. The regulations passed give us indications not just into the risk-averse nature of regulators but also the fact that they often have great difficulty perceiving how a technology will develop even in its most elemental forms—they interpret it using the language and products of the day and therefore cannot grasp the changes that will be brought forth by the new technology. In the UK, the "red flag laws" were passed (similar laws were passed in parts of the USA), whereby anybody driving a "horseless carriage" had to have someone walking 60 yards ahead carrying a red flag[28] and warning people about the oncoming vehicle. In Pennsylvania, a law was passed unanimously by both legislative houses (although eventually vetoed by the Governor) whereby anybody with a horseless carriage, upon chance encounters with cattle or livestock, by law had to "immediately and as rapidly as possible... disassemble the automobile", and "conceal the various components out of sight, behind nearby bushes until equestrian or livestock is sufficiently pacified". In 1896, the red flag laws were repealed and Lord Winchelsea symbolically ripped up a red flag in front of Parliament; enthusiasts of the new horseless carriages drove from London to Brighton to celebrate. When conceptualising the development of blockchain technology, it is important to understand that blockchain-based currencies are not just currencies without a central bank in the same way that the internal combustion engine is not just a "horseless carriage".[29] Blockchain technology has the power to change our very notions of what constitutes money.

Writing for the World Economic Forum, Niepelt (2016) recently opined:

> Should central banks oppose the new technology? If central banks don't join forces, they risk being cut out from intermediation and surveillance. They also run the risk that payment service providers may move to other currency areas with an institutional environment that is more appealing for buyers and sellers. Neither can be in the interest of monetary authorities, even if the technical and legal challenges of engagement are huge.
>
> Central banks increasingly are under pressure to keep 'their' currencies attractive. They should let the general public access electronic central bank money, not just financial institutions (Niepelt 2015). To do this, they should embrace the blockchain.[30]

Blockchain technology has sparked the interest of many who would like to see money returned to the market in such a way that the individual can choose how they receive payment for goods or labour. There is now a substrate on which any recusant can develop their own money, either as a standalone "application" or as a form of money which is embedded in a specific network, a trading platform, or prediction market for instance. Just as the market will use blockchain to produce forms of

---

[28]Locomotive Act 1865.

[29]For one of the first examples of a more elaborate blockchain network where the functionality goes well beyond the monetary aspects, see the evolution of Vitalik Buterin's initial papers *from* Buterin, Vitalik (2014a). Multisig: The Future of Bitcoin. *to* Buterin, Vitalik (2014b). A next-generation smart contract and decentralized application platform. White Paper.

[30]See here https://www.weforum.org/agenda/2016/10/blockchain-cryptocurrencies-and-central-banks-opportunity-or-threat

money that have hitherto gone unthought of, so central banks have also considered how the current monetary system might be advanced using blockchain technology. Chief Economist of the Bank of England, Andrew Haldane, in his speech "How low can you go?",[31] adumbrated how blockchain might allow central banks to pursue radical monetary policy such as negative interest rates—the *reductio ad absurdum* of all modern monetary economics—which would be difficult using traditional means. Orthodox monetary economics has traditionally been unnerved by the zero bound in interest rates,[32] the concern being how interest rates can go below zero when the natural inclination for a substantial portion of the population would likely be to withdraw their cash from banks and store it in a way that does not incur the negative interest rate penalty. The use of blockchain to implement a central bank controlled digital currency would mean that negative interest rates and other forms of financial repression could be programmed into the money itself with nowhere to run and nowhere to hide for the saver. All of the innovations hitherto considered in this chapter could be brought to bear so that radical monetary policy can be implemented in ways which avoid the inconveniences, from the central bankers' point of view, of our current system.

In *The Fatal Conceit*, Hayek wrote that the "The curious task of economics is to demonstrate to men how little they really know about what they imagine they can design".[33] With a central bank issued blockchain-based currency not only would central banks have the ability to monitor transactions in real time but they would also be able to essentially programme the money to operate as they wish. Additionally, assets could be confiscated or funds withheld at their behest. Whereas Nakamoto designed Bitcoin to be a currency with no caretaker, the technology employed for this can be adapted for a currency which gives a caretaker considerable control over the money itself.

Writing in Bloomberg, Deputy Governor of the People's Bank of China Fan Yifei stated "Digital currencies have shown considerable promise...[our research] suggests that the best way to take advantage of these innovations is for central banks to take the lead, both in supervising private digital currencies and in developing digital legal tender of their own".[34] Over the coming years, money will take a form which is not possible to predict, but the Austrian School at least gives us the methodology to

---

[31]See the full speech here http://www.bankofengland.co.uk/publications/Pages/speeches/2015/840.aspx

[32]For a fuller discussion, please see IMF working paper WP/15/224 (Agarwal and Kimball 2015) *Breaking Through the Zero Lower Bound.*

[33]See Chapter 5 p. 76, the full quote is as follows "If we had deliberately built, or were consciously shaping, the structure of human action, we would merely have to ask individuals why they had interacted with any particular structure. Whereas, in fact, specialised students, even after generations of effort, find it exceedingly difficult to explain such matters, and cannot agree on what are the causes or what will be the effects of particular events. The curious task of economics is to demonstrate to men how little they really know about what they imagine they can design".

[34]See here https://www.bloomberg.com/view/articles/2016-09-01/on-digital-currencies-central-banks-should-lead

understand the developments as money itself becomes less a defined "token" used by society and more a feature of particular networks or in other cases a miscellany of assets on distributed ledgers wherein the assets can be synthesised and programmed according to the needs of the market economy at any given moment. As state authorities pursue their own adaptations of blockchain currencies, it is likely that they will miss the broader point that the very nature of "money" is being redefined, and it is being redefined in ways which cannot be predicted—to try to do so would be an instance of Hayek's fatal conceit.

Banking has certain characteristics which define it.[35] The changes in the ledger system that are now possible are not a continuation of the familiar technological "disruption" similar to retailers selling online rather than through catalogues, or movies being streamed over the internet rather than television, but rather a philosophical shift in the very nature of what constitutes money and credit. Other forms of financial technology, or "fintech", have made changes in how lending occurs. Examples include peer-to-peer lending—the lending, however, still occurs by moving the money from one bank ledger to another; the peer-to-peer aspect is merely the intermediary.[36] The implementation of blockchain technology will not just provide adjunct services through the interosculations of the banking sector, but potentially replace the entire ledger system upon which it relies and operates.

The title of this chapter is "Blockchain—The New Intellectual Battleground Within Economics". The battle is not about whether blockchain will or will not become used but rather what type of economy it will lead to. We have seen that in less than a decade since the origination of Bitcoin, a complete ecosystem of monetary structures has already started to emerge. The intellectual battleground is now who will get to control these technologies, will they remain a function of Hayekian free market competition, or will the state see fit to ingurgitate their innovations and refashion them in a way more conducive to a *dirigiste* economy.

3 Blockchain and Austrian Business Cycle Theory

Before looking at how blockchain technology will likely affect the business cycle, it is worth providing an outline of Austrian Business Cycle Theory in a way that synthesises the main developments in this line of thinking from the late nineteenth century to the present day. In a purely free market, lenders would provide credit to

[35]For instance see "The New Lombard Street" (2010) by Perry Mehrling for a good description of the banking system, taking into account recent developments such as the shadow banking system. This can be compared with Walter Bagehot's 1873 classic "Lombard Street: A Description of the Money Market".

[36]For an interesting summary of peer-to-peer lending, see *The Business Models and Economics of Peer-to-Peer Lending* by Alistair Milne and Paul Parboteeah (European Credit research Institute No. 17 / May 2016).

borrowers at an interest rate which is set by the market.[37] Market interest rates would be constantly shifting, just like prices in other areas, in order to re-calibrate following changes in demand and supply, in this case the demand and supply of savings.[38] If the number of people wishing to borrow increases relative to the number of people wishing to lend, strictly speaking if the demand for the quantity of credit increases relative to the pool of loanable funds, then the interest rate rises so that the market can factor this; the rise in interest rates is itself a damping factor on credit growth as well as an incentive for more savings, and thus loanable funds, so that a new equilibrium can be found.

In our current monetary system, rather than interest rates being a function of the demand and supply of credit, they are rather a function of what economists at central banks deem to be the "optimal" rate of interest for the economy.[39] When a central bank lowers interest rates in order to stimulate an economy out of recession, the Austrian School posits that rather than stimulating the economy it is in fact distorting it. When prices are set in other areas of the market, the distortions caused are apparent to the broader Neoclassical Synthesis, for instance if the state were to set the price of rubber or butter, then the mismatch between demand and supply would be predicted by orthodox microeconomics. When interest rates are set by a central bank then by definition there is a differential relative to the rate of interest which is a function of demand and supply. As Mises (1944: 251) put it:

> True, governments can reduce the rate of interest in the short run. They can issue additional paper money. They can open the way to credit expansion by the banks. They can thus create an artificial boom and the appearance of prosperity. But such a boom is bound to collapse soon or late and to bring about a depression.

The macroeconomic approach of the Neoclassical Synthesis implies a difference in the epistemic nature of interest rates relative to other prices given that it is accepted that no central planner would have the requisite knowledge of the wider economy to be able to set price controls in rubber or butter but implied that central banks do have this knowledge with respect to interest rates. For the Austrian School, any setting of interest rates by central banks also relies on the same pretence of knowledge on the part of the monetary economists as for other economic central planners. In the IMF outline on the Austrian School, it is expressed as follows by Oppers (2002 p. 4):

> The coordination between the intertemporal spending plans of consumers and the investment plans of entrepreneurs has its basis in the market for 'loanable funds'. This is where consumers offer their savings (the willingness to forgo consumption) to entrepreneurs who

---

[37]See Roger Garrison's "Time and Money: The Macroeconomics of Capital Structure" (2001) for an exposition of Austrian Business Cycle Theory compared to other related theories from other schools of economics.

[38]I will avoid using the term "natural rate of interest" since it has been used by different economists to convey often incompatible ideas.

[39]See for example this outline of monetary policy by the Bank of England (http://www.bankofengland.co.uk/monetarypolicy/Pages/how.aspx).

invest in production technologies to produce future output. After Wicksell, Austrians call the price that clears the market for loanable funds and, thus, makes the intertemporal allocation of resources internally consistent, the 'natural' rate of interest. At this rate of interest, the savers' total reward for their patience—the interest payment—is exactly equal to the expansion of future output made possible by the added value of the longer, more roundabout production processes.

When interest rates are brought lower than they would be under free market circumstances, there are several effects. Initially, more bank credit is produced than would otherwise have been the case. When interest rates are set by the market then loanable funds match investment and thus time preferences are coordinated; the suppressing of interest rates by central banks distorts the time preferences of the economy. Mainstream economics is generally agnostic on the homogeneity of capital; the heterogeneity of capital, however, is fundamental to understanding Austrian School business cycle theory and developed primarily through Mises and Hayek[40] following von Böhm-Bawerk's (1884) initial explications.[41] As an excess of bank credit is generated through artificially low interest rates and time preferences become distorted, the capital structure becomes extended; entrepreneurs invest in projects with longer rates of return as the lower interest rates allow for levels of investment at costs below that which would naturally occur. Rather than "overinvestment", the term "malinvestment" is used to convey the idea that the credit expansion has actually distorted the capital structure—the distortions to the economy are qualitative as well as quantitative.[42]

Eventually, the economy reaches a point where the dislocations caused can no longer be sustained with more artificially cheap credit, what is known as a *katastrophenhausse* occurs—the resources in the economy must purge the malinvestment that took place during the boom period, the distortions caused in the capital structure by artificially low interest rates, and the only way this can happen is through a painful restructuring of the economy. A recent example is the housing bubble in the USA leading up to the 2008 crisis, the low interest rate policy of the Federal Reserve from 2002 to 2004 resulted in malinvestment, in other words more was invested in housing than would have been the case had credit come only from loanable funds (the aggregate savings of the economy) rather than credit created ex nihilo as a result of central bank low interest rate policy. The result was a dramatic surge in housing production[43] which diverted resources from other sectors of the economy into the bubble. The solution that central banks have pursued is a further period of artificially low interest rates thereby exacerbating the

[40]See especially Hayek's Prices and Production (1931) and Mises ([1912] 1980 and 1999).

[41]In *The Positive Theory of Capital* (1891), written 7 years after *Capital and Interest,* von Böhm-Bawerk outlines the heterogeneity of capital by using the metaphor of a growing tree; the tree grows in different ways at different stages and exogenous manipulation will distort its natural growth patterns.

[42]See, for example, Murray Rothbard's "America's Great Depression" (1963) for an elaborate analysis of the formation of a bubble.

[43]See The Economics of Housing Bubbles by Mark Thornton (2006).

malinvestment. In Human Action, Mises (1949) succinctly described the eventual effects of a boom built from such a foundation, "There is no means of avoiding the final collapse of a boom brought about by credit expansion. The alternative is only whether the crisis should come sooner as the result of voluntary abandonment of further credit expansion or later as a final and total catastrophe of the currency system involved".

Institutions such as the Bank for International Settlements have drawn lessons from aspects of Austrian business cycle theory. Claudio Borio (2011), Head of the Monetary and Economic Department at the Bank for International Settlements, in BIS Working Paper 346[44] outlined some of the historical development of the "natural rate of interest" view as well as the consequences of a deviation of the natural rate:

> The distinction between market and natural interest rates, and the key role played by credit, was already commonplace when John Stuart Mill (1848) was writing, and was the main preoccupation of thinkers such as Wicksell (1898) and those that followed him.

He then continued:

> It is hard to imagine that goods markets can be in full equilibrium, and hence growth can be sustainable, in the presence of such credit booms (Borio and Lowe 2002, 2004). If anything, the subsequent full-blown financial crisis suggests that the unusually rapid credit expansion was a sign that market rates were below the natural rate. Indeed, the expansion of credit was part and parcel of Wicksell's 'cumulative process' resulting from market rates lower than the natural rate. And while Wicksell saw inflation as the inevitable outcome, others, such as Hayek (1933), argued that the distortion would be reflected in relative prices, in this case between consumer and investment goods. This suggests that it would be important to develop formal analytical models in which such a gap is reflected also in unsustainable asset price booms.

Later concluding:

> We have argued that the fundamental weaknesses in the international monetary and financial system stem from the problem of 'excess elasticity': the system lacks sufficiently strong anchors to prevent the build-up of unsustainable booms in credit and asset prices (financial imbalances) which can eventually lead to serious financial strains and derail the world economy. Reducing this elasticity requires that anchors be put in place in the financial and monetary regimes, underpinned by prudent fiscal policies.

The concept of *katastrophenhausse* as the endpoint of growth in artificially cheap credit is different to the concept presented by Hyman Minsky, known as a Minsky Moment, whereby credit becomes so extended that it becomes unsustainable. In the Minsky model,[45] as credit becomes more extended, the leverage structure of the economy moves from hedge finance to speculative finance to ponzi finance as credit becomes increasingly disproportionate to GDP. The heterogeneity of capital in

[44]Austrian School tendencies are far from alien to the BIS which has cited the work of Hayek several times.

[45]For a useful outline, see *Minsky's Theory of Financial Crises in Global Context* by Martin H Wolfson (2001) see also Minsky (1982) and Minsky (1986).

Austrian capital-based macroeconomics means that the different phases which Minsky catalogues lead to progressively more distortionary effects not just on asset prices but on the very real capital structure of the economy. The key consequence is that for Minsky the appropriate response is stimulus so that the effects of the Minsky Moment are mitigated whereas for capital-based macroeconomics any further stimulus will delay the reallocation of resources that needs to occur for recovery to take place.

How does blockchain technology fit into this theory? There are two aspects: first during the initial boom period when the artificially cheap credit is causing the misallocation of resources to take place, second following the *katastrophenhausse* when resources must be reallocated as efficiently as possible so that the economy can return to a sound footing and revitalise growth. As we have seen, Friedrich von Hayek wrote during the 1970s about how competition in money would provide a solution to the gratuitous increases in the quantity of money that were occurring following the end of Bretton Woods in 1971. Hayek's perspicacity on this was not widely appreciated at the time, but a plurality of currencies would do much to mitigate the harmful effects of central bank-induced misallocation of resources due to artificially cheap credit as there would be other networks through which trade could occur. If radical monetary policy such as negative interest rates is pursued by central banks, then more widespread trading on blockchain(s) would make substitution out of the currency viable and easy, likely forcing a tighter monetary policy on the central bank. In fact, the familiarity people would develop with blockchain technology when using a central bank issued currency in this format would likely make the transfer to alternatives easier. Writing for the The National Bureau of Economic Research Raskin and Yermack (2016) also drew this conclusion:

> Algorithmic digital currencies such as bitcoin appear to be viable competitors to central bank fiat currency, and their presence in the marketplace may pressure central banks to pursue tighter monetary policy.

Friedman and Schwartz (1987 p. 312) criticised Hayek's *The Denationalisation of Money* by pointing out that there is no law preventing voluntary exchange between two parties using any medium they choose and yet the adoption of competing currencies has not been widespread. Prior to Bitcoin, there were no realistic alternatives to the current monetary ledger structure. On a blockchain-based economy what constitutes "money" would be continuously evolving and therefore consumers and firms could easily move out of a central bank currency into a near-money asset on the blockchain such as gold—a commodity with which one would currently not be able to pay for goods at the local supermarket but which would likely have a high degree of moneyness on a blockchain economy. The European Central Bank (2012 p. 35) reinforces this idea with their view that a substitution effect could be deleterious to monetary policy instruments:

> In this regard, a widespread substitution of central bank money by privately issued virtual currency could significantly reduce the size of central banks' balance sheets, and thus also their ability to influence the short-term interest rates. Central banks would need to look at

their existing tools to deal with this risk (for instance, trying to impose minimum reserve requirements on virtual currency schemes).

In the traditional economics discourse when a central bank is forced to tighten during a recession, it is procyclical. In the Austrian tradition, it is loose monetary policy which caused the malinvestment and what the economy needs to recover is free market interest rates which match the demand and supply of savings and loans—in other words time preferences must be coordinated by interest rates just as prices coordinate preferences for goods in other parts of the economy. In a recession, counter to what is posited by mainstream economics, further manipulation of interest rates by central banks will lead to increased distortions in the capital structure of the economy. The IMF (He et al. 2016 p. 34), in their guide to blockchain currencies, outlined how a higher prevalence of digital currencies could restrict monetary policy[46]:

> More generally, in an economy with a high share of VCs, the ability of monetary policy to manage the business cycle could be diminished. Some of the challenges would be similar to those faced by countries that are heavily dollarised. The current generation of VCs does not allow for an expansion of the money supply in response to negative demand shocks. This would tend to exacerbate recessions and could lead to a deflationary spiral, as during the Great Depression under the gold standard.

From an Austrian School position, the matching of time preferences through normalised interest rates will lead to a capital structure which reflects the desires and constraints of consumers in complementary time periods. As Mises (1944: 251) put it with respect to the gold standard,[47] which also restricted credit creation:

> In a market economy the rate of interest has a tendency to correspond to the amount of this difference in the valuation of future goods and present goods. True, governments can reduce the rate of interest in the short run. They can issue additional paper money. They can open the way to credit expansion by the banks. They can thus create an artificial boom and the appearance of prosperity. But such a boom is bound to collapse sooner or later and to bring about a depression.
>
> The gold standard put a check on governmental plans for easy money. It was impossible to indulge in credit expansion and yet cling to the gold parity permanently fixed by law. Governments had to choose between the gold standard and their—in the long run disastrous—policy of credit expansion.

Credit markets on a blockchain free of influence by central banks would likely take a different form to even Austrian School-inspired "free banking". Hayek's *Conceit of Knowledge* prefigured the idea that we should not try and predict the exact nature of how genuinely free credit markets might develop on a blockchain substrate, but we can take it as an assumption that the underlying economic nature of interest rates will not change; people and institutions will lend to each other at a rate

[46]Note that "VCs" are "virtual currencies".

[47]The issue of deflation, which surrounds this, was addressed from an Austrian School perspective in Selgin, G (1997): *Less than zero: the case for a falling price level in a growing economy* in which he challenges the assumption in much of modern economics that deflation is harmful.

that reflects the demand and supply of savings as well as, of course, the creditworthiness of the borrower. In such an environment where different assets have varying degrees of moneyness, it matters not whether people lend to each other in gold, silver, bitcoin, or indeed any other asset or even asset derivative. What matters is that the interest rates are set by the free market rather than by central banks. As long as this is the case then any credit markets taking place on blockchains will serve to mitigate the effects of artificial credit expansion by central banks and help to realign time preferences once a recession arrives. If the standard Austrian axioms are accepted—that resources must be reallocated following a recession so that the capital structure can return to an undistorted state, that further stimulus will delay this necessary adjustment, and that the best way to achieve the re-ordering is through the unhampered interactions between agents in a free market, then the ability to trade on blockchains using assets that are not manipulated by a central bank will accelerate the readjustment process and will mean that it can occur with greater transparency.

If the public is restricted to using a central bank-managed blockchain currency, then the radical monetary policy which might be implemented will mean that the distortionary boom can be continued for longer.[48] The detailed central planning that would be enabled by blockchain technology would mean that a central bank could employ measures other than the manipulation of interest rates in its monetary policy. As we have seen, on a blockchain currency, it is possible to program into the currency how it may be used as well as other features. A central bank seeking further stimulus following a recession could employ this so that low, zero, or even negative interest rates are augmented by further control in how money is spent in the economy or how assets are exchanged. One of the reasons given for the failure of monetary policy to deliver the expected gains following the near-collapse in 2008 is that there has not been sufficient fiscal stimulus to accompany it. With blockchain technology, the control afforded by central banks would allow another form of stimulus where they deemed appropriate—direct control over the programming of the money itself.

Finally, it is worth noting our present circumstances given years of artificially cheap credit. In their analysis, "Debt and (not much) Deleveraging" (Dobbs et al. 2015), McKinsey plotted global debt levels showing that during the period of supposed deleveraging since 2007 debt levels in fact rose by $57 trillion to more than $200 trillion in total. As one would predict using Austrian analysis, the years of artificially cheap credit pursued as a policy by central banks has resulted in a considerable global debt bubble which has distorted both asset prices and capital structure. While the credit has indeed coagulated in certain areas, particularly the bond market, there is a bubble across many asset classes globally including broad

[48]In Bank of England Chief Economist Andy Haldane's speech "How Low Can You Go?", he set forth this very point (note that the ZLB he refers to is "zero lower bound") "These questions do not have easy answers. That is why work on central bank-issued digital currencies forms a core part of the Bank's current research agenda (Bank of England 2015). Although the hurdles to implementation are high, so too is the potential prize if the ZLB constraint could be slackened. Perhaps central bank money is ripe for its own great technological leap forward, prompted by the pressing demands of the ZLB". http://www.bankofengland.co.uk/publications/Pages/speeches/2015/840.aspx

stock market indices. The cyclically adjusted price-to-earnings ratio of stocks, otherwise known as the Shiller P/E, is now at levels roughly the same as in 1929 just before the Wall Street Crash—the long-term average is 15 and now stands at 29.9.[49] Austrian School analysis would suggest that we are now in a credit bubble considerably larger than any other since the 1920s and that the coming financial peripeteia will uncover that there is a bubble across most asset classes globally. Let us hope that the currently inchoate blockchain trading networks come to fruition so that in the event of a global *katastrophenhausse,* a systemic banking failure, there are mechanisms through which trade can occur.

4 Conclusion

In the Origins of Money, Carl Menger (1892 p. 12) stated:

> And hence there runs, from the first essays of reflective contemplation of a social phenomena down to our own times, an uninterrupted chain of disquisitions upon the nature and specific qualities of money in its relation to all that constitutes traffic. Philosophers, jurists, and historians, as well as economists, and even naturalists and mathematicians, have dealt with this notable problem, and there is no civilised people that has not furnished its quota to the abundant literature thereon. What is the nature of those little disks or documents, which in themselves seem to serve no useful purpose, and which nevertheless, in contradiction to the rest of experience, pass from one hand to another in exchange for the most useful commodities, nay, for which every one is so eagerly bent on surrendering his wares? Is money an organic member in the world of commodities, or is it an economic anomaly? Are we to refer its commercial currency and its value in trade to the same causes conditioning those of other goods, or are they the distinct product of convention and authority?

Blockchain technology constitutes one of the most innovative developments in ledger systems since the invention of modern accounting techniques during the Renaissance. It is already bringing about, and will continue to bring about, significant changes not only in how we use money but in how we conceptualise money itself. Within the three areas which we have examined—the Austrian School conception of the nature of money, the fatal conceit, and the Austrian business cycle theory—blockchain technology complements the Austrian framework and in fact realises some of the concepts which have hitherto not been given sufficient attention in economics such as competing currencies. The fact that on a blockchain money itself becomes programmable—in a sense assets themselves more widely become programmable—as well as the ease with which moving between different forms of "money", or indeed from asset to asset, means that the neoclassical notions of money as a static unit of account for the economy will need to be updated with more traditional Austrian concepts.

[49]See Robert Shiller's Irrational Exuberance (2000); the updated 2015 version includes commentary on the current valuations of bonds and stocks.

As blockchain technology develops and the related protocols become progressively optimised as well as being more widely used, there will be increasing attention to Austrian School ideas with respect to money. Some of the very ideas that are axiomatic to Keynesianism, at least with respect to monetary policy, become not just impractical but largely nonsensical as blockchains become more widely adopted in finance and other sectors. Monetary stimulus, one of the cornerstones of modern macroeconomics, will become increasingly untenable if trading on private blockchains occurs more frequently as it relies on central bank manipulation of the money supply. This is likely to happen not just because people wish to use another form of "money", but because trading in general on blockchains will be more efficient and hitherto unthought of money systems will be embedded into these new frameworks. For the Neoclassical Synthesis, this implies a weaker economy as monetary authorities will increasingly lack the ability to stimulate the economy through interest rate manipulation and other instruments of monetary policy; for the Austrian School it will mean the possibility of a revitalised economy as interest rates become increasingly set by the market and monetary "stimulus" becomes impossible, thus allowing free exchange and genuinely free markets.

References

Agarwal, R., & Kimball, M. (2015). *Breaking through the zero lower bound* (IMF Working Paper. Middle East and Central Asia Department WP/15/224).

Ali, R., Barrdear, J., Clews, R., & Southgate, J. (2014a). The economics of digital currencies. *Bank of England Quarterly Bulletin, 54*(3), 276–286.

Ali, R., Barrdear, J., Clews, R., & Southgate, J. (2014b). *Innovations in payment technologies and the emergence of digital currencies. Bank of England Quarterly Bulletin, 54*(3), 262–275.

Bagehot, W. (1873). *Lombard street: A description of the money market*. London: P S King and Son.

Böhm-Bawerk, E. v. (1884). *Capital and interest: A critical history of economical theory* (William A. Smart, trans.). London: Macmillan and Co.

Böhm-Bawerk, E. (1891). *The positive theory of capital*. Auburn, AL: Ludwig von Mises Institute.

Borio, C., & Disyatat, P. (2011). *Global imbalances and the financial crisis: Link or no link*? (BIS Working Papers No 346 Monetary and Economic Department).

Borio, C., & Lowe, P. (2002, July). *Asset prices, financial and monetary stability: Exploring the nexus* (BIS Working Papers No 114).

Borio, C., & Lowe, P. (2004, July). *Securing sustainable price stability: Should credit come back from the wilderness?* (BIS Working Papers No 157).

Buterin, V. (2014a). *Multisig: The future of bitcoin*.

Buterin, V. (2014b). *A next-generation smart contract and decentralized application platform* (White Paper).

Cerf, V. G., et al. (2012). Brief History of the Internet. *The Internet Society*.

Dobbs, R., Lund, S., Woetzel, J., & Mutafchieva, M. (February 2015). Debt and (not much) deleveraging. *McKinsey Global Institute*.

European Central Bank. (October 2012). *Virtual currency schemes*. Frankfurt am Main.

Friedman, M., & Schwartz A. (1987). *Has government any role in money*? (p. 312). University of Chicago Press. ISBN 0-226-74228-8.

Garrison, R. W. (2001). *Time and money: The macroeconomics of capital structure*. London: Routledge.
Hayek, F. (1931). *Prices and production*. London: Routledge.
Hayek, F. (1933). *Monetary theory and the trade cycle*. New York: Harcourt, Brace & Co.
He, D., Habermeier, K., Leckow, R., Haksar, V., Almeida, Y., Kashima, M., Kyriakos-Saad, N., et al. (2016) *Virtual currencies and beyond: Initial considerations* (IMF Staff Discussion Notes January 2016 SDN/16/03).
Hicks, J. (1935, February). A suggestion for simplifying the theory of money. *Economica*.
Iansiti, M., & Lakhani, K. (2017). *The truth about blockchain*. Boston, MA: Harvard Business School Publishing.
Keynes, J. (1936). *The general theory of employment, interest and money*. London: Macmillan. (reprinted 2007).
Machlup, F. (1970). Euro-dollar creation: A mystery story. *Banca Nazionale del Lavoro Quarterly Review, 23*(94), 219–260.
Mankiw, G. (2014). *Principles of economics* (7th ed.). Nashville, TN: South-Western College Pub.
Mehrling, P. (2010). *The New Lombard Street: How the fed became the dealer of last resort*. Princeton: Princeton University Press.
Menger, C. ([1892] 1999). *On the origins of money*. Auburn, AL: Ludwig von Mises Institute
Mill, J. S. (1848). The principles of political economy with some of their applications to social philosophy, 7th edition, 1871 as reproduced. J. M. Robson (Ed.), Toronto: University of Toronto Press, 1965.
Milne, A., & Parboteeah, P. (2016). *The business models and economics of peer-to-peer lending* by European Credit research Institute No. 17/May 2016
Minsky, H. (1982). *Can "It" happen again?: Essays on instability and finance*. New York: Routledge.
Minsky, H. (1986). *Stabilizing an unstable economy*. New Haven: Yale University Press.
Mises, L. ([1912] 1980). *The theory of money and credit*. Indianapolis: Liberty Classics.
Mises, L. (1944). *Omnipotent Government: The rise of the total state and total war*. New Haven: Yale University Press.
Mises, L ([1949] 1998). Human action. 5th ed. Auburn, AL: Ludwig von Mises Institute
Mises, L. (1999). *Human action*. Auburn, AL: Mises Institute.
Nakamoto, S. (2008). *Bitcoin: A peer-to-peer electronic cash system*. (http://bitcoin.org/bitcoin.pdf)
Niepelt, D. (2015). Reserves for everyone—Towards a new monetary regime? VoxEU, January 21.
Niepelt, D. (2016). Blockchain, cryptocurrencies, and central banks: Opportunity or threat? *World Economic Forum* published in Collaboration with VoxEU.
Oppers, S. (2002). *The Austrian theory of business cycles: Old lessons for modern economic policy?* (IMF Working Paper 02/02). Office in Europe.
Peters, G. W., & Panayi, E. (2016). Understanding modern banking ledgers through blockchain technologies: Future of transaction processing and smart contracts on the Internet of money. In P. Tasca, T. Aste, L. Pelizzon, & N. Perony (Eds.), *Banking beyond banks and money: A guide to banking services in the twenty-first century* (pp. 239–278). Switzerland: Springer.
Radford, R. A. (1945). The economic organisation of a P.O.W. camp. *Economica, 12*(48), 189–201.
Raskin, M., & Yermack, D. (May 2016). *Digital currencies, decentralized ledgers, and the future of Central Banking* (NBER Working Paper No. 22238).
Rosenfeld, M. (2012). *Overview of colored coins* (White paper, bitcoil.co.il).
Rothbard, M. ([1963] (2000). *America's great depression* (5th Ed.). Auburn, AL, Ludwig von Mises Institute.
Selgin, G. (1997). *Less than zero: The case for a falling price level in a growing economy*. London: Institute of Economic Affairs.
Shiller, R. (2000). *Irrational exuberance*. Princeton, NJ: Princeton University Press.
Sinclair T. A. (transl). Revised and re-presented by Trevor J. Saunders (2000); *Aristotle—The Politics*. Pearson; Rev Ed.

Snell, D. (2007). *Ledgers and prices: Early Mesopotamian Merchant Accounts* (Yale Near Eastern Researches). New Haven and London: Yale University Press

Swan, M. (2015). *Blockchain: Blueprint for a new economy*. Newton MA: O'Reilly Media, Inc..

Szabo, N. (1997). Formalizing and securing relationships on public networks. *First Monday, 2*(9).

Thornton, M. (2006). *The economics of housing bubbles*. Auburn, AL: Ludwig von Mises Institute.

Walport, M. (2016). *Distributed ledger technology: Beyond blockchain* (A report by the UK Government Chief Scientific Adviser).

Wicksell, K. (1898). *Interest and prices* (R. F. Kahn, Trans.). London: Royal Economic Society, Macmillan, 1936.

Wolfson, M. (2001). Minsky's theory of financial crises in global context. *Journal of Economic Issues, XXXVI*(2), 393–400.